Intervention before Interventionism

Intervention before Interventionism

A Global Genealogy

Patrick Quinton-Brown

OXFORD
UNIVERSITY PRESS

OXFORD
UNIVERSITY PRESS

Great Clarendon Street, Oxford, OX2 6DP,
United Kingdom

Oxford University Press is a department of the University of Oxford.
It furthers the University's objective of excellence in research, scholarship,
and education by publishing worldwide. Oxford is a registered trade mark of
Oxford University Press in the UK and in certain other countries

© Patrick Quinton-Brown 2024

The moral rights of the author have been asserted

All rights reserved. No part of this publication may be reproduced, stored in
a retrieval system, or transmitted, in any form or by any means, without the
prior permission in writing of Oxford University Press, or as expressly permitted
by law, by licence or under terms agreed with the appropriate reprographics
rights organization. Enquiries concerning reproduction outside the scope of the
above should be sent to the Rights Department, Oxford University Press, at the
address above

You must not circulate this work in any other form
and you must impose this same condition on any acquirer

Published in the United States of America by Oxford University Press
198 Madison Avenue, New York, NY 10016, United States of America

British Library Cataloguing in Publication Data

Data available

Library of Congress Control Number: 2023948989

ISBN 9780198886457

DOI: 10.1093/oso/9780198886457.001.0001

Links to third party websites are provided by Oxford in good faith and
for information only. Oxford disclaims any responsibility for the materials
contained in any third party website referenced in this work.

Acknowledgements

The original title of this book, then a doctoral dissertation for the Department of Politics and International Relations at the University of Oxford, was 'Ideologies of Intervention'. What prompted it was an attempt to escape the shadow of a particular interventionism, under which a generation of International Relations (IR) scholars have come to know a 'sovereignty-intervention' debate, and which must now be undone in an international context very different from the one in which it gained currency. When we describe the age of liberal interventionism as over, what we have in mind is neither the end of responsible sovereignty nor the withering of internationalism at large, but a renunciation of once-dominant interpretations of what it means to intervene. It is for the purpose of tracing alternative interpretations, particularly interpretations rooted in the values and practices of the Global South and non-alignment, that this book was written. It was completed in August 2023 and subsequent events, including, following the abhorrent Hamas attacks on 7 October, the horrific and ongoing destruction of Gaza, have only confirmed the urgency of this task.

My deepest intellectual debt is to my supervisor, Andrew Hurrell, who has been a constant source of inspiration and guidance and who, over several years, provided extremely valuable criticism. I am also greatly indebted to my assessors, Edward Keene and Karma Nabulsi, whose comments on the thesis proved pivotal at an early stage, as well as to Neil MacFarlane and Jennifer Welsh, who provided crucial feedback as examiners and mentors. The manuscript was then revised for publication during a postdoctoral fellowship at the Asia Research Institute (ARI) of the National University of Singapore. To colleagues in the Identities research cluster, the Inter-Asia Engagements cluster, and the Asian Peace Programme, I am grateful both for feedback on key chapters and for providing ideal conditions in which to write and exchange ideas across disciplines. I would also like to acknowledge the generous financial support of the William and Nona Heaslip Foundation, Trinity College, Toronto, and St Antony's College, Oxford, as well as that of the Social Sciences and Humanities Research Council of Canada, the Canadian Centennial Scholarship Fund, and Oxford's Department of Politics and International Relations.

The project has benefitted from the support of friends, teachers, and colleagues at the University of Oxford, the National University of Singapore, and now Singapore Management University. At Oxford, I owe a very special debt to Margaret MacMillan for her kindness, grace, and many recommendations, as well as her wonderful sense of humour. Those in and around the university who provided advice or support, both during and after graduate work, include: Richard Caplan; Martin Ceadel; Neta Crawford; Sam Daws; Louise Fawcett; Rosemary Foot; Timothy Garton Ash; Roger Goodman; David Malone; Luigi Marini; Anand Menon; Karolina Milewicz; Jeanne Morefield; Kalypso Nicolaïdis; Patricia Owens; Adam Roberts; Dorian Singh; Sophie Smith; Kate Sullivan de Estrada; and Tia Thornton. Special thanks are also due to Aimee Burlakova of the St Antony's College Library and to Michael Ignatieff, whom I first encountered ten years ago at Massey College, Toronto, and whose generosity and thought, even where divergent, has been highly impactful on all that has followed. Teaching for the International Relations MPhil programme during the 2022–2023 academic year allowed for thought-provoking discussions with undergraduate and graduate students, including four supervisees: Sam Bither; Ladislav Charouz; Tierney Hall; and Naji Safadi. I am very grateful to University College for providing such a stimulating environment in which to work and socialize.

In Singapore I would like to thank in particular: Kanti Bajpai; Simon Chesterman; Jamie Davidson; Sabina Insebayeva; Amit Julka; Yuen Foong Khong; Kishore Mahbubani; Michelle Miller; Swapna Kona Nayudu; Joel Ng; Nilufer Oral; Yongwook Ryu; Xuefeng Sun; Kesava Chandra Varigonda; Yang Yang; and Graham Zhao. My deep gratitude goes to Tim Bunnell for his support at every turn, including unexpected ones. My warm thanks to Naoko Shimazu for lunches, brunches, and the chance to present before ARI's Inter-Asia Engagements cluster. And Will Bain provided comments, mentorship, and camaraderie, including during the darkest days of the pandemic, for which I am eternally grateful. My thanks as well to participants of the IR Brown Bag Lunch session at the Lee Kuan Yew School for Public Policy for their comments on a version of Chapter 6. I would also like to thank all my new colleagues at Singapore Management University and the School of Social Sciences for their very warm welcome.

A book manuscript workshop, funded by the National University of Singapore and ARI, afforded the basis of some of the most important changes. Out of the detailed feedback from Will Bain, Courtney Fung, Chris Reus-Smit, and Robbie Shilliam emerged new formulations, as well as cuts, that greatly enhanced the final product. Robbie also participated in our Conceptual Vocabularies and the Bandung Spirit workshop, supported by ARI and where a version of Chapter 3 was presented, and I am deeply grateful for his encouragement and advice. I would also like to thank Quỳnh Phạm and Naoko Shimazu for their participation and excellent comments at that workshop. Related arguments were helpfully tested out before the IR Colloquium of the University of British Columbia, hosted by Katharina Coleman, and the Global Humanitarian Research Academy, hosted by Andrew Thompson, Fabian Klose, Johannes Paulmann, and Stacey Hynd. For cherished Zoom calls and other meetings that sustained the project in various ways I would also like to thank: Antony Anghie; Barbara Arneil; Michael Barnett; Johanna Bockman; Timothy Brooke; Adom Getachew; Brian Job; Arne Kislenko; Thomas Peak; Miguel Mikelli Ribeiro; Meera Sabaratnam; and Ricardo Soares de Oliveira. Heloise Weber provided suggestions and recollections that enriched the introduction in particular.

At Oxford University Press I would very much like to thank Dominic Byatt for his embrace of the project and enthusiasm, Phoebe Aldridge-Turner for her forbearing management, and all their colleagues, including Rajalakshmi Ezhumalai, who assisted with production, as well as Anthony Mercer, who provided superb copyediting. An extensively modified version of Chapter 7 was published as 'Two Responsibilities to Protect' in *Millennium: Journal of International Studies* 51, no. 2 (2023): 405–430. I also thank Research England under the Enhancing Research Culture funding stream for financially supporting the creation of the index.

The cover of the book is a reproduction of 'World Day of Solidarity with the Struggle of the People of Angola' by Lázaro Abreu Padrón, an offset lithograph poster published by the Organization of Solidarity with the Peoples of Asia, Africa and Latin America (OSPAAAL) in 1970. It is because of Mike Stanfield, his friendship, and his spectacular collection of OSPAAAL posters and publications—the largest in the world—that I was so fortunate to come across it. I would also like to thank Olivia Ahmad at the Quentin Blake Centre for Illustration for her assistance in accessing related materials.

To my family, for their boundless love and patience, I have incurred my greatest debt. To Martina, the most beautiful thing in my life, this book is dedicated. It is hers as much as mine.

Contents

Introduction	1
1. Reconstituting intervention: Contestation and the Princeton Conference	24
2. Dictatorial intervention and the UN Charter	53
3. Anti-colonial intervention and the Bandung Spirit	85
4. 'Friendly' intervention and the Special Committee	123
5. Emancipatory intervention and the New International Orders	162
6. Liberal intervention and the Responsibilities to Protect	194
Epilogue	232
Bibliography	247
Index	276

Introduction

We lived, once, in an era of interventionism. During the mid-twentieth century a strongly sovereigntist interpretation of international politics attained global predominance over the course of decolonization, the Cold War, and a Third World protest against Western-dominated order. This was a time, the story goes, when intervention, for any reason, in whatever form, was absolutely proscribed within the norms and rules of the society of states—when 'good fences made good neighbours'. In just a few decades, however, following the collapse of the Soviet Union, there emerged an internationally legitimate practice of intervening for higher purposes—of 'saving strangers' in places far away.[1] To talk thereafter about intervention was most usually to consider a particular set of problems and ideas: the dilemma of what to do about appalling human rights violations across borders, the international use of force as a right or duty, and the limits of the sovereign equality of states.

Our ways of thinking about and debating intervention remain indebted to these sorts of ideas, even if it is increasingly clear that the politics and projects with which they are associated have faded from shared concern. It seems obvious to many, not least since the invasion of Ukraine and the COVID-19 pandemic, that non-interventionism is returning to centre stage—the dominant discourse once again is about defending state borders and putting up walls. At a recent high-level meeting to commemorate the seventy-fifth anniversary of the United Nations, Xi Jinping was not alone in declaring that 'the world stands at a new historical starting point'.[2] To quote the foreign ministers of the BRICS countries (Brazil, Russia, India, China, and South Africa) in their June 2021 statement on multilateral reform: a more 'equitable and representative multipolar international system', committed to 'sovereign equality' and 'non-interference in the internal affairs of any country', is taking root in the relative decline of the United States.[3] But this shift is not only a story of emerging powers: it is also a story of 'European sovereignty', Trump,

---

[1] Wheeler 2000.
[2] 21 September 2020, A/75/PV.3: 56.
[3] BRICS 2021.

Intervention before Interventionism. Patrick Quinton-Brown, Oxford University Press. © Patrick Quinton-Brown (2024).
DOI: 10.1093/oso/9780198886457.003.0001

Brexit, and populist nationalism as an enduring transregional phenomenon.[4] And it of course encompasses, and has exposed in greater moral and political complexity, changing perceptions of the injuries and ongoing destructiveness of interventions assumed of late: calamity in Afghanistan and the ruins of Libya, for example.[5]

At a global level, the broad reassertion of the non-intervention principle—often regarded as the normative foundation of Bandung, of the Non-Aligned Movement (NAM), and of the Group of 77 (G77) coalition plus China—raises a series of difficult questions, not least about the management of interdependence and challenges shared by all. One familiar response is to prepare for deglobalization, decoupling, and all the effects of a more general return to geopolitics that restricts the solidarity or potential solidarity of states with respect to international justice. On this account a contemporary shift to non-interventionism is a problem because it implies a return to old-style power politics and sovereigntism, if not a retreat from global governance in general. The world on offer is not, or so it seems, a world safe for internationalists. 'Traditional', non-interventionist conceptions of sovereignty, entrenched in the Cold War and resurfacing in a plausible New Cold War, appear to stand in tension with cherished international responsibilities, like those of UN Charter provisions to promote and encourage respect for human rights.[6]

This book is about statespeople and their ideas about what constitutes intervention and non-intervention in international relations. Over the last eighty or so years, these ideas have changed drastically. The liquidation of European colonial empire, the rise and fall of superpower rivalry, and the emergence of new centres of power have involved political struggle encompassing rival points of view not just on how to manage intervention but on the nature of intervention itself. By recovering an interpretation rooted in the coalitional identities of countries of Asia, Africa, and Latin America, its overarching goal is to provide a reply to prevailing narratives of the international sovereignty–intervention debate, the ideological work performed by those narratives in politics, and the meaning of intervention as a globally institutionalized vocabulary. It proposes a problematization of beliefs engendered by the liberal-interventionist moment on the basis of actual interstate practice and alternative visions seen. A view from within historical non-aligned and Southern contestation ought to cultivate a more radically global evaluation of international-societal change and the questions and choices before us in

---

[4] Macron 2017.
[5] See e.g. Grovogui 2014.
[6] See e.g. Glanville 2014: especially 132–226.

an age of hegemonic transition. How are we to make sense of reorganizations of intervention and non-intervention in the global order, particularly given the connections and connectivity of contemporary international life? Whose conceptions of the nature and legitimacy of intervention have triumphed, and been triumphed over, in the shared norms and rules of states? In what precisely has and should a global non-interventionism consist?

Beyond the Responsibility to Protect

Recently the dominant way of approaching these issues has been through the lens of cosmopolitan or liberal-solidarist duties, including the Responsibility to Protect (RtoP).[7] The trend arose in the context of a new preponderance of American power and decisions to act forcibly in places like Kosovo (in 1999), as well as tragic decisions not to do so—most memorably in Rwanda (in 1994).[8] But even if we are to recognize, as we should, that this approach illuminated a very important and recurrent 'post-Westphalian' debate over the conditionality of state sovereignty, we must still admit that in accounting for the functions of intervention as an organizing concept of world politics, 'sovereignty as responsibility' is not enough.[9] Yes, the Responsibility to Protect is one part of the story, and yes, longer histories might be told of related liberal arguments.[10] But sovereignty as responsibility does not help us come to terms with the more diverse functions of intervention and non-intervention historically, and it has too little to offer us presently. To achieve a better and more global understanding of these concepts in contemporary international society, it is not enough to trace the emergence of intervention as a legitimate exception to the rules and laws of sovereignty, its non-suspension, and the non-use of force.

Rather we need a much more genealogical understanding that picks up where this dominant approach left off, that meets the much discussed 'death of RtoP' and 'end of humanitarian interventionism' in a way that exposes, for instance, not only the imperial or hierarchical complicities of intervention through bygone eras, but the normative and practical contributions of

---

[7] ICISS 2001. See e.g. Bellamy and Dunne 2016. On intervention and cosmopolitan justice, see e.g. Tan 2016.
[8] Haass 1999.
[9] Deng et al. 1996; Bellamy 2014; Thakur and Maley 2015. See also Getachew 2019a.
[10] Swatek-Evenstein 2020; Klose 2016; Heraclides and Dialla 2015; Rodogno 2012; Simms and Trim 2011; Bass 2008. On humanitarian intervention in classical European thought, see Welsh and Recchia 2013, and in relation to nineteenth-century liberalism particularly, see Doyle 2015. See also Mantena 2010: especially 21–56.

non-intervention with respect to multilateralism and the pursuit of justice.[11] We need to say something more deeply critical about the plural and contested logics of intervention and non-intervention, how they have changed and evolved in shared normative infrastructures, and how their contingent uptake or displacement cultivated distinct moral horizons, which seem marginalized in recent political thought. It should decentre the liberal-interventionist account by unmasking its presuppositions and ethnocentricities. And, while acknowledging debates at earlier historical junctures and other settings, it should start when the formal membership of international society began to encompass the entire globe: in 1945.

We ought to revisit this period in particular because it was one of heightened East–West geopolitical tensions, but also of South–North encounters around grave injustice, inequality, and the management of cultural difference that have a clear bearing on the present. The so-called 'revolt against the West' is not to be understood in a straightforwardly Bullian sense—that is, as a threat to the viability of international order or of order as an essentially European or Atlanticist contrivance.[12] Rather we have to approach the 'Third World challenge', and intervention's place within it, as bound up in processes of contestation and exchange that have transformed a much more contingent society of states.[13] As a set of struggles for recognition, rights, and duties, Southern resistance to Western-dominated order involved a significant shift in the content of prevailing norms and rules.[14] And this relates in important ways to what is happening now, not just in terms of Great Power competition and resurgent politics of neutrality, captured by notions like the New South and Active Non-Alignment, but also of how the world can and should be governed.[15] If an 'exit from hegemony' seems well underway, it is in no small part because of attempts at rule-making that counter existing arrangements and offer global alternatives.[16] As power diffuses further from a Western core, and emerging and developing states contest centralized or hierarchical conceptions of order, a type of revolt is being waged again.

Classical scholars of the intervention problem—R. J. Vincent and Nicholas Wheeler, for instance—have of course explored mid-twentieth-century global order before, yet so much of this writing has neglected if not

---

[11] On the vanished era of RtoP, see Ignatieff 2021.
[12] Bull 1984a: 19–34; Bull and Watson 1984. For a trenchant analysis of the revolt, particularly as a revolt involving international 'interventions' in support of national liberation movements in Asia and Africa, see Adebajo 2016.
[13] Dunne and Reus-Smit 2017.
[14] See e.g. Crawford 2004; Eslava, Fakhri, and Nesiah 2017; Acharya 2018.
[15] Fortín, Heine, and Ominami 2023.
[16] Cooley and Nexon 2020. On the crises of liberal internationalism, see Ikenberry 2020.

outright forgotten the debate that, at the time, was most prominently fostered by the non-Western world: not just 'whether intervention' but 'what is intervention?'[17] Before asking how far intervention has been embraced, or non-intervention unseated, as legitimate practice, it must first be established: what does it mean to intervene in the discourse of international society, according to whom, at what times? Historically, in fact, the answer is not at all obvious. In 1968, for instance, when the *Journal of International Affairs* published its special issue on intervention, the word was 'extremely common in discussions of international politics' but its wide usage had 'not resulted in common understanding', making it 'as misunderstood now as "balance of power" or "splendid isolation" were decades ago'.[18] Intervention once invited a series of rich and unusual questions: about military force and the promotion of human rights of course, but also dependence and peaceful coexistence, race and self-determination, domestic jurisdiction, and the structures and agents of the world economy, for example. And scholarship that did lay emphasis on such meanings before the new millennium—the work of M. S. Rajan and Caroline Thomas, for example—seems today largely overlooked, belonging to a world that most chose to leave behind.[19]

Those who have emphatically not overlooked that world, and who have long resisted the one that came to replace it, have also kept us alive to the critical purchase of global theorizing in terms of an analytics of difference.[20] Influential strains of postcolonial and decolonial scholarship, faced with the temptation to withdraw from the interconnected global and move towards the inward-looking national, insist on a rendering of non-Western international thought that is neither bleakly derivative of nor wholly removed from orthodox canons.[21] To paraphrase Robbie Shilliam, the imperative is to travel outside the intellectual terrain of the West precisely for the purposes of engaging and contesting our shared modern condition—for the purposes of engaging and contesting a modernity that has been shaped fundamentally by colonialism and imperialism, and circulated through an expanding capitalist market and system of states, but whose context must be recognized as global.[22] There have been several pivotal studies on sovereignty and intervention in decolonial and critical-discursive registers, but none broadly account for the coming into being of intervention in the genuinely global debates of

---

[17] Vincent 1974; Wheeler 2000.
[18] Quitter 1968: ix–x.
[19] Rajan 1961; Thomas 1985.
[20] See especially the various contributions in e.g. Pasha 2016.
[21] Shilliam 2011. On non-Western thought and the making of a more 'Global IR', see e.g. Acharya and Buzan 2020; Tickner and Wæver 2009; Bilgin 2008.
[22] Shilliam 2011: 4, 12–26.

the diplomatic community in and around the UN since its founding.[23] The next step in decolonizing intervention is to decolonize the intervention concept itself, and to do so in consonance with beliefs, norms, and institutions as conceived in the minds of statespeople—a concern usually associated with the so-called English School—but in a way that sharply deviates from particular values and modernist methodological positions associated with earlier works in that tradition.[24]

By exposing the profoundly contested and politicized character of the intervention concept in the way it is used, this book proposes a very different story from the one we came to know in the era of saving strangers, with a very different normative and theoretical agenda: it is by interpreting diverse meanings of intervention held by states, and by connecting those meanings to international-institutional contexts of domination, contestation, and co-constitution—and not just persuasion, diffusion, and rational incorporation—that we can establish the concept's role in globally organizing political authority. It is only within the scope of such historical or existing meanings and their institutional embeddedness, rather than within the strictures of cosmopolitan-liberal political theory or any posited and substantive conception of legitimacy, that accounts of global order and justice should be given.[25] Proposals for or against interventionism must accordingly come to terms with shared practices of those parts of the world that, in various degrees of emergence, have enjoyed increasing agency since the end of the Second World War, for which accommodation in the normative architecture of international relations is now a political imperative. To think in this way about a serial non-Western protest against Western conceptions of intervention, and non-intervention, is to show how interregional contests shaped the trajectories and functions of these concepts in international society as a whole, and to recover a series of alternative ideas about what intervention is, has been, and might become.

Core arguments

International Relations (IR) scholarship since the 1990s has usually approached intervention through the lens of the Responsibility to Protect and variations on conditional or defeasible sovereignty. Yet it seems doubtful that

---

[23] See e.g. Sabaratnam 2017; Orford 2003; Bartelson 1995. See also, again, Acharya 2018.
[24] Bevir and Hall 2020.
[25] On international society as a basis of debating global political justice, see Hurrell 2007: especially 298–319. On Western-centrism and the normative analysis of International Relations, see Hurrell 2018.

this framework is still capable of posing the right questions and generating the right sorts of answers. This book offers a new approach that provincializes the conventional debate, denaturalizes what it takes as universal or given, and lays out a set of alternatives at a time when non-intervention quite suddenly seems everywhere in the discourse of international society. It does so through a genealogy of intervention (and non-intervention) in the globalization of international society—a genealogy that starts in 1945, when the sovereign membership of that society begins to reach, for the first time, across the entire world.[26] Decolonization involves a proliferation of states seeking acceptance in a single order, but also contestations of that order, which produce significant shifts in international legitimacy and in relation to moral and legal rules and norms. To grasp the present crisis of intervention, these shifts should be explained through an excavation of competitive discursive practice, one that reveals the liberal-interventionist moment as a constitutive episode, but only one episode, in a broader story of the realization and reality of a post-Western world.

Writing in 1967, Geoffrey Barraclough predicted that when the history of the first half of the twentieth century came to be written in long-term perspective 'no single theme will prove to be of greater importance than the revolt against the West'.[27] This has, to mirror Giovanni Arrighi, also surely proven true of the second half of that century and, to draw from Andrew Hurrell, little suggests that the trend has since come to an end: the economic and political empowerment of a range of actors across Asia, Africa, and Latin America relates to a global ordering process 'interrupted, but not fundamentally dislodged' by an anomalous American unipolarity.[28] It is hence 'the diffusion of agency and political consciousness that has been the most important feature of the globalization of international society'.[29] If it is by now well established that the colonial encounter was central to the formation of modern international law and order, then core concepts like sovereignty and intervention have of course been shot through with the violence of the civilizing mission and structural processes of colonial exploitation.[30] But they have also been reconstituted in the context of anti-colonial resistance and the post-war ascent of Afro-Asia, when the revolt 'became powerful enough to shake the system'.[31] The latter process we too hastily think to know already:

---

[26] On theories of genealogy, see Bevir 2008 and the next section, 'The meanings of intervention in international relations'.
[27] Barraclough 1967: 153–154.
[28] Arrighi 2007: 1; Hurrell 2018: 93.
[29] Hurrell 2018: 94.
[30] Anghie 2005.
[31] Bull 1984b: 217. See Dunne and Reus-Smit 2017.

the success of the South's sovereigntist campaign, from the 1950s into the early 1980s, in which non-intervention became a 'categorical right with no strings attached'—precisely that which was overturned by Western, though not exclusively Western, assertions of humanitarian intervention and RtoP in the 1990s and 2000s.[32]

The reconstitution of non-intervention, in the norms and rules of mid-twentieth-century international society, was no doubt steered by the UN-based campaigns of the Non-Aligned Movement and G77. Yet prevailing understandings of this transformation, and the diverse practices around which it was organized, have been based on a highly caricatured view of both the demands and purposes of historical Southern coalitions and of the eventual demise and betrayal of the Third World project. Of particular importance is the way in which absolute non-interventionism is said to have become a 'shield' behind which states or 'quasi-states', mainly in the developing world, and guilty of the most heinous of crimes, could hide from international censure and accountability.[33] The emergence of such a 'sacrosanct' or 'absolute' sovereignty in decolonial UN-based processes, and sustained by superpower conflict and the threat of neo-colonialism, allegedly brought about a 'sovereignty-human rights deadlock' in international society.[34] As part of a historical story that legitimized a particular view of where post-Cold War order ought to be going, and of the concepts that would hold such a New World Order together, this assessment of the function of Cold War non-interventionism remains surprisingly resilient, even among critical historians of human rights.[35] But what it occludes are abiding political, moral, and legal logics of the Global South which embrace international responsibility and the prevention of large-scale human suffering, including through force if necessary, but which cannot be neatly assimilated into the intervention debate as it stands—framed as that debate still is, even after the international adoption of the RtoP framework, by a fundamentally liberal-solidarist tension between sovereignty and human rights.

One argument hence seems especially inimical to existing terms of the intervention debate and crucial to the process of its progressive recasting: in the context of the UN-based struggle of the 'Bandung powers', the

---

[32] Glanville 2014: 158.
[33] Thakur 2016a: 146; Jackson 1990. See also Thakur 2019: especially 'Origins, Meaning, and Evolution', 31–120; Evans 2008: 'The Problem: The Recurring Nightmare of Mass Atrocities', 11–30; Chopra and Weiss 1992.
[34] Chopra and Weiss 1992: 117, 95.
[35] Critical historians otherwise highly perceptive of reappropriations of political and legal vocabularies. See Moyn 2010: 84–119. See also the discussion on the 1965 Declaration on Non-Intervention in Moyn 2015.

non-intervention principle was understood not as a restraint on the international human rights regime, but as a continuation or extension of it.[36] Back then, non-intervention was understood as an integral part of a differently solidarist and internationalist design: one that contracted the scope of domestic jurisdiction and legitimated a series of international and collective actions against colonialism and extreme racism. These actions, justified as upholding new and existing humanitarian duties, took on moral but also material—at times outright coercive—forms. The view that these actions also abided by an unconditional rule of non-intervention might seem paradoxical, but it was not paradoxical in increasingly institutionalized practice. 'Sovereignty', wrote Georges Abi-Saab in a major 1960 article on intervention and the new states, 'indicates the unlimited discretion of the state, and domestic jurisdiction delimits the scope of this discretion.'[37] To be clear: the principle of non-intervention does always protect sovereignty as a right, but precisely because it imposes duties, and is unmistakeably compatible with duties, that constrain the range of sovereignty subject to unilateral decision.[38] The content and reach of those duties can only be established in the context of international laws, norms, and practices that specify both how sovereign states may properly behave in relation to affairs located essentially outside of their respective domestic jurisdictions and, as I want to emphasize, what constitutes an act of intervention.

True, in 1965 and again in 1981, the UN General Assembly did very explicitly declare that 'no state, or group of states, has the right to intervene, directly or indirectly, for any reason whatsoever'.[39] But what did it mean to intervene in 1965, and in 1981, and hence what sorts of activities, exactly, were being deemed inadmissible in international life? And might answers to these questions rather suggest that international activities ordered as 'non-interventionary' then, have come to be reordered as 'interventionary' now? Because in the 1960s and 1970s it was clearly not as if non-aligned states, most having been subject to colonial-racist exploitation, sought a non-solidarism—one that embraced an absolute sovereignty with unqualified jurisdiction, for example, or that denied the existence of shared international

---

[36] Wight 1957: 248.
[37] Abi-Saab 1960: 87.
[38] This is not only 'an empirical finding; it is a conceptual requirement on any findings that are to be coherently described using the concept of a right'. The question is not whether state sovereignty is limited in international society—it always is—but specifying how it is limited, with the understanding that while '[s]overeignty provides for a certain range of unilateral decision ... the range of sovereignty is not itself subject to unilateral decision'. The content of those rules 'that specify what may be unilaterally decided may not itself be unilaterally decided ... It is international laws, practices, and norms that specify how states may properly behave.' See Shue 2004: 11–29.
[39] A/RES/2131(XX); A/RES/36/103.

responsibilities—even if they did set up an absolute non-interventionism. To see why categorical non-intervention need not imply non-involvement in the international prevention of large-scale human rights abuses, we must contextualize the relationship of a newly declared international duty to refrain from intervention 'for any reason' and 'in any form' with previously declared programmes of internationalist and humanitarian responsibility, such as those of the Declaration on the Granting of Independence to Colonial Countries and Peoples of 14 December 1960.[40]

Here a core contention of my account is that, in the norms and practices of an increasingly post-Western international society, non-intervention became the corollary not just of sovereignty, but of the right of self-determination that legitimized sovereignty. Such a meaning of the non-intervention concept was not about a bland indifference towards the international, or a wholesale retreat to the state, even if the adoption and consolidation of the nation state was of course very central to the Third World project. Nor was it simply, as many detractors claimed at the time, a reproduction of Soviet doctrine or proletarian internationalism.[41] A crucial part of the story of course does involve a triangulation of self-determination, national liberation, and their entanglements with international-socialist theorizing, and, true, practices of international socialism and their roles in shaping the rules and norms of historical international society have been frequently downplayed. But what seems more generally underappreciated is rather the 'worldmaking after empire' which expressed a view of decolonization that was more than a view of gaining statehood, that sought to counter and replace hierarchical world order, its global colour line, and its structural dominations, and that conjoined nationalism and internationalism in a manner compatible with a single society of states—a society in which liberal capitalism and socialism coexisted, whose rules were to apply regardless of regional spheres of influence or other arrangements unique to the duelling ideologies.[42]

The anti-colonial redescription of the intervention problem, in tandem with the anti-colonial redescription of sovereignty, was a historic normative achievement of the non-aligned and developing world. As a matter of international-societal change, it seems grossly misunderstood. By the mid-1960s, for instance, and by virtue of the way in which the meaning of intervention had been reconstructed, the use of force to deprive peoples of

---

[40] A/RES/1514(XV).
[41] On Third World radicalism and the idea of national liberation, see MacFarlane 1985a. On Soviet doctrine and strategy, see Allison 1988, 2013: 24–43, and, in relation to socialist theories of international law, Socher 2017.
[42] Getachew 2019b.

their national identity came to violate the principle of non-intervention. All states were to uphold the right of self-determination, with absolute respect for human rights and fundamental freedoms, and consequently—it was widely believed—shared a duty to contribute internationally to the elimination of racial and colonial oppression. Far from being an idea whose design and effect was to preserve established political power, or to uphold state values as neatly extricated from human values, non-intervention in influential strains of discursive practice served emancipatory purposes. It befitted a growing intergovernmental movement that contributed morally and materially to both international and collective action against mass atrocities and large-scale human rights abuses—in Southern Africa most evidently. Yet to refer to these robustly internationalist actions as interventionist actions would be mistaken. Postcolonial international society went an astonishingly long way towards recognizing the legitimacy of, for instance, international support for national liberation and the international prevention of crimes against humanity, at the same moment that it entrenched the total inadmissibility of intervention in the domestic affairs of states. It is not, of course, that highly controversial questions about the limits of active support for self-determination were wholly resolved in the UN or in the Global South itself; important contradictions with respect to international support for anti-colonial struggle abroad could easily be found in relevant UN declarations and other institutional achievements. But the redefinition of the intervention concept in anti-colonial practice at large reaffirms the contradiction between intervention and human rights.

A non-interventionist era was understood by a majority of statespeople, representing more than half of the world's population, as an internationalist and solidarist era—an era that saw the accretion of shared norms and rules gradually diminish the scope of abstract sovereign privilege, and that exhibited a degree of political solidarity, rooted in the newly independent and developing world, with respect to the enforcement of law and morality on a global scale. The coalitional activism of Asia, Africa, and Latin America was about humanitarian responsibility through respect for self-determination and sovereign equality. Internationalism in an age of non-interventionism might sound like a contradictory idea now, but it was a coherent vision once. It was coherent on account of knowledges that, in high-level debates around prevention of mass atrocities, rapidly lost political currency at the end of the Cold War: knowledges of dynamic domestic jurisdiction, of the right to self-determination, and ultimately of what constitutes intervention, particularly as something other than either the use of force across borders or, in a much more ordinary sense, international involvement.[43] And as those knowledges slipped from view, as they came to be replaced, the meaning of the international implementation of shared responsibilities blurred mendaciously into the historically separate activity of suspending state sovereignty—a resurrection, in fact, of the logic of trusteeship against which the revolt against the West was originally waged. The liberal-interventionist moment can be exposed as a moment of reappropriation as successful as the anti-colonial one before it. Tracing the rise and fall of a more non-aligned theory of intervention might hence enliven us to the possibilities of the concept in international relations today.

The meanings of intervention in international relations

My aim, in short, is to map out a series of international struggles over what statespeople do and might do with the concept of intervention in global ordering. This ought to involve a focus on the diplomats as meaning-makers of the Global South, and on revolt in international society as reconstitution of our shared global vocabularies. In calling into question a deeply held and deeply felt political story, that of how liberal interventionism diffused and cascaded as an international norm, the approach recovers a plurality of meanings in discursive campaigns with institutional effects. Assessing the legitimacy of intervention is no longer a developmentalist account of global convergence upon any single, higher understanding, but about global contestation and evaluative redescription, as a part of an ongoing and intrinsically unequal process in which states have competed to structure their international interactions. It therefore reflects the basic purpose and interpretivist commitments of a genealogy.

By genealogy I mean a historical narrative that explains some aspect of society—in this case international society—by showing how it came, contingently, into being.[44] Amia Srinivasan makes crystal clear that while some critical genealogies free us, practically, from the grip of some dominant ideology by exposing its epistemic deficiencies, others are more interested in how our representational systems function: what work our representations perform in society and politics, whom they serve or exclude, which practices they arise from, and how power operates through those practices, feasibly as separate from concern with the epistemic standing of the representations under analysis.[45] Hence to genealogize, for some, is to critique ideology. For others it

---

[43] See Chapter 6.
[44] Bevir 2008: 263.
[45] Srinivasan 2019. On the genetic fallacy, see ibid.: 127–131.

is to reveal what representational systems *do*. But then there is the additional possibility that the practical promise of critical genealogizing lies above all in its account of how representational practices change and transform, and of transformation as a matter of situated agency and conscious artifice. To understand genealogy in this third way, argues Srinivasan, is to understand it as a guide to what she calls worldmaking, particularly insofar as 'it not only diagnoses our representations in terms of the oppressive function they serve, but moreover shows us the role that agential powers—individuals, groups, and institutions—have played in the emergence and continued dominance of those representations'.[46]

A genealogy of intervention in global order concerns the agential powers of statespeople, as seen through multiple discursive practices, in transforming the normative infrastructure of international society. It takes an interest in large-scale institutional change in relation to historical confrontations among practitioners, and in light of diverse meanings that institutionalization helps to organize or sustain.[47] Such a theory of genealogy undertakes an ideology critique insofar as it seeks to correct epistemically deficient assessments of international society that have been central to the liberal-interventionist project. But it also goes further than ideology critique. It reflects on the power-inflected functions of discursive and institutionalized practices of intervention—in legitimizing or delegitimizing political action over time, and at specific points of time, for example. And it alerts us to the worldmaking encompassed by global ordering. It shows how the rules of the game are the result of the contingent agency of its players, whose practices, traced across historical self-descriptions, can be conceived of as competing for institutional uptake in an arena of politics. This other dimension of genealogizing provides a guide to contesting current meanings of intervention and unlocking new degrees of shared understanding in an era of profound geopolitical and normative turbulence.

By tracing how the concept of intervention emerged in the historical understandings of actors themselves, in other words, we might take forward the global intervention debate in the present. In this, we should start by noticing how contemporary scholarly perspectives on the subject adopt common, Western-centric foundations. While turn-of-the-century liberal-solidarist arguments are often read as rebuttals to older, pluralist ones, in equally if not more important ways these accounts are in agreement. Not only is this true of their interpretation of state practice in Cold War international

---

[46] Ibid.: 145.
[47] Consider in relation to Reus-Smit (2018) and his conception of 'diversity regimes' as organizing or managing, and not just subsuming, difference. See also Phillips and Reus-Smit 2020.

society, and of the traditional sovereigntism allegedly espoused by newly decolonized states, it is also and much more fundamentally true in terms of the way intervention is treated as 'an event, something which happens in international relations: it is not just an idea which crops up in speculation about them'.[48]

While the story that follows is of course concerned with events called intervention, it is not directly concerned with the incidence or scale of intervention, as if distinct from its practice in global-political discourse. We should of course be interested in specific events or activities deemed interventionary or non-interventionary, particularly the weight of these cases on what is argued and believed. But it is not as if the terms within which acts of intervention are evidenced can be easily presumed over time or place.[49] To achieve a satisfactory understanding of intervention and its function in the society of states, the task of classification must be assumed differently: intervention is of course an event, but it is also an evaluation of a particular set of actions, something that is practised in the discourse of international society. A more global genealogy suggests that what has changed most significantly over time are international standards and perceptions of what counts as intervention, outside of which any turn towards, or away from, interventionism is impossible to understand. It hence provides a corrective to much reification and essentialism in some of the most influential studies in the discipline, which themselves can be related to processes of discursive change in international society.[50]

What Vincent, Wheeler, and others did not show is that defining 'intervention' is of course a deeply political question, tied to the legitimation of power, and plainly unresolved in the diplomatic community of the UN. Nor was this the path taken, for instance, in a recent and very important special issue on intervention in the *Review of International Studies* which, in not 'wanting to get bogged down' in 'the difficulty of defining the term', specified 'as a working guide' the kind of definition taken up by IR scholars in the 1970s: that of 'coercive interference'.[51] Albeit a 'social practice' embedded in the emergence of modern international order, whose character varies over time and is shaped by, most notably, the changing nature of international hierarchy, intervention remains conceptualized as a modality of coercive reordering of the global.[52] It is defined as coercion that mediates conflicts and contradictions between sovereign territoriality and transnational social

---

[48] Vincent 1974: 3.
[49] See generally Connolly 1993.
[50] On inadvertent naturalism in concept formation, see Bevir and Blakely 2018: 65–85.
[51] Macmillan 2013: 1041.
[52] Lawson and Tardelli 2013: 20. On the hierarchical origins of our modern practice of intervention, see Keene 2013. On the colonial-modern function of intervention, see Shilliam 2013.

forces.[53] Hence even 'post-traditionalist' analyses have yet to provide a full account of the changing constitution of intervention as a shared vocabulary of the global community of statespeople.[54] For all their differences, and in spite of their clear erudition, existing major works on the subject have in fact shared a tacitly naturalist view of what it is to intervene in international relations.[55]

The genealogy, then, is emphatically not a rejection of intervention language simply as apology for empire.[56] To the contrary, it meets the arguments of those who might seek to do away with this concept—as outdated or oppressive or violent—and demonstrates its enduring attractiveness as a more open-ended global vocabulary, including as anti-imperialist vocabulary, to be put to use in a society of states that must be defended in the face of extraordinary pressure and political division.[57] Nor is it a familiar communitarian or relativist rejoinder to the cosmopolitan position, as construed in much recent liberal political philosophy or radical-liberal accounts of international law.[58] It no doubt acknowledges the complicities and 'conceit' of contemporary liberal interventionism, but it also submits that conceit is much more than a matter of mere hubris: the more profound conceit of modern humanitarian intervention is that of its depiction of historical international society, particularly its depiction of Southern internationalism as a pure sovereigntism or inherent anti-solidarism.[59] Such a post-Cold War framing of the sovereignty–intervention debate characterizes only one theoretical departure among many historically influential others, which taken together have more to do with the 'Bandung moment', its meanings, and its normative legacies than with those of the unipolar moment.[60] And while Afro-Asian and later Southern practices do emerge out of rejections of Western-dominated order, it is of course not necessary to see their plausible and actual applications—against hegemonism, racism, and international hierarchy, for example, and in favour of coexistence, development, and humanitarianism—as either inherently anti-Western or logically, morally, or, certainly now, politically dependent on their origins.

To genealogize intervention is to trace the changing conditions of what it means to intervene, within which international institutionalization can

---

[53] Macmillan 2013.
[54] See Little 1987.
[55] These issues are illustrated in Chapter 1.
[56] For a discussion of recent interventionism as a technology of rule, see e.g. Mallavarapu 2015.
[57] Consider in relation to Jahn 2021.
[58] On 'illiberal' communitarian, relativist, and other objections, see Tesón 2003.
[59] Compare with Menon 2016.
[60] Phạm and Shilliam 2016; Lee 2010; Tan and Acharya 2008.

be better explained and achieved. It is through the discursive practices of statespeople, through comparing and connecting patterned self-descriptions concerning 'what intervention is', that we can write a narrative that is both more global and attentive to contestability and contingency, while also avoiding the excesses of previous perspectives in relation to material and discursive forces. To explicate intervention in discursive practice is not to show that, as relatively stable arrangements of beliefs and actions, practices somehow pushed states into zombie-like compliance, to uncover the shifting contents of intervention as merely hypocritical, nor to isolate some confined formulation as a harbinger of the good. Rather, by historicizing the effects of normative contestation, and by measuring the relationships of multiple ideational structures to the semantic fields of the political, it is to restore a focus on the meanings that shape international action.

Organization of material

Chapter 1 is about reconstituting intervention in analyses of global ordering. It illustrates different ways of formulating the concept through a discussion of the Princeton Conference on Intervention and the Developing States of 1967; conclusions drawn there by James Rosenau came to influence, among others, English School writers like Vincent and Wheeler. In doing so it traces the descent of the classical definition of intervention ('dictatorial' or 'coercive interference') in academic circles, drawing together a wider range of existing definitions on a spectrum between two poles: on one side, the international use of force, without consent of the affected state; on the other, the outcome of foreign constraint or pressure, inclusive of various forms of dependence.[61] Because intervention is a profoundly contested and contestable concept, scholars cannot, as they have, adopt a purely 'analytic' and 'operational' view in assessing its evolution in international society, nor is there a single acceptable definition to be pulled from 'traditional international-legal publicists.'[62] In fact intervention as coercive interference seems hegemonic both in the sense of having been conventionalized in a Western-dominated academy, but also in the sense of expressing the values of particular Great Powers. What became the prevailing definition, in the English School and beyond, corresponded directly with actual conceptions held by a US-led coalition, at the expense of alternative Asian, African, and Latin American conceptions common throughout the Cold War.

[61] Oppenheim 1937: 248; Lawrence 1920: 120.
[62] Rosenau 1968, 1969; Bull 1984c.

But it is not enough to simply provincialize or disparage. The question must be: how to better understand the intervention concept if we recognize its contested and evaluative nature? A genealogical approach provides a corrective to Rosenau and the ostensibly value-neutral approach exemplified by his paper at the Princeton Conference. Using Princeton as a foil, we can begin to see how intervention, as a vocabulary of the global society of states, is always expressive of contingent and intersubjective practices, exposes a pervasive normativity in social-scientific inquiry, and is never an objective or neutral description. Struggles to institutionalize and conventionalize its meaning betray a politics of discourse. Subsequent chapters explore such discursive contests among statespeople since 1945, in a narrative of large-scale change that reorients the study of intervention around a new set of debates.

Chapter 2 focuses on San Francisco and the drafting of the UN Charter. San Francisco's adoption of what I call the dictatorial theory of intervention shows how, from the very beginning, post-war order was marked by a South–North confrontation on the meaning of state-based non-intervention. What should we make of the fact that statespeople chose to inscribe into the Charter the minimalist interpretation with which most academics are familiar and that they take for granted—the interpretation of Oppenheim and Lawrence—at the expense of a widely proposed alternative—the interpretation of Calvo adopted at Buenos Aires and Chapultepec if not clearly Montevideo? It might also surprise and initially puzzle us to learn that the conference's sponsoring powers—the US, UK, Soviet Union, and Republic of China—voted in secret to oppose 'any reference to non-intervention' (non-intervention between states) 'anywhere in the Charter'.[63] San Francisco becomes a story of the failed attempt of a Latin American-led coalition to reconstitute intervention according to a logic of the effect of foreign pressure on state 'personalities' and state 'destinies'.[64] To take account of this failed bid is also to observe a certain double ordering of intervention in the UN Charter. If Article 2 (4), the Charter's expression of non-intervention as an obligation of states, worked to preserve imperial privilege and an agreeable distribution or balance of influence among major powers, then we might identify in Article 2 (7), the Charter's expression of non-intervention as it was to order the rights of the UN towards its members, a plausible means of furthering the same sort of political programme—one prone to colonial and racist applications with respect not just to its denial of the compulsory jurisdiction of international courts, but also to its rejection of conceivable powers available to the General Assembly and other UN organs.

---

[63] FRUS 1945: I, Document 229.
[64] Language that reappears but comes to be, I argue, practised differently at places like Bandung.

This is precisely opposite to the function of the intervention concept as theorized in terms of a solidarist internationalism, in terms of the Bandung Spirit—a spirit to be associated with the Asian-African Conference of 1955, but also other intergovernmental meetings in the following decades, especially of the Non-Aligned Movement. The anti-colonial redescription of intervention becomes one of the most significant internationalist achievements of the Cold War period. Chapter 3 is concerned with an emerging Third World identity that seeks to reorder intervention in a manner that reduces the external vulnerabilities of smaller states while also expanding the content and scope of shared international duties. For Afro-Asian governments, non-intervention is, yes, one of the five principles of the Panchsheel, but comes to be comprehended in a context not limited to the Panchsheel. Its discursive practice in relation to the promotion of human rights and self-determination—understood in the South as the single most important and prerequisite human right, and clearly institutionalized as such—is both about narrowing the band of legitimate action available then to imperial and larger powers, and about broadening the band of legitimate resistance against foreign domination, particularly in relation to iterations of colonial domination and extreme racism. Issues once resigned by a Northern coalition to the essentially domestic become repossessed by the international. Violations of the non-intervention principle and human rights invite international and collective responses.

Some of the clearest applications of this logic appeared at the Belgrade Conference of the non-aligned countries in 1961 as well as, in strains that frequently divided the countries of the Global South, at meetings of the Afro-Asian Peoples' Solidarity Movement and eventually the Tricontinental Conference of 1966. A more moderate non-aligned theory was used to legitimate international and UN-based moral, diplomatic, and material sanctions on apartheid-era South Africa, for example. In a more radical and Tricontinentalist formulation, 'full support' for the national liberation movements, in South Africa and much beyond, by 'all means necessary' and across existing political borders, became a universal responsibility allegedly consistent with a declaration that 'no state has the right to intervene, directly or indirectly, for any reason whatever' in 'any form'.[65] We might hence be tempted to ascribe a veritable interventionism to the Third World revolutionaries. But to do so would be to misconstrue highly controversial knowledges of self-determination, and of domestic jurisdiction, that rendered these actions internationalist but not technically interventionist. The anti-colonial

[65] These vocabularies and their institutionalizations are explored in Chapter 3.

theory of intervention, in moderate and radical versions, enjoys through this period considerable popularity at meetings and summits of the developing world. In its general form, it is circulated globally in friction with previous formulations written into major international agreements.

In picking up this interpretation in the UN, non-aligned and Southern states were seeking, quite self-consciously, to progressively redevelop the function of non-intervention as contained in the Charter. A politico-legal struggle emerges especially in the 1960s and 1970s, defined by an encounter between the South's anti-colonial theory of intervention and the West's late defence of the dictatorial theory, which is also a struggle over the positioning of self-determination at the heart of what it is to intervene. Chapter 4 considers this process in relation to the Friendly Relations Declaration, and particularly the meetings of the Special Committee on Friendly Relations and the writing of the first UN Declaration on Non-Intervention in 1965. In places like Mexico City, in some of the most contentious global meetings since San Francisco, statespeople convene to ask specifically 'what is intervention?' in a manner that not only departs from the content of Article 2 (4), but also from Article 2 (7) as originally conceived: constantly in the crosshairs is the legitimacy of various types of international action to promote human rights and national liberation processes. Dictatorial intervention slips, the West does bend, and there is a broadening of perceived manifestations of intervention as an act, such that intervention is increasingly practised as an effect of foreign pressure on self-determined futures.

Accordingly, our account of the 1965 Declaration must not be satisfied with its adoption of a categorical stance against intervention alone. Instead it should explain the Declaration with reference to multiple competing discursive practices. It should reveal both its role in processes of legitimating the UN-based struggle against colonialism and extreme racism, as well as its connection to unresolved normative conflicts having to do with foreign support in so-called wars of national liberation (not only did it refer to the duty of all states to contribute to elimination of racial and colonial oppression but debate in the General Assembly made extensive reference to the Vietnam War). In fact a Western coalition would vote against subsequent UN resolutions on non-intervention, the record shows, because of perceived links to radical 'non-interventionist' agendas and logics adopted at the Tricontinental.[66] Yet it ought still to be admitted that for many, even most, the new era of

---

[66] Moderate developing states, including members of the Organization of American States (OAS), would vote in favour of the 1965 Declaration and draw attention to its rejection of international subversion and exports of revolution. See especially the section 'The Tricontinental's "total respect for the sovereignty of all states"' in Chapter 3.

non-intervention in the middle of the twentieth century was an internationalist one in relation to a range of significant cases. 'It would occur to no one', the Tunisian delegation was comfortable to argue in the General Assembly, 'to accuse of intervention in the domestic affairs of a third country a state which gave active support to the peoples of Southern Rhodesia, the Territories under Portuguese administration, South Africa, Palestine, and all the other countries still under colonial rule ....'[67]

Like 1965, 1970 is a story of the anti-colonial theory of intervention in circulation but not consensus. Of course total agreement does not emerge on the various implications of intervention as the denial of self-determination, or on the precise management of self-determination as belonging to nations and peoples. But, overall, there is a global shift: we might explain it as a shift from approaching non-intervention as a problem of freedom from physical violence, to approaching non-intervention as a problem of freedom to determine one's own future without foreign pressure. Such a conception of intervention, written into a landmark statement on the foundational principles of the international legal order, implied a peaceful coexistence or 'good neighbourliness' that was neither shorn of humanitarian and human rights-based commitments, nor liberal-solidarist or cosmopolitan in the typical sense. So a 'friendlier' (as in Friendly Relations) conception of intervention is about an alternative discretion, one rooted in a commitment to international law even as it diverges from certain traditional international-legal conceptions of intervention as 'coercive' or 'dictatorial interference' construed as the use or threat of force. It shows once again how international action to promote and encourage respect for human rights, including through UN-based collective action and enforcement measures, is not necessarily inconsistent with sovereign equality or the principle of non-intervention. Rather it is intervention that, on account of its renegotiated nature as foreign pressure at the expense of self-determination, constitutes a violation of universal human rights.

Through the 1970s and early 1980s, such a Bandung-based conception of intervention is developed further and the UN becomes the scene of another protest, another attempt at contestation and international-institutional change, led by the developing world against Western-led order. There remains a great deal of disagreement concerning the responsibilities of good neighbours in respect to self-determination and emancipation more generally. Conditions of meaning change in tandem with new problems, technologies, and redistributions of power. It is in part for this reason that we see a call for a second non-intervention declaration in the General Assembly,

[67] A/C.1/SR.1402: 291.

which is eventually adopted in 1981—a loose Southern coalition, joined by the Soviet Union, votes for, and a Western coalition votes against. New constitutive pillars emerge; one is the New International Economic Order (NIEO). The language of intervention serves a new role in the context of development, the control of natural resources, the nationalization of various forms of property, the regulation of transnational corporations, and the creation of producers' associations and price controls. Within the NIEO we should also locate the New World Information and Communication Order (NWICO). The NWICO's attempt at regulating international information flows, 'false news', defamation, and propaganda—and at launching countermeasures, including a news agency pool much like a producer's association—is no doubt related to the appearance of new communications technologies. Here self-determination becomes a path towards unencumbered development in international-economic but also international-communicative networks. Chapter 5 examines how, for the G77, a still more broadly emancipatory logic of intervention appears in the UN's Second Non-Intervention Declaration. And it provides an alternative reading of the intervention problem at the end of détente: while the intensification of the Cold War clearly does coincide with a Third World malaise and fragmentation of the solidarist-internationalist programme, the 1970s and early 1980s is not only a story of the Cold War polarization of languages of self-determination and human rights through, for instance, the Reagan Doctrine on the one hand and Soviet justifications of, for example, its war in Afghanistan on the other.

The debates of the 1990s and early 2000s are the most familiar to us. In the context of horrific crimes and tragedies in Eastern Europe and Northern and Central Africa, as well as the unipolar moment, a theory of liberal intervention achieves new political currency. But the key point is not that human rights would serve, as they had before, as a basis for qualifying sovereign privilege or would bestow, as they had before, corresponding responsibilities to states and the international community. Nor is it about the emergence of liberal or classical humanitarian intervention as a singular international norm, the meaning and appeal of which experiences ever-increasing convergence among states. Rather it is about a large-scale discursive retreat from a model of international humanitarian protection rooted in respect for self-determination and sovereign equality. Chapter 6 shows how the meaning of what it is to intervene became decoupled from self-determination, which enabled the historical contradiction between human rights and intervention to be circumvented in the practices of states. It is this decoupling that, from a genealogical perspective, represents the most significant change during the early post-Cold War period. True, by 2005 there is a kind of coming together among smaller and larger states around self-described intervention for humanitarian purposes. But it is only a partial overlap: it conceals a set of very crucial differences in interpretation that had previously been expressed in a language of unconditional respect for self-determined futures. We should further expose that set of differences by, among other things, studying the clash of two conceptions of sovereignty as responsibility or, eventually, two Responsibilities to Protect: one best characterized as Southern, and one as Northern.

This age of interventionism was a shift away from what states believed and practised during the Cold War, but not for the reasons we commonly assume. Yes, the use of force for humanitarian purposes is being advocated in this period, but what seems salient is not simply the reappearance of a coercive internationalism. It is rather that a new legitimacy is achieved in relation to international humanitarian protection as an issue of suspending, rather than occurring outside of the scope of, the essential domestic jurisdiction of states. The liberal-interventionist moment also involves an often overlooked reconstitution of what it means to intervene; the notion of intervention comes to be employed much more loosely in international debate, taking on a more ordinary meaning as international involvement. Consider intervention's changing relationship with consent; significant is the fact that it becomes so broadly reasonable in these settings to speak of 'intervention by invitation' or intervention as UN-based peacekeeping and peacebuilding.[68] Key discursive moves along these lines are surveyed: for example, in Kofi Annan's 1999 address on the intervention concept and various reports on the RtoP concept from 2001 onward, as well as in Organisation of African Unity (OAU)/African Union (AU) and non-aligned documents. Having clarified post-Cold War discursive practice, we can locate the apogee of liberal interventionism in 2011, but also see that the decline of a defeasible understanding of sovereignty need not imply the end of the collective responsibility of states to bring international relief and redress in humanitarian emergencies.

The Epilogue provides a synthesis of the previous chapters and presses further the case for a genealogical reading of the global intervention debate. It presents an alternative framing of our present crisis of interventionism: one that understands historical liberal interventionism in terms of an elaborate rhetorical redescription, and a counterstruggle against Southern-oriented order, which supplanted previous understandings and brought about a confusion that was also an ideological feat. The fall of interventionism must no longer be confused with the fate of internationalism. The Epilogue then

[68] See the first section in Chapter 6.

considers additional implications of the genealogy for an increasingly divided and multipolar world. A new agenda, one that steers clear of bloc politics and fragmentations of the global, is in part about coping with and anticipating different or returning domains of contestation: the neo-imperial or neo-hegemonic, for example, as well as the environmental and digital commons. Another part is about relating those contestations to processes of legitimating political action. Whatever its substance, the new agenda must involve a certain sensibility in conceiving of discursive and institutionalized pathways into a still viable global order, one that relates to a longer-standing intellectual tradition of pluralism, but unlike the ways that we might expect. How, if at all, are we to proceed with the vocabulary of intervention in the continued evolution of post-Western global order?

1
Reconstituting intervention

Contestation and the Princeton Conference

When we write about intervention in International Relations, we usually have in mind a particular sort of event, with particular characteristics, fitting into a particular frame—humanitarian intervention by 'kind-hearted gunmen' to halt the effusion of blood.[1] We examine intervention with adjectives. But most would go further to say that even if stripped of those adjectives, the concept has something like a constant core: intervention is a 'discrete act' of 'coercive interference'—a temporary, non-consensual involvement in the internal affairs of a state. It comprises the threat or the use of force.[2] This is also the kind of definition offered by a positivist international-legal tradition, which construes intervention as 'dictatorial interference'.[3] For many it is not that we are afraid to call war by its name, but that intervention is veritably different from full-blown warfare; it exists in the space between war and peace.[4]

Less typical is an acknowledgement that this was not always so. This chapter seeks to resolve a puzzle, and in doing so tries to say something about the way we ought to go about approaching intervention as a term used in global political discourse. In 1967, James Rosenau opened a conference at Princeton University devoted to 'the function of the concept of intervention'.[5] 'So many diverse activities, motives, and consequences are considered to constitute intervention that the key terms of most definitions are ambiguous and fail to discriminate empirical phenomena', Rosenau would say of the early literature. In the face of such extreme contestation, 'discipline' was

---

[1] Brownlie 1973: 139. See e.g. Murphy 1996: 8–20; Wheeler 2000: 1–2; Roberts 2002; Holzgrefe and Keohane 2003: 18; Welsh 2004: 3; Weiss 2007: 5–8; Seybolt 2007: 5–6; Heinze 2009: 7–10; Simms and Trim 2011: 4.

[2] According to Marc Trachtenberg, intervention has historically 'referred to the use of force in those exceptional cases where a line had been crossed and national sovereignty, the legitimacy of which was recognised in principle, need not be respected'. Quoted in Reus-Smit 2013a: 1062. See also e.g. Macmillan 2013; Recchia and Welsh 2013: 1; Finnemore 2003; MacFarlane 2002: 13; Haass 1999; Cutler 1985; MacFarlane 1985a: 1; Walzer 1977: 86–109.

[3] Bull 1984c: 1. See e.g. Oppenheim 1948: 272–273; Hershey 1927: 236; Lawrence 1913: 124.

[4] 'In its strict sense, intervention means coercion short of war' (Wight 1978: 191).

[5] The Princeton Conference on Intervention and the Developing States took place from 10 to 11 May 1967.

Intervention before Interventionism. Patrick Quinton-Brown, Oxford University Press. © Patrick Quinton-Brown (2024).
DOI: 10.1093/oso/9780198886457.003.0002

Reconstituting intervention: Contestation and the Princeton Conference 25

required 'so that words have the same meanings and ideas the same referents'.[6] Summoned from across political science, economics, international law, journalism, and government, more than 200 delegates arrived in New Jersey for two days of deliberation. But as the conference came to a close, as they all assembled to review their progress, they could agree on just one thing: that a satisfying definition had not been found, that researchers ought not to sacrifice 'relevance for precision'.[7] Rosenau had been calling for a properly 'scientific' definition of intervention that would plainly 'recognize an interventionary act when it occurs', and create space for scholarship preoccupied with 'neutral predictions of behavior' and the conditions of its occurrence.[8] The rejection was, as Rosenau himself admitted, 'vigorous'.[9] Confronted with the prospect of a 'narrow and precise technical meaning', conferees fell back on something Rosenau would call the concept's 'common-sense' meaning.[10] And in 'rejecting a particular operational definition, they thus rejected operationalization as a whole and affirmed the legitimacy of using the concept in a variety of ambiguous ways'.[11]

Why? What happened at Princeton and what might this story tell us about the empirical study of shared concepts in international society? At stake here is the reconstituting of intervention in a prominent strain of English-language IR literature. It is notable that, from the mid-1970s into the early post-Cold War period, something in the academic conversation changed. A small but influential covey of scholars, first from so-called 'English School' circles, and then from cosmopolitan political-theoretical and radical international-legal groups, were circumventing the fact of contestation rather than theorizing or historicizing it. Anglophone scholars had attempted to determine a substantive, essential meaning of intervention in the 1960s, having until that point achieved 'no agreement whatsoever' on the phenomena designated by the term.[12] But a relatively stable designation did become prominent in the decades that followed. Hereafter the boundaries of academic inquiry did become 'monochromatic' and more or less 'fixed', but for reasons Rosenau would not have recognized, and probably would have repudiated: it was through a politico-normative spiral that intervention came to be treated as an act or event with a precise core or 'essence', and it was on account of a similar sort of politico-normative spiral, or at least on account of the

---

[6] Rosenau 1968: 176.
[7] Quoted in ibid.: 171.
[8] Rosenau 1969: 155–156.
[9] Rosenau 1968: 165.
[10] Ibid.: 174.
[11] Ibid.: 175.
[12] Rosenau 1969: 155, 152.

politico-normative nature of the dispute, that no single realization of intervention emerged from Princeton in 1967.[13]

It is on these grounds that this chapter makes the following argument: there was a feeling, once, that contestability captured something profound about the intervention concept in world politics. In confessing the fact of the term's contested meanings, scholars felt inclined to think of the intervention problem not merely as a struggle for or against the enlightened use of force, but as an encounter of multiple internationalisms and multiple politics. What was lost from the 1970s onwards, when a shift in practising intervention as academic inquiry moved towards developmental stories of singular international norms, and diagnoses of their diffusions or cascades, was a distinction between intervention in two senses that emerge out of the 1967 story: namely intervention in its 'empirical' sense on the one hand and its 'operational' sense on the other.[14] Conflated, then, was intervention for 'analytic' purposes and the more 'common-sense' meanings of intervention in the fray of actual political use.[15] Taken together, these observations suggest that, first, the relationship of intervention as fact and intervention as value is more complex and less dichotomous than Rosenau would have us believe; second, we need to admit that all applications of the concept are bound up—inexorably, though to varying degrees—in normative-political contests; and third, where some formulations achieve dominance, and where one evaluative description is replaced by another, we should recognize a dynamic by which contestation becomes reconstitution. In short, I intend to use the Princeton Conference as a means of illustrating certain basic insights of anti-naturalist explanation and concept formation. In doing so I want to expose not only the naturalistic tendencies of prevailing writings, but also the complicities of the classical academic definition of intervention with historical foreign policies of Western Great Powers and recurring politics of colonialism and vassalage.

Before history's end

What was being debated at Princeton and how could attendees ever have settled on 'the legitimacy of using the [intervention] concept in a variety of ambiguous ways'?[16] Before answering this question, and to better contextualize it, we should first establish: what did the intervention conversation

---

[13] Moore 1972: 83–114; Vincent 1974: 4; Rosenau 1969: 155.
[14] Rosenau 1968: 173.
[15] Rosenau 1969: 161.
[16] Rosenau 1968: 175.

sound like in the Western academy of the Cold War? Compared with the consolidation and hegemony of the 'new interventionism' of the 1990s, it seems difficult to overstate the relative discord of interventionisms and non-interventionisms in the 1960s.[17] We will begin by registering different definitions of intervention in the academic literature of the period; these exemplify an array of conceptual choices that were available at the Princeton Conference. We will then consider the rejection of the Rosenau proposal, the political commitments of that proposal, and its unlikely intellectual trajectory, before prescribing an approach that faces squarely these issues in a history of global ordering.

In the 1960s, intervention had become a research question primarily in the context of decolonization and the appearance, in global diplomatic circles, of the new and developing states. This was a time when Cyril Black—notably an attendee at the conference—was predicting 'ten to fifteen revolutions a year for the foreseeable future in the less developed societies' and Robert McNamara, then President of the World Bank, warned of rampant intrastate violence: 'at the beginning of 1958 there were 23 prolonged insurgencies going on around the world, as of February 1966, there were 40'.[18] One might have expected that given the risks of civil war and superpower proxy conflict, to say nothing of the various other dimensions of historical anti-colonial resistance, there was a strong sense of the intervention concept's remaining a 'cornerstone' not a 'derelict' in the international scene.[19] Yet just a few years before Rosenau's presentation, Manfred Halpern observed:

> It is an illustration of the unstable character of the present international system that there is no agreement on the definition of the two acts most likely to destroy the sovereignty, independence, and equality of any participant in the system, or perhaps even the system itself—namely, aggression and intervention.[20]

Intervention was, in the United States for instance, of course being tied to the problem of the Vietnam War.[21] Yet perhaps there above all, in the drama of the draft, its meaning was broken up and its purposes became elusive. Writing for the *New York Times* in 1967, Don Oberdorfer quoted Zbigniew Brzeziński's view that 'intervention is justified whenever its absence will

---

[17] Glennon 1999.
[18] Quoted in Moore 1969: 209.
[19] See the original programme of the Princeton Conference in Box 167-016, Lincoln Gordon Papers, John F. Kennedy Presidential Library, Boston, MA.
[20] Halpern 1964: 250.
[21] A series of influential publications on the concept were written under the auspices of the Civil War Project of the American Society of International Law which referred specifically to the Vietnam War. See e.g. Fisher 1964; Falk 1968; Moore 1974.

create regional instability of expanding proportions' and President Johnson's invocation of a 'guardian at the gate' against expanding Russian and Chinese power.[22] However Oberdorfer also observed the appearance of a 'new non-interventionism' in the 'growing frustration of Vietnam', captured by Senator J. William Fulbright's caution against 'the US becoming an "imperial power" like ancient Rome'.[23] Synonymous with the period's youthful protests against established domestic order, interventionist and non-interventionist literature was, in the 'Global Sixties', a counterculture with many hues and currents, a rally in many directions—an issue of national security and the spectre of communism, sure, but other things too, including pacifism, anti-militarism, peaceful coexistence, anti-racism, self-determination, and certainly the ideals, if not yet the record, of the new governments representing the new states.

In the academic sphere, two of the main groups to consider the definition of intervention in world politics were the political scientists and the international lawyers. And while there were different approaches to the study of intervention—for example, as a strategy or policy (how to understand intervention as strategic recommendation, as a foreign policy decision), as a moral issue (whether intervention was right, when, how), as a legal issue (whether it was legal and under what circumstances)—it was sometimes believed that these sorts of questions ought to be, and logically could be, preceded by something more essential and constant: what was the content of intervention as an event? Six types of answers, drawn from historical academic literature and imaginable on a spectrum, express provisionally a period of academic contestedness that I want to compare to a period of political contestedness in actual international society.

The first type of answer was an argument that sounds very familiar: that intervention is essentially an act of international coercion or force.[24] In this most straightforward form, intervention occurred with the arrival of American marines in Saigon, Soviet tanks and artillery in Budapest, and Anglo-French bombing sorties over the Suez Canal Zone. '[I]ntervention is always dictatorial, involving the threat if not the exercise of force. It is quite distinct from diplomatic protest, or mediation, or an offer of friendly assistance.'[25] And if intervention involves force, then force, to adapt Mao's dictum, grew out of the barrel of a gun. Here the Roosevelt Corollary to the Monroe

---

[22] Yet Brzeziński also warned that the United States should not become 'overinvolved in conflicts with "revolutionary nationalism," admittedly a commonplace feature of the world scene' (quoted in Oberdorfer 1967).
[23] Quoted in Oberdorfer 1967.
[24] See especially Lawrence 1913: 124.
[25] Wight was writing in the mid-1950s. See Wight 1978: 191–192.

Doctrine became an interventionist doctrine insofar as it prescribed 'police action' as international military action in places like Cuba, Nicaragua, Haiti, and the Dominican Republic.[26] Writing in 1963, Ian Brownlie introduced similarly the problem of humanitarian intervention with reference to classical writers on the law of nations, who 'stated in very general terms that a war to punish injustice and those guilty of crimes was a just war'.[27]

In a second type of argument, armed violence was not intrinsic to the act itself, but one modality of coercive interference among others. Wrote Max Beloff: intervention is 'the attempt by one state to affect the internal structure and external behaviour of other states through *various degrees* of coercion'.[28] Military force undoubtedly constituted intervention, but intervention at its extremity; lesser forms of intervention also coerced, but without military involvement (economic sanctions was the most common example). Or, outside of intervention as coercion in greater or lesser degrees, there was concern for coercion in particular categories, such as the 'more subtle modalities of coercion' sometimes branded as 'indirect aggression' that posed a special threat to peaceful coexistence among states and superpowers.[29] When Quincy Wright, a prominent participant at the Princeton Conference, spoke of 'subversive intervention', he meant any tactic of the fifth column intended or likely to incite aggression, local sedition, or armed revolt against foreign governments: paramilitary activities, political assassinations, and sabotage, but also manipulation of radio and press, spying, bribery, and secretive training.[30] Beloff went even further: intervention occurred through 'subversion, propaganda, non-recognition, and the expression of moral support and sympathy'.[31]

Beloff's view blurred into a third type of argument: in place of a logic of coercion was adopted a logic of pressure, according to which the will of states was affected not through force but through constraint. Intervention hence took on still more diplomatic, informational, and psychological forms—it could manifest through 'active measures' of propaganda, disinformation, media manipulation, and related meddling in foreign electoral processes.[32] 'Political intervention' occurred via direct efforts to undermine a foreign

---

[26] On intervention as 'international police action' and 'enforcement' see e.g. Brownlie 1963: 338–349. See also Lillich 1967, 1969, 1973.
[27] Brownlie 1963: 338. Later, in 1974, Brownlie would define humanitarian intervention as 'the threat or use of armed force by a state, a belligerent community, or an international organization, with the object of protecting human rights' (Brownlie 1974: 217).
[28] Beloff 1968: 198. Emphasis added.
[29] McDougal and Lasswell 1959; Wright 1960: 524.
[30] Ibid.: 521–535.
[31] Beloff 1968: 201.
[32] Fenwick 1941.

government, including premature recognition of a portion of a country as sovereign at the expense of its parent state.[33] But it might also occur through the foreign pressure of international resolution-making, complaints, and formal inquiries; one example cited was Afro-Asian-led 'collective intervention' through the UN General Assembly, by means of verbal and resolution-based condemnations of particular members in relation to colonialism.[34] The pressure-based outcomes of discrete international involvements were to aid theorists in separating benign 'influence' (of normal diplomatic exchange, for instance) from desirable 'mutual involvement' (say, among cooperative trading partners) and illegitimate 'intervention', in direct or indirect forms.[35]

Fourth, and relatedly, theories of intervention concerned inducement. 'Actions varying from the *donation of foreign aid* to the use of military force are described as interventionary in the international system', Richard Little would observe of the early literature.[36] Michael Cardozo focused on what he called 'intervention through benefaction' when he and others, including David Baldwin, described a series of technical, military, developmental, and diplomatic forms of aid to which conditions were tied or attached.[37] 'When the United States offers "technical assistance" to a country this assistance may involve advice on legislation, legal procedures, social structure, land tenure, and policy towards unions', and hence it was controversially argued by some, like Andrew Scott, that '[o]ne nation cannot help another nation modernize and at the same time, cling to the time-honoured principle of non-intervention'.[38] For Hans Morgenthau, writing in *Foreign Affairs* only a few weeks before the Princeton Conference, the economic and financial aid from major industrialized states provided to new and poverty-stricken states had 'drastically reduced the traditional legal significance of the consent of the state intervened against'.[39] Yet in particular 'what makes this aid a lever for intervention is the fact that in most cases it is not just an advantage which the new nations can afford to take or leave, but a condition for their survival ... the supplier of foreign aid holds the power of life and death over them'.[40]

Fifth, if 'donor control' and 'dollar diplomacy' amounted to intervention as 'pressing from the outside', then so too did more aggregate or macro-scale relations of a world market economy, amounting to entire interventionary

---

[33] Rosenau 1969: 163.
[34] Wight 1978: 236.
[35] Wriggins 1968.
[36] Little 1975: 1.
[37] Cardozo 1964; Baldwin 1969.
[38] Scott 1968: 208.
[39] Morgenthau 1967: 426.
[40] Ibid.: 426–427.

Reconstituting intervention: Contestation and the Princeton Conference 31

systems, including through core–periphery interactions among states.[41] According to Hans Singer, patterns of economic intervention included 'the drastic effects of a rich nation's balance of payments problem on poor nations and the continuous elimination of markets for primary materials by protectionist agricultural policies and by production of synthetic substitutes'.[42] Dependency theory, so influential in Latin American social science through the 1960s and 1970s, took hold in a strand of American Marxist thought.[43] Dependency theorists, and those who often thought like them, offered novel interpretations of intervention as an intrinsic feature of historical capitalism:

> The Leninist or neo-Leninist theory of imperialism or dominance and dependence encourages one not merely to recognise a high incidence of intervention by the advanced capitalist countries in the affairs of the Third World countries, but also to see intervention as systematic or structural in nature, a built-in feature of present arrangements.[44]

Entrenched and unequal patterns of trade sustained the mere illusion of free choice in a state's pursuit of its own economic, political, and cultural potential. To take the point even further: if power inequalities were everywhere, and everywhere institutionalized, so too was intervention, playing out in a broad range of conceivable forms, burrowed deep into the relationships of every small power with every larger one. 'A Great Power intervenes in the domestic realm of other states when it says "yes" and when it says "no"; indeed, by its sheer existence.'[45]

This was, admittedly for most, the 'height of definitional vagueness' because it seemed to suggest that even 'non-action constituted intervention'.[46] One way of reading such 'non-action' was as saying 'no' to specific courses of action (in fact a particular way of acting at the expense of some proposed or plausible alternative). To quote John Norton Moore, the 'withdrawal of assistance previously begun with respect to each of these modalities may also have internal effects which are sometimes characterised as intervention'.[47] Otherwise intervention was construed as the absence of any policy at all, or at least the absence of its conscious consideration (a more generous interpretation of

---

[41] Baldwin 1969: 425.
[42] See especially the definition of intervention offered by Singer, then of the UN Industrial Development Organization, in McNemar 1969: 307–308.
[43] See e.g. Cardoso and Faletto 1979; Frank 1967.
[44] Bull 1983: 307.
[45] To quote Halpern further: 'if the American economy sneezes, the world's economy, and especially countries depending on the export of a single raw material, catch pneumonia' (Halpern 1964: 251).
[46] Rosenau 1969: 153.
[47] Moore 1972: 108.

a 'failure to act'), in grossly asymmetrical relations. Hence, in this sixth area of thought, intervention might be taken without intent.[48]

To summarize, as we moved across a spectrum of Anglophone academic writings in the Cold War, the concept of intervention became more abstract, and more a meditation on hierarchy and the condition of power inequality itself. Arguably this was a rational, albeit radical, conclusion. And as we will see, it was also a conclusion that would become central to a genuinely global political debate carried on among states.[49] But to influential academics at the time it was also an unhelpful one, leading to 'absurd' judgements without sensible proportions, that would serve as a licence for 'undisciplined thought' and 'special concern', marked by 'the absence not only of clarity and communication, but also of direction'.[50] As Stanley Hoffmann noted some years later, '[i]n the widest sense, to be sure, every act of a state constitutes intervention'.[51] Yet to accept as much would be to render the topic 'practically the same as that of international politics in general from the beginning of time to the present', a never-ending sequence of classifications, of 'distinction upon distinction' that would be of 'little use'.[52] The same basic point was raised by James Rosenau in November 1967.

The politics of analytic meaning

We have established then that intervention was—far from what contemporary literature would suggest—a highly contested concept. Through the 1960s it was commonplace to use the term in its 'infinite shades' and in 'a variety of ambiguous ways'.[53] If that spectrum is taken to exemplify the range of ideas available and actually deployed at the Princeton Conference—a conference that set out to assess the 'usefulness of the term' given its 'constant use' but elusive meaning—we might begin to understand not just why conference attendees failed to 'generate agreement on a specific use of the word', but also why we ourselves ought to doubt the feasibility of any single and substantive definition of the term in an analysis of international society.[54] The point that needs to be illustrated now is that the process of defining intervention is always a normative and political contest, at the same time as an analytic one.

[48] Ibid.
[49] See especially Chapter 5.
[50] Rosenau 1969: 153, 164, 155; 1968: 173.
[51] Hoffmann 1984: 8.
[52] Ibid.: 7; Rosenau 1969: 155.
[53] Friedmann 1969: 207–208. Rosenau 1968: 175.
[54] McNemar 1969: 306. For a report on the conference, including summaries of conference panels and general discussion, see ibid.: 306–311.

The Princeton Conference was titled 'Intervention and the Developing States'.[55] And at Princeton, an important faction of the conference recognized itself first as part of a parallel debate occurring between members of international society, and second as providing a reply to a normative challenge posed by developing states since the founding of the United Nations.[56] 'Reasonable and responsible leaders from developing nations have applied the label of "intervention" to almost every conceivable form of influence during the last twenty years', argued David Baldwin in his paper presentation. If we were to 'understand what the developing states are really complaining about', the subject matter needed to be related to pressure, if not influence in its multiple forms.[57] 'Only a very broad definition of intervention will allow us to discuss the matter in a way that is relevant to the concerns of these nations.'[58] When other participants retorted that such a definition was 'absurd' or 'undisciplined', that leaders of the developing world were evidently not so reasonable, or not so responsible, those participants were in fact adopting arguments then deployed by certain key Western Great Powers.[59]

Writing just five weeks after Princeton, Rosenau admitted that the 'vigorous reaction' to his own paper presentation had become 'an inescapable part of [his] thinking on the problems posed by the concept of intervention'.[60] He would not seek to revise his definition, but instead to diagnose why it had been so widely rejected, and to demonstrate how 'the experience of the Princeton conference' encapsulated a problem for the literature as a whole: 'As memory fades, the fact that absence of communication marked the deliberations is likely to be obscured, and there is a lesson in this fact which it seems important to try to understand.'[61]

That lesson, believed Rosenau, was that conferees had failed to distinguish between two specific senses in which the term could be used. On the one hand was intervention in its 'operational' sense: how the word was being used by statespeople for the purpose of *doing* international relations, how 'actors in the political arena use the term'.[62] On the other was intervention in its 'analytic' sense: how 'intervention' was to be used by academics for the purpose of analysing international relations, for observing and explaining intervention as behaviour or an event. An analogous distinction could be made, suggested

---

[55] Ibid.: 306.
[56] Mapping out and explaining this challenge is the task of the coming chapters.
[57] Baldwin 1969: 426.
[58] Ibid.
[59] Rosenau 1969: 153; 1968: 173. See especially Chapter 4.
[60] Rosenau 1968: 165.
[61] Ibid.: 165–166.
[62] Ibid.: 175.

34 Intervention before Interventionism

Rosenau, between intervention in its 'common-sense' meaning (by which he meant intervention in 'everyday conversation' or 'common discourse') on the one hand, and what he called its 'empirical' meaning on the other, as a technical meaning that was purely descriptive rather than normative, and which could therefore be run through more properly scientific models.[63] This latter meaning would have to 'be broad enough to identify those phenomena that are generally associated with the term and yet not so broad that it fails to discriminate them from other aspects of international politics'.[64]

What Rosenau was trying to say was that if contestedness or 'ambiguity' characterized existing academic debate on the intervention concept, then contestedness could be attributed to the absence of a self-conscious distinction between specialized terminologies.[65] An analyst had to be careful not to 'slip into popular rhetoric without knowing it', or else they would greatly reduce their 'chances of successfully probing the complex processes in which he [sic] is interested'. Intervention was 'particularly susceptible to confusion in this regard' and 'the proceedings at Princeton succumbed to it'.[66] If only the conferees had realized that Rosenau sought an analytic definition, the Princeton Conference would surely not have devolved into 'two days analysing the problems of world politics rather than the problems of intervention'.[67] If only the terminology of intervention in International Relations had been more clearly differentiated, researchers might have been more willing 'to forego the luxury of common-sense analysis' and accept 'the rigors of a technical language and the boundaries of a specialized set of concepts'.[68]

Rosenau was not oblivious to the fact that the meaning of intervention was disputed in international politics and international law. He conceded that 'economic intervention' was being 'protested by Africans', for example, and 'cultural intervention' derided 'by Europeans'.[69] But a properly scientific definition of intervention had to remain the same 'irrespective of whether it is approached from a moral, legal, or strategic perspective' and it therefore necessitated a kind of bracketing of 'popular rhetoric'.[70] Interventions 'embrace moral questions and legal standards, but they also find expression in the activities of identifiable human beings'.[71] Hence what 'officials and citizens call "intervention" may be the complex result of multiple processes for

[63] Ibid.: 174.
[64] Ibid.: 173.
[65] Ibid.: 166.
[66] Ibid.: 174.
[67] Ibid.: 172.
[68] Ibid.
[69] Ibid.: 175.
[70] Ibid.: 167.
[71] Rosenau 1969: 160.

Reconstituting intervention: Contestation and the Princeton Conference

the analyst, and he [sic] will never comprehend these processes if he allows the subject of his investigation to define his terms for him'.[72] In short, actors' beliefs about intervention were to be logically removed from the causal conditions of its occurrence and differentiated from its constitution as an act or event:

> The Russians have a doctrine of 'intervention' and so do the Chinese and Cubans, with the result that controversy over the strategy and tactics of 'intervention' is a persistent feature of the Communist world. Similarly, Latin Americans have long complained about the 'interventions' launched by the colossus to the North, and in the United States itself recent months have witnessed the mushrooming of debate over the propriety of 'intervention' … Obviously, however, its meaning in such usage is not necessarily the same as that of the analytic concept to which the intervention label is also given.[73]

Yet to think that it was valid to extract a single, truly scientific explanation of intervention among states from outside the beliefs and meanings of those actors themselves reflected a series of flawed philosophical assumptions then common to behaviouralism and to naturalist conceptions of rationality more generally in Anglo-American social science. These issues have been examined in detail elsewhere.[74] For our purposes what is important to say is that Rosenau failed to fully appreciate the theory-embedded character of intervention as a political concept and the distortive effects of formal conceptual language in empirical inquiries of world politics.[75] The fundamental problem with Rosenau's paper was its presumption of a neutral description of intervention, at an absolute level of analysis, divorced from the historical self-interpretations of the actors being studied and explained. Such a naturalist explanation of the intervention problem is fallacious, first because meanings of intervention are always value-laden, and second because agents as people, including statespeople, act on their beliefs and preferences.

It is the first of these two subpoints that we must focus on. In other words, that conferees were so hopelessly confused, as Rosenau suggested, seems unlikely. Much more probable is that their rejection of an ideal-scientific conceptualization, sterilized of ordinary or common-sense meanings, had to do with the value judgements implicit in any substantive definition of the term,

---

[72] Rosenau 1968: 175.
[73] Ibid.
[74] A very clear explanation is contained in Bevir and Blakely 2018: 18–43.
[75] On rationalism and the politics of discourse, see Connolly 1993. For a reply to the naturalist ambition of concept formation without situatedness, and outside of history, see Bevir and Blakely 2018: especially 66–80. See also Bevir and Kedar 2008.

including Rosenau's own, and the political implications of those value judgements in ongoing global debate. The political implications become especially apparent in a study of global norms and rules. Rosenau had claimed at Princeton that there were 'two characteristics that appear to be necessary attributes of interventionary phenomena' in international relations.[76] First was its 'convention-breaking' character—by which he meant that intervention is a 'sharp break with then-existing forms', it is always 'finite and transitory'. Second was its 'authority-oriented' nature—it is 'directed at changing or preserving the structure of political authority'.[77] Let us explore the normative and political stakes of each in turn.

First, if intervention had to have a clear 'beginning (when conventional modes of conduct are abandoned) and an end (when conventional modes are restored or the convention-breaking mode becomes conventional through persistent use)', then this would mean that behaviour would 'no longer [be] regarded as interventionary' when 'the presence of the intervening actor in the target society remains undiminished'.[78] It is easy to see how this was not some benign or innocent composition. In fact Rosenau explicitly admitted that his definition 'narrows the concept of intervention in such a way that it is not equivalent to colonialism or imperialism' as these phenomena 'involve the continued presence of the intervening actor in the target society'.[79] We could add that excluded too was any history of successful conquest, while all unsuccessful attempts at conquest or colonization were included. Was this not then a victor's definition, convenient for the seat of empires, at the expense of the oppressed and the colonized? Commenting on Rosenau's paper, Michael Brecher noted 'that many of the penetrative acts about which the developing countries are most concerned lack the sharpness of a break with convention which is necessary to fall within the proposed definition'.[80]

Similarly, must intervention necessarily be 'directed' at changing or preserving the 'structure of political authority', or might it reasonably take on other aims? Rosenau gave the example of the Marshall Plan, which he claimed was 'directed at the policies or capabilities of other nations and not at their authority structures', and therefore did not constitute interventionary behaviour.[81] But to accept such an 'authority-oriented' definition would also be to constitute as non-interventionary additional economic patterns of intervening in the affairs of others, including through terms of

[76] Rosenau 1969: 161.
[77] Rosenau 1968: 167.
[78] Ibid.
[79] Ibid.: 170.
[80] See McNemar 1969: 307.
[81] Ibid.

Reconstituting intervention: Contestation and the Princeton Conference 37

trade—notably the explicit concern at the Princeton Conference of Hans Singer (of the Prebisch-Singer hypothesis and then of the UN Industrial Development Organization).[82] And it would be to invite difficult questions about intent and motivation. Rosenau's definition appeared to exclude, for example, forcible humanitarian missions in which protection was believed to be the sole or primary aim (in which, say, regime change became an unintended consequence of higher objectives). Then there was the distinction between affecting the 'structure of political authority' and affecting political authority at large—over domestic affairs, for example—the latter of which presumably verged on foreign influence or pressure, understandings which Rosenau was rejecting outright.[83]

And so we can see that Rosenau's value-neutral analytic definition was in fact evaluative and politicized. It was even deeply politicized on account of the evaluative implications that its pretention towards universal validity and exclusively 'scientific' meaning would serve to entrench but also conceal.[84] Since many in the audience held strong and diverse views about the constitution of intervention, moving in parallel with a global ordering debate among states, let us say they rejected Rosenau's theory of the term as either too inclusive or too exclusive. He had not and could not capture the single 'precise' meaning of intervention in international relations, and instead proposed a technical meaning that, albeit sophisticated, represented his own limited moral point of view (even insofar as it was intended to yield lawlike explanations according to specific formalities and logics of discovery).[85] It was because of the empirical diversity and political and normative character of the intervention concept that, to use the words of one conferee, the conference refused to sacrifice 'relevance for precision'.[86]

To put it another way, the true lesson of the Princeton Conference was not about a failure to comprehend analytic meaning at all, but rather about how intervention, as a concept used in both international relations and its study, proves inescapably and controversially appraisive. To call something 'intervention' is to both describe it and ascribe value to it. There can be no such

---

[82] Singer included in his conception of 'economic intervention' the 'virtual monopoly on modern technology that the richer countries have. This results in efforts to save labor and substitute capital—the exact opposite of the requirements of the developing countries.' See the summary of Singer's presentation in McNemar 1969: 307–308.

[83] Rosenau 1969: 159–160.

[84] Rosenau's paper was eventually titled 'Intervention as a Scientific Concept' (see ibid.). A properly scientific understanding of intervention, I am suggesting instead, entails an understanding that objects of the social sciences, unlike those of the natural sciences, are engaged in processes of self-interpretation. See Taylor 1985.

[85] Rosenau 1968: 166.

[86] Quoted in ibid.: 171.

thing as a neutral yet substantive definition of intervention, just as there is no such thing as a neutral yet substantive definition of democracy, freedom, aggression, or, say, security.[87] It was in this sense that Rosenau was wrong to suggest the conferees had succumbed to 'undisciplined thought' and forgone 'clarity', even if they had failed to reach agreement on a precise meaning of the term.[88] Rather, what was occurring at Princeton, and what surely occurred in the academic literature of the 1960s, was a reasonable dispute, wherein some degree of mutual understanding was present, but imperfect, and where, in light of their relation to deeper commitments, constitutive arguments clashed in an ongoing process which could not be resolved through rational argument alone.[89] Analytical contests over the correct use of shared terms of global order discourse are also normative and political contests.[90]

Such a process of contestation is unassimilable by ahistorical or naturalist explanation. To know and better explain what it is to intervene in the realm of international relations, it would rather be necessary to attempt to map out, at multiple levels of abstraction, different patterns of the concept's use; but this would be, to use Rosenau's words, a differently 'empirical' endeavour in the realm of 'common discourse'.[91] At the international-societal level, I would now like to argue, it would have to involve a mapping of competing practices of intervention in the global-political discourse of states, bearing in mind the above lesson of failed attempts at ideal consensus in the discourse of academics as an analogy to international struggles to make and remake shared norms and rules. It would need to be genealogical insofar as it seeks to account historically for the coming into and out of being of rival meanings of intervention, drawing attention to logics and possibilities thus far unseen, and it would need to be hermeneutical insofar as it emerges out of a pragmatic dialogue with the languages of those being studied.[92] For any inquiry to assume a formal analytic or otherwise reified and essentialist meaning of intervention, while also proclaiming itself a detached and objective analysis of large-scale social change, would be to defeat itself even on its own terms, to accept a profound bias cutting to the heart of its assessment of global normative

---

[87] On essentially contested concepts in International Relations theory, and on international society itself as a contested concept, see Keene 2000. See Gallie 1955–56; Connolly 1993. On security as a contested concept, see e.g. Baldwin 1997 and Buzan and Hansen 2009. On decolonizing the concept of war, see e.g. Barkawi 2016.
[88] Rosenau 1968: 173; 1969: 155.
[89] See especially Connolly 1993: 10–35; 1984: 149–154. See also Freeden 1996: 62–67.
[90] Connolly 1993: 39.
[91] Rosenau 1968: 174.
[92] On critical genealogies and their uses, see Srinivasan 2019. On 'fusions of horizons' and the image of a conversation, see Gadamer 2004: 302–306. On comparison and undistortive human understanding, see Taylor 1995.

convergence. And yet so often from the mid-1970s into the early 2000s this is exactly the sort of analysis that we received.

Intervention for the Great Powers

We first saw it in John Vincent: 'Intervention is a word used to describe an event, something which happens in international relations: it is not just an idea which crops up in speculation about them.'[93] Vincent's *Nonintervention and International Order*, published in 1974 and recognized as 'the best general account of the rule of non-intervention', made a broad normative-political argument, but one concerned with the regulation, not the constitution, of intervention as an act.[94] Vincent posited a force-based definition to tell a story of how states have both violated and upheld the principle of non-intervention. And based on the lessons of this long-term history, we were to become non-interventionists. His preface admitted as much openly:

> What provoked this inquiry was the prevalence of the view that the contemporary world is not a world in which a principle of non-intervention can obtain in international relations. Its ultimate purpose is to reply to the prevailing view and to state a case for non-intervention principally by meeting the arguments of those who would dethrone it.[95]

For pluralists like Vincent, there were powerful and obvious moral reasons why coercion ought to be restrained in international society, but it was not immediately clear why the concept of intervention, given its multiplicity of meanings, needed to be associated with the international use of force. Vincent admitted that he was approaching the question of intervention through what he called the 'factual basis' of the 'international political environment in which law operates': one that had witnessed, as a consequence of the 'arrival of nuclear weapons' and an 'all-enveloping ideological conflict' between the United States and Soviet Union, an irremediable 'diminution of the significance of state borders'.[96] 'Specifically', wrote Vincent, 'it is in the international law of internal war that the simple doctrine of non-intervention is held to have received a challenge to which it cannot effectively respond.'[97]

---

[93] Vincent 1974: 3.
[94] Bull 1984c: 6.
[95] Vincent 1974: vii.
[96] Ibid.
[97] Ibid.

As we have begun to develop, and will develop further in the coming chapters, uses of the term intervention throughout the period of Vincent's research were often framed by decolonization and anti-colonial revolution. In such a context, 'intervention' was subject to competing interpretations. Yet, like for Michael Walzer, who would write on intervention in conversation with the idea of just war, a major concern for Vincent had to do with 'proxy conflict' among superpowers (as Walzer's preface of *Just and Unjust Wars* reads: 'I did not begin [this book] by thinking about war in general, but about particular wars, above all about the American intervention in Vietnam'[98]). While it was clear that Vincent was attempting to probe the morally and not just strategically persuasive reasons for non-interventionism in relation to internal or civil war, his was a moral inquiry occurring on just one of two levels. The first level was easier to understand: the moral question of whether, in ordinary or special circumstances, intervention was right or wrong. The second level, exemplified by Princeton, was totally overlooked: this was the moral question of intervention's constitutive limits.

So Vincent intended and curated his history as a lesson in right, but it was a lesson in right that ignored contestation in the society of states. Acknowledging unresolved academic debates regarding intervention's definition, he noted that intervention had been variously understood in terms of the type of subject that embarks upon intervention, the object or target that 'suffers' intervention, and the activity of intervention itself, only to conclude that 'the use of threat of force will be taken as a guide to the incidence of intervention.'[99] 'Here, no pretence will be made to encompass the whole field of interventionary activity in a single definition, and intervention will be understood as coercive interference.'[100] Citing none other than James Rosenau himself, Vincent went on to 'select an approximate definition of intervention' as a 'discrete event having a beginning and an end' which is 'aimed at the authority structure of the target state' and which could be said to 'break a conventional pattern of international relations.'[101] Having stipulated this conception of intervention, 'non-intervention might be said to be the circumstance in which intervention does not occur' (when temporary, 'convention-breaking', and 'authority-oriented' coercion is absent).[102]

That is, for all their clear interest in the normative and historical, Vincent and members of the English School at the time were in fact not open

---

[98] Walzer 1977: xix.
[99] Vincent 1974: 8.
[100] Ibid.
[101] Ibid.: 13. Vincent cited Rosenau 1969.
[102] Ibid.

to exploring situated and evaluative dimensions of concept formation. In a footnote, Vincent said so explicitly: while 'no study of intervention would be adequate' unless it took 'the values at stake in interventionary situations' and 'the reasons for our concern about intervention' into account, he considered the arbitration of value problems an exercise 'separate from the task of definition'.[103] Vincent was probably aware of the controversies lurking beneath the surface of Rosenau's proposal. He had, after all, revised the manuscript of *Nonintervention and International Order* at Princeton's Center of International Studies (at the time directed by Cyril Black, who had attended the Princeton Conference) and had it read twice by Richard Falk (who also attended the Conference and was particularly sensitive to the positions of the developing world).[104]

But bracketing the problem of contestation in fact appears to have been a core objective of his research project: to impart a definitive meaning for intervention—as Vincent put it, 'to fix its place in knowledge about international relations'—would be to facilitate an inquiry into a more practical ethics pertaining to 'the international law of internal war'.[105] He sought neither 'to discover a legal definition which might satisfy those who seek to restrain its occurrence by law' nor, 'given disagreement about the concept of intervention, about the sorts of activities that are to be called intervention and what it is that makes them similar', to provide a definition that captured 'the whole of reality'.[106] By dismissing its common-sense meaning altogether, *Nonintervention and International Order* was at base a meditation on the imprudence of intervention in its analytic sense, and in its arguably Western liberal sense of coercive interference.[107] And yet at the same moment, and incongruously, it sought to account for an empirical history of non-intervention in the rules and norms of international society and, more incongruously still, in the evolving practices of statespeople.[108]

Remarkably it was by these sorts of means that Rosenau's definition found a second life in the study of International Relations. A new trend began to emerge in academic writing about the intervention problem: this trend was of course not naturalist in its self-description or stated objectives, but its attempt to trace the legitimacy and evolution of intervention in international society rested on a conceptualization that was naturalist in origin and contained naturalist assumptions. In a valuable survey of existing literature on intervention

---

[103] Ibid.: 4.
[104] Vincent 1974: viii. See e.g. Falk 1962; 1966; 1984.
[105] Ibid.: 4.
[106] Ibid: 3–4.
[107] On Western liberal conceptions of intervention, see especially Chapters 1–3.
[108] For a survey of traditionalist versus behaviouralist literatures on intervention, see Little 1987.

in 1987, Richard Little described an influential set of essays in which authors, providing almost no reference at all to previous literature on the meanings of the concept, gave the impression that they were 'starting from a tabula rasa'.[109] For this 'traditionalist' school of thought, for whom there could be no reasonable understanding of the subject 'which is divorced from the conception of intervention employed by practitioners', there was extraordinary aversion to the beliefs and self-interpretations held by statespeople from beyond the West.[110] Its assessment of non-intervention in global order proceeded as if the content of the concept was self-evident or commonly understood, being inversely tied to intervention as a particular sort of event.

True, one other approach of the school involved, as Hedley Bull put it, adopting a definition of intervention rooted in international law and the writings of 'traditional international legal publicists'.[111] But the overwhelming question that ought to have been posed to him in reply was: which ones? Which definition, according to which publicist, from which part of the world? In 1963, when Louis Henkin observed before the American Society of International Law that 'international law speaks less than clearly to foreign "intervention"', he was echoing the opinion of previous speakers who had appeared at the Society's podium, like Ellen Ellis, who explained thirty years earlier that 'intervention is a term with respect to which there has been little consistent usage in international law. While the difficulties of the text-writers and others have had to do essentially with the question of its legality, much of the difference of opinion on that point has resulted from a lack of agreement as to the nature of intervention itself.'[112]

Bull insisted that scholars take as their starting point the Oppenheim-Lawrence thesis of 'dictatorial or coercive interference' that related most clearly to the threat or use of military force.[113] Yet the Brazilian jurist Accioly seemed to reject the dictatorial thesis when he offered an alternative view of intervention as influence or pressure: 'intervention may be defined by the interference of a State in the internal or external affairs of another

---

[109] Little 1987: 53. Little was referring to Bull 1984d.
[110] Little 1987: 53.
[111] Bull 1984c: 1.
[112] Henkin 1963: 154; Ellis 1933: 78. The Thomases indexed various types or outcomes of intervention covering armed force, economic sanctions, economic pressures, propaganda, and 'mere expressions of opinion', as well as, for instance, intervention by recognition or non-recognition (of new states or governments) and asylum (of political dissidents) as intervention. See Thomas and Thomas 1956: 215–414. Accordingly, the principle concerning the duty of non-intervention remains to this day, argues Vaughan Lowe, 'one of the most potent and elusive of all international principles' (Lowe 2007: 104). On the contested definition of intervention in international law, see Chesterman 2001: 7–44; Higgins 1984; Winfield 1922.
[113] Bull 1984c: 1. Bull cited Oppenheim 1948. On the dictatorial theory in the practice of states, see Chapters 2–4.

State not dependent on it, with the intention of imposing on it a certain way of proceeding'.[114] And Carlos Calvo, in his highly influential treatise and what became known as the Calvo Doctrine, condemned two types of intervention—'diplomatic' as well as 'armed'—as methods of enforcing private pecuniary claims.[115] As if to anticipate a Bull, a Vincent, or, as we will see, a Nicholas Wheeler, the nineteenth-century Argentine publicist had written this in a review of his contemporaries:

> The conclusion which results from the diverse citations which we have made is that there exists almost as many different opinions as there are authors. Some admit and approve intervention; others condemn and repudiate it; these make of it a right, those attach to it the idea of a duty; others see only a simple act, a brutal act, having its place in history, born of certain necessities and occurring under certain identical circumstances ... Right or duty, no author furnishes us clear, irrefutable data on which one can base fixed and precise rules; *it is not then in the writings of publicists that the guiding thread can be sought*.[116]

In this way the English School's choice to insist on dictatorial interference came to resemble intervention by and for the Great Powers. At the height of decolonization, it might have been thought that the South was asserting its rights 'in so extreme a form that they seem incompatible with the idea of an international society or community with rights over its members', but, if in a sense the opposite was true—that these asserted rights were compatible with and understood to deepen, not dissolve, the society of states—to maintain that a 'basic condition of any policy that can be called interventionary' was its 'dictatorial or coercive' nature would not be to account for actual global order; it would be to pick a side.[117]

Intervention as the thing itself to be reordered

Wheeler's *Saving Strangers* was published in 2000, to great acclaim and in part as a response to Vincent's earlier argument. Much has been said of the pluralist-solidarist debate and its exposure of a 'conflict between order and justice', where 'the importance of these categories [pluralism and solidarism] is that each provides a very different understanding of the legitimacy

---

[114] Accioly 1968: 50.
[115] Calvo 1896: 267. For an application of the Calvoesque tradition in international society, see Chapter 2.
[116] Ibid.: 278.
[117] Bull 1984a: 7; 1984c: 1.

of humanitarian intervention'.[118] But while in some ways Wheeler's solidarist argument was a rebuttal to Vincent's pluralist one, in other and more fundamental ways these accounts were in agreement: 'This book focuses on the legitimacy of using force to end appalling abuses of human rights.'[119] More specifically, *Saving Strangers* investigated 'how far states have recognized humanitarian intervention as a legitimate exception to the rules of sovereignty, non-intervention, and non-use of force'.[120] Although a historical account of global international society, which argued that a new norm of humanitarian intervention had emerged in the 1990s, it too was premised on the notion that contestation—of the criteria to be met before an action constituted an instance of intervention—could be reasonably ignored.

Wheeler was no doubt interested in the empirical ways in which statespeople interpreted and deployed political language, but only in the sense of justifying and ultimately legitimizing intervention as a specific type of event in international relations, not as 'an idea which crops up in speculation about them'.[121] He related his approach to the work of Quentin Skinner, or at least to the contextualism for which he was most well known at the time. Of particular importance, for Wheeler, was Skinner's argument that 'any course of action is inhibited from occurring if it cannot be legitimated'.[122] The aim was 'to incorporate the Skinner thesis into a broad-based constructivist approach' concerned with the 'constraining role' played by laws, rules, and values over international actors and to make an 'inroad into the claim that states can always create a legitimacy convenient to themselves'.[123] For if, as Skinner argued, 'the range of legitimating reasons that any actor can invoke is limited by the prevailing morality in which she finds herself', if any actor 'cannot hope to stretch the application of the existing principles indefinitely', then correspondingly actors 'can only hope to legitimate a restricted range of actions'.[124] Wheeler's overall concern hence had to do with 'the power of legitimacy' in relation to evolving 'rules of the game', where the rules of interest were 'those that constitute international society' and the focus was on 'how far the

---

[118] Wheeler 2000: 11. See e.g. Wheeler 1992; Bellamy 2003; Welsh 2011. On the idea of a conflict between order and justice, see Foot, Gaddis, and Hurrell 2003. For a critical discussion of pluralist and solidarist views on humanitarian intervention, see Bain 2021. On the progressive reformulation of the pluralist element in contemporary English School theorising, see Williams 2015.
[119] Wheeler 2000: 2.
[120] Ibid.
[121] Vincent 1974: 3. In *Saving Strangers*, Vincent's influence was everywhere: 'the writer who really started me thinking about humanitarian intervention was R. J. Vincent' (Wheeler 2000: 12). See also Vincent 1986.
[122] Skinner 1988: 117.
[123] Thereby relegating the view that 'prevailing norms and rules of any international order' are simply dictated by the most powerful states in the system. See Wheeler 2000: 4–11.
[124] Ibid.: 7; Skinner 1988: 117.

society of states recognizes the legitimacy of using force against states who grossly violate human rights'.[125]

Assessing norms and rules in terms of their 'constraining role' is one very important dimension of interpretivist methodology, but it elides distinctions between contextualist and intentionalist theories of meaning, and reflects only a selection of Skinner's own writings on how we use and understand political language in legitimation processes.[126] Skinner's work on techniques of conceptual change, particularly rhetorical redescription, would have provided—I hope we can now begin to see—a much stronger basis for assessing the evolution and function of intervention in international relations.[127] '[A]ll attempts to legislate about the "correct" use of normative terms', wrote Skinner in 2002, 'must be regarded as equally ideological in character ... their application will always reflect a wish to impose a particular moral vision on the workings of the social world.'[128] Rhetorical redescription refers to the strategy by which one replaces 'a given evaluative description with a rival term that serves to picture the action no less plausibly, but serves at the same time to place it in a contrasting moral light'.[129] It is not, strictly speaking, 'a case of substituting one word for another', but a form of conceptual change involving a 'new description' and new 'moral character'.[130] In *The Genealogy of Morality*, for instance, it was Nietzsche's contention that a Christian revolt succeeded in 'overturning the moral world of antiquity' by rhetorically redescribing core normative vocabularies.[131]

What might it mean to incorporate this other Skinnerian thesis and related ideas of his 'genealogical turn' into a study of the globalization of international society?[132] What might it mean to analyse the redescriptions, or reconstitutions, by which a more global revolt—the revolt of the newly independent and smaller states against Western-led order—has been waged and institutionalized? Amia Srinivasan explains that the key move, for critical genealogists, involves understanding our representational practices—'our beliefs, values, and concepts'—not just in terms of their epistemic merits—their aptness, for example—but rather in terms of their function, in terms

---

[125] Wheeler 2000: 6, 4. Wheeler was drawing from Thomas Franck and referencing the work of Inis Claude and John Searle. See Franck 1990; Claude 1966; Searle 1995.
[126] See e.g. the discussion in Lamb 2009. On contextualist, conventionalist, and intentionalist theories of historical meaning, see Bevir 1999: 31–52. See also Bevir 2009.
[127] Skinner 2002: 175–187.
[128] Ibid.: 182.
[129] Skinner cites the analysis of ancient rhetoricians to whom the technique was known as *paradiastole*.
[130] Skinner 2002: 183–184. Even where disputants argue about the range of circumstances in which to apply a term, rather than about its core characteristics, the outcome of such debates contribute to conceptual change. Ibid.: 186.
[131] Ibid.: 185; Nietzsche 1989.
[132] Lane 2012.

of what they do.[133] A critical genealogy, far removed from revelations of the validity or scientific reliability of any singular formulation of a concept, focuses on the purposes served by differing representations or designs: which activities they inhibit or sustain, whose dominations or positions they reinforce, and what sort of overall social order they come to establish.[134] One point is to draw our attention to the role of human agents in overturning and replacing existing evaluative descriptions with rival understandings.[135] Where such agency is exercised to redescribe prevailing moralities or rules, it could also be said to recast the range of actions available for reasonable legitimation, thereby transforming the function of those prevailing rules.[136] A skillful revolt in politics and society might therefore involve 'a conscious attempt to change our representational practices'.[137]

The dynamic of revolt as reconstitution—reconstitution of 'our beliefs, values, and concepts'—is a strange and disorienting omission in the most influential accounts of the intervention concept in global order.[138] If we readily acknowledge the 'power of legitimacy' in relation to moral and legal 'rules of the game', then it follows that we should be concerned with dynamics of redescription, including rhetorical redescription and other processes of the conscious change of our practices, that can be located in international nets or structures of power, and explained in terms of redistributed agency.[139] Closing our eyes to such contestation not only slips into a form of ethnocentric reasoning, and of thinking about global justice uprooted from actual understandings of the global diplomatic community; it also fails to provide a compelling empirical account of international-societal change. A critical-genealogical account of intervention would in contrast draw our attention to how our representational practices—or what I am calling our discursive practices—have competed and evolved.[140] Sustained at the level of international society, it would explain how intervention has been contested and redescribed in the beliefs expressed by states. In tracing the rise and fall of influential ways of interpreting, it would accordingly be concerned not only with 'who prevailed', but also 'what was argued', 'what was at stake', and 'how

---

[133] Srinivasan 2019: 142.
[134] Ibid.
[135] Ibid.: 145.
[136] I am referring and linking now to the earlier Skinner thesis. See Skinner 1988.
[137] Srinivasan 2019: 144.
[138] Ibid.: 142.
[139] Franck 1990; Searle 1995. On the technique of collective legitimation through the UN, see Claude 1966.
[140] By discourse I simply mean collections of statements through which social meaning is made. By practice I mean a patterned and socially meaningful set of actions. When we are speaking of language itself as a patterned enactment, we are conceiving of discourse as practice, and understanding practice through discourse. For a clear discussion, see Adler and Pouliot 2011: 6, 16.

the dispute proceeded'. For only once we clarify the changing conditions of what it is to intervene might we appreciate whose understandings, of which activities, have been constrained and legitimated, and to what extent, through global-international rulemaking.[141]

To return to *Saving Strangers* and related studies: we might in fact explain turn-of-the-century liberal solidarism as part of an analogous process of redescription in academic International Relations—as part of the process of reconstitution and contestation that has formed the focus of this chapter. In other words, against the backdrop of an intellectual history of the Princeton Conference, English School and related literatures might be seen to demonstrate the basic mechanism or dynamic by which much critical genealogy proceeds—by which some discursive practices, through their practitioners, achieve dominance and become conventionalized or institutionalized, in a process akin to a struggle.[142] In prominent strains of American constructivist thought, for example, exemplified by the writings of Martha Finnemore in 2003, 'the purpose of intervention' would again be conflated with 'changing beliefs about the use of force'.[143] In a discussion of her methodology, Finnemore specified the 'boundaries on the kinds of events I was willing to include in the category of "intervention"', and that in particular, 'military action had to be involved … Intervention by other means, for example, diplomatic or economic, *even if states call it intervention*, is not central to my inquiry'.[144] And yet the same study sought to assess the function of intervention in 'the changing character of international society', concluding that what had changed over time was 'not the fact of intervention'—the fact of intervention as a particular kind of event—'but its form and meaning. What have changed are state understandings about the purposes to which they can and should use force.'[145]

The point is the opposite of saying that the sprawling interventionist literature that we have come to know so well (the debate around the international legitimacy of humanitarian intervention and the related notion of the Responsibility to Protect) was unsuccessful.[146] As is widely acknowledged, liberal-interventionist studies—including radical international-legal and

---

[141] On international institutionalization and the management of global cultural diversity, see Reus-Smit 2018; Phillips and Reus-Smit 2020.

[142] On conceptualizing political argument—given its legitimating function in historical society—in a language of struggle rather than a language of rational debate, see Tully 1983. Tully cites Foucault's inversion of Clausewitz: if politics is a continuation of war by other means, then '[p]eace itself is a coded war' (Foucault 2003: 50).

[143] Finnemore 2003.

[144] Ibid.: 11–12.

[145] Ibid.: 2.

[146] For an introduction to this vast literature, see e.g. Bellamy and Dunne 2016.

cosmopolitan-theoretical studies—became indispensable reference points at the turn of the century, and made clear analytical achievements.[147] Yet they can also be seen as bound up in a successful academic redescription that imposed 'a particular moral vision on the workings of the social world' and on the workings of world politics, not only in the sense of justifying intervention, but in the sense of reconstituting it.[148] In a 1992 article for *Millennium*, Wheeler noted the 'growing interest, especially among liberal opinion in the West, in the idea of permitting a legal right of humanitarian intervention in international society'.[149] Adam Roberts later referred to 'humanitarian war', an 'oxymoron which may yet become a reality', in relation to a plausible 'new consensus' on humanitarian intervention and the revitalized purposes of NATO after the collapse of the Soviet Union and the Warsaw Pact.[150]

By the end of the Cold War, the concept of intervention was becoming more positively valued, and took on more flattering connotations—as Stefano Recchia and Jennifer Welsh would put it, 'for present-day supporters of the practice intervention is no longer an act that a target society "suffers", but rather something that it benefits from'.[151] Linklater and Suganami spoke of a related 'transformation of political community' and many observed a shift within the English School itself to champion a certain liberal solidarism, in which intervention served as enforcement both of existing international rules and of an emerging international society built around individuals rather than states.[152] But as the pendulum swung from pluralism towards solidarism, the academic conception of intervention, as a particular sort of fact or event, did not change. In the early 1970s, Vincent sought to 'fix its place' in the study of International Relations.[153] By the early 1990s, it appeared as if he had largely succeeded: a dictatorial or coercive theory of intervention rose to hegemony and, to put it one way, we forgot about Princeton.[154]

At the beginning of this book I noted the 1968 special issue of the *Journal of International Affairs* (on intervention) which announced that 'usage

---

[147] Consider the writings of Fernando Tesón, for example, who examined humanitarian intervention as if its legal validity flowed from the moral and philosophical basis of law itself. Still, his was not an argument about actual state practice around 'what is humanitarian intervention'. It was primarily an argument about the legitimate use of force. See Tesón 1988. Compare to liberal-cosmopolitan positions concerning military intervention such as e.g. Beitz 1980; Booth 1995; Caney 2005: 226–262.
[148] Skinner 2002: 182.
[149] Wheeler 1992: 1.
[150] Roberts 1993, 1999.
[151] Recchia and Welsh 2013: 1. Recchia and Welsh were quoting Vincent 1974: 3.
[152] Linklater 1998; Linklater and Suganami 2006: 223–258; see the discussion in Hurrell 2007: 57–94.
[153] Vincent 1974: 4.
[154] In an essay co-authored with Peter Wilson and posthumously published in 1993, Vincent would notably argue that 'the principle of non-intervention no longer sums up the morality of states'. See Vincent and Wilson 1993: 129.

of the term has not resulted in a common understanding of [its] meaning.'[155] In 2013, a new and important special issue on the concept appeared, this time for the *Review of International Studies*. On the face of it the issue was a firm rejection of any analytic meaning: it set out to explain intervention as a 'social practice', one that evolves and changes over both time and place—this much, as I have suggested, sounded exactly right.[156] Yet the same issue went on to specify that 'as a working guide' for intervention's historical-sociological study in the ordering of the modern world, the concept should be 'taken to refer to "discrete acts" of "coercive interference" in the "domestic affairs" of other states, and which do not change the formal juridical status of the intervened party (as would, for example, annexation or colonisation)'.[157] Not 'wanting to get bogged down' in the question of 'the difficulty of defining the term', there was a pivot back to John Vincent—back, in fact, to the definition offered by James Rosenau in 1967.[158]

Rather than escaping analytic meaning, much of what we think and write about intervention remains entangled with an inadvertently naturalist mindset: 'whereas major war and formal empire negate the dynamic between territoriality and transnationalism that drives the modern world', intervention 'rests upon it'—its function is in 'coercively facilitating the settlement of tensions between territorial and transnational forces' that order world politics.[159] Even arguable 'post-traditionalist' works, with an explicit focus on practice and discourse, remain bewitched by a dictatorial theory of intervention, as a 'specific modality of coercion' and an 'ordering practice' that is itself 'constitutive of modernity's dynamic and expansive nature'.[160]

Yet it seems difficult to deny how this sort of stipulative approach breaks with what studies of intervention in international society have always promised to be doing: accurately and honestly assessing its international functions, depicting its evolving global debate, and accounting for related cultural convergence, norm development, and institutionalization. From the vantage point of the newly independent and developing states in whose name

---

[155] Quitter 1968: ix.
[156] Macmillan 2013: 1041.
[157] Ibid.
[158] Ibid. For a broader definition of intervention (as 'transgressions of a unit's realm of jurisdiction') that deviates from the state sovereignty frame, see Reus-Smit 2013a in the same issue.
[159] Macmillan 2013: 1044.
[160] Ibid.: 1047. The trend can also be seen in earlier and more overtly post-structuralist arguments of scholars like Cynthia Weber, for whom a process of justifying historical interventions, as acts of coercive interference, constructs and reconstructs sovereignty or 'writes the state'. See Weber 1995: 125. Here practices of intervention and non-intervention were understood in terms of stabilizing what it means to be a state at particular times and places. A generation of scholars came to be preoccupied with exploring sovereignty, not intervention itself, as a discursive construct. See also e.g. Forbes and Hoffman 1993; Bartelson 1995; Malmvig 2006.

the Princeton Conference had convened, it would not be hard to argue that the conflation of technical and common-sense meanings effaced an entire field of deliberation and, consciously or not, set up a kind of ruse, one that bent all paths towards a Western liberal logic. Scholars may therefore have misrepresented the purposes of one of the most essential and controversial concepts of global order. Intervention in global order is not simply a story about the control of international coercion, for humanitarian or other reasons, but about reconstitutions of what it means to interfere in the affairs of others, such that our inherited interventionism is only one possible formulation among a range of alternative practices. There can be no convincing explanation of large-scale change in international society that does not grapple with the contingencies and contestation of statespeople's beliefs about shared concepts. Ultimately, intervention is not just a coercive ordering practice; it is the thing itself to be reordered.

Intervention, reconstitution, and the revolt against Western-led order

This chapter was about intervention as a concept and the contested nature of its global practice. It used James Rosenau and his paper presentation at the Princeton Conference as a foil for an anti-naturalist form of explanation and concept creation.[161] Rosenau's proposal betrayed an ahistorical and instrumentalist understanding of the intervention concept that must now be abandoned. Analytic meaning, as we have seen, proves confused in its value-free and neutral scientific pretensions, as well as ethnocentrically distortive. It should be replaced by a restored focus on meanings in the 'common discourse' of states.[162] Starting from the self-interpretations of practitioners, we should look at historically contested meanings that come to be re-evaluated over time, precisely through redescriptions. The uptake in the mid-1970s of the Rosenau definition, in English School circles and beyond, is a testament to an inadvertent naturalism in International Relations at the same moment that it is a demonstration of such a redescriptive or reconstitutive process. That is, the uptake of a coercive theory of intervention in Anglophone academia might be understood as an illustration of the basic dynamic by which much critical genealogy proceeds—by which our

---

[161] For an introduction to anti-naturalist interpretivism, see especially Bevir and Blakely 2018.
[162] Rosenau 1968: 174.

discursive practices transform, and consequently transform our politics and society, in processes led by situated agents.[163]

Narrative explanation based around shifting discursive practices maps out, in greater inclusiveness, the changing conditions of what it is to intervene. A genealogy shows how intervention is expressive of contingent points of view. It is also a guide to the reconstitution of those points of view in and through political relations. Even arguments that have claimed or tried to stand above the fray, it should now be clear, bear marks of the battle. What interests us are not only the apparent victories—the institutionalized or conventionalized achievements—of any one form, but the annals of the confrontation itself, and the normative logics or conceptual strategies to be pulled from its campaigns. The evolution of intervention in international society must be exposed as bound up in crises of legitimation and explained in a language of political struggle and inequality, rather than a language of purely rational debate.[164]

The cult of dictatorial or coercive interventionism is a case in point. The English School, in picking up the Rosenau definition, seized upon intervention as an extension of Great Power politics, at the expense of reasonable alternatives, even where scholars claimed neutrality or aspired to a view from nowhere. Underlying the use of the classical definition was, in the Cold War, a certain Western traditionalism and, in the optimism of the early post-Cold War period, a familiar liberal solidarism. The latter notably redescribed the international use of force for humanitarian purposes as humanitarian intervention. But few if any acknowledged the reality of smaller-power and developing world contestations that broadened the meanings of intervention and came to be etched into the rules and norms of international society. Those other meanings continue to be overlooked. There is hence good reason to believe that fundamental errors committed by both behaviouralists and traditionalists have also been committed by arguable post-traditionalists who approach intervention as a 'social practice'.[165] While intervention has been understood as a forcible practice across boundaries, including one that arbitrates crisis and orders the globe, there has been surprisingly little interest in the global ordering of intervention as a concept. Rather than capturing its empirical functions as shared vocabulary, much of what we think and write about intervention remains basically entangled with a naturalist or quasi-naturalist thesis that Rosenau once called analytic.

---

[163] Srinivasan 2019: 140–147.
[164] Tully 1983: 505–507.
[165] Macmillan 2013: 1041.

The fuller picture that I have put together, then, is that intervention is not only 'a word used to describe an event'; it is a normative-political concept that is practised and repractised in international discourse.[166] To put the argument through multiple sieves that relate to key steps that I have taken in this chapter: contrary to conventional wisdom, intervention is, by virtue of its evaluative nature, 'something that crops up in speculation' about international relations.[167] But it is not a coercive 'ordering practice'.[168] It is the thing itself that is ordered, in contestations that are also reconstitutions. More specifically it is the thing that has been reordered, through contestation, and at the global level of the society of states. Even more specifically it is the thing to be globally reordered, according to the diverse beliefs of statespeople, and in relation to norms and institutions that have reflected and managed those beliefs. All this I take to be the methodological basis of a global genealogy of intervention traced since the founding of the United Nations, which should restore a focus on the meanings that shape international action, and challenge and alter hegemonic terms of understanding.

If intervention is a function of the knowledge embodied by discursive practice, then we must move now from a type of scholarship whose primary effect was to establish the worth of one specific practice, to a type of account that seeks to decipher historical contests between practices, and teaches us to think again in terms of contests. The coming chapters aim to cultivate a deeper appreciation for contingency, contrivance, and diversity in shared pathways to global governance—precisely those themes that we cannot afford to ignore in an increasingly strained and multipolar context that might seem to imply not just an abidingly post-Western world, but a waning or fragile global order. The Princeton story warns us clearly against developmental narratives of any singular interventionism in terms of diffusion or retreat. Contestation refers here to conditions of meaning, and my aim is to establish a history of the ways and processes through which meaning has been disturbed and remade. I want to do so also in the spirit of a protest, one that reimagines revolt as a history of our present dilemma.

---

[166] Vincent 1974: 3. Compare to Rosenau 1969.
[167] Vincent 1974: 3.
[168] Macmillan 2013: 1047.

2
Dictatorial intervention and the UN Charter

Between 1939 and 1945, much of the old international order had become discredited. Attempting to construct a new framework in its place was the United Nations—not yet the international organization, but the Allied alliance of 1942 after whom the organization was to be named. The forty-six nations who had declared war on the Rome–Berlin–Tokyo Axis, their governments the original voice of 'we, the peoples, of the United Nations', were seeking to preserve and defend international society by remaking it—to impart new ideas of what to do and what not to do in the relations of its states, to lay down new international rules, norms, and laws.

And to these United Nations, the meanings and limits of intervention were of central concern. For to greater and lesser degrees, global war had trampled upon the domestic and reached into the exclusive affairs of all participants. Its outbreak was itself marked by extreme interventions that breached the Covenant of the League of Nations. To name an obvious few: when Italy invaded Ethiopia, Mussolini claimed that this war would liberate populations that since millennia had been 'at the mercy of a few bloody and rapacious chiefs', that Italy was exercising 'the right and the capacity of extending that high protection which the very Covenant of the League of Nations, in its Article 22, recognizes as the civilizing mission incumbent upon the more advanced nations'.[1] When Japan launched its attack on Northeast China, Tokyo referred to its Mukden pretext and supposed self-defence.[2] And when Germany occupied Czechoslovakia, Hitler asserted the inalienable right to self-determination of minorities, who, under alleged Czechoslovak oppression, were in need of protection by the German Reich.[3]

---

[1] Mussolini 1936: 30; United States Department of State (*Papers Relating to the Foreign Relations of the United States*, cited henceforth as FRUS) 1935: I, Document 568.
[2] FRUS 1931: I, Document 10, Document 14, Document 55.
[3] See e.g. Shirer 1960: 384–396.

Hence, when an international conference was called to draft a charter for a general international organization, there was a shared interest in reordering the concept in a way that would preserve a newly won era of peace. Divergences between governments were widespread, but the incentive to address globally, and not just regionally, the problem of intervention was overwhelming. It was in this sense not surprising that when the United Nations Conference on International Organization opened at San Francisco in April 1945, non-interventionism was being described by participants as one of its 'most important questions'.[4]

The San Francisco episode provides an ideal starting point for a genealogy of intervention or non-intervention in international society. In speaking of the founding of the United Nations (UN), I am concerned again with the contingent design of intervention in the context of power-political choice, whereby interstate practice of the concept reflects the exclusion of alternatives, which can be documented in conference transcripts, resolutions, and voting records. Here questions about the meaning of intervention are formally raised and provisionally answered through the contents of the Charter. Because of what participants were trying to do—to determine nothing less than a comprehensive post-war global order—a whole series of discursive practices came together at San Francisco, and out of them emerged a set of important codifications that structured a global debate among states in the Cold War and post-Cold War eras. San Francisco is therefore a story that deserves a detailed, micro-level analysis: it recounts, in broad terms, the construction of an institutionalized framework of thinking about intervention within which subsequent discursive developments occur.

I want to argue that this framing is best understood at the intersection between two discursive practices influential at this particular moment in history. Each of these practices, in rival terms describing but also evaluating intervention, in a process of reconstituting and not just regulating intervention as an act, may be interpreted in official viewpoints adopted throughout the conference. The first—what I will call a theory of 'dictatorial intervention' (to draw on the language of 'dictatorial or coercive interference' in juridical interpretations emphasized by its adherents)—confronted a theory of 'effective intervention' espoused by a primarily Latin American-led coalition of smaller states (the logic of which I explain below).

While conference participants largely converged over intervention-related rights belonging to the UN as an organization, there was much disagreement over the rights to be allocated to the organization's members. Collective

---

[4] The official Canadian report referred to non-interference in the domestic affairs of states as 'one of most important questions before the Conference' (Canadian Department of External Affairs 1945: 18).

actions sometimes recognized as interventionary were to be undertaken by particular masters (the Security Council through its members) when 'international peace and security' was breached or threatened—this much was clearly agreeable to all.[5] Less agreeable was whether states themselves could unilaterally intervene and exactly which means, if any, of doing so— armed force, economic sanctions, propaganda bombardment, sedition, international criticism, tied aid, diplomatic threats, etc.—could be considered legitimate. Intervention had two significant meanings at San Francisco that came to be reflected in two different articles: Article 2 (4) and Article 2 (7). It is to the former, pertaining to the question of intervention occurring between states, that I devote most of my attention, for it was here that the most heated disputes emerged, with the most surprising consequences.

If the practice of the smaller powers advocated a broad, more 'effective' proscription to international interventionary activities, then what do I mean by 'broad', what do I mean by 'effective'? First I mean 'broad' in the sense that it prohibited not only armed force, but also a wide range of other means of interfering with the sovereignty, independence, or even 'personality' of the state.[6] The argument usually adhered to the following sort of logic: all states have a right to determine their own futures—their own 'destinies'—and accordingly all states have a duty to refrain from intervention, whether direct or indirect, for whatever reason, in the domestic affairs of another state.[7] Consequently, all forms of armed interference but also political, economic, and cultural interference are to be condemned in relations between states. I lay emphasis on 'effective', then, in the sense that this theory of intervention referred not to the means, but to the effect or outcome, of foreign constraint. Here, in line with an inter-American legal tradition associated with Carlos Calvo, it is not the form but the outcome of foreign constraint or pressure, in relation to a spectrum of political, economic, and cultural elements, that defines the character of an interventionary act.[8] Intervention is the effect or outcome of foreign pressure on the liberty of states, if not nations or peoples, over their own affairs.[9]

In contrast, a dictatorial theory of intervention attempted to order intervention, at least between states, with reference to the use or threat of armed force. In doing so, it seemed to drastically narrow the scope of

---

[5] See Chapter VII of the UN Charter.
[6] See e.g. UNCIO 1945: VI, 457.
[7] See e.g. UNCIO 1945: III, 245.
[8] Calvo 1896: I, sec. 110.
[9] The relationship between effective intervention—espoused here by a Latin American-led coalition— and evolving discourses of self-determination—espoused especially by the new states of Asia and Africa— is explored in Chapter 3.

the fundamental duty of non-intervention by placing unarmed interferences of a more political, economic, or cultural nature out of the reach of related international rules. It therefore excluded from its interpretation things like the use of economic inducements and dependence, propaganda, and plausibly a range of fifth column activities like espionage, sabotage, or the political manipulation of proxy actors. This resonated with a particular interpretation of the 'dictatorial interference' argument made by Oppenheim and Lawrence—the conceptualization with which IR scholars are today so familiar—that implied that the essence of intervention was not about pressure but about coercion.[10] Intervention was described less as an abstract effect or outcome—less as the abstract effect or outcome of foreign pressure against the independence or personality of a UN member state—than as a coercive pattern of behaviour enumerated, not always but usually, in military terms.

In the end, the Great Powers, and with them the arguments of the dictatorial understanding, would prevail. The institutional result was a remarkable double ordering of the intervention problem in the UN Charter, the meaning of which will become clearer as this chapter continues. The Charter was of course signed and eventually ratified by all participants, but diplomatic compromise or capitulation is not to be confused with cultural convergence or persuasion. We can and should show that the conference's most controversial decisions were not really made in its meeting rooms, but quite literally in Secretary of State Edward Stettinius' private penthouse at the Fairmont Hotel, where smaller-power proposals sought hegemonic assent—the assent of the US, the USSR, the UK, China, and France. I am proposing, then, that to ignore the play of discursive practice is to risk mischaracterizing global debate and to misunderstand the function initially performed by the intervention concept in the early post-war years. Although the creation of the UN is often felt as a broad-minded achievement, where cultures joined hands and breathed life into common principles, for many the mode of realizing intervention in the UN Charter was one of diminution if not oppression.

Sponsoring powers' proposals

By 1944 the so-called 'Big Three' (the US, the USSR, and the UK) had already met to prescribe the structure of the international organization they hoped to create, especially at Dumbarton Oaks in September 1944 and at Yalta the following February. Not all attendees were drawn from the West: Republican

---

[10] Oppenheim 1912: 305; Lawrence 1913: 124–125. See Chapter 1.

China was also present at the first of these meetings—though we should note that Chiang Kai-shek's government was a less-than-equal participant behind closed doors (to treat the 'pigtails' as a victorious Great Power, Churchill has been quoted as saying, would reflect 'a wholly unreal standard of values').[11] Agreements made at Dumbarton Oaks formed the basis of a draft Charter that served as the sole agenda item at San Francisco, a meeting itself jointly sponsored by the US, the USSR, the UK, and China. When delegates arrived for the Conference on International Organization (the San Francisco Conference), then, they were not gathering around a blank slate, but replying to a template provided by their hosts.[12]

There was no explicit inclusion of the word 'intervention' in the Dumbarton Oaks Proposals signed on 7 October 1944. But while the four governments stopped short of inserting a non-intervention provision, the meaning of intervention was openly deliberated in 1944 and agreements over issues like domestic jurisdiction and the use of force were understood to have set boundaries around interventionary activities in the post-war order.[13] We can explore the contested nature of those boundaries by examining suggestions made by working groups of official Dumbarton Oaks delegations. Such suggestions spoke to the long history of the non-intervention principle in major international treaties and constitutional documents, not least in the Covenant of the League of Nations that the Proposals set out to improve on.[14]

For instance, one proposal for member states 'to refrain from the use of force or threat to use force in its relations with other states and *from any intervention in the internal affairs of other states*, except in performance of its obligation to contribute to the enforcement procedures instituted by the Executive Council' appeared in an American draft in December 1943.[15] Related provisions calling for member states to 'respect political independence' (a concern of importance 'particularly among the smaller states') and 'respect and maintain the territorial integrity and political independence of each other against external aggression' (where the scope of 'aggression' was not limited to armed force) also appeared in official Chinese plans for the general international organization, including those as late as August 1944.[16]

---

[11] See Stettinius 1975: 53, quoted in Hilderbrand 1990: 59, 123. The inclusion of France created a 'Big Five' and eventually a Permanent Five ('P5').
[12] United States Department of State 1945: 26.
[13] See Robert Hartley's recollection of the debate around non-intervention at Dumbarton Oaks ('the problem arose out of defining what constituted intervention') contained in FRUS 1945: I, Document 222.
[14] Particularly Article 15 (8) of the *Covenant of the League of Nations*. See Rajan 1961: 20–31.
[15] The statement was prepared by the Informal Political Agenda Group on 21 December, directly after President Roosevelt's return from the Cairo and Tehran conferences (FRUS 1944: I, Document 366).
[16] Ibid.: Document 475, Document 410.

The record of informal American consultations with Latin American states, too, makes the following very clear: that the Big Three were aware of a smaller-power plea for non-intervention to be ordered as a duty not just of the hypothetical UN organization itself, but of all states as members towards each other. Such a non-interventionism would emulate existing norms and rules in the inter-American system. On 15 September 1944, for instance, during a meeting in Washington, DC with ambassadors from Colombia, Brazil, Peru, Mexico, Uruguay, Venezuela, and Chile, Secretary of State Cordell Hull assured his guests that the United States was at Dumbarton Oaks precisely to insist upon 'principles already established in the Inter-American community; for example, non-intervention and non-discrimination'.[17]

Yet, contrary to Hull's suggestion, as it became clear that the intervention concept was subject to various and occasionally radical interpretations ('sometimes the failure to act is intervention', reportedly contended the British delegation at Dumbarton Oaks), the term disappeared from draft proposals.[18] Washington's early call to prohibit 'any intervention' between state members became conspicuously missing in future iterations of American planning documents, which were revised according to new recommendations by Hull himself and President Roosevelt.[19] And related attempts by China to introduce a broad definition of aggression were short-lived after London voiced its opposition.[20]

True, there was broad agreement on limiting the intervention rights of the UN itself, and this might have seemed, at first blush, to placate demands for a non-intervention clause. But a non-intervention principle intended to ward off the organization's becoming a kind of suprastate was very different from a non-intervention principle intended to govern activities between its members. One shared understanding was, yes, non-interventionist in the sense that states refused to surrender their sovereignty to a new and experimental international body like the UN. To the Big Three, the rights and duties available to the organization were to be those of an association of sovereign states, perhaps centred around a Great Power concert and a more general assembly of members, but never a 'world government'.[21] And, yes, this was an especially important concern for Roosevelt, who in the final years of his

---

[17] Hull claimed during this 15 September meeting that, at Montevideo, he had accepted a policy of non-intervention 'in spite of the feelings of other members of the United States Delegation'. See ibid.: Document 494.
[18] FRUS 1945: I, Document 222.
[19] FRUS 1944: I, Document 390.
[20] The Chinese group preferred to 'see "aggression" defined' by an 'illustrative but not comprehensive' list. See ibid.: Document 476, Document 475. On reordering intervention through codifications and enumerations of non-aggression at San Francisco, see 'A Latin American-led revolt' later in this chapter.
[21] United States Department of State 1945: 100.

Dictatorial intervention and the UN Charter 59

presidency sought to succeed where Woodrow Wilson had failed, and who saw in the founding of a general international organization a personal and grand-strategic legacy.[22] If the Charter was ever to be ratified by the US Senate (if it was ever to avoid the fate of the Covenant of the League), senators had to be assured that the organization's interventionary and coercive capacities were essentially under American control (I discuss the Security Council's veto power in the coming paragraphs).[23]

But what needs to be stressed is that there was strong opposition to managing *interstate* behaviour by reference to the non-intervention principle at the same time that there was strong support for managing, by reference to that principle, the activities of *the organization itself* towards its members. States of course conferred on the UN and what came to be called the Security Council primary responsibility for the maintenance of international peace and security. Yet if a strain of organization-led interventionism entered the Proposals, its character was relatively moderate, having been marked by the collective refusal of the four participating governments to turn down other, more robustly internationalist paths that might have, and later would, gain the support of the majority of the organization's members.

To illustrate: in 1944, a particular UN-based humanitarian interventionism was advocated for inclusion in the draft Charter. The paragraph was the handiwork of maverick American diplomat Benjamin Cohen.[24] At least one September draft of the Joint Formulation Group at Dumbarton Oaks laid out an unequivocal right of the UN organization to undertake interventions on the grounds of 'humanity and justice':

> It is the duty of each member of the Organization to see to it that conditions prevailing within its jurisdiction do not endanger international peace and security and, to this end, to respect the human rights and fundamental freedoms of all its people and to govern in accordance with the principles of humanity and justice. *Subject to the performance of this duty the Organization should refrain from intervention in the internal affairs of any of its members.*[25]

Yet such a humanitarian interventionism was all too much for the Allies present. Not because of a perceived vulnerability to coercive or armed UN interventions—these seemed a political implausibility—but rather because of more probable exposure to UN interventions in other forms, including

---

[22] See e.g. Gowan 2003.
[23] On approaches to collective security and the failures of the League, see e.g. Ceadel 2013.
[24] See Lasser 2002: 280. Cohen's original formulation is in FRUS 1944: I, Document 440.
[25] FRUS 1944: I, Document 440. A similar proposal later presented by France at San Francisco to include humanitarian intervention provision would notably also fail. See UNCIO 1945: VI, 498.

political, economic, and communicative or cultural forms. Sir Alexander Cadogan claimed that a humanitarian intervention provision might enable the General Assembly to engage in invasive criticisms of members.[26] After Ambassador Gromyko voiced a similar concern, claiming that the international promotion of human rights was simply 'not germane to the main tasks of an international security organization', the Americans set aside the Cohen provision.[27] It would be erased from subsequent drafts and Cohen himself would not be asked to attend the San Francisco Conference.[28]

Instead, according to the final Proposals, the organization was empowered to intervene when and only when the Security Council deemed 'international peace and security' to be threatened or breached.[29] First, the Proposals empowered the Security Council to use all diplomatic, economic, and other measures not involving the use of armed force to give effect to international action mandated with the maintenance or restoration of the peace. Second, if such pacific measures failed, the Council reserved the right to intervene through unlimited military enforcement action by air, sea, and land. In every instance, the authority to monitor and control what was meant by 'threats' or 'breaches' to 'peace' and 'security' was granted to members of the Council, bound by a certain crucial voting formula.[30]

This crucial voting formula was definitively settled as a non-negotiable item at Yalta and announced as an additional provision to the Proposals on 5 March 1945. The decision was to appoint (not to elect) five permanent Council members who were to wield veto powers over matters of substance as well as procedure. Early American plans to include Brazil as a sixth permanent member were dashed when the idea of expanding the membership of the Council faced objections primarily from the Soviet Union.[31]

And in some ways, the exclusion of Brazil exemplified a trend running through Dumbarton Oaks and into San Francisco, whereby the sponsoring governments in their design of the new international organization deviated from the inclusivist ideals so crucial to its outward appearance. 'Where questions of power and security are concerned', it was thought 'most unwise to raise theoretical issues like sovereign equality', and better instead to favour 'common sense and safety first rather than status for the smaller countries.'[32]

---

[26] FRUS 1944: I, Document 440.
[27] Ibid.
[28] Ibid.: Document 460.
[29] See Dumbarton Oaks Proposals, Chapter VIII, Section B.
[30] See generally Lowe et al. 2008.
[31] See e.g. discussions of Brazil as a permanent member in FRUS 1944: I, Document 429.
[32] I am quoting a 30 September 1944 telegram that was written by Jan Smuts to Churchill, which was notably then forwarded by Churchill to Roosevelt. See ibid.: Document 464.

Dictatorial intervention and the UN Charter   61

'Common sense', 'safety first' formulations (of the intervention problem, like Council arrangements) were, a critical view might begin to suggest, formulations that retained or expanded Great Power control.

Here three examples should be cited. First: by the end of the meeting at Dumbarton Oaks, the article that eventually became Article 2 (7) of the UN Charter appeared in the Proposals as Section A, paragraph 7, slated into Chapter VIII ('Arrangements for the Maintenance of International Peace and Security including Prevention and Suppression of Aggression'):

> The provisions of paragraphs 1 to 6 of Section A should not apply to situations or disputes arising out of matters which by international law are solely within the domestic jurisdiction of the state concerned.[33]

This wording and location had important consequences. Placed in Section A, the article referred to the pacific settlement of disputes, and specifically disputes not yet considered to constitute a threat or breach to international peace and security (the subject matter of Section B). It provided that whether a certain matter was within the domestic jurisdiction of a state was to be determined by international law, rather than by a decision of the Council itself—as was the case with an otherwise similar article of the League Covenant—or by the self-judgement of the state concerned.[34] It also laid down the criterion of 'solely' within domestic jurisdiction: the article hence referred to matters unshared by the evolving scope of international law or by obligations that states expressly undertook towards other states under treaties or agreements.[35]

But for many, what was even more significant was this: by being inserted into Chapter VIII, the article regulated interventionary activities of the UN organization itself, and specifically the Security Council—it had no bearing on interventions undertaken by states in other states.[36]

Second: to address this 'between-states' dimension of the intervention problem, the Proposals appeared to dedicate just a single article: 'All members of the Organization shall refrain in their international relations from the threat or use of force in any manner inconsistent with the purposes of the Organization.'[37] Such a formulation would narrow the theoretical

---

[33] Dumbarton Oaks Proposals, Chapter VIII, Section A, paragraph 7.
[34] Article 15 (8) of the League Covenant, on which the Dumbarton Oaks reservation was based, held that the League Council itself was to determine, according to the prescribed standard of international law, whether a matter was 'solely within the domestic jurisdiction' of a state. For a discussion, see Rajan 1961: 20–31.
[35] I return to this general point in Chapter 3. See ibid.: 32–35. See also Davies 1946.
[36] See e.g. Goodrich and Hambro 1949: 110–111.
[37] Dumbarton Oaks Proposals, Chapter II, Article 4.

scope of illegitimate intervention insofar as it excluded a range of activities—informational, cultural, economic, and otherwise—explicitly recognized as interventionary by other states that would become founding members of the UN (among them, as I will show, those Latin American countries whom Hull had informally consulted and who would later claim to speak on behalf of the interests of smaller countries in general). Again it was not that the drafters had been unaware of alternative formulations; to add to our examples, China argued that the section that would become Article 2 (4) should explicitly forbid the 'provision of arms and munitions, or financial or technical assistance to the nationals of another state, calculated to create civil commotion or to overthrow the government of such state'.[38] The point is rather that these other forms of intervention were chosen to be omitted from the Charter's proscription.

And third: while the Proposals did list the 'sovereign equality' of 'all peace-loving states' among the organization's principles—the language having first appeared in the Moscow Declaration on General Security signed by all four sponsoring powers in 1943—the meaning of 'sovereign equality' was itself highly contested.[39] Its consequences for the precise constitution of intervention were difficult to ascertain. Multiple meanings of 'sovereign equality', with very different implications, appeared in sponsoring powers' planning documents and eventually in the preparatory work of the San Francisco Conference.[40] According to tentative British proposals for the international organization, for instance, two principles followed from sovereign equality: 'in the first-place members must agree to respect each other's political independence, and secondly all members enjoy equality of status, though not necessarily equality of function'.[41] But to the Soviet Union, sovereign equality was understood merely as a principle holding that the organization must be 'open to membership by all peace-loving states, large and small'.[42] And in private meetings of the American delegation at the San Francisco Conference, Harley Notter is on record as having said 'we interpret sovereign equality as embodying the principle of respect for territorial integrity'.[43] For his part, John Foster Dulles (who helped to prepare the Dumbarton Oaks

---

[38] FRUS 1944: I, Document 410.
[39] See Dumbarton Oaks Proposals, Chapter II, Article 1, and Chapter I, Article 2.
[40] According to the report of Committee I/1 to Commission 1 at the San Francisco Conference, the phrase 'sovereign equality' was assumed by committee members to include multiple elements, one of which was notably 'that the personality of the state is respected, as well as its territorial integrity and independence' (UNCIO 1945: VI, 457).
[41] FRUS 1944: I, Document 410.
[42] Ibid.: Document 403. American and Chinese draft outlines for the international organization did not include the words at all. Ibid.: Document 410, Document 390.
[43] FRUS 1945: I, Document 224.

Proposals and would serve as a senior adviser to the American delegation at San Francisco) had written in an academic article titled 'Conceptions and Misconceptions Regarding Intervention' published years earlier that 'there may be and should be, one type of [sovereign] equality, that is, equality of opportunity', such that 'when we find states which have failed to grow up, then we cannot claim for those states in their relation with other nations, a complete equality any more than in society individuals who have failed to grow up are as a practical matter the equal of other members of society'.[44]

As the Peruvian delegation would put it during formal conference debate in 1945 concerning what would eventually become Article 2 (1) of the Charter: 'sovereign equality' was a 'newly coined phrase that has no technical or scientific meaning'.[45] The error of its ambiguity would have 'a tremendous importance and effect', for by using it, the founders of the United Nations organization would put aside the 'main idea, the idea of [state] personality', which would also be to 'put aside the idea of sovereignty' as construed by smaller states.[46] The 'elements that ought to be respected in states are not only the political elements embodied in the physical state, and the material element, that is the territory ... the small countries chiefly ask respect for their moral personalities'.[47] This language of 'respect for personality' had been accepted in the Declaration of Lima of 1938 and 'the word "personality" regarding states was put in the Act of Chapultepec'.[48] To recognize as much might also be to see how a particular theory of intervention had been written into key agreements and proposals of the countries of the Americas, but not in those of the sponsoring powers. 'It seems to me that the Chapultepec Act is as deserving of respect as the Moscow Declaration; perhaps it will even have the same importance in the sequence of the events of the world.'[49]

Intervention as the effect of foreign pressure

To better understand intervention in an increasingly global international society, we should read what followed Dumbarton Oaks as the beginning of a revolt. It was not that the so-called lesser powers disagreed with the 'Greats' in their adopting of larger responsibilities over universal collective security—in light of the role played by the four governments in ending the

[44] Dulles 1929: 102–103.
[45] UNCIO 1945: VI, 66–67.
[46] Ibid.: 67.
[47] Ibid.
[48] Ibid.
[49] Ibid.

world war, as well as their superiority in military capability, this much was to be expected—but that certain other dimensions of the Proposals, including in regard to non-intervention, had been arranged without the sort of consultation expected of good neighbours, even less wartime allies.

In October 1944 the Brazilian ambassador to Washington, DC reported that President Getúlio Vargas and members of his Foreign Office were 'considerably embarrassed by having to admit that they knew nothing other than what they had seen in the press' regarding the progress of the Dumbarton Oaks Conference.[50] Having been excluded from this foundational exercise in post-war global ordering, and apprehensive of what the Proposals contained (or did not contain), nineteen Latin American governments agreed to meet separately in Chapultepec Castle, Mexico City, in early 1945.[51] Joined by the United States, they did so to take a pre-emptive stance on normative issues that would preoccupy the San Francisco Conference, and to reinforce a long-standing Pan-Americanism. Chapultepec put forward, as is well known, a regionalist answer to the collective security question so central to a hypothetical post-war international organization, but it was also implicated in a broader redescription of the intervention concept.[52]

A core aspect of Chapultepec was its state-based non-interventionism.[53] In codifying and extending regional norms sheltering the domestic affairs of states from the interference of other states, the Act of Chapultepec reaffirmed certain fundamental principles proclaimed at earlier inter-American conferences, including: 'the condemnation of intervention by one State in the internal or external affairs of another' (adopted at the Seventh International Conference of American States, 1933, and the Inter-American Conference for the Maintenance of Peace, 1936) and 'the recognition that respect for the personality, sovereignty and independence of each American State constitutes the essence of international order sustained by continental solidarity, which historically has been expressed and sustained by declarations and treaties in force' (adopted at the Eighth International Conference of American States, 1938).[54] The Act's signatories declared that 'every State has the right to the respect of its individuality and independence, on the part of the other members of the international community', and, to prescribe a code of inter-American solidarity and reciprocal assistance consistent with this

---

[50] FRUS 1944: I, Document 493.
[51] See e.g. Gellman 1979: especially chapter 14; Smith 1994: especially chapter 3.
[52] Chapter VIII of the UN Charter would come to order the involvement of regional organizations in the maintenance of international peace and security. This was another crucial choice in San Francisco's ordering of the intervention problem, but not the choice of primary interest in this chapter.
[53] Inter-American Reciprocal Assistance and Solidarity Act (Act of Chapultepec).
[54] Ibid.

non-interventionism, that 'every attack of a state against the integrity or the inviolability of the territory, or against the sovereignty or political independence of an American State, shall ... be considered as an act of aggression against the other States that sign this Act'.[55]

What I am saying then is that Chapultepec should be understood as committing the US and the Latin American states to a regionalist system of collective self-defence from foreign—and it would often be assumed, Soviet—acts of aggression, yet from within a broader framework of non-interventionism among states. While a mutual security guarantee was a relatively new idea in the region, the latter framework was much older, and expressive of an unorthodox and often-forgotten discursive practice.[56] I want to devote a little space to laying out this point in more detail. There can be traced through the modern history of intervention in the Americas the basic logic of a non-Western theory of intervention that came to be picked up by many in 1945. This theory construes intervention as a particular kind of effect.

To introduce that theory through a historical illustration: we might say that bitter and cautionary memories of foreign interference—first European, then American—had long spurred the integration of a robust non-interventionism into inter-American public law, beginning as early as 1826 at meetings like the Congress of Panama. It was as if, to draw from a speech made by the Cuban delegation at Montevideo in 1933, the concept of intervention had come to be understood in the region as a 'congenital vice': the Americas were colonized by Europeans and new nation states were born out of resistance to European empire, but these newly liberated nations soon became subject to a kind of ingrained North American interventionism. This occasionally befell through arrangements that verged on quasi-annexation, as with the Platt Amendment, to take one example. Intervention was hence the 'curse of America' and the 'curse of curses' for its smallest countries, which encompassed foreign influence and control through bayonets and marine landings, but also, very crucially, through other kinds of means.[57]

According to this sort of story it was in 1868 that the Calvo Doctrine came to challenge the Monroe Doctrine: whereas the latter proscribed military intervention in territories of the Americas by non-American states, such as historical European efforts to seize Venezuelan territory as a matter of a forcible debt recovery, the former attempted to proscribe a much wider range of international action—American and non-American—including in

---

[55] Ibid.
[56] For comprehensive discussions of non-intervention in the history of international law in the Americas, see for example Scarfi 2017; Lorca 2015: especially chapter 9; Thomas and Thomas 1956.
[57] The Cuban delegation at Montevideo is quoted in Connell-Smith 1966: 89.

reference to the collection of public or contractual debts.[58] Calvo condemned absolutely both 'diplomatic' and armed intervention in the domestic affairs of states.[59] He recognized that intervention constituted more than only armed force or the threat thereof. For Calvo the type or form of intervention is of little importance: the key point is the effect of foreign constraint or pressure.[60] And this theory of intervention became a Latin American discursive practice, particularly a practice that clashed with American doctrines that evolved and changed: in December 1904, President Theodore Roosevelt enunciated his Roosevelt Corollary, first as a defence of coercive interference in the Dominican Republic, and second as a basis on which to justify subsequent use of armed force. 'Chronic wrongdoing' was to require 'intervention by some civilized nation', like the United States, as an exercise of 'international police power'.[61]

Calvo's interpretation of intervention—an expression of what I am calling the theory of effective intervention—can be seen as a certain negation, then, of a dictatorial or coercive tradition associated with the legal traditions of North America and Europe:

> Certain publicists give the name of intervention only to [armed intervention] objecting that if the interposition on the part of one state in the affairs of another is not violent but peaceful, limited purely to advice, it resolves itself into an amicable interposition, or good offices, or even in mediation, which is not intervention. This is, according to my view, to take the result for the act itself. The form under which intervention takes place does not alter its character.[62]

It is true that by the mid-1930s, Franklin Roosevelt's Good Neighbor Policy expressed a new strain of American non-interventionism. The early nineteenth-century policy of his fifth cousin Theodore had been abandoned, and Washington was pulling away from former President Hoover's endorsement of the Clark Memorandum, which reserved an American right to the pre-emptive use of force under a doctrine of self-preservation.[63] The American practice of intervention had in this way been altered; the forcible, 'civilizing' sentiments of its older formulation were replaced by an appeal

---

[58] Calvo 1896: I.
[59] Compare with the narrower Drago doctrine, written by Argentine foreign minister Luis María Drago in response to the German, Italian, and British blockade of Venezuela in 1902. For a discussion, see Hershey 1907.
[60] Thomas and Thomas 1956: 68–69.
[61] Theodore Roosevelt's annual message to Congress of 6 December 1904 in FRUS 1904: XLI.
[62] Calvo 1896: I, sec. 110.
[63] The Clark Memorandum is reprinted in Dozer 1976: 116–122.

to the etiquette of good neighbourliness.[64] At the Montevideo Conference of December 1933, Secretary of State Cordell Hull did clearly accept that 'no country has the right to intervene in the internal or external affairs of another'.[65]

Yet, far from embracing the Calvo Doctrine, Roosevelt's Good Neighbor Policy in context contradicted its most novel elements. From a particular Latin American perspective, then: to say that the Good Neighbor Policy as practised was an articulation of non-intervention, properly understood, would be an overstatement if not a lie.

The crucial fact of December 1933 is that Washington attached reservations to the Montevideo Convention that are expressive of the same formulation of state-based non-interventionism that appeared in the Dumbarton Oaks documents (and eventually, I am beginning to suggest, the UN Charter). In a telegram for President Roosevelt and Acting Secretary of State William Phillips, Hull recalled the acrimony of the Latin Americans over Article 8, the non-intervention article, in particular, for which 'the demand for a unanimous affirmative vote was very vociferous and more or less wild and unreasonable'.[66] During a meeting of the subcommittee on the Rights and Duties of States, Hull delivered a speech that was incorporated verbatim as a formal reservation of the United States:

> I feel safe in undertaking to say that under our support of the general principle of non-intervention as has been suggested, no government need fear any intervention on part of the United States under the Roosevelt administration. I think it unfortunate that during the brief period of this Conference there is apparently not time within which to prepare interpretations and definitions of these fundamental terms that are embraced in the report. Such definitions and interpretations would enable every government to proceed in a uniform way without any difference of opinion or of interpretations.[67]

By qualifying that there was 'not time within which to prepare interpretations and definitions of these fundamental terms that are embraced in the report', Washington voted in favour while also protecting its rights according to 'the law of nations as generally recognized and accepted'.[68] Yet it was also under

---

[64] Roosevelt, argues Alan McPherson, had previously 'backed occupations, boasting that he had written Haiti's 1918 constitution and calling its inhabitants "little more than primitive savages"'. He was now 'following prevailing political winds'. McPherson 2016: 121. Roosevelt is quoted in Grandin 2006: 32.
[65] The Convention on Rights and Duties of States, signed by the United States, is reprinted in e.g. Carnegie Endowment for International Peace 1940: 121–123.
[66] FRUS 1933: IV, Document 115.
[67] Ibid.
[68] Ibid. See also e.g. Appendix 21 in United States Department of State 1934: 20.

'the law of nations as generally recognized and accepted' that Washington had earlier rejected the Calvo Doctrine.[69] In clinging rather to the treatises of Oppenheim and others, American policymakers interpreted intervention by exclusive reference to 'dictatorial or coercive interference': to 'big stick' operations and occupations like those that had been conducted by American marines in Nicaragua, Haiti, and the Dominican Republic.[70] Two days after the Montevideo Conference ended, Roosevelt clarified what Hull's delegation had meant when it adopted the Convention on the Rights and Duties of States: 'The definite policy of the United States from now on is one opposed to *armed intervention*.'[71]

This seems like such an important point, with such significant implications for our understanding of San Francisco and an incipient global debate around the ordering of intervention, that I want to provide further evidence. The Roosevelt administration's interpretation of intervention was, observed Gordon Connell-Smith in 1966, 'a very narrow one: the actual employment of armed force. Only with such a narrow definition could it have protested that it was not intervening in Cuba in 1933.'[72] To quote again the Cuban delegation at Montevideo: of Sumner Welles' activities as President Roosevelt's special envoy to the country, and particularly Welles' use of non-recognition and sedition to bring down a foreign government of which he did not approve, 'it is impossible to maintain silence when it is affirmed the United States did not wish to intervene in Cuba … If by intervention we understand the last stage of intervention, properly speaking, the actual, physical occupation of a country … perhaps then the statement would have been correct.'[73] But the threshold of intervention proper was not simply whether troops had been dispatched abroad. The Additional Protocol Relative to Non-Intervention adopted at the 1936 Buenos Aires Conference, for instance, referred to the inadmissibility of intervention 'directly or indirectly, and for whatever reason, in the internal or external affairs of any of the Parties', and Article 15 of the Organization of American States (OAS) Charter, adopted at Bogotá in 1948, would eventually specify, after years of contestation, that non-intervention 'prohibits not only armed force but also any other force of interference or attempted threat against the personality of the state, or against its political, economic, and cultural elements.'[74]

---

[69] See Connell-Smith 1966: 83–91.
[70] On these interventions and their resistance, see McPherson 2014.
[71] Quoted in Connell-Smith 1966: 90.
[72] Ibid.
[73] Quoted in ibid.: 88–89.
[74] See Pan-American Union 1949: 298; United States Department of State 1948: 169–170.

Commenting on Buenos Aires, Roberto Córdova, the Mexican jurist (later judge of the International Court of Justice) and diplomat (who notably served as adviser of the Mexican delegation at Chapultepec and San Francisco, as well as the country's chief delegate at Bogotá), would explain in a public address that: 'the connotation of the principle of nonintervention with the words "directly or indirectly"' was, to Latin American delegates at least, 'not only the armed intervention of one country in another, but that other intervention ... consisting of intervention which we might call peaceable but which has the same effect as ... political, preventative, or repressive interventions'. He added, 'I am convinced that in the mind of the Mexican delegation which proposed the wording of the Protocol [of 1936], those words refer clearly to that class of unarmed intervention.'[75] Conversely, in the mind of the American delegation, direct intervention meant the official deployment of armed forces, while indirect intervention meant the threat of such action. According to Bryce Wood in his influential 1966 study of the Good Neighbor Policy: 'This interpretation by the United States delegates is strongly supported by the failure of a committee of the [Buenos Aires] Conference to agree on a convention concerning pecuniary claims which would have bound the signatories to refrain from force and from "diplomatic intervention" for the collection of public or contractual debts.'[76]

'To Mexicans', in short, 'the test of "intervention" was not the means employed, but the effectiveness of the use of any means whatever by the United States to cause a Latin American state to change its policy against its will, in what that state regarded as "internal affairs"', including through the actions of 'United States corporations'.[77] For Córdova, who was serving as Agent to the General Claims Commission between Mexico and the United States (from 1937 to 1940), the political and normative stakes would become undeniable after the Mexican oil expropriation decree of 1938. Subsequent American and international boycotts of Mexican goods, lasting until the outbreak of the Second World War, surely counted among the unarmed but nonetheless effective interventions emphasized in his speech. From one view, such non-violent abstentions from trade might have been construed as legitimate actions for the purposes of protecting national property and nationals abroad.[78] From another, only once Mexicans had been freed from 'economic

---

[75] Quoted in Wood 1961: 163.
[76] Wood 1961: 162. See United States Department of State 1937: 232–234.
[77] Wood 1961: 164
[78] Global contestation of non-intervention in relation to issues of economic dependence, nationalization, permanent sovereignty over natural resources, and the transnational corporations is explored further in Chapter 6.

vassalage' could they regard themselves as citizens of a fully sovereign state and the United States as a 'Good Neighbor'.[79]

A Latin American-led revolt

The San Francisco Conference opened just one month after Chapultepec. To those involved in its design, it was clear that the Rooseveltian blueprint of global order had been based around a general prohibition of state-led intervention, but only intervention in the descriptive sense afforded by traditional Western jurisprudence. A Rooseveltian global ordering of intervention would therefore resemble in significant respects an earlier Rooseveltian regional ordering of intervention reflected in the Good Neighbor Policy. Neither vision denied itself the privilege of political, economic, and cultural sanctions and inducements that, from the Latin American view, constituted intervention against the personality of the state or its political, economic, and cultural elements. This difference in interpretation—between an Oppenheim-Lawrence theory of coercive interference and what I am calling a more Calvo-esque theory of intervention as the effect of foreign pressure—should be exposed as a struggle in the founding of the UN.

It was also clear that subtleties in the meaning of intervention would prove consequential in deciding whom post-war global order would most benefit and endanger. Concerns over intervention in multiple forms—directly and indirectly, in local and presidential elections, diplomatic recognition, natural resource extraction, patterns of uneven economic development, the management of public services, domestic monetary and fiscal policy, and the application of domestic laws—were of course the problems of the so-called 'banana republics' and most underdeveloped territories of Latin America, but they also counted among the challenges facing states and still-dependent peoples elsewhere in the world, including in Asia and Africa.[80] Hence there must additionally be a sense in which, while the Act of Chapultepec and earlier agreements like Montevideo and Buenos Aires were first and foremost Latin and Pan-American documents, their conception of what it meant to intervene, and accordingly what was meant by non-intervention as a duty of states, spoke for a group and increasingly self-conscious coalition of smaller powers from beyond the Western hemisphere.

Non-intervention was a principle, asserted Ecuador, 'without which the Charter of the world organization would be shorn of ideals'.[81] Unless 'internal

[79] Wood 1961: 162.
[80] Evolving Asian-African understandings of the intervention concept are explored in Chapter 3.
[81] UNCIO 1945: I, 369.

and external sovereign rights of states are respected within the limits imposed by the obligations arising from the interdependence of members of the international community', and 'unless the principle of non-intervention is upheld as the full expression of that respect', the covenant of any future association of states would be 'susceptible to becoming disjointed and falling apart'.[82] To quote the Mexican delegation in Commission I and Mexico's official proposals for the Organization: the principle of non-intervention was so 'vitally important ... to all of the small nations of the world' that, as 'the cornerstone of the Inter-American System', it ought 'to be in the foreground [of what] the New World can offer as a contribution of its own to the formation of International Organization that is created'.[83] Specifically, to quote again the Mexican proposals:

> The incorporation of such a principle ... could be effected—following the terminology used in the 'Convention on the Rights and Duties of States' [the Montevideo Convention] and in the 'Additional Protocol relative to Non-Intervention' [the Buenos Aires Protocol]—as follows:
> 'No state has a right to intervene, directly or indirectly, and whatever be the reason, in the domestic or foreign affairs of another.'[84]

The world organization ought to be inspired 'by the spiritual values as well as the positive institutions of the Inter-American regional system'.[85]

Smaller-power contestation of intervention was perhaps most noticeable in formal amendments to draft Paragraph 4, Chapter II, of the Dumbarton Oaks Proposals (whereby UN member states were to refrain 'from the threat or use of force' against each other). What might have seemed like an incontrovertible, even innocuous paragraph was interpreted as something more potentially insidious: Paragraph 4 relegated non-intervention between states to the prohibition of force, but only force, and hence did not clearly prohibit other interstate activities construed as interventionary in Latin American tradition. Brazil's proposed amendment, submitted on 9 May, referred instead to 'foreign influence':

> All members of the Organization shall refrain in their international relations from any intervention in the foreign or domestic affairs of any other member of the Organization, and from resorting to threats or use of force, if they are not in accord with the methods and decisions of the Organization. In the prohibition

---

[82] Ibid.
[83] UNCIO 1945: VI, 125; III, 65–66.
[84] Ibid: III, 66.
[85] Ecuador in ibid.: I, 372.

against intervention there shall be understood to be included any interference that threatens the national security of another member of the Organization, directly or indirectly threatens its territorial integrity, or *involves the exercise of any excessively foreign influence on its destinies.*[86]

This principle of non-intervention, explained official Brazilian comments, had 'already been extensively recognized among the American nations ... and even in a certain manner accepted by the Assembly of the League of Nations', particularly by a resolution adopted on 10 October 1936.[87] That resolution had appointed a Special Committee to Study the Application of the Principles of the Covenant, including the question of bringing the Covenant into harmony with the Treaty of Non-Aggression and Conciliation concluded at Rio de Janeiro three years earlier.[88] The Treaty of Non-Aggression, also known as the Saavedra Lamas Treaty or the Argentine Pact, stated that in a case of non-compliance by any state engaged in a dispute, the contracting states 'will in no case resort to intervention, *either diplomatic or armed*'.[89]

A group of smaller powers were coming together, as early as 1945, to resist a narrow, dictatorial theory of state-based intervention, and promote a rival discursive practice that would grant all members of the UN the broader protections already enjoyed by Latin American states under inter-American regional agreements. Their indictment seems so clear, in fact, that inattention to concerted attempts to revise the meaning of intervention as a duty of states should be seen as an omission in important English-language historical commentaries on the San Francisco Conference.[90] Venezuela wished to see incorporated into the new Charter, 'in an explicit manner if possible', the duty of states 'to abstain from any attempt at intervention ... whether political or social'.[91] That was the understanding Venezuela had always upheld 'as a member of the American community', but its appeal was 'not specifically American'.[92] The Iranian delegation also distinguished between intervention and the use of force in its proposed amendment of Paragraph 4: 'All the member states of the Organization should refrain from intervening in their international relations, either directly or indirectly, in the internal affairs of

---

[86] UNCIO 1945: III, 237 (emphasis added).
[87] Ibid.: 236.
[88] 'Resolution on the Application of the Principles of the Covenant and the Problems Connected Therewith' contained in League of Nations 1936: 40.
[89] Emphasis added. Treaty of Non-Aggression and Conciliation. It had been signed by Brazil, Argentina, Chile, Mexico, Uruguay, and Paraguay in October 1933, and unanimously approved at Montevideo in December 1933, where all countries present, including the United States, agreed to accede.
[90] See e.g. Goodrich and Hambro 1949: 98–122. Chapter 4 showcases comments of the American delegation during the Friendly Relations process that corroborate this point.
[91] UNCIO 1945: I, 517.
[92] Ibid.

the other States and from the threat or use of force in any manner inconsistent with the purposes of the Organization.'[93] In a reference to an 'indirect form of intervention of certain peoples with the affairs of others', Uruguay gave the example of 'the former requiring of the latter ... the election of a certain government'.[94] And Mexico quoted from *The International Law of the Future*, a document prepared in 1944 by a team of nearly 200 distinguished American and Canadian lawyers, notably writing in their capacity as private citizens: 'Instances have not been rare in the past in which a powerful state has sought to impose its will on a less powerful state with respect in the latter's disposition of its own economy ....'[95]

Beyond official proposals to amend Paragraph 4, we can show in the proceedings of San Francisco at least three additional tactics of contesting intervention as a duty of states. One was to prepare a 'Declaration of the Duties and Rights of Nations', for which Cuba had submitted its own draft, Panama had advocated in line with a statement adopted by the American Institute of International Law, and others had proposed in parallel to and in coordination with a declaration on the rights of individual human beings (as an early version of a universal human rights declaration).[96] The Cuban draft read as follows: 'every state has the right to independence, to secure its well-being and its free development without interference by other states, provided that in the pursuit of those objectives it does not violate or infringe upon the rights of other states' and therefore 'direct or indirect intervention by a state in the internal or external affairs of another state for any reason whatsoever is inadmissible'.[97] Panama's proposed declaration similarly held that every state 'has the right to independence in the sense that it has a right to the pursuit of happiness and is free to develop itself without interference or control from other states' and Mexico suggested that to adopt such a declaration would be to generalize the agreement of the Ministers of Foreign Affairs of the American Republics, at Rio de Janeiro in 1942, that international conduct must be 'inspired by the policy of the good neighbor'.[98]

A second approach to broadening state-based non-interventionism was through a codification of acts of aggression and mechanisms for related

---

[93] Ibid.: III, 554. Similar amendments were proposed by Ecuador and Mexico. See ibid.: 422, 179.
[94] Ibid.: III, 32.
[95] Ibid.: III, 67. See Carnegie Endowment for International Peace 1944: 49.
[96] UNCIO 1945: III, 496–499; ibid.: 266–270; Ecuador in ibid: 404–405; Mexico in ibid.: 176. See also similar Dutch arguments in favour of a 'statement on fundamental rights and duties of states' in ibid.: 323–324. On Latin American influence on the emerging UN-based human rights regime, see e.g. Glendon 2003; Obregón 2006; Sikkink 2015.
[97] Ibid: III, 495–499.
[98] The Declaration of the Rights and Duties of Nations, adopted by the American Institute of International Law in 1916, is contained in ibid.: III, 272–273. Mexico was again quoting from *The International Law of the Future*. See ibid.: 69; Carnegie Endowment for International Peace 1944: 49.

dispute settlements, much like what had been attempted in the League of Nations, through a study of the principles of the Covenant in relation to the Saavedra Lamas Treaty. At San Francisco, the Philippines proposed that a state was to be determined an aggressor if, yes, it declared war on another state, or attacked without a declaration of war, but also if it was found 'to interfere with the internal affairs of another state'.[99] Interference was explicitly described by the Philippines as occurring through 'arms, ammunition, money or other forms of aid to any armed band, faction or group' as well as 'establishing agencies in that nation to conduct propaganda subversive of the institutions of that nation'.[100] Bolivia, similarly, proposed that: 'a state shall be designated an aggressor if it has committed … [i]ntervention in another state's internal or foreign affairs'.[101] In Committee III/3, a Bolivian motion to enumerate a list of acts considered aggression was quickly defeated. Among the grounds cited: 'within the list there were several points which would require definition, e.g. *when "intervention" was to be considered aggression*'.[102]

And a third type of argument stressed the sanctity of state 'personality', or specifically the moral personality of the state, a charge led by chair of the Peruvian delegation Victor Andrés Belaúnde. This concept of state personality, as previously noted, had been included in the Act of Chapultepec and was being juxtaposed against territorial integrity or political independence. According to Belaúnde, all states constituted a 'living synthesis of moral values' and 'the elements of the state most worthy of respect are its cultural values, which are the essence of personality'.[103] To refrain from intervention against the personality of the state was hence to refrain from force against 'material attributes', but also excessive foreign influence against its political, economic, and cultural elements.[104] 'When the ideas of sovereignty and territorial integrity are dealt with only in relation to the use of force', as was the case with draft Paragraph 4, Chapter II, and eventually Article 2 (4) of the UN Charter, 'there is not the absolute respect which in other cases would have been established'.[105] For our purposes, an emphasis on respect for state personality appeared to accommodate an understanding of the intervention concept intended to defend cultural traditions from the outcome of foreign pressure.

---

[99] UNCIO 1945: III, 538.
[100] Ibid.
[101] Ibid.: III, 585.
[102] UNCIO 1945: XII, 342. The motion was notably supported and amended by the Philippines. See ibid.: 348–349. Emphasis added.
[103] UNCIO 1945: VI, 67–68.
[104] Ibid.: VI, 68.
[105] Ibid.

A double ordering of intervention in the Charter

American delegates, the records show us, carefully contemplated this broad and effective non-interventionist plea. On 15 May 1945, Virginia Gildersleeve asked whether her delegation would agree to the inclusion of some reference 'to respect for treaties or to obligation on members to refrain from intervention'. It was, she explained, 'extremely difficult' to 'take a firm stand against the demands of the smaller states' on this and related matters, including 'the problem of enumerating human rights in the Charter'.[106] The following day Green Hackworth, the American jurist and later judge and President of the International Court of Justice, who had also advised at Dumbarton Oaks, noted the possibility of a backlash 'if no provision were made in the Charter in which members of the Organization would be obligated to refrain from intervention', referring specifically to 'the non-intervention agreements in a number of Latin American agreements'. In his words, 'non-intervention clauses have been a focal point in major agreements with the Latin American countries' and 'opposition on the part of the United States to the insertion of a similar provision in the Charter would be unfortunate'.[107]

Their colleagues had less sympathy. Isaiah Bowman asked whether existing Latin American agreements were not 'in themselves a sufficient offset' to make unnecessary 'any provision in the Charter for an obligation to refrain from intervention in the internal affairs of other countries'.[108] The suggestion was that, while the non-interventionism of Montevideo, Buenos Aires, and Chapultepec did not apply universally, it did apply regionally, and surely that was already enough of a concession for the Latin American countries. 'The problem', said Robert Hartley, 'arose out of defining what constituted intervention'.[109] Moreover, to pick up an interventionist argument commonplace in inter-American history—in regard to the international police action of the Roosevelt Corollary, for example, but also through more 'indirect' and less coercive means—were not certain interventionary acts, perhaps undertaken by enlightened states in addition to enlightened international organizations, necessary for maintaining law and order? According to Commander Stassen in related discussions of the delegation a month earlier: 'wars broke out' because of excessive non-interventionism, 'because nations took cover under the concept that their actions fell only within their domestic jurisdiction'.[110]

---

[106] FRUS 1945: I, Document 219.
[107] Ibid.: Document 224.
[108] Ibid.
[109] Ibid.: Document 222.
[110] Ibid.: Document 148.

In fact a parallel and more authoritative discussion on state-based non-intervention had already occurred in the Committee of Five (composed of senior delegates of the conference's host governments plus those of France, meeting nightly in Stettinius' penthouse at the Fairmont). Jean-Pierre Cot writes that the Penthouse meetings were 'obviously essential to the success of the Conference' and 'each of the Five Powers had a right of veto' on proposed amendments and requests from other governments.[111] The most important decision-making dynamic at San Francisco was hence this: to solve a controversial problem in and around the Committee of Five was to effectively determine the outcome of any concurrent debate in its constituent delegations. To quote Daniel-Erasmus Khan:

> Apart from the official structure of the conference, an unofficial one existed. Its most effective element was formed by consultations among the five principal powers which occurred throughout the conference. The influence of the five powers was dominant everywhere. Wherever a difference sharpened and approached a critical threshold, all participants at the conference were aware of the fact that a veto by the Five—or only one of the Five—could ruin the entire project.[112]

And although formal minutes were not taken of these secretive meetings, there is incidental documentation of positions taken there. Leo Pasvolsky, a trusted member of this inner ring, special assistant to Cordell Hull, and probably the single person with the greatest claim to authoring the final Charter text, elaborated on the committee's decisions in briefings to the American delegation.[113] Pasvolsky recalled first that discussions on the intervention concept had occurred at Dumbarton Oaks, but that no 'satisfactory formula' had been found there.[114] Next, when non-intervention appeared in more than a dozen proposed amendments, it was doing so in a form that the Committee of Five had no interest in recognizing. According to Pasvolsky, only Australia's proposed amendment on the matter had been considered acceptable.[115] This amendment read: 'All members of the United Nations shall refrain in their international relations from *the threat or use of force* against the territorial integrity or political independence of any member or state, or in any other manner inconsistent with the purposes of the United Nations.'[116]

---

[111] Cot 2011. See also Schlesinger 2003: chapter 7.
[112] Khan 2012: 18.
[113] See Schlesinger 2003: chapter 3.
[114] FRUS 1945: I, Document 224.
[115] Ibid.: Document 219.
[116] Ibid. It would eventually be adopted as Article 2 (4).

Eventually the sponsoring powers formalized their decision: Pasvolsky reported that the Committee of Five had 'agreed that any reference to non-intervention would be opposed'.[117] And to the dismay of Gildersleeve and Hackworth, the US delegation faithfully towed the line: Stassen moved that 'the American delegation accept the decision of the Committee of Five to oppose reference to non-intervention anywhere in the Charter. It was so agreed.'[118]

The meaning of intervention, at least as it informed a duty of states, was now 'the threat or the use of force', and the extent to which this force embraced political, economic, and other forms of pressure seemed doubtful. Brazil's proposed amendment of Paragraph 4 (prohibiting 'any excessively foreign influence' on state destinies) failed in early May.[119] A subsequent Brazilian amendment, arguably also encompassing a theory of effective non-intervention, this time as a separate paragraph to be added to Chapter II, read: 'All members of the Organization shall endeavor to practise the policy of the Good Neighbor.'[120] This too failed. Finally Brazil offered an amendment to extend Article 2 (4) to cover 'the threat or use of economic measures'.[121] It was rejected by Committee I/1 on 4 June.[122]

With respect to the meaning and inclusion of non-intervention as a duty of the UN organization, there might initially be some confusion. After all, despite the sponsoring powers' decision that no reference be made 'anywhere in the Charter' to the non-intervention principle, the duty not to intervene would ultimately be addressed by Article 2 (7), which held that '[n]othing contained in the present Charter shall authorize the United Nations to intervene in matters which are essentially within the domestic jurisdiction of any state ....'[123] How might this much be explained? I have been arguing that, at San Francisco, a primary site of the concept's global ordering, wherein major discursive practices clashed without rational settlement, had to do with the rights and duties of states. Here, through Article 2 (4), the framers and signatories of the Charter embraced not only an interpretation of 'force' confined to 'armed force', but an interpretation of 'intervention' confined to 'coercive' or 'dictatorial' interference.[124] Yet their concerns around non-intervention as a duty of the UN organization were very different.

---

[117] FRUS 1945: I, Document 229.
[118] Ibid.: Document 224.
[119] UNCIO 1945: III, 237.
[120] UNCIO 1945: VI, 559.
[121] Ibid.: 334.
[122] Ibid.: 335.
[123] UN Charter.
[124] On the 'correct and prevailing view' of the meaning of the word 'force' in Article 2 (4) as limited to 'armed force', see e.g. Dörr and Randelzhofer 2012.

This was clearly the case, first, in relation to preventative and enforcement measures taken by the Security Council under Chapter VII, which were not to be prejudiced by UN-based non-interventionism.[125] The following position stood for the majority of Latin American governments: 'Although the Government of Uruguay adheres to the principle of non-intervention, it considers collective intervention justified in the case of a state which constitutes a threat to the peace.'[126] On the composition and structure of the Security Council, some smaller powers did clash with the Great Powers, particularly in relation to the Northern bent of the P5 and the compatibility of any right to veto with the avowedly democratic aims of the new organization.[127] But on the whole there was agreement on the legitimacy of collective intervention, through surgical and forcible measures as well as through measures not involving the use of armed force, to maintain or restore international peace and security.[128]

What, however, of legitimate intervention to further other purposes of the organization? What were the interventionist competences, if any, of the General Assembly, the Economic and Social Council, and its other organs, for example? The Dumbarton Oaks Proposals contained a prohibition on UN-based intervention in affairs 'which by international law are solely within the domestic jurisdiction of the state concerned', but by placing this prohibition in Chapter VIII, Section A, the Proposals suggested it was a formula applicable only to activities concerning the pacific settlement of disputes, especially the formal investigations and recommendations of the Security Council.[129] One very important development, then, during the San Francisco meeting, was the transfer of this non-intervention provision to Chapter I, Article 2, concerning general principles. Much has been said about the implications of this move for the political promise of the new organization and the development of international law.[130] What is important for our purposes is its implications for the changing conditions of what it meant to intervene.

Smaller and larger powers alike sought guarantees that the UN would not control or influence their domestic affairs. Liberia's comments, for instance, reflected an anti-imperialist hesitation towards UN-based interventionism:

> whatever study eventually may be given to the economic, social, and other humanitarian problems, relating to members of the United Nations, envisaged in

---

[125] UN Charter.
[126] See Pan-American Union 1945: 137, 140. Quoted in Fenwick 1945: 661.
[127] See e.g. Egypt's proposed amendments in UNCIO 1945: III, 457–459.
[128] Chapter VII, UN Charter.
[129] As had also been the case with Article 15 of the League Covenant.
[130] See e.g. Davies 1946; Rajan 1961; Gilmour 1967.

Paragraph 3, Chapter 1, of the Proposals, the principle should emerge and be made crystal clear that this should not imply that a nation or the General Assembly may either interfere or intervene in the internal affairs of another state. The state itself must reserve the right to determine the necessity for any such action; otherwise it would be relegated to the status of a dependency.[131]

The Australian delegation, led by Minister for External Affairs Herbert Evatt, was also adamant about the need for a domestic jurisdiction clause—'insane', even, according to Senator Tom Connally, who took note of the country's insistence and leadership on the issue.[132] Given the traditional Oppenheim-Lawrence thesis of intervention as coercive interference and its centrality in much Western thinking at the time, Evatt's use of the language of intervention might have seemed peculiar, even incorrect—in committee discussions, Australia's use of the term seemed to proscribe all cultural, educational, and communicative activities by the organization in relation to the exclusive affairs of states, reflected in Evatt's assertion of 'an overriding principle or limitation' controlling 'each and every organ and body' of the UN, not only in terms of 'recommendations' but also 'discussions' on 'matters of domestic concern or jurisdiction'.[133]

Evatt explained his goal as the adoption of a 'clause specifically banning intervention by the Organization' such that issues like 'immigration or customs laws would be clearly excluded by that provision from consideration' by the General Assembly, but also by bodies like ECOSOC (UN Economic and Social Council).[134] Australia had in mind, Evatt admitted openly, the question of refugees and its own racial demographics: Japan's earlier attempts to pressure Australia into changing its immigration policy—the enduring White Australia Policy—haunted the Australian government. Evatt now feared a similar dispute with China.[135]

A similar concern around the General Assembly's 'right of discussion' as opening a means 'to interfere with the principle of sovereignty' was notably also raised by Gromyko of the Soviet Union.[136] In doing so, Gromyko as much as Evatt seemed to have adopted a theory of the intervention concept as the outcome of foreign pressure. This much was reflected in a row between the two men over an early June formula adopted by Committee II/2, which

---

[131] UNCIO 1945: I, 450.
[132] FRUS 1945: I, Document 242. For a memo regarding the Australian position, see UNCIO 1945: VI, 463.
[133] UNCIO 1945: V, 535.
[134] Ibid.
[135] UNCIO 1945: VI, 438–439.
[136] UNCIO 1945: V, 525.

would have allowed the General Assembly the right to discuss 'any matter within the sphere of international relations'.[137] The stakes of this row were extremely high: at one point Gromyko contended that unless it could be made clear that UN interventionism was to be the sole reserve of the Security Council, strictly in cases of threats to the peace, breaches of the peace, or acts of aggression, the Soviet Union would not sign the Charter.[138] Gromyko's insistence contributed to the eventual removal of the words 'international relations' and the addition of the phrases 'within the scope of the present Charter' and 'relating to the powers and functions of any organs provided for in the present Charter' into Article 10—a compromise reached within the Committee of Five just six days before the conference ended.[139] The sponsoring powers' domestic jurisdiction clause, which had been amended by Evatt, and should have the effect of assuaging Gromyko because of its placement in the principles section at the beginning of the Charter, read:

> Nothing contained in the present Charter shall authorize the United Nations to intervene in matters which are essentially within the domestic jurisdiction of any state or shall require the Members to submit such matters to settlement under the present Charter; but this principle shall not prejudice the application of enforcement measures under Chapter VII.[140]

The official Canadian commentary on the San Francisco Conference would later confirm, with reference to the Australian amendment, that 'the protection accorded to the domestic jurisdiction of member states is now very complete as it is clear that there can be no interference in the domestic economy or internal legislation of members'.[141] Yet, as the supplement to the report of the rapporteur for Committee I/1 observed: 'It is evident that the subject we are dealing with is not the intervention of one state in matters which fall within the domestic jurisdiction of another, but that we are dealing with the relations of the Organization and its members with respect to domestic and international jurisdiction.'[142]

In short, we can see that a certain double ordering of the intervention concept had been inscribed in the UN Charter, such that, through Article 2 (4), intervention came to be treated as armed or coercive interference, but in Article 2 (7) intervention took on a much broader meaning—encompassing

---

[137] Ibid.: 534.
[138] The episode is recounted in Schlesinger 2003: chapter 14.
[139] Ibid.; UNCIO 1945: V, 536.
[140] Article 2 (7) of the UN Charter.
[141] Canadian Department of External Affairs 1945: 19.
[142] UNCIO 1945: VI, 486.

not only 'interference in the domestic economy' and the 'internal legislation' of states, but also 'recommendations' and 'discussions' of any matter considered 'essentially within the domestic jurisdiction of any state'.[143] It was hence in relation to Article 2 (7) that the meaning of non-intervention seemed to be more that of the outcome of foreign pressure or influence. One difficult issue of course, which is still to be explored, had to do with the precise scope or demarcation of 'domestic jurisdiction'.[144] For now, what is important to know is that at San Francisco John Foster Dulles, representing all four of the sponsoring powers, argued that domestic jurisdiction ought to be defined neither by any particular UN organ nor by the explicit criterion of international law, as had been the case in analogous provisions of the League Covenant and Dumbarton Oaks Proposals, but rather to evolve 'with the state of the world, the public opinion of the world, and the factual interdependence of the world'.[145]

Perfection as visualized by the small states

Carlos Romulo, who served as head of the Philippines delegation, recounts in his memoirs the fruits of an attempt to resist the rule of Great Power unanimity or vetoes. One morning, he and Herbert Evatt were invited to join Secretary Stettinius for breakfast.

> ... after the amenities, Stettinius asked us, 'Do you want the United States in the United Nations?' Evatt answered, 'Well, Mr. Secretary, of course we do.' And I said, 'Without the United States in the United Nations it will be another League of Nations, and it will fail.' 'I'm glad to hear your statements with this regard,' Stettinius said, 'because I've asked you here to persuade you to stop fighting the unanimity rule. I must tell you that the American government is bent on having that unanimity rule in that Charter. And I must also tell you that if that unanimity rule is not in that Charter, the United States will not be a member of the UN. If you do not believe me, you can ask Senators Connally and Vandenberg.'[146]

In 1945, the United Nations were seeking the respite of peacetime. The UN organization emerged as an answer to the prevention of war's recurrence,

---

[143] UNCIO 1945: V, 535; Canadian Department of External Affairs 1945: 19.
[144] I explore this issue in Chapter 3.
[145] Quoted in Rajan 1961: 44. M. S. Rajan also shows us that Greek and Belgian amendments in favour of determining jurisdiction by the international law criterion and relatedly of the principle of compulsory jurisdiction were rejected by Committee I/1. See ibid.: 42–47.
[146] Romulo 1986: 15. See also Romulo 1961: chapter 16.

but an explanation of its contested institutional design involves compulsion, inequality, and conflict as much as persuasion and negotiated resolution of common problems. Romulo, Evatt, and others relented because they had few other options. The organization could not function without Great Power involvement and the sponsoring governments were already wielding de facto vetoes in the conference proceedings. When, at another point during the conference, smaller-power delegates had assembled again to discuss unanimity, Connally literally tore up before them a copy of the draft Charter. 'You may, if you wish, go home from this Conference and say that you have defeated the veto. But what will be your answer when you are asked: where is the Charter?'[147]

The location of the final plenary meeting was in the San Francisco Opera House. There the Charter passed unanimously and ceremoniously but with only the semblance of consensus often of interest to developmentalist and liberal convergence stories. In a closing address, Stettinius proclaimed, 'Every nation represented here has had a part in the making of the Charter. Sentence by sentence, article by article, it has been hammered out around the conference tables.'[148] In another, Gromyko stated that there had been 'difficulties' and 'different viewpoints' but that 'as a result of the work of the Conference, all the main difficulties were overcome.'[149] Still, in the midst of the exultation, it was easy to miss one line in the speech of Prince Faisal bin Abdulaziz, Minister of Foreign Affairs and later King of Saudi Arabia: 'This Charter does not represent perfection as visualized by the small states.'[150]

Certainly, regarding the intervention concept, all final decisions had worked out overwhelmingly in favour of the sponsoring powers: abstention from nakedly force-based interventions, but only force-based interventions, had become a responsibility of state members. Consequently, arguable direct and indirect intervention through economic, cultural, communicative, and other activities seemed tacitly legitimated. Simultaneously, those organs of the organization over which the P5 did not exercise absolute authority, including the General Assembly, would now be barred from intervening by any means at all. The Security Council would have the right to intervene for the purposes of maintaining international peace and security, but it would abide by the rule of unanimity in every case.

Put another way, when a group of smaller states banded together to contest the meaning of intervention, the Great Powers refused to budge. A Latin

---

[147] Quoted in Russell 1958: 736–739.
[148] UNCIO 1945: I, 658.
[149] Ibid.: 696.
[150] Ibid.: 708.

American-led coalition sought broad protections on domestic affairs that would globalize the non-interventionist guarantees won by inter-American regional agreements like those of Buenos Aires and Chapultepec, but what they received instead was a narrower order that systematically undercut smaller-power agency: that resembled merely the early, Rooseveltian iteration of the Good Neighbor Policy and that gutted the General Assembly, ECOSOC, and other organs of the UN. The constitution of non-intervention as a duty of states came to correspond to the dictatorial thesis of Western legal scholars like Oppenheim and Lawrence, at the expense of a proposed alternative associated with Latin American jurists like Calvo. Only as a duty of the organization had non-intervention been theorized in terms of the outcome of foreign influence or pressure.

A critic, listening in on the conference, might have argued that the Committee of Five was satisfied with this configuration of global order for obvious reasons. And to better appreciate the subsequent rise and fall of a more non-aligned and Southern theory of intervention in the globalization of international society, it seems necessary now to better foreground the imperial–ideological origins of the post-war global order.[151] It is not only that figures like Jan Smuts—the South African premier and white nationalist—had penned the majority of the preamble of the Charter and saw in its rules the basis of enduring empire and international racial hierarchy, but also that rival figures—Jawaharlal Nehru to name just one—sought to make use of its institutional machinery in processes of decolonization.[152] From this view the stakes of the intervention debate were about freedoms not limited to freedoms from physical violence. It would be easy for our critic to argue that the Great Powers of 1945 understood diverse interferences in the domestic affairs of others to be necessary in the maintenance of a hegemonic and colonial distribution of influence. A move towards an effective theory of state-based non-interventionism risked becoming a strategic constraint and circumvention of existing international hierarchical codes. On similar grounds, those Great Powers had attempted to prohibit an activist UN at large. The risk of UN-based organizing for social, economic, and humanitarian purposes, for example, was also the risk of interfering with an imperial status quo.

The discursive shift away from intervention as armed or coercive interference towards intervention as foreign pressure, and eventually intervention as the deprivation of self-determination (the focus of Chapter 3), is a process that took place over thirty years. It marks one of the most important

---

[151] See especially Mazower 2009, 2012.
[152] Ibid.

and misunderstood dimensions of the concept's function in historical international society. And it was complemented by the emergence of international duties to promote universal human rights and to prevent crimes against humanity, meaning that a range of related international activities through the UN were no longer understood to constitute intervention in affairs essentially within the domestic jurisdiction of states. From an evolving Southern view, the sponsoring powers could not have it both ways: a wide, UN-based non-interventionism that undercut those organizational forums and activities most likely to benefit smaller and newly independent powers, including in their incipient international struggle for decolonization and humanitarianism, and a narrow, state-based non-interventionism that exposed those smaller powers to foreign and structural domination, including manifestations of imperialism and extreme racism that increasingly seemed an appalling abrogation of shared international responsibilities.

3
Anti-colonial intervention and the Bandung Spirit

W. E. B. Du Bois left San Francisco disappointed, having served as a non-governmental consultant to the US delegation.[1] He was disappointed because conferees had redrawn the global colour line, because international society subsisted still in an era of Jim Crow: 80 per cent of the world's population and an estimated one-third of the world's surface remained under Western domination, and there was little to suggest that obstinate European colonialism was inconsistent with the rules of a new international order.[2]

Some colonies—India, for example—had been present at the conference. But given that colonial delegations were virtually hand-picked by their respective metropoles, and that, as we have seen, San Francisco was largely a story of the sponsors' de facto vetoes, those colonies could hardly voice, even less institutionalize, a serious argument against empire. True, the national liberation agenda may have found a following in progressive civil society, but it remained ostracized in the global diplomatic community.[3] On his way back to New York, Du Bois wrote in a letter to Arthur Spingarn: 'Not a whisper against colonialism could be heard except from Molotov.'[4] Then in a letter to the editor of the *American Mercury*: 'Nothing was done at San Francisco to face or settle the colonial problem. Rather, colonial imperialism was strengthened.'[5]

True, the development of self-governing institutions was to be fostered by the UN's Trusteeship Council, but only according to 'continual processes' structured by 'stages' and 'gradations' set by the colonial powers themselves, with no prearranged or binding timetable—this was 'a denatured "shell" of a Trusteeship system', which placed no obligation on imperial powers to

---

[1] On e.g. the National Association for the Advancement of Colored People (NAACP) and the founding of the UN, see Anderson 2003.
[2] Du Bois 1995: 639.
[3] See e.g. Sherwood 1996; Lauren 2011: 165–194.
[4] Quoted in Aptheker 1978: 14.
[5] Ibid.: 13.

Intervention before Interventionism. Patrick Quinton-Brown, Oxford University Press. © Patrick Quinton-Brown (2024).
DOI: 10.1093/oso/9780198886457.003.0004

make use of its machinery.[6] Meanwhile Chinese and Philippine attempts at inserting a racial equality clause—virtually identical to the Japanese proposal rejected at the Paris Peace Conference—had been ignored.[7] To speak of any serious Charter commitment to universal human rights was a 'contradictory statement', argued Du Bois, because the document appeared to sanction a most fundamental abuse of human rights: colonial rule itself.[8]

This basic nexus—of race, human rights, and empire—proved enormously influential in the coming decades. And what matters here for the constitution of international-societal concepts like intervention is not just that the European metropoles lost hold of their colonies, but that global knowledges that once sustained those metropoles began to fall out. On the one hand, of course, the collapse of European empire is about the devastating costs of world war and violent conflict, or its possibility. But on the other, it is important to recognize the effects on hierarchical international order of emerging anti-colonial identities and practices cutting across Asia, Africa, and Latin America. The Global South, as an identity formed at places like Bandung and Belgrade, and as a way of practising the intervention problem, is the focus of this chapter. Although manifested in different sizes, colours, religions, and political orientations—socialisms, traditional theocracies, and free market capitalisms—the countries of the Global South or Third World, 'ignored, exploited, scorned' like the Third Estate, seek to expose Western imperial domination not as some paradigmatic modernity, but as a violation of responsibilities located outside of essentially domestic jurisdiction.[9] In the process, shared conditions of what it is to intervene in international relations are changed in new and significant ways.

In Chapter 2 I was especially interested in showing how a particular discursive practice of intervention—what I called dictatorial intervention, in relation to a duty of states—took hold in post-war international society. Here I want to look at how the dictatorial theory was challenged by a new formulation, which came to perform global ordering work in subsequent decades. If dictatorial intervention was an attempt to narrow state-based non-interventionism to the threat or use of force, an anti-colonial redescription

---

[6] Urquhart 1998: 121, quoted in Anderson 2003: 55. The Philippines had successfully inserted the word 'independence' into the trusteeships section, but this provision was qualified by the 'particular conditions' of the territory in question. See Bain 2003: 108–140.
[7] UNCIO 1945: III, 498. On the Japanese racial equality proposal, see Shimazu 2009.
[8] Quoted in Aptheker 1978: 14.
[9] Sauvy 1986: 83. For a discussion and defence of the meaning and appropriateness of the terms 'Global South' and 'Third World', see Grovogui 2011.

Anti-colonial intervention and the Bandung Spirit 87

of intervention provided for a broad non-interventionism that was also a solidarist internationalism.[10]

Clearly the substitution of the dictatorial theory of intervention with what has been called the effective theory of intervention continued to have special appeal to smaller states and former colonies for whom independence had only recently been won. And an emerging Global Southern coalition certainly did declare that no state has the right to intervene 'directly or indirectly, for any reason whatever', such that 'armed intervention and all other forms of interference or attempted threats against the personality of the state' were condemned; this much would initially appear to be a continuation of Latin American organizing at San Francisco.[11] It might therefore sound as if I am going to argue that a more Calvo-esque, Latin American practice became 'Third World' or 'Southern' when it was picked up by the new states of Asia and Africa in 1955.[12] But the reality was more interesting and complicated than this.

An anti-colonial reordering of the intervention problem successfully reconciled the international responsibility to promote human rights with the international responsibility of non-intervention in domestic matters. The historical institutionalization of particular international rights and duties, by which certain matters were transferred outside of, and no longer belonged essentially or solely to, the domestic jurisdiction of states, legitimated the emergence of a 'Bandung UN'.[13] A new global preoccupation had to do with the common bonds of nations and peoples in a struggle for self-rule and state personality, whereby a just international order was built on respect not simply for territorial integrity and political independence, but also for self-determination. Were matters concerning the treatment and national identity of those still living under colonial rule to be located within the domestic affairs of the metropole? Or might the progressive development of international law and norms, for example, restrict the legitimacy of colonial governments taking cover behind the non-intervention principle in ways previously available? One formula was: if certain matters of human rights were no longer essentially located within domestic jurisdiction, then the UN could legitimately contribute to a global international struggle against colonialism and extreme racism without violating the duty of non-intervention. A more

---

[10] On solidarist internationalism and the 'Bandung Spirit', see Weber and Winanti 2016.
[11] A/RES/34/101. I explore the 1965 and 1981 UN Declarations on Non-Intervention in subsequent chapters.
[12] See Chapter 2.
[13] Wight 1957: 248.

striking one was: if 'intervention' was the outcome of foreign pressure on self-determined futures, and not just the threat or use of force, then internationalist activities contributing to the elimination of colonialism and extreme racism were not properly acts of intervention at all. Multiple strains of anti-colonial discourse were used to justify international and collective action, including action of a coercive nature, for the purposes of preventing colonial atrocities and crimes against humanity, such as apartheid.

This chapter provides a broad sweep of Third World organizing in the early Cold War period to draw out and evaluate different logics of anti-colonial intervention. It focuses on extra-UN diplomacy (a treatment of intra-UN contestation follows in Chapter 4) and on encounters in cross-regional forums both of states and of representatives of colonized and neocolonized nations and peoples. The first part looks at the crystallization at the Bandung Conference of a set of influential arguments regarding intervention, human rights, self-determination, and domestic jurisdiction. It goes on to survey evolving practices of anti-colonial intervention as developed and applied in the early summits of the Non-Aligned Movement. Finally I include a discussion of the Tricontinental Conference of 1966 to exemplify a strain of anti-colonial intervention in its most radical form, which claimed to express a more complete understanding of the principles of Bandung and non-alignment, but which often came to divide opinion within the Global South, not least in Latin America where the Tricontinental had been hosted.

By the end of the chapter I hope to have illustrated how global political debate from the 1950s into the 1970s became a scenario in which roles normally associated with the Global North and Global South came to be switched. The anti-colonial reordering of intervention serves to demonstrate that, through much of the Cold War, a loose group of Northern states played a non-interventionist role in the face of an internationalist, and seemingly interventionist, Southern group. This non-aligned and Southern practice is of course highly interventionist from the point of view of rival discursive practices, and was constantly derided as such by its detractors. But it would be better and more accurately described as internationalist and even, in particular formulations, coercive internationalist. Learning to untangle interventionism from internationalism in these historical settings is helpful in making sense of the historical evolution of international society, the solidarist ambitions of its members, and the institutionalization of its core vocabularies. It enables a recovery in intergovernmental practice of a logic of humanitarian internationalism that is neither a humanitarian interventionism nor a denial of legitimate international coercion and enforcement. A core understanding of the anti-colonial theory is that to commit 'intervention' is, by the nature of the act itself, to violate universal human rights.

From the Panchsheel to the Ten Principles

The Asian-African Conference took place from 18 to 24 April 1955, welcoming twenty-nine states, exclusively from the world's two largest continents, to discuss matters of common concern.[14] Sponsored by the Colombo Powers—Burma, India, Indonesia, Pakistan, Ceylon—it was a project of newly independent states (Indonesia as host had declared independence just ten years earlier and parts of the city of Bandung were still being rebuilt after burning down during its national revolution).[15] Still, the conceivable fractures among these actors were many: invitees were stratified not only by religion, skin colour, culture, and styles of national governance, but also in terms of bloc alignment. Of the five sponsoring powers alone, three could have been described as neutralist-socialist (India, Indonesia, and Burma), while the other two were clearly pro-West and anti-communist (Pakistan and Ceylon). Of the invitees, a number had signed mutual security and economic agreements with the United States or Britain. Others, such as the People's Republic of China and North Vietnam, were at the time close allies of the Soviet Union. A straightforward neutralism was hence not synonymous with the appeal or purposes of 'Bandung'.[16] Its appeal and purposes were very different.

Scholars today approach the conference as a platform of a global self-awakening of colonized and formerly colonized peoples—culturally and spiritually, as well as politically and institutionally.[17] Such a self-awakening was a possibility for which there was cautious optimism in 1955: France had been defeated by the Việt Minh in Indochina, the Korean War had come to a halt, and the Geneva Accords had coincided with a temporary ease in hostilities between superpowers. The stage seemed to be set for realizing a narrative about a common struggle against unjust hierarchical designs—about, to quote Sukarno's opening address, 'brothers and sisters' once 'blockaded, physically and intellectually', but no longer.[18] The question of 'who we are' was hence in a significant way also a question about 'how the

---

[14] See e.g. Mackie 2005; Prashad 2007: 31–50; Lee 2010.
[15] See Ewing 2019.
[16] For a provocative critique of this and 'other fables' of Bandung, see Vitalis 2013.
[17] Phạm and Shilliam 2016.
[18] Indonesia 1955: 23, 26. On the symbolic and cultural legacies of Bandung, see Shimazu 2014. See also Adelman and Prakash 2023.

world ought to be'.[19] If, as Antony Anghie writes, '[t]he origins of Bandung can be traced to African and Asian countries' fear that they were left out of the major deliberations at San Francisco' and 'that this inaugural omission could signal their ongoing exclusion from any major role in the management of international affairs', then we should show how, as Quỳnh Phạm and Robbie Shilliam write, 'attendees at Bandung introduced anti-colonialism and anti-racism as constitutive principles of a new world order rather than as background aspirations in a bipolar rivalry of great powers'.[20]

How exactly did the intervention concept fit into this defiant vision of global reordering? If a series of well-known cases of historical anti-colonial and anti-racist actions would appear to contravene the principle of non-intervention as laid out so far, how was intervention coming to be retheorized? I want to start by revisiting the meeting transcripts of the conference's Political Committee, which shed a good amount of light on both these questions.[21]

Bandung's approach to non-interventionism is commonly said to have been based on the concept of the Panchsheel, also known as the Five Principles of Peaceful Coexistence. Yet this seems only partly right. The Five Principles were originally understood as the basis of good neighborly relations between India and China in relation to the Tibet region. Hardly limited to bilateral application, however, Nehru and Zhou explained that the Five Principles referred to appropriate behaviour 'in international relations generally', and offered a model to be emulated by others.[22] According to the Panchsheel, if a lasting peace and coexistence in the society of states were ever to be achieved, the principle of 'mutual non-interference in internal affairs' would have to be adopted alongside 1) 'respect for territorial integrity', 2) 'mutual non-aggression', 3) 'equality and mutual benefit', and 4) 'peaceful coexistence'.[23]

The Five Principles were not wholly new or original. As Nehru was fond of claiming, for instance, they were Asian values 'as old as our thought and culture', reflected perhaps in the teachings of ancient Buddhism, the Five Precepts of its lay devotees, and the rock edicts of Ashoka.[24] But aside from the origins of the Panchsheel—what one former Indian diplomat and journalist

---

[19] Phạm and Shilliam 2016: 13–14. On the legacy of Bandung for contemporary international order, and for the contemporary regional order of Asia particularly, see Tan and Acharya 2008.
[20] Phạm and Shilliam 2016: 11.
[21] Unpublished and verbatim transcripts of the meetings of the Political Committee of the Asian-African Conference (cited henceforth as TMPCAAC) are held at the St Antony's College Library, Oxford.
[22] Quoted in Jansen 1966: 128.
[23] Agreement on Trade and Intercourse between the Tibet Region of China and India.
[24] See Jansen 1966: 128–129; Anghie 2017: 538.

of the period called its 'confectionary wrapping' pulled, all too conveniently, from an array of contradictory cultural artefacts—what we surely want, for genealogical purposes, is its meaning, and particularly its meaning in context, as it was being practised by states.[25] In this vein the choice to arrange in the Panchsheel a specific pillar of 'mutual non-interference in internal affairs' beside and not within other pillars, such as 'mutual non-aggression' and 'respect for territorial integrity', reflected an interpretation of intervention based on outcomes of influence or pressure rather than means by which that pressure occurred.[26] As a theory of what it means to intervene, the Panchsheel appeared to accept an effective intervention and hence to correspond to a number of Latin and inter-American documents whose conception of a state-based duty of non-intervention was not limited to Article 2 (4) of the UN Charter.[27]

Still, to say that a practice of effective intervention was adopted at Bandung would be an oversimplification.[28] No doubt the Bandung version of non-intervention went beyond Oppenheim-Lawrence, but I think we can also show how it moved beyond Calvo too. It is not as if an arguably Latin American tradition of intervention—intervention as the outcome of foreign pressure rather than armed force—enters Southern practice when it is picked up by Afro-Asia in 1955, and then becomes promoted by the non-aligned states in various bodies of the UN. What needs to be shown is that a kind of anti-colonial theory of intervention, emerging at Bandung, is shaped by concerns around universal human rights and a particular delineation of 'domestic' and 'international' affairs. As Amitav Acharya has rightly shown, '[t]he key issue at Bandung was non-interference', and though it 'also focused on human rights', 'there was no hint of anyone using non-intervention to mask human rights abuses at home'.[29] If the promotion at once of human rights and non-intervention sounds like a contradiction, I want to show how this is true in terms of some iterations of non-intervention as historical discursive practice, but not others.

---

[25] Jansen 1966: 128–129.
[26] Anghie 2017: 541; Acharya 2014: 411. See Chapter 2.
[27] In a speech on the Five Principles fifty years later, Boutros Boutros-Ghali would himself observe that the third principle of the Panchsheel (non-intervention) corresponded with Article 2 (7) of the UN Charter, not Article 2 (4), which corresponded most closely with the Panchsheel's second principle (mutual non-aggression) (Boutros-Ghali 2004).
[28] Consider in relation to the idea that 'Westphalian sovereignty' and Westphalian norms of non-intervention had been adopted at Bandung. For a discussion, see Kim 2018. On an 'Eastphalian' alternative to Westphalia, see Fidler, Kim, and Ganguly 2009. Notably, on the Westphalian myth 'from below', and in relation to humanitarian intervention specifically, see Peak 2021.
[29] Acharya 2018: 78; 2014: 410.

Part of the confusion has to do with the relationship of intervention to the Panchsheel Treaty, the centrality of references to the Panchsheel in the construction and maintenance of a Third World identity, and the common assumption that the Panchsheel was endorsed in the Bandung Communiqué's section on world peace and cooperation.

Nehru and Zhou did proclaim that the Five Principles ought to guide behaviour 'in international relations generally', but, as Nehru would later say in Bandung's Political Committee, the Panchsheel was not intended 'to prevent all the ills of the world', nor, in 1954, all the ills of its practitioners. Rather '[i]t is something which meets the needs of the day.'[30] The concept was originally formulated as the basis of the 1954 Agreement on Trade and Intercourse between the Tibet Region of China and India and was no doubt concerned with outcomes of foreign pressure that risked crisis in contexts like Tibet. There were diverse applications for such a formulation of non-intervention in the region. To illustrate: when on 29 June 1954, Zhou met with U Nu to discuss the Five Principles,[31] one issue had to do with insurgencies that had broken out within Burma, involving multiple communist factions and ethnic groups, as well as Kuomintang Chinese nationalist forces. U Nu pondered a type of foreign involvement to quell the civil unrest: 'the Burmese Communist Party respects the Chinese Communist Party very much. If you utter a sentence, they will listen.' This Zhou could not accept: 'Then that will become interfering with others' internal affairs.'[32] Earlier in the same meeting, Zhou took the view that 'the prime minister of one country appealing to the people of another country is also interference in another's internal affairs ... According to the reaffirmed principles in the joint statement from China and India, we can say it is appropriate for the relationship between China and Burma.'[33]

But the agenda at Bandung was in many ways very unlike the agendas of Indian and Chinese cooperation over Tibet or friendly Sino-Burmese relations. Most notably, respect for fundamental human rights was not listed among the Five Principles, nor was respect for another associated concept that would become so central to the Bandung deliberations: that of self-determination. Of course it is not hard to imagine the perceived risks of adding human rights and self-determination to the Five Principles in 1954, particularly insofar as the Principles were often taken as a guide to the relations of 'new states', often with contested borders as well as minorities with nationalist aspirations, no less states already experiencing or soon to

---

[30] Quoted in Jansen 1966: 128; TMPCAAC 1955: 281.
[31] Wang 2014.
[32] Ibid.
[33] Ibid.

experience ethnic conflicts.³⁴ And yet it is the consanguinity of these ideas that proves so critical to the success of Afro-Asia's anti-colonial campaign against Western-dominated order.

So it is undoubtedly true that Nehru and Zhou brought with them to Bandung their Five Principles, and it is also true that the Panchsheel was acclaimed by others gathered there—U Nu, for instance, asserted at Bandung that 'the acceptance and strict observance of these [Five] principles by all nations would make for lasting peace, and for the happiness of mankind.'³⁵ But it should be remembered that the Five Principles were themselves contested during the conference proceedings, including those of its Political Committee. There, for example, Pakistani Prime Minister Mohammad Ali Bogra proposed two additional principles to the Panchsheel, calling the promise of peace according to the Five Principles alone 'a fallacy' and construing his seven principles (which he called 'the Seven Pillars of Peace') as a bare 'minimum that all nations must be prepared to accept and follow.'³⁶ Asserted Iraqi Foreign Minister Muhammad Fadhel al-Jamali: 'to take the Five Principles and enunciate them as our goal is not adequate at all.'³⁷ And Zhou Enlai is on record as saying: '*we can reformulate these five principles so as to make them agreeable to all the delegates ... the points on which we can all agree are no longer five.*'³⁸

They were in fact ten. And it is the interlocking logic of these principles that speaks to the constitution of the interventionary act to which Bandung sought to attach restrictions. Taken together, the Ten Principles of Bandung reordered the meaning of the five derived from the Panchsheel; five would not suffice, and each of the ten were to be construed in the context of all the others for the promotion of 'good neighbourliness' and 'friendly cooperation.'³⁹

In particular the Bandung version of non-intervention—a principle of peaceful coexistence according to the Panchsheel—was to be interpreted in relation to an overarching commitment to human freedom, the final communiqué's section on the Ten Principles having premised that 'peace and freedom are interdependent.'⁴⁰ Chair of the Lebanese delegation Charles Malik, in his 1955 Mars Lectures at Northwestern University delivered after

---

[34] See generally Anghie 2013.
[35] TMPCAAC 1955: 239.
[36] Ibid.: 256; Indonesia 1955: 110.
[37] TMPCAAC 1955: 259.
[38] Ibid.: 323.
[39] See 'Promotion of World Peace and Cooperation' in *Final Communiqué of the Asian-African Conference*, reprinted in Romulo 1956: 92–102.
[40] Ibid.

his return from Bandung, recounted that 'the whole problematic of an age' appeared concentrated in that single turn of phrase: not just that freedom and peace were interrelated, or that freedom was conducive to peace, or peace conducive to freedom, but that there could be no peace without freedom, or freedom without peace. Argued Malik: emancipation in conformity with purposes and principles of the UN Charter, and the question of how to foster such emancipation and from which sorts of oppression or dependence, 'constituted the soul of the Conference' or the political and normative platform that came to be known as the Bandung Spirit.[41]

The right to self-determination, adopted in Article 1 (2) of the Charter (which defined as a purpose of the UN organization the development of 'friendly relations among nations based on respect for the principle of equal rights and self-determination of peoples'), thus became linked to the duty of non-intervention.[42] Historians like Roland Burke have analysed in more detail the place of universal human rights at Bandung. It is not just that the conference 'declared its full support' for human rights, but that human rights became a frame through which to comprehend problems of peace, with the right to self-determination as its necessary and even principal element.[43] By 1955, as Burke and others have shown, self-determination was already being called 'the essence of all human rights' and, in spite of Western opposition, was soon to be adopted as the first and primary article in the International Covenants both on Civil and Political Rights and on Economic, Social, and Cultural Rights.[44] The Bandung final communiqué, in declaring its 'full support of the principle of self-determination of peoples and nations as set forth in the Charter', and taking note of related UN resolutions, explicitly described self-determination as 'a prerequisite of the full enjoyment of all fundamental human rights.'[45]

The understanding then was that the pursuit of peace, necessarily entangled with the advancement of freedom, encompassed respect for human rights which, in emerging practice, was necessarily entangled with an international struggle for national liberation. One of the seven principles proposed at Bandung by Pakistan was: 'the right of self-determination of all peoples and abhorrence of colonial exploitation in any shape or form.'[46] Egypt also proposed seven principles at the conference, counting among them '[t]he full respect of all states of their international obligations' and '[t]he liquidation of

[41] Malik 1955.
[42] UN Charter, Article 1 (2).
[43] *Final Communiqué of the Asian-African Conference.*
[44] See Burke 2010: 35–58; Jensen 2016: 43–46; Getachew 2019b: 71–106.
[45] *Final Communiqué of the Asian-African Conference.* See TMPCAAC 1955: 107.
[46] TMPCAAC 1955: 254.

colonialism', which 'has always been a source of friction and unrest'.[47] In the end, immediately after asserting the interdependence of freedom and peace, the final communiqué's section on the Bandung principles would read: 'the right of self-determination must be enjoyed by all peoples in freedom, and independence must be granted with the least possible delay to those who are still dependent peoples'.[48]

To be sure, then, Zhou did understand the conference's Ten Principles—the first principle being 'respect for fundamental human rights and for the purposes and principles of the Charter of the United Nations'—as an extension of the Five. He argued at Bandung that to successfully 'oppose racial discrimination and to demand fundamental human rights, to oppose colonialism and to demand for national independence, and to firmly defend their territorial integrity and sovereignty', countries would need to adhere to the Five Principles of Peaceful Coexistence.[49] The pillars of the Panchsheel were hence explained in 1955 as reinforcing an international process of decolonization—even if, in 1954, they did not contain provisions concerning human rights or the struggle for national liberation through self-determination. Nehru also supported such a progressive interpretation of the Panchsheel, having recalled that at the 1954 Colombo Conference 'the Prime Ministers discussed the problem of colonialism which they felt still existed in various parts of the world; they were of the view that the continuance of such a state of affairs was a violation of fundamental human rights and a threat to the peace of the world'.[50]

It is true then that the Afro-Asian description of intervention adhered more to the tradition of Calvo than of Oppenheim-Lawrence, but also true that it was unsatisfied with the Calvo-esque interpretation alone. At Bandung the Indonesian delegation understood the principle of non-intervention as having been recognized 'in many bilateral and multilateral agreements such as the Convention of Rights of Montevideo' of 26 December 1933, the 'Protocol Relating to Non-Intervention of Buenos Aires' of 23 December 1936, as well as 'the Bogotá Charter' that established the Organization of American States in 1948.[51] Non-intervention was also widely cited in Political Committee debates concerning the inadmissibility of foreign subversion, propaganda, and other non-forcible forms of 'pressure', including the pressure to participate in military blocs or formal alliances.[52] Still, the non-interventionism of

---

[47] Ibid.: 265.
[48] *Final Communiqué of the Asian-African Conference.*
[49] Quoted in Chen 2017: 184.
[50] TMPCAAC 1955: 219.
[51] Ibid.: 253.
[52] See e.g. Nehru's comments in ibid.: 214–222.

Bandung was not the non-interventionism of Montevideo, Chapultepec, or Bogotá—at least as discussed in Chapter 2. Non-interventionism was, yes, about insulating the personalities and destinies of smaller states, and in this way did refer more to the outcome of foreign pressure rather than to the threat or use of force. Yet for an emerging Afro-Asia, the new non-interventionism was also fundamentally concerned with the yielding of a particular range of abstract sovereign privileges, though not sovereignty per se, to what at least one participant called 'liberalism'.[53]

Domestic jurisdiction, human rights, and self-determination

Gamal Abdel Nasser, in one of his first major conference appearances, submitted to his fellow delegates at Bandung the issue of the dependent nations of North Africa. In doing so he offered a crucible for an anti-colonial theory of intervention. The basic problem facing colonized peoples and their allies was the 'groundless' belief that cases of colonial violence and oppression were said to belong essentially to the internal affairs of their respective European metropoles.[54] Solidarist international action was said to 'constitute intervention in the domestic jurisdiction' of the pressured metropole.[55] '[W]ith regard to Algeria', Nasser explained, France held that 'Algeria is an integral part of the French Union. The French Government bases the fantastic claim on the provisions of the French Constitution.'[56]

The domestic jurisdiction argument had already become a well-worn defence of colonialism in political debate in the early 1950s and would endure into the following decade. As newly independent Morocco would observe in a UN plenary meeting, two years after delegates at Bandung declared their support for the country's right to self-determination: Western invocations of Article 2 (7) had become a kind of 'shy and disguised veto' of the 'old imperialist countries'.[57] UN records strongly support the Moroccan assessment: domestic jurisdiction was a colonial-power trope used to reject international as well as UN-based 'interventions' of various forms, including intervention

[53] Ibid.: 146–147.
[54] Ibid.: 143.
[55] Ibid.
[56] Ibid. François Mitterrand, then Interior Minister, five months prior to the opening of the Asian-African Conference asserted: 'Algeria is France; from Flanders to the Congo there is only one law, one nation, one parliament. The Constitution wills it so, we will it so ... The only negotiation is war.' Quoted in Ansprenger 1989: 229.
[57] A/C.1/SR.834: 130.

through speech, and intervention through reports and recommendations to specific governments.[58] I discuss UN-based contestation in more detail in Chapter 4, but because this 'little veto' was so relevant to what was happening at Bandung, I want to share a few illustrations.[59]

In February 1957, during UN debate on the Algerian question, France reasserted that it 'never admitted and would never admit any competence on the part of the United Nations in a problem which France regarded, under international law, as an essentially domestic matter'.[60] The UK delegation agreed:

> in accordance with Article 2, paragraph 7, of its Charter, the UN was precluded from intervening in the domestic affairs of any Member State, and the General Assembly had no right, under the Charter, to discuss any matter or adopt any resolution in that field. The question of Algeria was incontestably within the domestic jurisdiction of France and, as such, was outside the competence of the General Assembly.[61]

A similar point had been made earlier in relation to the question of Tunisia.[62] As Anthony Eden himself had declared, 'any attempt to go outside the four corners of the Charter was bound to weaken the United Nations, which had never been intended to be an organ qualified to intervene, as was being attempted at the present time, between a metropolitan country and a dependency for whose foreign affairs it was responsible by virtue of certain treaties'.[63]

Yet, to quote the Ceylonese delegation in 1957, 'if that theory were accepted, that would sound the death knell of all liberation from colonial bondage'.[64] The obstacle had to do with a theory of effective intervention that was also conceived with a certain wide and presumably static conception of domestic jurisdiction. For if the duty not to intervene was absolute, and the line between international and domestic jurisdiction unchanging, could international support for national liberation exist at all except as a breach of international rules and values?

---

[58] For case studies of UN practice in the 1950s, see Rajan 1961: 135–222. Writing in 1956, and in direct response to the Afro-Asian proposal to place the Algeria question on the agenda of the UN, Quincy Wright would ask, 'Is discussion intervention?' See Wright 1956.
[59] Chile's rebuke of Article 2 (7) in the context of racism in South Africa. Quoted in Rajan 1961: 235.
[60] A/C.1/SR.830: 99.
[61] A/C.1/SR.834: 125.
[62] See Rajan 1961: 172–176.
[63] A/C.1/SR.538: 201.
[64] Ceylon's reply to the idea of the Algerian conflict as a 'purely domestic' affair of France. A/C.1/SR.839: 158.

Iraq's comments in Bandung's Political Committee, delivered by Muhammad Fadhel al-Jamali, responded to this question not through the lens of dictatorial intervention, nor the lens of effective intervention, but through that of a more progressive and newer anti-colonial intervention—the outlines of which were coming into view by 1955:

> France considers it as a part of metropolitan France and therefore she considers the affairs of Algeria as the affairs of her internal jurisdiction. No one is therefore entitled to speak about Algeria except France. *Well, we cannot interfere with the internal affairs of France, but we can invoke the right of self-determination of the people. We can invoke human rights.*

Such a move promised to legitimate a human rights-based programme of public discussion and censure in the General Assembly, but it might also open the possibility of legitimating a wider range of other forms of international solidarity. Al-Jamali continued:

> The people of Algeria are being discriminated against and they are being treated brutally. They are machine-gunned. Bombed. There is complete extermination, complete destruction ... We have been going to the United Nations year after year asking for the judgement of the civilized world. But in the United Nations not all things move smoothly and there are influences which sometimes make right and justice sink before power ... Is it not true that the people of Asia and Africa must come together and go to the help of these people?

In the face of anti-colonial solidarity, France would claim domestic jurisdiction over its so-called Departments, but such abuses or misuses of the non-intervention principle were to 'yield before justice, before liberalism, before common sense'.[65]

The qualification of sovereign privilege to a particular sort of 'liberalism' and 'justice' was, I am beginning to suggest, 'common sense' in the Global South. To draw from comments made by the Afghan delegation at Bandung: to insist on effective non-intervention alone would be 'contrary to the very principles of liberty, equality, and fraternity which represent the traditional spirit of the French people' and crucially, we should add, emerging norms and practices of international society.[66] A more anti-colonial theory of intervention involved two moves. The first was to assert the transfer of issues of

---

[65] TMPCAAC 1955: 145–146, 147.
[66] Ibid.: 155.

human rights out of the domain of the domestic—out of the jurisdiction of the sovereign state—and into the domain of the international. Just five months after Bandung, during General Assembly discussion of an Afro-Asian proposal to place the question of Algeria on the UN's agenda, Prince Wan Waithayakon of Thailand closed his remarks 'by recalling the words of Mr [René] Cassin, who ... had declared that in the matter of human rights the competence of the United Nations was an established fact and that the provisions of Article 2, paragraph 7, could not be invoked against such competence.'[67] The question of Algeria was one of respect for human rights, and 'the question of human rights had ceased to be a domestic matter.'[68] The second move was more directly about the right to self-determination—increasingly an international legal standard, and not just a political principle—and its promotion and realization as a responsibility shared by states and the UN.[69] To promote self-determination against the overt domination of a privileged minority was not to intervene or violate sovereignty, but to promote the 'first human right' at the heart of a seemingly more 'popular' and legitimate sovereignty.[70] As Krishna Menon of India put it during the same UN meeting: '[w]hen France had conquered Algeria, the sovereignty which resided in the Algerian people had not been extinguished; it had merely become latent, and could be revived once again by just such a national movement.'[71]

Already in 1950, India and its allies had invoked the first of these two moves in the case of the treatment of people of Indian origin in the Union of South Africa.[72] When South Africa—supported by, among others, Australia and Greece—argued that the UN and its members had 'no competence to intervene' in such 'domestic affairs', one particularly effective reply was that 'human rights and fundamental freedoms were matters of such international concern as to be removed beyond the sphere of domestic jurisdiction', hence international action to prevent large-scale human rights violations was neither a violation of Article 2 (7) nor an abrogation of non-intervention as a duty of states.[73] States speaking in favour of a liberal draft resolution on the matter—Bolivia, Chile, Cuba, Haiti, Iceland, and Iraq—provided the following formulation: 'the defence of fundamental human rights was one

---

[67] A/BUR/SR.103: 11.
[68] Ibid.
[69] On the evolution of the right of peoples to self-determination from international political principle to international legal standard, see generally Cassese 1995.
[70] For a discussion in international law, see e.g. Roth 2000: especially 413–430.
[71] A/BUR/SR.103: 11.
[72] See United Nations Department of Public Information 1950: 398–407.
[73] Ibid.: 400. The Australian and Greek positions are summarized in ibid.: 400.

of the primary duties and obligations of the United Nations, and concern for the observance of fundamental human rights in a country *did not mean interference in the domestic affairs of that country*'.[74] The decision at Bandung to deplore 'the policies and practices of racial segregation and discrimination, which form the basis of government and human relations in large regions of Africa and in other parts of the world' as a 'gross violation of human rights' should be interpreted in this discursive context.[75] This is even more so when we note that the Bandung final communiqué specifically:

> extended its warm sympathy and support for the courageous stand taken by the victims of racial discrimination, especially by the peoples of African and Indian and Pakistani origin in South Africa; applauded all those who sustain their cause; reaffirmed the determination of Asian-African peoples to eradicate every trace of racialism that might exist in their own countries; and pledged to use its full moral influence to guard against the danger of falling victims to the same evil in their struggle to eradicate it.[76]

The second move—having to do with promoting human rights through respect for legitimate sovereignty, particularly on the basis of the collective right of peoples to self-determination—was made in Political Committee discussions concerning Algeria, but also quite clearly concerning Palestine. The nature of the Palestinian question, as Syrian Foreign Minister Khalid Bey al-Azm put it, was not merely that of a 'change of regime' or a 'coup d'état', but of something 'far deeper and graver': the 'national existence of a people' who had been left 'with no sovereignty and no independence', symbolized in the suffering of the more than half a million Palestinians displaced and dispossessed between 1947 and 1948.[77] The forcible expulsion was asserted 'a matter of imperialism, naked imperialism, in black and white' at the same time that it was conceived as a humanitarian catastrophe.[78] Accordingly, to come to the aid of the Palestinians was not to intervene in the domestic affairs of states: 'let us not forget that the question of Palestine is not a local or a regional one. By its very nature, it is an international catastrophe which must

---

[74] Ibid.: 407. Another approach was to argue that the question was outside of domestic jurisdiction because the situation involved a potential threat to international peace and security, a point raised in 1950 by e.g. the Egyptian delegation. See Rajan 1961: 236–237. The logic returned in more well-known Security Council debates on e.g. sanctions against South Africa and Rhodesia. For a discussion of domestic jurisdiction, threats to international peace, self-determination, and human rights in relation to the latter case, see McDougal and Reisman 1968.
[75] *Final Communiqué of the Asian-African Conference*.
[76] Ibid.
[77] Ibid.: 55.
[78] Ibid.: 50.

evoke the sympathy of the world at large.'[79] If there could be no peace without freedom, then '[w]e claim, and rightly claim—I do not think anyone resists our humble submission—that the people of Palestine are entitled to benefit from human rights and to benefit from the principle of self-determination.'[80]

Of course the precise scope and applications of 'self-determination', 'peoples', and international anti-colonial responsibility in this and other cases were not wholly resolved, and, true, there was also heated debate at Bandung over the meaning of colonialism in relation to superpower imperialisms and satellites.[81] Ceylonese Prime Minister Sir John Kotelawala's condemnation of the 'new colonialism' of the Soviet Union was, after all, among the conference's most explosive moments, nearly 'spell[ing] disaster' for unanimity.[82] Much discussed among statespeople was the final communiqué's denunciation of colonialism 'in all its manifestations'.[83] And certainly one way to interpret the phrase—the interpretation common in internal American memos of the period, for instance—was as a tacit reference to Soviet infiltration, the Cominform (to be dissolved one year later), spheres of influence, etc.[84]

But an alternative interpretation, the interpretation that as we will see had the greatest impact in the politics of global ordering in this period, referred to manifestations of colonialism and imperialism that followed a fundamentally racist and white supremacist logic. This other reading we might better appreciate by quoting Nehru's reply to Kotelawala at Bandung: condemning the 'aggressive propaganda' and 'subversion' originating from 'both groups' standing across the Iron Curtain, Nehru noted that, 'speaking technically', such behaviour 'was not colonialism', that the 'use of the word is incorrect', and the conference instead ought to refer to such activity as 'interference', with the understanding that it 'obviously goes against the idea of two countries existing peacefully together' and 'the so-called Five Principles', that in fact 'it is entirely opposed to them'.[85] When, then, did sustained intervention, as the outcome of foreign pressure or of foreign pressure against self-determined futures, become colonialism in its most politically significant manifestation? Here we would need to turn to Carlos Romulo's opening address at Bandung and his comments on what he called 'Western racism':

---

[79] Ibid.: 52.
[80] Ibid.: 83–84.
[81] On Bandung and enduring tensions between external and internal sovereignty, particularly in the multi-ethnic states of postcolonial Asia and Africa, see Anghie 2013: 541–551. See also e.g. Senaratne 2013.
[82] See e.g. the comments of conference chairperson Ali Sastroamidjojo in TMPCAAC 1955: 192–195.
[83] *Final Communiqué of the Asian-African Conference*.
[84] See e.g. Secretary Dulles in FRUS 1955–1957: XXI, Document 50.
[85] TMPCAAC 1955: 221, 345.

I do not think in this company I have to labour the full import of this pernicious doctrine and practice. I do not think I have to try to measure the role played by this racism as a driving force in the development of the nationalist movements in our many lands.[86]

The racial-hierarchical and white supremacist constitution of empire—and the central place of this iteration of empire in historical Third World practices of self-determination—has been discussed in detail elsewhere.[87] When the final communiqué affirmed that 'the subjection of peoples to alien subjugation, domination, and exploitation constitutes a denial of fundamental human rights' and declared colonialism 'an evil which should speedily be brought to an end', it helped lay the groundwork for legitimating a range of related anti-colonial international actions that were not considered interventions.[88] My point then is that, within prominent discursive practice that we can associate with Bandung, human rights and self-determination had become fundamental in determining what it meant to intervene in international relations.

Belgrade and the 'moral violence of nations'

So far I have introduced a main thrust of the Global South's solidarist internationalist project in terms of its legitimation in the rules and norms of international society.[89] Pivotal to that process of legitimation was a particular redescription of intervention, one that departed both from the classical definition of 'coercive interference' as the use or threat of force and from the Calvo-esque outcome of pressure, and moved towards a conception of intervention as foreign pressure at the expense of self-determination. But I have said too little about the substance of anti-colonial action, including what Sukarno in his opening speech called the 'moral violence of nations'.[90] Did this moral violence imply mere declarations of sympathy or condemnation (in the General Assembly and at cross-regional conferences, for example) or did it extend to support for liberation by other, more tangible means? What was the substance of solidarity and what might this tell us about the historical

---

[86] Indonesia 1955: 115. See Romulo 1956: 24–25, 68–69.
[87] See e.g. Getachew 2019b; Crawford 2004: 291–342; Grovogui 1996.
[88] *Final Communiqué of the Asian-African Conference.*
[89] See generally Weber and Winanti 2016. Additional dimensions of this project, including the international-economic and informational-communicative, are covered in subsequent chapters.
[90] Indonesia 1955: 24.

importance and enduring theoretical salience of radical versus moderate iterations of the theory of anti-colonial intervention?

To these questions Bandung stopped short of providing a clear answer—to be sure, the final communiqué said nothing of, say, collective action through international sanctions against colonial and white minority regimes, the transfer of supplies, or the provision of financial or material assistance to national liberation movements, or still more direct forms of confrontation. One part of a good explanation is that such a position would be likely to be perceived by the liberal-democratic West as a shift further towards the international-political far left, into the arms and arms shipments of the Soviet Union, which had officially supported the right of colonized peoples to self-determination since the Bolsheviks took power in 1917, and long portrayed itself as a 'natural ally' to liberation movements worldwide.[91]

Yet a robust commitment to anti-colonialism and anti-racism was not necessarily an alignment; rather we should better appreciate how anti-colonialism was always the premise of a non-alignment. This was one conclusion to be drawn from the events of 1956. On the one hand Nasser's decision to nationalize the Suez Canal and the ensuing British–French–Israeli invasion of Egypt seemed to signal that no matter the degree of international moral indignation, colonial powers would cling on forcefully to old imperial privileges. On the other, the creation of the UN Emergency Force, the decision of the United States to break from its historic allies on the issue, and the eventual withdrawal of British, French, and then Israeli forces, can be read as a victory not only of a new precedent in UN peacekeeping, but also of the idea of European colonial empire as anachronism.[92] Moreover, at about the same moment that Israel intervened in the Egyptian Sinai, Red Army tanks of course rolled into Budapest, inviting denunciations of Moscow's 'fraternal military assistance' and socialist duty justifications as yet another guise of empire.[93] The point is: the role of ally to self-determination in a global cold war could not be easily claimed by just one of two sides.[94] To the contrary, both superpowers were seizing upon self-determination and seeking to champion the idea as it enjoyed new prominence in international

---

[91] See generally MacFarlane 1985b.
[92] Louis 2008.
[93] Roy Allison describes the Soviet intervention in Hungary as a major step in the development of a doctrine of socialist or proletarian internationalism that, given fuller expression during the invasion of Czechoslovakia and centred around a 'socialist commonwealth', came to be known, especially in the West, as the Brezhnev Doctrine (Allison 2013: 24–43). For a broad analysis of Soviet theories of intervention, see also Thomas 1985: 52–63.
[94] See generally Westad 2005.

society. They nonetheless embarked on so many campaigns widely decried as interventions and hence denials of self-determined futures.

About three months earlier, Nasser had met with Nehru and Yugoslavia's Tito in the Brijuni Islands. The meeting, writes Vijay Prashad, was the 'Third World's Yalta'.[95] If the Yalta Conference is taken as a symbol of the Allied agreement to partition Europe into 'spheres of influence' after the anticipated surrender of Nazi Germany, then Brijuni was its inverse: a repudiation both of regional spheres of influence and of bloc politics. The Nasser–Nehru–Tito communiqué adopted at Brijuni had four main components: 1) a commitment to the ten (not five) Bandung Principles, 2) a call for nuclear disarmament, 3) advocacy for economic cooperation and development, and 4) an argument to the effect that peace could never be achieved if the world was divided into powerful blocs.[96] Non-alignment has often been understood in its geopolitical sense, as if Third World governments were identifying themselves solely on the basis of a decision not to line up formally behind a superpower, which was a Cold War security imperative or military non-alignment.[97] In many respects this could not be further from the truth; in addition to the fact that many non-aligned states were not (and are not) neutral states, and that Cold War belligerents clearly did not respect traditional neutrality as a recognized status, non-alignment was always deeply involved in anti-colonialism, and it would be wrong to present the non-aligned as passive isolationists rather than agents in their own right, which they undoubtedly became.[98] As Prashad shows, vocabularies of neutrality, neutralism, non-alignment, and peaceful coexistence, while sometimes mooted at Brijuni in their negative sense—in terms of withdrawal from conflict, of refusing to pick a side—had a positive face as well.[99] It is from within the positive face of non-alignment that we must trace the descent and branching out of intervention language in the discursive practices of the Third World.

In September 1961, twenty-five governments—from Afro-Asia primarily, but also from Eastern Europe (Yugoslavia) and Latin America (Cuba)—met at Belgrade for the first summit of the self-described 'non-aligned countries'.[100] Belgrade, like Bandung, was partly about refusing to be 'dragged

---

[95] Prashad 2007: 95.
[96] 'Text of the Nehru-Tito Joint Statement', *New York Times*, 24 December 1954.
[97] For a discussion of the various historical meanings of non-alignment, see Jackson 1983: 3–11. See also Willetts 1978: 1–57.
[98] Willetts 1978: 19–20.
[99] Prashad 2007: 95.
[100] Bolivia, Brazil, and Ecuador joined as observers. For an introduction to the Non-Aligned Movement and its summits, see Dinkel 2019 and Čavoški 2022. See also e.g. Mišković, Fischer-Tiné, and Boškovska 2014; Rajan 1990; Singham and Hune 1986; Singham and Trân 1976. On the South in world politics more generally, see Alden, Morphet, and Vieira 2010.

in' or to be tied 'to Europe's troubles and Europe's hatreds and Europe's conflicts'.[101] But, like Bandung, Belgrade was also absorbed in eminently global normative contestation and the choices involved in global ordering.[102] For Kwame Nkrumah, non-alignment did not refer to a sort of 'negative neutralism' whereby the Third World withdrew itself 'entirely from the international problems of peace and war'.[103] It was not, said Sukarno, 'the sanctimonious attitude of the man who holds himself aloof', nor, said Tito, 'a third bloc'—'would it be logical for us, who are fighting against the vision of the world into blocs, to create a third bloc?'[104] Instead, the purpose of non-alignment was to 'make the Great Powers realise that the fate of the world cannot rest in their hands alone'.[105] Continued Tito as host: smaller states could not 'reconcile themselves with the status of observers'; they had 'the right to participate in the solving of problems, particularly those which endanger the peace and the fate of the world'.[106] The Belgrade meeting had been convened 'for the purpose of asserting this right'—so that 'greater numbers' could articulate 'as simply and as strongly as possible, their views regarding the question as to what the relations among peoples and states should be like'.[107]

Or as Ibrahim Abboud of Sudan put it succinctly, non-alignment sought to establish 'a firm foundation for the creation of an ideal international society'.[108]

In seeking to create an ideal international society, Belgrade shared much in common with Bandung (to which the participants and the conference made glowing references and claimed lineage), but it also further diversified and branched out the theory of anti-colonial intervention.[109] 'Peaceful co-existence', explained Haile Selassie, 'is not merely the absence of war. It embraces non-interference and non-intervention in the domestic affairs of others' and it recognizes, as Louis Lansana Beavogui of Guinea put it, 'that the struggle of a colonial people for liberation cannot and must not be regarded as the private concern of the ruling powers'.[110] 'It is not necessary here to point out that the right of nations to determine their own fate, as expressed

[101] Nehru's speech at Bandung, quoted in Phạm and Shilliam 2016: 13.
[102] It is in this normative sense that a line can be drawn from Bandung to Belgrade. On the politics of non-alignment as a rival to the politics of an evolving Afro-Asianism, see e.g. Lüthi 2016. See also Willetts 1978: 10–17.
[103] Nkrumah's speech at Belgrade, in Yugoslavia 1961: 99.
[104] Ibid.: 27, 20.
[105] Ibid.: 21.
[106] Ibid.: 19.
[107] Ibid.: 19, 20, 18, 21.
[108] Ibid.: 52.
[109] See e.g. the references to Bandung as precedent in speeches by Tito, Sukarno, Nasser, U Nu, Haile Selassie, Mohammed Daoud Khan, Osvaldo Dorticós Torrado, Prince Norodom Sihanouk, and Ben Youssef Ben Khedda in ibid.: 18, 38, 40, 68, 80, 87, 119, 183, 234.
[110] Ibid.: 95, 223.

in the UN Charter, the Declaration of Human Rights, and the International Covenants on Human Rights must be observed ... these facts are known to all of us.'[111] Hence it would be 'a gross injustice', claimed Somalia's Aden Adde, 'to regard as an unwarranted intervention any support granted to colonial peoples struggling for self-determination.'[112]

Important components of the anti-colonial theory were reflected in the first operative paragraph of the Declaration of the Heads of State or Government of Non-Aligned Countries (the Belgrade Declaration):

> The participants in the Conference solemnly reaffirm their support to the 'Declaration on the Granting of Independence to Colonial Countries and Peoples,' adopted at the 15th Session of the General Assembly of the United Nations and recommend the immediate unconditional, total, and final abolition of colonialism and resolved to make a concerted effort to put an end to all types of new colonialism and imperialist domination in all its forms and manifestations.[113]

The Declaration on the Granting of Independence to Colonial Countries and Peoples (Resolution 1514 (XV)), recalling influential formulations contained in the Bandung final communiqué, read: 'the subjection of peoples to alien subjugation, domination and exploitation constitutes a denial of fundamental human rights' and 'all peoples have a right to self-determination; by virtue of that right they freely determine their political status and freely pursue their economic, social and cultural development.'[114] Accordingly the participants at Belgrade demanded not only that 'an immediate stop be put to armed action and repressive measures of any kind directed against dependent peoples to enable them to exercise peacefully and freely their right to complete independence', but that 'any aid given by any country to a colonial power in such suppression is contrary to the Charter of the United Nations.'[115] And there was another formulation adopted in the Belgrade Declaration that seems deeply underappreciated in the context of evolving discursive practices of intervention: that 'the vast majority of people are becoming increasingly conscious

---

[111] Mohammad Daoud Khan of Afghanistan, ibid.: 83.
[112] Ibid.: 229.
[113] 'Declaration of the Heads of State or Government of Non-Aligned Countries' in ibid.: 257. Resolution 1514 (XV) has been much discussed. Chris Reus-Smit for instance writes of a 'tectonic shift in international legitimacy' having to do with the Resolution and other events of the period. See Reus-Smit 2013b: 153, 151–192.
[114] A/RES/1514(XV).
[115] 'Declaration of the Heads of State or Government of Non-Aligned Countries' in Yugoslavia 1961: 257.

of the fact that *war between peoples* constitutes not only an anachronism but also a crime against humanity'.[116]

The argument coming through again and again, and supported gradually more by agreements at the UN and meetings of the non-aligned states, had to do with self-determination at the heart both of global humanitarian duty and the duty not to intervene. Landmark resolutions like 1514 (XV) had begun to codify a new reality of the anti-humanitarian nature of all forms of alien subjugation, domination, and exploitation, and the constitution of colonialism and intervention as violations of fundamental human rights. So the use of Article 2 (7) and non-intervention language to suppress the international struggle against colonialism and associated racial discrimination was losing the legitimacy it might once have had in international relations. International and UN-based action to promote human rights was, in spite of interpretations bearing on the Charter as it was originally conceived, becoming more tolerable from the standpoint of the global normative standards of the diplomatic community.

But if the means by which solidarity should be realized were left ambiguous at Bandung and unspecified in resolutions like 1514 (XV), the precise character of international anti-colonial and anti-racist action was a more prominent feature of discursive practice in 1961. It was significant, for example, that the Belgrade Declaration called on participating countries 'to extend to the people of Algeria *all possible support and aid*' in their 'just and necessary' struggle for freedom.[117] And it is on the basis of defining the substance of a widely accepted international anti-colonial and anti-racist responsibility that a rift between radical and moderate strains of thinking can now be more coherently brought into view.

In this respect a dominant theme at Belgrade was that declaratory forms of international solidarity were not enough; to shame or censure in UN forums and regional meetings would not put an end to war and oppression; '[e]xperience during the last decade [on matters of apartheid] has shown that mere verbal condemnations are totally inadequate'.[118] 'Has not the time come', offered Prime Minister Saeb Salam of Lebanon, 'to implement, practically, the resolution adopted by the United Nations General Assembly in its last session [Resolution 1514 (XV)]', and if so, argued Nasser, 'it seems to me that we can give more than just moral efforts ... The same can be said with regard to racial

---

[116] Ibid. Emphasis mine.
[117] Ibid. Algeria joined as a formal participant at the Belgrade Conference and was represented by the country's provisional government.
[118] Aden Adde in Yugoslavia 1961: 231.

discrimination, which we can face with more than protests.'[119] Louis Lansana Beavogui of Guinea similarly called on participants 'to furnish tangible assistance to all peoples fighting for their independence from colonial rule'.[120] And while to very different effect, it should be noted that some degree of disillusionment with 'moral efforts alone' was shared by moderates like Nehru ('a fear creeps in upon my mind that we may not be able to get out of the rut of meeting together, passing long resolutions and making brave declarations, and then going home and allowing the world to drift to disaster').[121]

The emphasis of Nehru's 1961 speech and non-aligned vision was on disarmament and the escalating risk of thermonuclear war ('nothing is more important or has more priority'), and of course we should not dismiss more straightforward meanings of coexistence as survival or the more cautious interpretation of the aspirations of what came to be officially known as the Non-Aligned Movement. (Nehru warned that the 'moral force' of those statespeople who had gathered in 1961 was 'not military power' and 'not economic power': 'we must realise both our actual strength and our potential strength that we have, and also the lack of strength that we have' in attempting to organize dialogue and disarmament on the greatest scale.)[122] But changes in the overall tone and character of the anti-colonial discursive record, including at Belgrade, would become important for what happened next in relation to the meaning of intervention in international society. Nkrumah's speech was, from one view, a direct reply to Nehru's own. His more 'positive neutralism', which foregrounded a more international-coercive struggle against colonialism that was 'no less important than the problem of disarmament', also seemed embedded in a dense convergence of international opinion: 'I believe that there exists a sufficient and intense identity of views among us to make it possible for us to act in concert in the complete eradication of colonialism, oppression, and racial discrimination, in the achievement of a disarmament agreement, and generally in the cause of peace.'[123]

The case was most persuasively made in relation to South Africa but also other cases across Southern Africa, where dependence and extreme racism were most clearly linked, and where international struggle had already adopted coercive elements, the public justification of which was becoming prevalent in and around the UN. Tito argued, for instance, that 'acts of

---

[119] Ibid.: 130, 51.
[120] Ibid.: 224.
[121] Nehru in ibid.: 110.
[122] Ibid.: 108, 113.
[123] Ibid.: 99, 102, 99.

savagery committed by the Portuguese armed forces against the barehanded populations of Angola are causing indignation throughout the world', and hence '[e]very form of assistance should be extended to the people of Angola in their struggle for independence'.[124] 'We find the same or a similar case in South Africa … The treatment of the autochthonous populations by South Africa's colonialist rulers constitutes a brutal offense against human dignity and humane principles.'[125] 'The African states have already imposed direct sanctions in the economic and diplomatic fields' against Pretoria, as Haile Selassie noted, but it was widely believed at Belgrade that 'to be adequately effective the policy of sanctions should be implemented by a larger number of nations' and even 'more severe sanctions should be applied'.[126] To quote again Tito as host: we 'cannot confine ourselves to expressions of indignation and protest, but must take more effective and concerted action, such as will compel the protagonists of this unheard-of arbitrary rule to bow to the decisions of the United Nations'.[127]

The Tricontinental's 'total respect for the sovereignty of all states'

Versions of the anti-colonial theory of intervention—that sought more tangible and coercive forms of international action in support of self-determination—were being heard elsewhere too. At the founding of the Organisation of African Unity (OAU) at Addis Ababa in 1963, it was declared that one purpose of the organization was 'to eradicate all forms of colonialism from the continent of Africa', a decision that crystallized similar agreements made at previous pan-African conferences and meetings.[128] True, Nkrumah's vision of an African High Command ('to guard our own freedom as well as to win freedom for our oppressed brothers, the freedom fighters') did not come to fruition, but as Oji Umozurike argued in an article published in 1979 on the OAU and the domestic jurisdiction clause of its Charter, the organization nonetheless 'encouraged the liberation movements' and gave them both 'material and moral support as demanded by the resolutions of the General

[124] Ibid: 159.
[125] Ibid.
[126] Haile Selassie in ibid.: 92; Aden Adde in ibid.: 232; Tito in ibid.: 159.
[127] Ibid.
[128] Article 2 (i) (d), OAU Charter. See also Article 3 (6). Consider similar purposes and declarations at e.g. the Conference of Independent African States held in Accra in 1948, the All-African Peoples' Conferences held in Accra (1958), Tunis (1960), and then Cairo (1961), as well as the various Pan-African Congresses.

Assembly of the UN'.[129] Article 3 (2) of the OAU Charter did refer to the principle of 'non-interference in the internal affairs of states' but members saw no impediment in this to international anti-colonial action across the continent.[130] Much to the contrary, at Addis Ababa for instance, we find this astounding formulation by Fulbert Youlou of the Congo (Brazzaville):

> The countries which have attained independence must resolutely unite and act in common so as to ensure that territories that are still dependent accede to independence in their turn with the least possible delay. To this end, it is desirable to establish a 'Monroe Doctrine' for Africa, that is to say to secure Africa against any direct interference by a non-African power ... .[131]

The thesis of collective support for wars of national liberation found uptake within the organization's radical circles. The OAU's Liberation Committee, established in 1963 and based in Dar es Salaam, self-described its purpose as the use of 'all means at its disposal to restore elementary human rights to the oppressed peoples of Africa' in the 'absence of an immediate peaceful solution', and claimed, in meetings of the UN General Assembly's Special Committee on the Declaration on the Granting of Independence to Colonial Countries and Peoples, that 'the total decolonization of Africa remained a top priority on the OAU's agenda ... the fight for liberation raging throughout the occupied territories of Africa would be waged to the bitter end'.[132] It would not be hard to see African solidarity against the raids of white supremacist countries into the OAU's 'Frontline States', recognized as an ad-hoc committee in 1975, as cut from the same cloth; if on the one hand there is the more familiar story of Julius Nyerere's humanitarian interventionism in Uganda from 1978 to 1979, then on the other it seems tempting to tell a story of Julius Nyerere's solidarist internationalism, his acting as chairperson of the Frontline States until 1985, and his sheltering and assisting of liberation movements engaged in full-blown struggle against South Africa and Rhodesia.[133]

I want to focus a little more on this sort of radical argument. I want to emphasize that moderate positions were also being adopted—at the OAU, for instance, the moderate, functionalist views on African unity of the

---

[129] 'Address delivered by Kwame Nkrumah' in Organisation of African Unity 1963b; Umozurike 1979. See also Imobighe 1980.
[130] Article 3 (2), OAU Charter.
[131] 'Address delivered by Fulbert Youlou' in Organisation of African Unity 1963b. See also e.g. the call for collective anti-colonial action in 'Resolution on Colonialism' in Organisation of African Unity 1963a.
[132] A/6700 (Part II).
[133] On Tanzania's arguable interventionism in Uganda, see Wheeler 2000: 111–139. See also Thomas 1985: 90–121.

Monrovia group were always set against the radical views of Nkrumah and the Casablanca group—and I want to acknowledge too that certain capacities of implementation (of the Liberation Committee for example) were of course severely limited in the face of, for instance, overwhelming financial strains.[134] But I also want to stress just how important the radical formulation became as a matter of global order contestation and how deeds scorned as high intervention by some were being legitimated by others in terms of a theory rooted in self-determination, human rights, and shifting domestic jurisdiction.

And of all the meetings of the Third World in the 1960s, the Tricontinental Conference of January 1966 provided the most fervent articulation of this specific strain of anti-colonial intervention. Though not strictly a meeting of governments, it is easy to forget the influential role played by the statespeople who did gather at Havana and just how extensive its resolution-making, often directly on matters of global order, became. A total of seventy-three resolutions were taken over the course of thirteen days, through which also emerged the Organization of Solidarity with the Peoples of Asia, Africa and Latin America (OSPAAAL), which was tasked with aiding, culturally and propagandistically, liberation movements worldwide.[135] While of course there were quarrels over, for instance, different socialist doctrines (quarrels that, as Jeffrey Byrne notes, were bitterly resented by a large majority of developing countries), and while Tricontinentalist visions of support for armed revolutionary movements sowed fierce divisions among the non-aligned (particularly insofar as those movements were located in Asian, African, and Latin American states that had already achieved legal independence), the conference laid claim to an internationalism located at the nexus of race and empire.[136]

In short, the prominence at the Tricontinental of proletarian internationalisms and intracommunist doctrinal difference has often overshadowed logics that were in fact embedded in shared and more globally institutionalized vocabularies. The radical South might hence be seen as entangled in formalistic debates about the rules and norms of international society, not just as having put those vocabularies aside in favour of deeper revolutionary

---

[134] On the Monrovia and Casablanca groups, as well as Nkrumah's 'expansionist' interpretation of the self-determination principle, see Umozurike 1979: 197–198. On the OAU Liberation Committee, see Mononi 1975.
[135] See OSPAAAL 1966.
[136] The conference met during the Sino-Soviet split and was attended by representatives of both the People's Republic of China and the Soviet Union. For a view on political and ideological schisms and other diverging trends in relation to Tricontinentalism, non-alignment, and evolving Afro-Asianism, see Byrne 2022. On OSPAAAL as supplanting a beleaguered Afro-Asian Peoples' Solidarity Organization (AAPSO), and Sino-Soviet competition in the history of AAPSO, see Friedman 2015.

112 Intervention before Interventionism

commitments.[137] When the revolutionaries gathered in Havana, one self-avowed objective was to harness 'the powerful drive of world public opinion' and reject 'the outdated pretensions' and 'false legal arguments' of colonialists, neocolonialists, and racists: for whether their normative designs took on 'the title of "spheres of influence", at other times "balance of power"', or 'the Monroe Doctrine, the truth is that the original purpose and final result is the imperial domination of weaker countries'.[138] According to conference documents, 'revealing and denunciation of the thousand faces of imperialism and the unmasking of its tactics' were 'important tasks' in 'orienting [the people] correctly in the struggle to halt the aggressors'.[139]

The most decisive argument along these lines was about legitimate armed struggle, including through armed assistance to the liberation movements of strangers, as an inescapable condition of ending colonialism. 'We do not think we will shock this assembly by stating that the only effective way of definitely fulfilling the aspirations of the peoples, that is to say of attaining national liberation, is by armed struggle', argued Amílcar Cabral in his speech before attendees.[140] Here were the makings of a theory, taken up by Cabral, that because imperialism was intrinsically an act of dehumanizing violence, colonized peoples could not be emancipated except through the threat or use of armed force.[141] 'The essential instrument of imperialist domination is violence ... imperialist domination implies a state of permanent violence against the nationalist forces.'[142] Violence was permanent in the sense that behind any façade of peace in colonized society was the constant threat of the colonizer's police, its jails, its soldiers, and the arsenal of the metropole and its allies as a kind of international gendarme—the coercive instruments that established colonized society were also integral to its material and psychological maintenance. To quote Cabral again: 'On a Tricontinental level, this means that we are not going to eliminate imperialism by shouting insults against it. For us, the best or worst shout against imperialism, whatever its form, is to take up arms and fight.'[143]

---

[137] Compare to Mahler's view of Tricontinentalist discourse in relation to a global struggle for racial justice and black internationalist thought—see Mahler 2018. On the Tricontinental Conference, and on Tricontinentalism in relation to the Global South, see Parrott and Lawrence 2022.
[138] 'Antecedents and Objectives of the Movement' in OSPAAAL 1966: 18, 19.
[139] Ibid.
[140] Cabral 1970.
[141] Taken up in the sense that theories of violence as a unifying force, but also as a humanizing or cathartic force, were influential in much anti-colonial thinking at the time. See e.g. Fanon 1963.
[142] Cabral 1970.
[143] Ibid. Compare with arguments openly concerned with doctrines of e.g. Maoist 'people's wars' in the speech of Wu Xueqian, head of the Chinese delegation and later Foreign Minister, contained in Organization of American States 1966: 77–85.

Hence the Conference's General Declaration proclaimed 'the right of peoples to meet imperialist violence with revolutionary violence' and the 'duty of the peoples of Asia, Africa, and Latin America, and the progressive states and governments of the world, to give material and moral support to peoples fighting for their liberation.'[144]

Yet this was not the first time the basic maxim of 'colonialism as permanent aggression' had appeared in the documents and discourse of the Third World, or in UN debate. Ali Mazrui, writing for *International Organization* in 1964, observed that it had also become 'an important theme in Afro-Asian argumentation mainly following India's annexation of Goa.'[145] To quote Krishna Menon, in his brazen defence and UN-based legitimation of the Indian military action in December 1961: 'We consider colonialism permanent aggression … We did not commit aggression. Colonialism collapsed.'[146] Noted Mazrui: 'when the question of defining "aggression" comes up for discussion by a special General Assembly committee next year, "colonialism" will not necessarily form part of the definition', but 'the more militant attitude toward colonialism which now characterizes the General Assembly both reflects and helps to consolidate new attitudes toward that phenomenon'.[147] It even appeared to be undergoing 'a legal re-definition', particularly in tandem with 'the criteria of what constitutes domestic jurisdiction and external intervention and interference'.[148]

At the Tricontinental in 1966, we can similarly see, intervention was practised not as the use or threat of force, but as the denial of the national identities and self-determined futures of peoples, such that, went this radical argument, international and coercive support on their behalf did not constitute an act of intervention. In one resolution, a condemnation of the US House of Representatives' Resolution 560 (on individual or collective self-defence against 'international communism and its agencies in the Western hemisphere'), we find the allegation that Washington had ratified a policy of intervention 'as previously stated in the cynical Monroe Doctrine, and by which they arrogate the right to intervene in the internal affairs of any country in the continent, with total contempt for peoples, and ignoring the elementary rules of international relations, in violation of the treaties that express the right of

---

[144] OSPAAAL 1966: 157–158.
[145] Mazrui 1964: 505–506. On 'permanent aggression' see Mazrui 1963. See also Quincy Wright's account of the 'Goa incident', and the General Assembly's notable decision not to condemn it, in Wright 1962.
[146] Quoted in Goodwin 1972: 108. Menon might well have said 'intervention' instead of 'aggression'.
[147] Mazrui 1964: 505–506. For a legalistic refutation of the idea that the use of force for the eradication of colonialism can be justified on the basis of self-defence, see Dugard 1967.
[148] Mazrui 1964: 506. On wars of national liberation and laws of war, see Abi-Saab 1972. On the Third World 'battle' for legal recognition of 'wars of national liberation' in this period, see von Bernstorff 2019.

self-determination.'[149] The same resolution therefore proclaimed the 'duty of all countries to offer moral and material support' in line with 'the principle of total respect for the sovereignty of all states.'[150]

Colonialists and neocolonialists, claimed the General Declaration, 'ignore their international commitments. They try to mask their crimes inventing all kinds of fallacious arguments to violate the principle of self-determination' and indeed, suggested the General Resolution on Vietnam, 'the most elementary human rights.'[151] The Vietnam case, to which the Tricontinental devoted 'special and preferred attention' and described it as 'the most important problem of today's struggles of the peoples in the world', linked a radical version of the anti-colonial theory of intervention not only to the 'just war' as construed in Leninist and Maoist thought, but also to the problem of non-intervention in international and UN-based practice.[152] The 'crimes of aggression against Vietnam' were condemned 'as a blatant violation of the rights of the peoples to self-determination, of the 1954 Geneva Agreements on Vietnam, and of international law'.[153] 'Human conscience', the resolution continued, 'is deeply disgusted and indignant at the barbaric genocide [by] the North American aggressors' and 'the peoples of the three continents and of the whole world have the duty to support and help the just struggle of the Vietnamese people', and to 'develop in every way and in every aspect an active solidarity', with the understanding that 'genuine peace cannot be separated from independence.'[154]

Such an interpretation of the interdependence of peace and freedom was spelled out further by a specific resolution on the familiar concept of 'peaceful coexistence'.[155] 'Peaceful coexistence', it was now asserted, 'assumes the unrestricted respect for the principle of self-determination of the nations and sovereignty of all states, big and small.'[156] The principle of peaceful coexistence referred 'exclusively to the relations among states', not, in other words, to relations among for example 'the people victimised by imperialism against their oppressors'.[157] The resolution continued:

---

[149] US House Resolution 560 ('Defense Against Communism in the Western Hemisphere') was adopted on 20 September 1965. See 'Resolution Condemning the Resolution Adopted by the House of Representatives of the United States' in OSPAAAL 1966: 72–73.

[150] 'Resolution Condemning the Resolution Adopted by the House of Representatives of the United States' in OSPAAAL 1966: 73.

[151] Ibid: 157.

[152] 'Antecedents and Objectives' in ibid.: 23; 'General Resolution on Vietnam' in ibid: 129. On 'just wars' of national liberation in socialist theory, see e.g. Socher 2017.

[153] OSPAAAL 1966: 128.

[154] Ibid.: 128, 129.

[155] Ibid.: 76.

[156] Ibid.

[157] Ibid.

> The defence of the principle of peaceful coexistence conveys the repulsion of imperialistic aggression, of the criminal use of force against the people and of the decisive repulse of foreign intervention in the internal affairs of other states, all of which represents the violation of the principle of peaceful coexistence. It entitles the progressive and democratic states of the world to repel the aggressor and help the victims with all their means. When all the democratic and progressive states offer their most decisive help to the victimised peoples, they are keeping alive the principle of peaceful coexistence.[158]

Or, as Khaled Mohieddin of the United Arab Republic put it in his speech, 'the struggle of peoples against colonialism is closely linked with the cause of peace … Peaceful co-existence does not mean surrendering to acts of aggression and usurpation'.[159]

Nor did peaceful co-existence, in the radical theory, preclude coercive internationalism in favour of preventing the atrocities of racism tied up with denials of self-determination. Racial discrimination, propounded the General Declaration, 'is practiced by imperialists, colonialists, and neo-colonialists … and reveals itself in its most repulsive, brutal, and diabolic form in the policy of apartheid'.[160] Another resolution took aim at Rhodesia (Zimbabwe) and South Africa:

> The [Tricontinental] Conference proclaims the full equality of all men and the duty of all the peoples to fight against all expressions of racism and discrimination, and therefore, its full support to the struggle of the people of Zimbabwe against the racist government of Ian Smith and to the international movement of solidarity against the South African regime, and calls on all the countries represented at the Conference to impose a political and commercial blockade on South Africa, as well as a boycott on the shipment of arms and petroleum.[161]

Notably, about one year later, through its Resolution 2151 (XXI), the UN General Assembly would, in reaffirming 'the inalienable right of the people of Zimbabwe to freedom and independence, and *the legitimacy of their struggle for the exercise of that right*', draw 'the attention of the Security Council once again to the grave situation prevailing in Southern Rhodesia, in order that it may decide to apply the necessary enforcement measures envisaged under

---

[158] Ibid.
[159] 'Speech by Khaled Mohieddin, Head of the UAR Delegation, 5 January 1966' in Organization of American States 1966: 92.
[160] 'General Declaration' in OSPAAAL 1966: 157.
[161] Ibid.

Chapter VII of the Charter of the United Nations'.[162] The Security Council would agree to apply both selective mandatory actions in December 1966, the first time ever that the UN had taken such an action against a state, as well as comprehensive mandatory sanctions from 1968 until the collapse of the Ian Smith regime in 1979.[163]

A case of comparably broad interest at Havana was Angola. Osvaldo Dorticós Torrado, President of Cuba whose speech opened the Tricontinental, had asked at the Belgrade Conference, 1961: 'How can we speak here of respect for the rights of peoples and nations to self-determination and of respect for the sovereignty and integrity of states if we do not adopt resolutions condemning the Portuguese colonialist genocide in Angola?'[164] The Tricontinental's resolution on Angola would go much further than censure: by calling for the support of the armed struggle of the Angolan people 'by all possible means, including the supply of arms'.[165] Cuba's military action in Angola—particularly from 1975 onward, to halt a South African invasion condemned by all non-aligned states—I briefly discuss in the conclusion of this chapter.

Again there is feasibly much complexity to the individual arguments, and there can be no dismissing of the Tricontinental's obvious political functions in Cold War terms, emphasizing as the conference so often did 'Yankee imperialism' and class-based oppression that surely verged on an alignment.[166] But having discussed already the aims and approach of this genealogical project, I would only say again that I have a certain level of abstraction in mind: one that helps us to better grasp the contestation and reconstitution of intervention in the globalization of international society.[167] No doubt one very important way of reading the Tricontinental has to do with the way in which it attempted to persuade existing Third World vocabularies into an new ideological purity and to bring the Third World, precariously, into alliance with the Second World, but what I am trying to say is that the conference might fruitfully be interpreted as a meeting of practitioners who, in the words of its host, 'representing different philosophical ideas or positions and different religious beliefs', and 'in many cases of different ideologies', nonetheless stood united in a stance against 'colonialism and neo-colonialism, against

---

[162] A/RES/2151(XXI). Emphasis added.
[163] On the success and history of UN-based sanctions against Rhodesia, see e.g. Minter and Schmidt 1988.
[164] Ibid.: 121.
[165] See 'Resolution on Angola' in OSPAAAL 1966: 88.
[166] See generally Organization of American States 1966.
[167] See Introduction.

racism'.[168] In his closing speech, Fidel Castro called for 'a common strategy, a joint, simultaneous struggle' because 'the field of battle against imperialism takes in the whole world'.[169] Accordingly, 'Cuban fighters can be counted on by the revolutionary movement in any corner of the earth.'[170] 'Without boasting, without any kind of immodesty, that is how we Cuban revolutionaries understand our internationalist duty.'[171]

The difference between an interventionist and an internationalist

On the evening of 31 December 1965, at a social at Revolution Square in Havana held in the honour of delegates attending the Tricontinental to begin three days later, Fidel Castro spoke with delegations from North and South Vietnam. A North Vietnamese revolutionary is said to have approached Castro and presented him with a metal ring—allegedly made from the wreckage of an enemy plane that she herself had downed.[172] Castro reportedly clasped her hand and raised it to the sky, exalting the fighting spirit of Vietnamese women in resisting imperialism.[173] If the content of Tricontinental resolutions and speeches were somehow not enough to precipitate their widespread condemnation in an ongoing Cold War, then images of this sort surely sealed common assessments of the conference as 'terroristic and warlike'.[174] And while such condemnation is of course not surprising, the ways in which it would be formally expressed, and the ways in which Havana would formally respond, have been misunderstood as a matter of international-societal contestation.

I account for that correspondence here to summarize core components of the anti-colonial theory of intervention that I have introduced in this chapter.

The Council of the OAS held a special meeting in the afternoon of 2 February 1966 to reply to the Tricontinental. In building their case, the United States, joined by Latin American allies, turned to the non-intervention principle: their adopted resolution, making no mention of colonialism, neo-colonialism, or extreme racism, focused instead on what the Council called

---

[168] 'Speech by Fidel Castro, Prime Minister of Cuba, in the Closing Session' in OSPAAAL 1966: 165.
[169] Ibid.
[170] Ibid.
[171] Ibid.: 165, 167.
[172] Adapted from an English-language Radio Hanoi broadcast and quoted in United States Department of State 1966: 23.
[173] Ibid.
[174] Ibid.

the conference's 'pledge to give financial, political, and military aid to communist subversive movements in this hemisphere, the same as in other parts of the world'.[175] The Council hence resolved to condemn 'empathetically the policy of intervention and aggression of the communist states and other participating countries and groups' that was allegedly adopted at 'the so-called conference of solidarity among the peoples of Asia, Africa, and Latin America'.[176] The OAS resolution was followed by a letter dated 7 February 1966 to the President of the UN Security Council, which made essentially the same claim: it ought to be better known to the international community that the Tricontinental's commitment to assisting and fomenting supposed liberation movements struck 'against the sovereignty and political stability of state members of the United Nations' and 'the fundamental principles of international law'.[177]

Three days later, Castro replied with a letter of his own—addressed to UN Secretary-General U Thant.[178] Requesting that this letter be circulated as an official document of the Security Council in order to give the OAS 'the reply it deserves', Castro railed against the indictment, which he claimed was in its origin more American than Latin American.[179] It was 'incredible that these governments should be so cynical as to accuse Cuba and the Solidarity Conference of the Peoples of Asia, Africa, and Latin America of interventionism' given that the governments 'in whose name the [7 February] letter was signed' were 'precisely the most servile henchmen of Yankee imperialism in Latin America', the sort who 'unhesitatingly supported' or 'issued mild and hypocritical protests' against the recent military intervention undertaken by the United States in the Dominican Republic, some of whom were now 'participating directly in the military occupation'.[180]

The stance taken at the Tricontinental was not about sanctioning intervention—at least in its traditional sense. Continued Castro: 'To proclaim the right of these peoples who are oppressed and exploited by the imperialists with the complicity, in each country, of the reactionary classes ... is not an act of intervention; it is precisely a struggle against intervention.'[181] To intervene is not simply to use or threaten to use force, but to effect foreign pressure

---

[175] 'Resolution Adopted by the Council of the OAS at the Meeting Held on the Afternoon on 2 February 1966' in Organization of American States 1966: 275–277.
[176] Ibid.
[177] S/7123: 1.
[178] S/7134.
[179] Ibid.: 1.
[180] Ibid: 1. On the US and OAS in the Dominican Civil War, see e.g. Gleijeses 1978. See also the discussion in McPherson 2004: 117–163.
[181] S/7134: 3.

through multiple means, and particularly pressure at the expense of the self-determined futures of peoples. A certain Tricontinentalist argument referred to the provision of every form of assistance to the national liberation movements, in the context of a shared duty to protect and promote fundamental human rights, particularly the right to self-determination. To be sure, this was a radical iteration of the anti-colonial theory of intervention, one that comprehended the substance of solidarist internationalism at an extremity, and that in its proclamation of a solidarist-internationalist responsibility embedded in the rules and norms of international society, bore limited similarities to the arguments made at Bandung and Belgrade. Diverse forms of moral and material action in favour of anti-colonialism and anti-racism would of course have been alleged to be interventionary according to practices adopted by colonial powers and their allies, as reflected in their use of Article 2 (7) in the UN General Assembly through the 1950s and 1960s. But in the evolving practices of statespeople, solidarity was not intervention properly construed; the limits of sovereign privilege and domestic jurisdiction had changed with the arrival of the moral and humanitarian predicates of the non-aligned and Afro-Asian movements.[182]

The Tricontinental decided 'to intensify the struggle *against intervention* and to assist the peoples fighting for liberty and independence.'[183] Absolutely, wrote Castro, the conference also 'emphasized the duty of states and progressive governments to support peoples who are struggling against interventionist and aggressive imperialism', including through 'the most violent revolutionary action', but 'the support of independence must not be confused with intervention'.[184] After all, there were historical precedents to be drawn from across the world for such forms of internationalist practice—precedents so widely accepted that members of international society had come to take them for granted not as denigrated or 'interventionist' in the pejorative sense of the word still predominant in 1966, but as among the most venerated developments in modern international relations:

> No one would think of accusing the French revolutionaries, who in the eighteenth century helped the people of North America to gain their independence from British colonial rule, of having been interventionists. The peoples of France, the United States, and the entire world recognised the undeniable merit of what those brave men did in fighting on American soil to win independence for the thirteen colonies.[185]

---

[182] I explore this point further in Chapter 4.
[183] S/7134. Emphasis added.
[184] Ibid.
[185] Ibid.

To invoke in this way a longer history of international anti-colonial solidarity was to allude not just to a neglected view of liberty—about the achievement of a more 'popular' and legitimate sovereignty, freedom through the nation state, as well as freedom as non-domination in the face of foreign rule—but also to progressive understandings of intervention and self-determination that, in historical international society, did not hew to a single ideological line.[186] Castro in fact cited the Panama Conference in the early nineteenth century:

> The militant, revolutionary solidarity of the peoples of Latin America assumed a very active form at the time of the struggle for liberation carried on by Bolívar, San Martín, and Sucre. The peoples of Latin America gratefully remember that solidarity. No one would think of describing the Latin American liberation movement of the last century as an act of intervention. In 1826, Simon Bolívar summoned the peoples of the Americas to the Panama Conference to discuss the most appropriate means of completing the liberation of the continent from Spanish colonial oppression. By the standards of Yankee imperialism ... that Conference could be regarded as violating the sovereignty of peoples and as frankly interventionist.[187]

The OAS was of course highly suspicious of the wider scope of colonial and neocolonial oppression that had been embraced at the Tricontinental, and saw itself as exposing 'militant, revolutionary solidarity' as a guise for 'communist subversion' in its own hemisphere.[188] Equally suspicious were moderate members of the Non-Aligned Movement and a majority of the developing states, which feared any attempt at the capture of the Third World's anti-colonial and anti-racist vocabularies by a socialist revolutionary vanguard. These states took great exception to the view that the Bandung Spirit moved ineluctably or naturally towards the East and away from the South. They clearly rejected any theory of intervention that legitimated 'active assistance' to insurgent groups seeking to overthrow recognized governments for the purposes of imposing a particular form of government.[189]

Yet the key point is that non-aligned and Global Southern practice at large—in radical and moderate iterations alike—dispelled the notion that

---

[186] Castro's letter reminds us that the anti-colonial theory of intervention might also be read, at an alternative level of abstraction, in terms of republican internationalism. On republicanism and its postcolonial revival in the Cold War, including its transformation in Nehruvian thought, see Ramgotra 2017. On the republican tradition of warfare, see Nabulsi 1999: especially chapter 6. For a historical republican interpretation of the non-intervention principle, see especially Mazzini 1870.

[187] S/7134: 3.

[188] Organization of American States 1966: 275–277.

[189] On the 'natural ally' thesis in the Non-Aligned Movement, culminating in a Castro–Tito clash and moderate triumph at the Havana Summit of 1979, see Čavoški 2022: 191–227.

non-intervention amounted either simply to the non-use of force or the non-use of pressure in international relations. The meaning of non-intervention in the domestic affairs of states was rather to be construed in the context of a human rights regime with the right to self-determination at its heart. This anti-colonial theory of intervention advocated by Asian, African, and Latin American peoples, and institutionalized as a shared duty of states, became integral to a process of legitimating a range of international activities against the inhumanities of white supremacist empire.

Essential to this manoeuvre was a particular reading of the concept of domestic jurisdiction. As far as liberation from colonial and racist oppression was concerned, it was believed that international solidarity did not qualify as intervention, because respect for the right to self-determination and other human rights and fundamental freedoms no longer belonged essentially to the domestic jurisdiction of states.[190] The anti-colonial theory rested on an understanding of the dynamic nature of domestic jurisdiction and of international-political and legal responsibilities arising at the expense of abstract sovereign privilege, but not of sovereign equality.[191] Explaining the emergence of a 'Bandung UN' involves recognizing how matters that once fell into the domestic were entering the international. Hence pleading Article 2 (7) provided no compelling shield to solidarist-internationalist organizing. International discussions of colonial and racial oppression were not interventions, and criticism, scrutiny, and resolution-making were not intervention either, because of their character as matters of shared responsibility and not simply because they failed to meet the threshold of coercion or force.[192]

International coercion was one element of this solidarist-internationalist project, and hence we hit upon another reason why the dictatorial theory of intervention is not enough to make sense of this era of global debate. Certainly, solidarity encompassed the enforcement and collective coercive action of the Security Council. To Afro-Asian and non-aligned states, UN-based sanctions against Rhodesia and, soon enough, South Africa was a matter of maintaining peace through the promotion of freedom. Yet for many, and of course far more controversially, solidarist internationalism also involved a coercive internationalism without Security Council authorization, as was the case of non-aligned sanctions against other racist and minority regimes in Southern Africa. Allegations of colonial atrocities and aggression appeared in relation to the use of force in Portuguese colonies, for example. Angola,

---

[190] On human rights as falling outside of domestic jurisdiction, particularly on account of legal obligations including in international treaty law, see e.g. Bossuyt 1985.
[191] See generally Rajan 1961. See also Rajan 1959.
[192] See Bossuyt 1985.

where a large-scale Cuban military mission would arrive in 1975 to halt a South African invasion and thereby contribute to a struggle against apartheid and foreign domination, is a case in point.[193] It seems significantly undertheorized in global order narratives that at the fifth non-aligned summit at Colombo in 1976, eighty-five members of the movement, notably now counting seven Latin American members, 'congratulated the government and people of Angola for their heroic and victorious struggle against the South African racist invaders and their allies; and praised the Republic of Cuba and other states which helped the people of Angola foil the expansionist and colonialist strategy of the South African regime and its allies'.[194]

For the non-aligned and Global South, in short, there was a great difference between an interventionist and an internationalist. That difference, I have been arguing, ought to be explained as a matter of historical discursive practice, in moderate and radical forms, in an increasingly post-Western and postcolonial international society. In Asia, Africa, and Latin America there were few other bases of international morality on which to fashion enduring political unity than a repudiation of the humanitarian abuses of white supremacist empire. A global anti-colonial and anti-racist front had hence begun to contest and reconstitute what it meant to intervene. It might be enough to quote Mexico, in the 1950 General Assembly debates over racism again in South Africa, that while non-intervention was a fundamental principle of international society, it could not be invoked to block the international promotion of human rights and prevention of large-scale abuses of those rights: 'It is a dangerous play on words and a sophism to speak of interference when the only thing involved is legitimate collective action.'[195]

---

[193] See generally Gleijeses 2003; 2016. See also e.g. Edward 2005.
[194] 'Political Declaration' in A/31/197: 24. Eighty-six nations participated at the summit, Belize with a special participating status, but not with full membership. On the contestation in international society of Cuba's use of force in Angola, and on Cuba's justification of its action in relation to interventionism and solidarist internationalism, see Quinton-Brown 2023a.
[195] Quoted in Rajan 1961: 238.

4
'Friendly' intervention and the Special Committee

In 1970, the UN celebrated its twenty-fifth anniversary. In 1945, it had just fifty-one members. Now the number was 127. The non-permanent membership of the Security Council had expanded too—from six to ten in 1966. I have been looking at discursive practices of intervention cutting across major Third World meetings in the early Cold War, but I want to look now at competitions for their uptake and institutionalization in the UN itself. Here no historical experience proves more important, for our purposes, than what began in December 1961 and ended in October 1970: the pulling together of the Friendly Relations Declaration, which set out to contribute, in a fundamental way, to the reinterpretation of legal principles underlying the UN Charter itself—to progressively develop them and to recodify them.[1]

The 1960s and 1970s involved a tumultuous campaign to institutionalize what it meant to intervene in international relations, not a pure and simple retreat to non-intervention as a political consensus. At no other point in history was the composition of the intervention concept so directly and systematically contemplated by UN member states, in a single forum and at such great length. In a major article for *Third World Quarterly* in 2016, Adekeye Adebajo wrote that the South–North debate over sovereignty and intervention could be summarized as a story of two cities: San Francisco and Bandung.[2] The genealogy so far has passed through both these crucial meetings, but to the list I propose we add Mexico City, New York, and Geneva. For decades the anti-colonial reordering of intervention was a palpable obsession for the Bandung group and growing Non-Aligned Movement. The number of related resolutions adopted by the General Assembly exceed what we commonly remember: developing states noted with satisfaction more than ten resolutions on the subject passed between 1957 and 1981.[3]

---

[1] The Declaration is experiencing a new wave of scholarly interest; see Viñuales 2020.
[2] Adebajo 2016.
[3] A/RES/1236(XII); A/RES/2131(XX); A/RES/2225(XXI); A/RES/2625(XXV); A/RES/3281(XXIX); A/RES/3201(S-VI); A/RES/31/91; A/RES/32/153; A/RES/33/74; A/RES/34/101; A/RES/35/159; A/RES/36/103.

Intervention before Interventionism. Patrick Quinton-Brown, Oxford University Press. © Patrick Quinton-Brown (2024).
DOI: 10.1093/oso/9780198886457.003.0005

The Non-Intervention Declaration of 1965—Resolution 2131 (XX)—was the most impactful, yet is today the most deeply misunderstood. At least as a starting point we ought to synthesize this anti-colonial campaign. And in this synthesis the meetings of the UN's Special Committee on Friendly Relations should be our guide—because it was there, during the drafting of a 'landmark' in the progressive development of UN principles, arguably the most serious undertaking of its kind since 1945, that the period's prevailing theories of intervention clashed and changed.[4] I would not purport to be drawing a legal conclusion here. My aim is rather to assess the lay of the discursive landscape of international society and to expose how intervention, as it appeared in the Special Committee, was closely linked to key decisions of the General Assembly that, while not legally binding, proved legally and politically significant.

As the Italian representative put it at Geneva in 1967, there was 'a demarcation line between actions and practices which should be condemned as constituting intervention and those which need not be so condemned'.[5] UN members had now tasked themselves with deciding exactly how that line was to be drawn, in light of contemporary developments that appeared to render the demarcations made at San Francisco outdated or oppressive.

This chapter is the first of two that will consider the twenty-five or so years between 1957 and 1981, particularly through the prism of key UN declarations and resolutions. These are lost decades: in still-lingering liberal-interventionist narratives of the sovereignty–intervention debate, the period is presented as a time when statespeople lived without 'purposes beyond themselves'.[6] So concerned were former colonies with the fragility of their new-found statehood that they turned inward, away from the international; according to this view, a logic of legitimate involvement across sovereign borders, and of humanitarian action, was repressed not only by Great Power vetoes and Cold War political pressures, but by a newly institutionalized understanding of non-intervention, of minding your own business. A yarn is spun that a 'state first' sovereigntist mentality took hold of the peoples of the South and prevented them from abandoning their supposed tribalism and from living up to, among other things, the ideals of mass atrocity prevention and global justice. The function of absolute non-interventionism is read on account of a presumed wall between state values and human values.

But to look seriously at the practice of this period suggests that an understanding of Third World states as dull and jealously indifferent sovereigntists

---

[4] See preambular paragraphs of A/RES/2625(XXV).
[5] A/AC.125/SR.73: 19.
[6] Evans 2008: 17. Evans was quoting Bull 1984a: 13.

is patently untrue. The direct opposite of what liberal-developmentalist stories suggest, it is not 'hard to find examples' of influential normative logics or institutionalized practices in which states 'looked beyond their own territorial and colonial borders, beyond their own immediate economic and security interests' so as to 'halt or avert new or continuing atrocity crimes', even if we qualify the scope of such behaviour to that which was described by some as interventionary.[7] A primary purpose of defining the limits of the intervention concept in this period—an age of non-alignment, in addition to bipolarity—was to insist that the international community was bound to promote and respect universal human rights, to act when strangers were suffering, and to expand the activities and jurisdiction of the international and the UN itself. In this it came up against interpretations both of international organization-based and state-based understandings of intervention that were associated with the drafting by major powers of Articles 2 (4) and 2 (7) of the UN Charter, and Western references to these articles, especially Article 2 (7), in the General Assembly.

If it was at San Francisco in 1945 that a theory of intervention as 'dictatorial' or coercive interference became predominant institutionalized practice as a matter of state-based duty in the UN, then the period leading up to the Friendly Relations Declaration should be construed as an encounter between the dictatorial theory of intervention and the anti-colonial theory of intervention as articulated at Bandung. That encounter came to structure the globally institutionalized character of the concept. By the time of the UN organization's twenty-fifth anniversary, the old formulation of intervention as physical coercion had lost its hold in international society: through the work of a more diverse and activist General Assembly, the dictatorial interpretation of intervention became thoroughly discredited. In the course of the Friendly Relations process, and in relation to non-intervention as a principle of international law, we see it slip from the hands of an outmanoeuvred and relatively fragmented Western coalition, replaced by something new. This something new is clearly not anti-colonial intervention in its Tricontinentalist sense, but it is, in very important ways, shaped by concerns having to do with both moderate and radical anti-colonial practices. It represents a kind of compromise among established and emerging or 'new' states. And this compromise involves an official retreat away from the idea that non-interventionism could serve as a restriction on certain forms of anti-colonial and anti-racist action in the UN and international relations at large.

---

[7] Evans 2008: 17.

What might we mean by an era of 'friendly' intervention? In what ways was it so friendly, or not? What was its precise relation to dictatorial intervention and anti-colonial intervention? The Friendly Relations process was highly formalized: as a study conducted by jurists who also served as state representatives in regular sessions, its attempt at defining intervention was a technical exercise conducted many times over. In accounting for these proposed normative designs, which involved a range of international-legal arguments, this chapter takes more and sharper turns than the previous two. But the purpose remains the same: to trace intervention in its reconstitution, according to the movement of discursive practices and their partial institutionalization in the agreements of states. First it gives a background on the Special Committee on Friendly Relations; second it provides an analysis of the Committee's attempts at Mexico City to define intervention; third, it provides a revisionist account of the 1965 UN Declaration on the Inadmissibility of Intervention that eventually broke the Committee's deadlock; and finally it gives a rereading of non-intervention as codified in the Friendly Relations Declaration in light of politically significant beliefs at the time.

Non-intervention as good neighbourliness

When on 18 December 1962 the UN General Assembly unanimously resolved, through Resolution 1815 (XVII), to undertake a study of 'the principles of international law concerning friendly relations and co-operation among states and the duties deriving therefrom, embodied in the Charter of the UN', to work towards their 'codification', 'progressive development', and 'effective application', the number of core international principles identified by its members was not ten (as it was at Bandung), not five (as it was in the Panchsheel), not sixteen (as it was in a Czechoslovak draft UN declaration on 'peaceful co-existence'), but seven:[8]

1. Prohibition of the threat or use of force
2. Peaceful settlement of disputes
3. Non-intervention
4. The duty to co-operate in accordance with the Charter
5. Equal rights and self-determination of peoples
6. Sovereign equality of states
7. Fulfillment in good faith of obligations assumed under the Charter[9]

[8] The Czechoslovak draft is contained in A/C.6/L.505.
[9] A/RES/1815(XVII).

In domestic life, good neighbours, enjoying friendly relations, are expected to knock or ask permission before entering one another's homes. It is not polite to spy through windows, guests should not take what is not theirs, they should refrain from prying open doors—at least in ordinary or non-emergency conditions. And in this way the promise to 'mind your own business' in domestic life is not only about safety from physical violence, but also about shared responsibilities and a broader discretion at the root of friendship and cooperation among citizens.

Still, for some, international good neighbourly relations remained comparable only to Roosevelt's interpretation of the Montevideo Convention on the Rights and Duties of States; the definite rule of the United Nations was one opposed to *armed intervention* between states.[10] I want to start by showing how, into the early 1960s, Washington continued to oppose the idea that the duty of non-intervention between states referred to something other than the prohibition of the threat or use of force (principle one of Resolution 1815 [XVII]), and how it held instead that non-intervention (principle three of that resolution) referred to the responsibilities of the UN organization, and the UN alone.[11] From this view, the import of non-intervention was strictly that of Article 2 (7) at San Francisco, where, as Chapter 2 showed, the Committee of Five had 'agreed that any reference to non-intervention [between states] would be opposed' so as to reject a series of Latin American amendments of Article 2 (4).[12]

I discussed previously why this double ordering of intervention in the Charter served the interests of the sponsoring powers in 1945, particularly insofar as those interests related to enduring forms of empire.[13] Yet by now, by the early 1960s, American insistence on a state-based duty of non-intervention as the non-use of force was surprising, not least because of the threat of subversive activities by its Cold War adversaries, both forcible and non-forcible, across its own borders and those of others, which a theory of intervention as the effect of foreign pressure seemed better suited to address. Putting that theory into stark relief was the 'little veto' of Article 2 (7) as deployed by 'status quo' powers against the 'Bandung powers' or 'have-nots' in the UN—the latter in an ascendant coalition, it was often argued at the

---

[10] Roosevelt's description of the duty of non-intervention as adopted at Montevideo is quoted in Connell-Smith 1966: 90. See Chapter 2.

[11] The final wording of Resolution 1815 (XVII) was equivocal on this point. It described the principle of non-intervention as '[t]he duty not to intervene in matters within the domestic jurisdiction of any State, in accordance with the Charter'. A/RES/1815(XVII).

[12] FRUS 1945: I, Document 229.

[13] See Chapter 2.

time, with the Communist bloc.¹⁴ In fact, in 1957 UN debate on a proposed 'Declaration on Peaceful Co-existence' (eventually adopted as the 'Declaration on Peaceful and Neighbourly Relations Among States') witnessed just such a deployment.¹⁵ In a right of reply to Albania, for example, France had noted that 'an allusion had been made to the Algerian question', as if French authority over Algeria, as opposed to the authority of the so-called national liberation movements, constituted 'an obstacle to peaceful co-existence'.¹⁶ But truly 'there could be no peaceful co-existence so long as certain States continued their attempts to distort the purpose of the United Nations' and 'intervene in the domestic affairs of other states' by using the UN 'as a propaganda centre for attacking the constitutions and frontiers of other states'.¹⁷

So from the very beginning of the Friendly Relations process, a bitter struggle was already underway between, on the one hand, practitioners of 'old' formulations of non-intervention that were cast, as a duty of states, in terms of the dictatorial theory, but as a duty of the UN organization in terms of the effective theory, and, on the other hand, practitioners of a set of 'new' formulations that were anti-colonial and based around self-determination, human rights, and a dynamic theory of domestic jurisdiction.¹⁸

Writing the Friendly Relations Declaration was an intricate, eight-year process, involving regular sessions of and exchange between the UN General Assembly's Sixth Committee and Special Committee, and I would not want to suggest I am accounting comprehensively for its principles or the historical

---

¹⁴ See Chapter 3. Chile's rebuke of Article 2 (7), quoted in Rajan 1961: 235. I return to Martin Wight's characterization of Afro-Asian states as 'have-not powers'—an allusion to E. H. Carr's characterization of the Axis powers—in the final section of this chapter (Wight 1957). For a discussion, see Hall 2017.

¹⁵ The proposed declaration on 'peaceful co-existence', introduced by the Soviet Union (see A/3673), was redrafted by India, Sweden, and Yugoslavia and adopted as the 'Declaration on Peaceful and Neighbourly Relations Among States' on 14 December 1957 (see A/RES/1236(XII)). On 2 December 1961, twelve delegations—Afghanistan, Cambodia, Ceylon, Czechoslovakia, Dahomey, Ghana, Indonesia, Iraq, Libya, Romania, the United Arab Republic, and Yugoslavia—recommended to the International Law Commission the inclusion of a question titled 'Consideration of principles of international law relating to the *peaceful co-existence* of states' in the provisional agenda of the General Assembly (A/C.6/L.492; emphasis added). Yet because the concept of 'peaceful co-existence' was to some 'merely a phase in the Soviet Communist struggle for world conquest' (see the comments of Henry Cabot Lodge Jr in A/C.1/SR.936: 409) or at least, argued many more, without 'a definite and generally accepted meaning' (see the summary of the Sixth Committee debate in A/5356: 7), it was replaced by the less contentious expression 'friendly relations and co-operation among states' in Resolution 1686 (XVI), adopted on 18 December. Some states and commentators claimed such a terminological revision in no way lessened the decision as one to codify the legal principles of coexistence. For a fuller discussion, see Šahović 1972: 9–50.

¹⁶ A/C.1/SR.937: 418.
¹⁷ Ibid.
¹⁸ I allude to a struggle between the older and the 'new' countries and their approach to the 'new international law' that came to be associated with the Friendly Relations process. See e.g. McWhinney 1966.

significance of their elaboration.[19] But as far as non-intervention is concerned as a matter of global order contestation, I think we can draw out the most significant moves, which relate to a historical tension between a Southern group versus a Northern group, and which took place in three key settings: Mexico City, 1964 (where the Special Committee held its first session), New York, 1965 (where the General Assembly adopted the Declaration on the Inadmissibility of Intervention, which became the basis of subsequent discussions in the Special Committee), and Geneva, 1970 (where, at the final session of the Special Committee, members struck a compromise). I will explore each before coming to a conclusion.

Mexico City: a return to Chapultepec?

When the Special Committee met at Mexico City in 1964, a total of five drafts on non-intervention would be put on the table: British, Czechoslovak, Yugoslav, and Mexican proposals, plus a joint draft by Ghana, India, and Yugoslavia.[20] Each attempted to reorder the concept for international life. Each made claims about state duties in addition to state rights. Some were broadly reconcilable with each other; others were mutually exclusive. None were adopted. But over the course of their amendment and justification, something did become clear: dictatorial intervention could no longer serve as a compelling reading of the non-interventionist obligation of states. Conditions of meaning were globally altered, and intervention became discursively repractised such that, as it was used among statespeople, it was no longer defined as the use or threat of force.

In plotting out areas of normative tension, the UK draft provides the ideal starting point. This might seem strange, given that it appeared to say almost nothing of the meaning of intervention at a higher level of specificity:

1. Every state has the right to political independence and territorial integrity.
2. Every state has the duty to respect the rights enjoyed by other states in accordance with international law, and to refrain from intervention in matters within the domestic jurisdiction of any other state.[21]

---

[19] See instead Viñuales 2020. See also e.g. Šahovic 1972; Anand 1972; Mani 1993. On anti-colonial legalism in the 1960s, including in relation to Friendly Relations, see Moyn 2021.
[20] A/AC.119/L.8; A/AC.119/L.6; A/AC.119/L.7; A/AC.119/L.24; A/AC.119/L.27.
[21] A/AC.119/L.8: 1.

Written commentary submitted with this draft explained that, admittedly, its wording did 'leave certain questions unresolved, as, for example, what is meant by "intervention" and what is meant by "matters within domestic jurisdiction".'[22] Yet the proposal was strengthened, not weakened, by what it left unsaid; that was its great advantage.

> In considering the scope of 'intervention' it should be recognised that, in an interdependent world, it is inevitable and desirable that States will be concerned with and will seek to influence the actions and policies of other states, and that the objective of international law is not to prevent such activity but rather to ensure that it is compatible with the sovereign equality of states and self-determination of their peoples.[23]

It would, claimed Ian Sinclair, the British delegate, 'therefore be impossible to give an exhaustive definition of what constitutes intervention', and any attempt 'to draw up even an admittedly non-exhaustive list of acts of intervention would lead the Committee into very real difficulties'.[24] Better to simply say that, in the 'context of inter-state relations', intervention 'connotes in general forcible or dictatorial interference', such that 'much of the classic conception of intervention has been absorbed by the prohibition of the threat or use of force against the political independence or territorial integrity of states in accordance with Article 2(4) of the Charter'.[25] Perhaps there were 'other forms of intervention, in particular the use of clandestine activities to encompass the overthrow of the Government of another State or secure an alteration in the political and economic structure of that state'.[26] But the difficulties involved in imagining these other forms, and the disagreements that would ensue among states, illustrated 'the dangers of attempting an exhaustive definition of what constitutes intervention'.[27]

There were several reactions. Significantly, within the West, divergent positions were appearing in a way that they had not at San Francisco—from the longer historical perspective, cracks were appearing in what was once more stable ground.

First, the United States proposed an amendment to the British proposal—this amendment was a more direct defence of the dictatorial interpretation. Yes, in 'an interdependent world', states should wish to 'influence the actions

---

[22] Ibid.: 7.
[23] Ibid.
[24] A/AC.119/SR.32: 18.
[25] Ibid.
[26] Ibid.
[27] A/AC.119/L.8: 8.

and policies of other states', but was it not precisely for this reason that the international community should want to enumerate intervention and distinguish it from influence or pressure?[28] It was hence recommended to delete everything after the second part of the draft's second paragraph, so as to make clear that:

> the obligation referred to springs from Article 2, paragraph 4 of the Charter, which constitutes a limitation on state action. The scope of the word 'intervention' is indicated by the wording of Article 2, paragraph 4. However, the concept of 'domestic jurisdiction' is not expressly included in Article 2, paragraph 4.[29]

The American delegation affirmed openly that 'intervention by one State in the affairs of another was illicit under the Charter only when it was accompanied by the threat or use of force'.[30] And what was meant by 'force'? Stephen Schwebel, serving at the time as the American delegate (later a judge of the International Court of Justice presiding over the very important 1986 case, *Nicaragua v. United States*, concerning among other things the limits of permissible intervention), explained: 'According to Judge [Sir Hersch] Lauterpacht, the term meant armed force, as opposed to economic or political pressure.'[31]

A second sort of reaction was exemplified by the arguments of Philippe Monod on behalf of France. To secure a definition of intervention 'precise enough and broad enough to be self-sufficient' would 'represent a major step forward in universal international law and at the same time the best means of cutting off one of the principal sources of international conflict'.[32] In particular it would be advisable to base such a definition on a less traditional idea of coercion, one that could encompass 'abnormal or improper pressure exercised by one State on another State in order to change its internal structure in a direction favourable to the interests of the state applying the coercion'.[33] Yet many 'were too often ready to see unlawful intervention': 'today reference was commonly made to economic or ideological intervention, with or without such improper coercion', and some—he referred to the Polish delegate—even

---

[28] Ibid.: 7.
[29] A/AC.119/L.26: 1.
[30] A/AC.119/SR.32: 25.
[31] A/AC.119/SR.3: 12. See also e.g. Sir Kenneth Bailey of Australia during separate Special Committee meetings concerning the principle of the prohibition of the threat or use of force: 'the force which a Member was prohibited from using or threatening, like the force which the Organization was authorized to use [under Chapter VII], was armed force, and nothing else' (A/AC.119/SR.10: 7).
[32] A/AC.119/SR.28: 8.
[33] Ibid.

sought to include in its remit the non-recognition of other states ('what he called the Hallstein doctrine.')[34]

So, while highly desirable, a universal definition of intervention was not possible 'in the present state of international relations'—any attempt to secure one would shatter under the force of its international controversy.[35] '[N]either the authors of the Charter nor, before them, those of the Covenant of the League of Nations', it was claimed, 'had tried to define intervention or its necessary corollary, domestic jurisdiction.'[36] If the Latin Americans had made 'more ambitious efforts to do so', through for instance 'Article XV of the Pact of Bogotá', they did 'more to emphasize than to solve the problem of the definition of intervention.'[37] The concept seemed interdependent with other principles which the Special Committee was called on to study: it was 'impossible to define intervention without defining domestic jurisdiction, and it was likewise impossible to define domestic jurisdiction without defining sovereignty which, conversely, had little meaning unless the sphere of domestic jurisdiction could be satisfactorily delimited.'[38] Monod took the liberty of comparing the problem of defining intervention to 'the symbol—dear to classical philosophy—of the serpent swallowing its own tail.'[39]

Yet when Monod referred to the 'indefinite nature of intervention' as inhibiting its global ordering potential, had he not downplayed the extent to which this was true of all terms of global-political discourse, and the ways in which, despite profound contestation, such concepts come to be internationally practised and institutionalized?[40] When at one point in his statement Monod observed an increase in the contestation of the concept at the international level, he was not necessarily observing a mounting incoherence or unreason:

> For two decades now the idea of intervention, which was itself bound up with the multiplication of sovereignties, had been undergoing an excessive inflation, and the concept of sovereignty had undergone a similar inflation.[41]

[34] Ibid.: 10. Soviet bloc delegations claimed the so-called Hallstein Doctrine was developed by West Germany to illegitimately pressure other states into the non-recognition of East Germany. The threat to sever diplomatic relations with other states, as a means of pressuring those states into the non-recognition of another state, was understood by those delegations as interventionary. See e.g. Poland in A/AC.119/SR.32: 28. See also McWhinney 1966: 24–25.
[35] A/AC.119/SR.28: 8.
[36] Ibid. The claim was questionable on several grounds. On the attempts of the authors of the Charter and the Covenant of the League to define and redefine intervention and domestic jurisdiction, see Chapter 2.
[37] Ibid.: 8.
[38] Ibid.: 7.
[39] Ibid.
[40] Ibid.: 9. See Chapter 1.
[41] Ibid.: 10.

The expansion of intervention's meaning since the end of the Second World War, like the expansion of sovereignty's meaning, could rather be seen in an ongoing process of contestation and reconstitution linked to the rise of a solidarist internationalism.

A third type of reaction seemed to accept the 'inflation' of meaning lamented by Monod as an improvement on traditional practices.[42] It picked up a version of the effective theory of intervention and referred to the substance of good neighbourly relations as they had developed in the inter-American system. At the expense of the British text and its American amendments, the Canadian delegation welcomed instead 'the Mexican proposal that the legal system elaborated by the Organization of American States should be taken as a model; that system was a history-making achievement of the countries of Latin America and of the great power which had co-operated with them in building it'.[43] In a 'progressive framework of peaceful means of settling disputes', the 'community of views and interests which had made the OAS instruments both possible and significant suggested what should be the major criterion for determining the possible scope of the Committee's efforts in elaborating the principle of non-intervention'.[44]

In addition to the Mexican proposal there were, again, alternatives put forward by Czechoslovakia and Yugoslavia, plus a three-power draft by Ghana, India, and Yugoslavia.[45] But to look closely at all four of these proposals is to see that, while divergent in narrow terms, they converged on a view of intervention as the outcome of pressure and of pressure against self-determined political, economic, and cultural futures. Moreover, all four of these proposals sought to move from an interpretation of the UN Charter in which the intervention problem was, in a sense, double-ordered—with two very different meanings across two paragraphs—to one in which it was single-ordered, such that the substance of non-intervention with respect to relations between states would correspond to the substance of non-intervention in Article 2 (7). The Burmese delegation explained that such a move should be considered within the remit of the Special Committee and its objectives in line with the goals of the UN organization:

> since one of the goals of the United Nations was the progressive development of international law, the committee should examine not only the purposes and principles of the Charter in themselves, but also the spirit underlying Article 2 (7). Nothing

---

[42] Ibid.
[43] A/AC.119/SR.31: 9.
[44] Ibid.
[45] A/AC.119/L.24; A/AC.119/L.6; A/AC.119/L.7; A/AC.119/L.27.

could be more destructive of friendly relations and co-operation than interference by one state in matters essentially within the domestic jurisdiction of another state.[46]

One exchange at Mexico City between India and the United States illustrated the stakes of the multiplied meanings of the concept in play. 'Since the United States delegation took the word "force" in Article 2 (4) of the Charter to mean armed force, it was presumably moving towards a further limitation of the principle of non-intervention.'[47] India's argument, in contrast, was that the principle of non-intervention, as contained in Article 2 (7) and as generally intended to order relations among states, had to be based on a liberal reading of the Convention on the Rights and Duties of States of 1933 and subsequent inter-American agreements. Such a reading, about 'pressure' and national or state 'personality', was more closely connected to Calvo than to Oppenheim or Lawrence, and departed from 'force' as defined by Judge Lauterpacht.[48] Hence non-intervention, claimed the Indian delegation, meant that 'not only armed force but also any other form of interference or attempted threat against the personality of a State or against its political, economic, or cultural elements is prohibited.'[49]

These words appeared verbatim in Mexico's working paper, and as Brajesh Mishra—representing India at Mexico City—noted, they also appeared in article 15 of the OAS Charter, which served as 'inspiration of the second part of paragraph one of the three-power [Ghana–India–Yugoslavia] proposal.'[50] By defining intervention in relation to armed force alone, '[t]he United States representative said in effect that his country's signature to articles 15 and 16 of the Bogotá Charter—which imposed obligations much more advanced and progressive than any under the United Nations Charter—had nothing to do with the latter.'[51] The 'protection given to the American States under the Bogotá Charter was thus not available to the Members of the United Nations—many of which would regret the fact.'[52]

Stephen Schwebel, exercising his right of reply, pledged that the United States 'had no intention of disavowing the purposes of the United Nations or

---

[46] A/AC.119/SR.31: 4.
[47] A/AC.119/SR.32: 8. The Indian delegation had strong views on the meaning of force: when Sir Kenneth Bailey of Australia argued that '[a]s applied to the international action of states, physical coercion was in fact the essential ingredient of force, as the word was defined in the dictionary', K. Krishna Rao of India, exercising a right of reply, reportedly read out from an Oxford Dictionary a definition of force in its non-material sense 'in the hope that his colleague would keep it in mind' in ongoing negotiations. See A/AC.119/SR.17: 12, 15.
[48] See the comments of Stephen Schwebel in A/AC.119/SR.3: 12.
[49] A/AC.119/SR.29: 15. This clause was inspired by the second part of paragraph 1 in A/AC.119/L.27.
[50] A/AC.119/L.24; A/AC.119/SR.29: 15; A/AC.119/L.27.
[51] A/AC.119/SR.32: 8.
[52] Ibid.

of denying to Member States the guarantees already enjoyed by members of the Organization of American States', but the delegation 'was not quibbling when it expressed certain objections to an excessively broad interpretation of the duty of non-intervention in the Charter'.[53] And yet, for our purposes, it must be noted that only two days earlier, in Special Committee discussions, the American delegation is in fact on record as having said 'it fully subscribed to the obligation it shared with its fellow American states on the subject of non-intervention, but it must be borne in mind that it was the United Nations Charter and not the OAS Charter which the Committee was considering'.[54] Moreover, the American delegation would assert very clearly at Mexico City that '[t]he travaux préparatoires of the San Francisco Conference did not support the interpretation that Article 2 (7) was even by implication applicable to intervention by states ... when the authors of the Charter had meant to refer in that paragraph to states, they had done so'.[55]

Still, Schwebel pressed his claim. The 'Indian representative had asked that the United States should take into account the evolution of international relations and the practice of States since 1945. But that was exactly what his country had done in the work of the Committee—and for the past twenty years'.[56] He implored the Indian representative 'to consider the role of the United States in building up the peacekeeping and nation-building functions of the United Nations, and the open hand it had extended giving aid and cooperation on a scale unknown in history', and asked him 'to consider whether any other great power in history which, for a time, possessed unprecedented, absolute power, had behaved with more restraint—in respect to intervention and otherwise'.[57] The United States was ready to contribute to a codification of a principle of non-intervention between states that involved 'the threat or use of force. However the ground became less certain if one tried to go further'.[58] He advanced an example based on paragraph 1 of the Ghana–India–Yugoslavia draft:

> That paragraph prohibited all 'interference' in the right of any state to choose and develop its own political, economic, and social order. But to take an actual case, India was at present having difficulty—temporary, it was to be hoped—in feeding its people, and the United States was sending it large quantities of wheat. Might not that action be interpreted as influencing India's economic and social order and

---
[53] Ibid.: 26.
[54] A/AC.119/SR.29: 12.
[55] A/AC.119/SR.32: 28. Compare to the main argument made in Chapter 2.
[56] Ibid.: 26.
[57] Ibid.
[58] Ibid.: 26–27.

strengthening the Indian Government against any possible revolution? If so, was it not a form of intervention, or at least of interference?[59]

Mishra's response to Schwebel—that 'so far as economic assistance in general was concerned and wheat deliveries in particular', the 'legitimate nature of such aid' would not be called into question by the three-power proposal, and that his delegation 'preferred to believe that they came within the context of international co-operation and were not motivated by other considerations'—can be seen as an application of the distinction between means and outcome that was so central to the writings of Carlos Calvo and to the theory of effective intervention.[60] But, arguably to an even greater extent, it was an application of a logic of self-determination as it had appeared in anti-colonial theories of intervention like those of the Bandung Conference. Such a delivery of emergency aid, particularly with the consent or invitation of the recipient state, was not an effect of foreign pressure; it realized, not obstructed, the right of all to freely determine their own political, economic, and cultural futures. Intervention as an evaluation of international action referred, to quote Yugoslavia at Mexico City, 'not only [to] the nature of the act itself, but also its effects', in the sense that it was 'a question of the organic, free, and unhampered development of states, i.e. the protection of the state from within'; 'in the case of the threat or the use of force', however, it was a question of 'the protection of the state from without'.[61] '[T]he course of developments over the past twenty years had made it possible to distinguish more clearly between the concept of intervention and the concept of the threat or use of force in conformity with Article 2 (4) of the Charter. The difference between those two concepts lay in the values they sought to protect.'[62]

Anti-colonial intervention versus dictatorial intervention

Which values did the concept of intervention seek to protect? Aside from the issue of broadening the scope of state-based duty, there was another difficulty: that of exceptions from a blanket rule of non-intervention, of pinpointing which types of international involvement were to be deemed

[59] Ibid.: 27.
[60] A/AC.119/SR.32: 30; United States, in ibid.: 27, 30. See Chapter 2.
[61] A/AC.119/SR.17: 8.
[62] Ibid.

legitimate in an era of non-intervention that would not be limited to the non-use of force.

The positive face of the non-intervention principle has always been harder to see. But I think we can show how at Mexico City, 1964, theories highlighted in previous chapters came together in a single setting: if Mexico City placed dictatorial and effective intervention on trial, so too did it adjudicate the merits of an anti-colonial intervention, in all its solidarist ambition. Ted McWhinney, the distinguished Professor of International Law and later President of the Institut de Droit International, observed in his review of the Committee's 1964 debates that the 'antinomies necessarily involved in any attempt at exhaustive definition of the legal scope of the principles of non-intervention' were 'clearly indicated in the course of the debate':

> the countries that seemed to be most adamant as to the need for widening the scope of legally *impermissible* interventions and so for restricting the pressures that any one state might exercise on another, were also insistent on establishing a special category of exceptions as to legally *permissible* interventions: the intervention would become lawful, under this special category of exceptions to the general rule, because in defense of a 'higher' right.[63]

The 'new' and smaller countries had no doubt proposed, for higher purposes, a category of permissible international activities construed by larger and 'status quo' countries as intervention, but to call such international activities 'permissible intervention' would be to misunderstand anti-colonial theory.[64] El-Sayed Abdel Raouf el-Reedy of the United Arab Republic explained: 'the systematic formulation of the principle of non-intervention was one of the most significant developments that had occurred in international law since the adoption of the Charter', and what needed to be better appreciated was that 'the principle of non-intervention complemented the principle of self-determination, a fact which had been recognised and recalled at Bandung in 1955'.[65] Within the value framework of Bandung had been shaped a certain 'positive national policy, the policy of non-alignment': the 'non-aligned countries had therefore given special attention to the principle of non-intervention at the Belgrade Conference of 1961 and had in their final communiqué expressed their determination that "no intimidation, interference, or intervention should be brought to bear in the exercise of the right

---

[63] McWhinney 1966: 23–24.
[64] Ibid.; Wight 1957; McWhinney 1966: 24.
[65] A/AC.119/SR.30: 20.

of self-determination of peoples"'.[66] The language of non-intervention, from the perspective of non-aligned states, legitimized an ongoing international struggle against colonialism and extreme racism, as an answer to the cry for freedom without which there could be no realistic hope of peace. It would be a mistake to label as intervention what was precisely the assumption of shared responsibilities: 'since 1945 the United Nations had always', claimed el-Reedy, 'rightly followed a liberal interpretation of Article 2 (7) of the Charter, which could not be invoked as grounds for prohibiting the United Nations from considering questions relating to human rights likely to affect international peace and security'.[67] From the 'fragments contained in the Charter and in post-Charter international practice' could be found a 'coherent formula which would reflect the law of the United Nations in its entirety'.[68]

The international promotion of human rights was fundamentally *not* at odds with respect for the principle of non-intervention on account of its complementary relationship with self-determination, but also on account of a particular understanding of the substantive and changing character of domestic jurisdiction. A key point being made at Mexico City was that while, yes, the principle of non-intervention is the corollary of sovereignty, sovereignty's basic relationship with obligation and the development of international law should not be misconstrued for any range of political purposes. Henri Jux Ratsimbazafy of Madagascar explained that 'it was true that the principle of sovereignty was still the keystone of inter-state relations', but 'significant progress in international law would be impossible without the gradual breaking down of the walls of national sovereignty'.[69]

> The efforts of the Special Committee itself were based on the assumption that States should recognize as mandatory the rules of international law, agree to limit their freedom of action in certain fields under multilateral agreements, and above all, transfer some of their powers to the appropriate organs of the United Nations. It was important to realize that any progress made by the United Nations must reflect in some degree a surrender of national sovereignty, and that such a process was in the interests of peace and stability.[70]

Hence, when the UN 'had undertaken the task of maintaining law and order in the Middle East and in Africa, and of speeding the process of

[66] Ibid.
[67] Ibid.: 21.
[68] Ibid.
[69] A/AC.119/SR.31: 6.
[70] Ibid.

decolonization, individual powers had been obliged to recognize a limitation on their freedom of action in those spheres'.[71] These voluntary acceptances of sovereign obligations—under the Charter, under multilateral treaties, under international law more generally—were at once a manifestation of sovereignty and its limitation, but not its violation.[72] Ratsimbazafy spoke of a 'patient conquest of areas of competence'.[73] He cited the 1923 Advisory Opinion of the Permanent Court of International Justice in the Tunis and Morocco Nationality Decree Case and its decision that 'whether a particular subject was within the exclusive competence of a state was an essentially relative question depending on the development of international relations'.[74]

That international relations had undergone drastic changes since 1945, and that processes of decolonization were having far-reaching international repercussions, including for the maintenance of peace and security, were among the original justifications of the Friendly Relations process. One indication of that far-reaching change, and of matters having been moved resolutely out of domestic jurisdiction, was that 'independent African States had not only affirmed the right of African countries still under foreign domination to self-determination but had proclaimed, in the Charter of the Organisation of African Unity, their "absolute dedication to the total emancipation of the African territories which are still dependent"'.[75] India noted further that 'some matters normally regarded as within the domestic jurisdiction of states might not, in view of their international repercussions, be essentially matters of domestic jurisdiction'.[76] Others referred to an internationalist faith that state prerogatives increasingly yielded to a shared responsibility to prevent 'crimes against humanity'.[77]

William Waldo Kofi Vanderpuye was serving as the Ghanaian representative at Mexico City. His comments approximated the arguments above and provided yet another illustration of the anti-colonial theory of intervention as it had been gaining ground in international society. First, 'the international character of a question was a consequence of the acceptance of international obligations concerning it'.[78] Second, 'in a matter not in principle regulated by

---

[71] Ibid.
[72] Ibid.
[73] Ibid.
[74] Ibid.: 7. For a fuller discussion of the case, see Elias 1983.
[75] United Arab Republic, in A/AC.119/SR.8: 9.
[76] A/AC.119/SR.29: 14.
[77] See e.g. the comments of Ghana's Kenneth Dadzie (later the fifth Secretary-General of UNCTAD), who also referred to a 'right of self-defence against colonialism, as reflected in the Declaration on the granting of independence to colonial countries and peoples', in A/AC.119/SR.10: 14–15.
[78] A/AC.119/SR.29: 6.

international law the right of a state to use its discretion might nevertheless be restricted by obligations undertaken towards other states'.[79] Hence:

> It followed that the principle of non-intervention could not be invoked with respect to such questions as apartheid in the Republic of South Africa, the oppression of Africans in Central Africa, the denial of the right of self-determination, and other colonialist and neo-colonialist practices which had been the subject of many resolutions in the General Assembly.[80]

Vanderpuye cited in that connection the Permanent Court of International Justice in the Nationality Decrees in Tunis and Morocco case, as well as the writings of Quincy Wright who, in *The Role of International Law in the Elimination of War*, demonstrated that domestic jurisdiction could 'not be defined on the basis of geography but only of law'.[81] The scope of domestic affairs 'in the legal sense had been continually reduced as the real interest of states in the territory of others had been recognized and given legal protection'.[82] For example, '[m]illions of people in Africa', as Kenneth Dadzie of the Ghanian delegation had argued in a separate Special Committee meeting, 'were still the victims of colonial oppression. The time had come when those who continued to commit that *crime against humanity* must be restrained by the force of the law.'[83]

So we can begin to appreciate what Joža Vilfan of the Yugoslav delegation was driving at when he argued that '[s]upport for the principle of non-intervention and the free development of nations was not, as was sometimes claimed, inconsistent with the idea of world integration'.[84] Intervention is not the handmaiden of globalization. Rather, intervention, by denying the right of peoples to self-determination, makes global integration impossible. Consider also the like-minded reply of the Mexican delegation: '[t]here was no doubt that the world was undergoing a process of integration, as the United States representative pointed out'.[85] Yet there existed 'a very wide margin for the application of the principle of non-intervention, which was in no way incompatible with the process of integration referred to by the United States representative'.[86]

---

[79] Ibid.
[80] Ibid.
[81] Ibid.; ibid.: 5; Wright 1961.
[82] A/AC.119/SR.29: 5.
[83] A/AC.119/SR.10: 14. Emphasis added.
[84] A/AC.119/SR.25: 7.
[85] A/AC.119/SR.32: 21.
[86] Ibid.

Still, many Western countries demurred from what they saw as a dangerous and unstable doctrine of national liberation. True, some were acknowledging—back in the 1960s—that 'the concept [non-intervention] could be viewed as an important derogation from the full freedom of action normally associated with national sovereignty'.[87] But even if there were good reasons to insist on a progressive reading of domestic jurisdiction in Article 2(7), or to abandon a conception of intervention limited to physical coercion or the threat or use of force, there were more potent reasons still to resist the anti-colonial theory: '[f]or example certain speakers had referred to the concept of self-determination embodied in Article 1(2) of the Charter as the main rationale for the formulation of such rules [of non-intervention]'.[88] And in particular 'the self-determination referred to in that paragraph was the self-determination of peoples, a concept which might not always coincide with the concept of the self-determination of states', and hence 'too rigid a formulation of the rules of non-intervention might lead to serious contradictions' when the Committee came to conclude its work in other areas.[89]

Part of the problem related, then, to familiar difficulties of the self-determination concept (who is the 'self' in self-determination, to which units does the concept apply and how, which 'people', which role for the 'nation', and which implications for territorial integrity, for example) that were being considered separately by the Special Committee.[90] Another part clearly related to a view that an anti-colonial theory was prone to being hijacked for the 'export of revolution' to capitalist countries or of 'counterrevolution to the socialist countries' (views that, according to the Soviet delegation at Mexico City, had been denied by Khrushchev himself four months earlier in Copenhagen, where he spoke of 'a policy of peaceful co-existence').[91] But while the anti-colonial theory involved a series of ambiguities and difficulties that would need further political and legal qualification, to confine our interest to these issues alone is to ignore the role it was playing in processes of legitimation. The crucial point was that anti-colonial intervention, across both its moderate and radical theses, indicted networks of power that, while of course of strategic interest in a global cold war, were also out of sync with international morality and convention in the society of states.

---

[87] Canada, A/AC.119/SR.31: 7.
[88] Ibid.: 8.
[89] Ibid.
[90] For a discussion of the problems created by self-determination in international society, and of recent political and legal strategies for their management, see Hurrell 2007: 122–142. See also Mayall 1990.
[91] See the comments of the delegate of the Soviet Union in A/AC.119/SR.28: 12.

New York: the Non-Intervention Declaration of 1965

I want to move on now from Mexico City—subsequent encounters, in the Special Committee and elsewhere, give us a sense of which battles, at the international-societal level, were coming to an end, and which ones continued to be fought. At its thirty-ninth meeting, the Special Committee unanimously adopted the following: 'the committee was unable to reach any consensus on the scope or content of this principle [non-intervention]'.[92]

About a year later, however, we did see something of a breakthrough, at New York in 1965, when a declaration on non-intervention was passed by the General Assembly. We tend to think we know the 1965 Declaration on the Inadmissibility of Intervention very well, but I want to show how so often it is mistakenly understood in the context of a global sovereignty-intervention debate. We tend to remember the Declaration as sovereigntist in a way that was also anti-solidarist, but surely that account is starting to sound incorrect due to the anti-colonial theory that in fact underpinned its co-sponsorship and much of its advocacy. The significance of 1965 for intervention in international society is twofold. First, it shows us how a dictatorial interpretation of the intervention concept was falling out of international practice. And second, it reflects how South–North disagreement, both before and after 1965, had to do with the international promotion—plausibly the international-coercive protection—of human rights, and particularly human rights inclusive of a central right to self-determination and as linked up with a struggle against colonial oppression and extreme racism. So we cannot, as we often have, read this moment simply according to its negative effects, having to do with the proscription of international action. We need to see how, in a way that was contested and not wholly resolved by its final text, its proper legacy has more to do with the positive face of non-intervention than its serving as a kind of bulwark for blocking legitimate international and collective action. In this way New York picked up where Mexico City left off.

We should start directly with the content of Resolution 2131 (XX) itself. Its fourth and final draft—sponsored by fifty-seven Asian, African, and Latin American states—was produced 'after very protracted and strenuous negotiations, which lasted several days'. It was an attempt to integrate a number of previous drafts (including Soviet drafts) and proposed amendments (including Western amendments) so as to produce a single text that would reach as

---

[92] See A/5746: 141.

near to unanimous agreement as possible.[93] And it was adopted 100 to none, with one abstention.[94]

The first thing to notice here is that a vote in favour of the 1965 Declaration could not be construed as a vote in favour of intervention as coercive or dictatorial interference. The operative parts of the adopted text declared explicitly:

> 1) That no State has the right to intervene, directly or indirectly, for any reason whatever, in the internal or external affairs of any other State. *Consequently, armed intervention and all other forms of interference or attempted threats against the personality of the state or against its political, economic, and cultural elements, are condemned.*[95]

We might note too that the preamble referred to non-intervention as proclaimed in the charters of the OAS, the Organisation of African Unity, and the Arab League, and affirmed at Montevideo, Buenos Aires, Chapultepec, and Bogotá, as well as in the decisions of the Asian-African Conference at Bandung and of the non-aligned countries at Belgrade and Cairo.[96]

When the Thai delegate made comments in the First Committee such as that 'intervention was not confined only to armed attacks ... the notion of non-intervention must encompass all activities, even those not involving armed force, which were calculated to impair the authority of the legal government of another sovereign state', the replies that emerged across multiple conceivable sides (US-aligned, Soviet-aligned, and non-aligned) focused less on the criteria by which to identify intervention than on the application of these criteria to specific cases.[97] In other words, the focus in the General Assembly was more about who had intervened and where, and in which armed and unarmed ways, than about coercive or dictatorial interference alone—all now seemed to accept that intervention meant more than armed force.

Why this rather sudden shift from dictatorial interventionism and what, now, was at the heart of global contestation? What we were beginning to see

---

[93] A/C.1/L.364 and Add.1; United Arab Republic, A/PV.1408: 5. See United Nations Department of Public Information 1965: 92.

[94] The UK abstained. In the First Committee, Australia, Belgium, the Netherlands, and New Zealand also abstained.

[95] A/RES/2131(XX).

[96] Ibid. Peru regretted that in the Soviet draft (A/C.1/L.343/Rev.1) no reference had been made to important inter-American legal instruments, because 'the struggle for Latin American independence had been a clear manifestation of the principle of non-intervention' in a longer history of how 'with the conquest of their national independence the peoples had become the sole arbiters of their own destinies' (A/C.1/SR.1397: 257).

[97] A/C.1/SR.1398: 264.

in 1965, and which was cemented by the passing of the Declaration itself, was the overtaking of the problem of intervention by anti-colonial politics and the globalization of political agency. This shift was marked by a change in international belief and practice such that the intervention concept served a new function in international society, one that was different, or in one sense opposite, from the role played in 1945. It was significant that the agenda item was originally sponsored by the Soviet Union; Washington accused Moscow of having introduced its draft resolution as 'a pretext for another attack on the US and the Western states generally', to be 'partly explained by the Soviet Union's competition with Beijing for primacy in Communist orthodoxy and militancy'.[98] Central to the controversy was of course the use of the anti-colonial theory of intervention as a lever by contending Cold War blocs or ideologies to achieve foreign domination—in a sense to use non-intervention as a pretext for unfettered interventionism. In debating the Declaration in the General Assembly, the United States delegation referred to 'the current Chinese communist doctrine of intervention, that of so-called "wars of national liberation", proposed not only against South Vietnam and Laos but against Thailand and even against non-communist governments in Africa'.[99] International efforts to support 'national liberation' were armed but not only armed, and they increasingly took on propagandistic, diplomatic, economic, and other dimensions. They were also in the main a communist conspiracy.

And yet at the same time there was in the global Cold War, and in the intervention debate as it unfolded at this time, a race to claim the mantle of international protector or liberator in various cases of alleged foreign rule. It is not that this race began in 1965, but that as a phase of global debate, the notion of international action to support self-determination and anti-colonialism was gaining a new legitimacy. From one view, this was about counter-interventionary action to fend off capitalist or communist imperialism: 'the United States', its delegation announced, 'had always been prepared to stand up against such interventions, as it had done in Greece and Korea, in support of peoples who cherished their liberty and wished to determine their own destiny'.[100] And it should be noted that a great deal of General Assembly debate on the Declaration had to do with Vietnam and what counted as 'intervention' in Vietnam, or even more specifically, what counted as intervention in the context of an ongoing Vietnamese revolution, as a struggle for independence against foreign aggression, or in the context of armed force across the borders of a South and a North Vietnam.[101] The point, just the same, was

---

[98] See United Nations Department of Public Information 1965: 89; A/C.1/SR.1396: 251.
[99] Ibid.
[100] Ibid.
[101] See especially A/PV.1408: 9–15.

that all sides were making use of the right to self-determination and a shared duty to eliminate colonialism in all its forms.

It was primarily Western diplomacy and Western drafts and amendments that provided the basis of what became the second operational paragraph of the resolution: '… no State shall organize, assist, foment, finance, incite, or tolerate subversive, terrorist, or armed activities directed towards the violent overthrow of the regime of another State …'.[102] We can see how the paragraph cut in two ways. It cut firstly in the sense that it at last abandoned dictatorial intervention and accepted the basic conception of intervention as the outcome of pressure against self-determined futures. US amendments to the original USSR draft were intended to 'deal explicitly with covert, subversive intervention and to emphasize the necessity of all peoples being allowed to determine their own destinies through the exercise of self-determination.'[103] British amendments aimed to show that the USSR draft 'failed to cover some forms of intervention', and hence that the General Assembly ought to adopt 'a declaration of the right of all states freely to choose and develop their own political, social, economic, and cultural systems'.[104] In short, one 'main change', to quote an American delegation that was now taking a very different line than it had at Mexico City, was to show that 'unlawful intervention meant more than simply armed attacks across international frontiers'.[105]

But it cut secondly in the sense that it seemed to reject the 'insidious encouragement of guerilla warfare', the 'secret training of armed bands', and the 'infiltration of agents' whose goal was to 'impose the will of another government' under the cover of 'liberation'.[106] Some examples cited by the American delegation included 'young people from many independent African States being trained in Communist China' and others 'trained in Cuba for the same purpose'.[107] It 'would be said that such activities were designed to aid the "people's revolution" or "national liberation movements"', but while that argument was 'plausible although objectionable' in the case of 'colonial territories', it was 'indefensible in the case of independent states where subversion *was fostered against the will of the people*'.[108] In its preamble, Resolution 2131 (XX) would refer to the OAU's Declaration on the Problem of

---

[102] A/RES/2131(XX). See US and UK amendments to the USSR draft declaration: A/C.1/L.350; A/C.1/L.351.
[103] United States in United Nations Department of Public Information 1965: 89.
[104] United Kingdom in United Nations Department of Public Information 1965: 90; see A/C.1/L.351.
[105] A/C.1/SR.1396: 252.
[106] United States, A/C.1/SR.1396: 2.
[107] Ibid.
[108] United Kingdom, A/C.1/SR.1398: 261. Emphasis added.

Subversion, though a stance against subversion was evidently not one against liberation.[109]

So the dictatorial was dropping out, but we can also start to see how, as a matter of globally framing debate, the anti-colonial was dropping in. This is not to suggest, in some neat or uncontentious way, that a single understanding had been universally accepted, but that the crux of Northern and Southern contestation referred to a theory of the intervention concept, based around self-determination, human rights, and international responsibility, that had been given new political impetus. What it meant to intervene had broadly changed. This move from intervention as physical coercion or the threat or use of force seems so important for our understanding of the function of non-intervention that I want to map it out even further. Rival interpretations of the anti-colonial ordering of intervention coexisted and left marks on Resolution 2131 (XX), and there is something to be said about how an era of non-interventionism was always bound up with a solidarity that was more than just words.

So it is true that the Declaration's first operative clause, the clause that we have come to know so well but remember in the singular, was written as follows:

> No State has the right to intervene, directly or indirectly, for any reason whatever, in the internal or external affairs of any other state

It also true that in a subsequent clause we find that:

> no state shall ... interfere in civil strife in another state

But misunderstood if not totally unacknowledged, in all its solidarist internationalism, is the remarkable achievement of clause three:

> That the use of force to deprive peoples of their national identity constitutes a violation of their inalienable rights and of the principle of non-intervention.

And just as uncommonly appreciated are the plausible implications of clause six:

---

[109] A tension in the OAU declaration had to do with, on the one hand, its non-tolerance of subversion, and on the other, its call to protect so-called 'political refugees from non-independent African territories, and to support them in their struggle to liberate their countries'. See the Declaration on the Problem of Subversion of 25 October 1965.

all States shall respect the right of self-determination and independence of peoples and nations to be freely exercised without any foreign pressure and with absolute respect for human rights and fundamental freedoms. Consequently, all States shall contribute to the complete elimination of racial discrimination and colonialism in all its forms and manifestations.[110]

That these clauses were also the ones most clearly advocated by non-aligned states speaks to an era of transition in global debate. Again I do not want to suggest that they were read in a universal way—even among the final draft's fifty-seven developing world sponsors, we could identify a spectrum of moderate to radical readings in line with those covered in Chapter 3—but I do want to survey some of the ways in which they were justifying international actions that prevented large-scale human rights abuses, particularly in relation to colonial oppression and extreme racism.[111] Grasping a revolt against Western-dominated understandings of intervention has non-trivial implications for our grasp of the function and potential of the concept.

Take for example Earle Edward Seaton, representing Tanzania, who spoke of how 'the ideal of a universal international society based on freedom and justice ... had gradually brought about the elimination from international life of such practices as piracy, slavery, capitulations, the forcible collection of debts', and now 'colonialism'.[112] It was 'the duty of the First Committee to examine the principles of international law from the viewpoint of international morality', and in particular the Tanzanian delegation 'did not consider assistance offered to oppressed peoples struggling against colonialism and apartheid to be a form of intervention, either direct or indirect'.[113] 'That view', argued Seaton, had also 'been upheld at the Second Conference of Heads of State or Government of Non-Aligned Countries, held at Cairo in October 1964' and 'a consensus of the views of the participating countries could be found in the declaration of that conference'.[114] The draft resolution submitted by the United Arab Republic 'faithfully reflected those views, and the delegation of Tanzania had therefore agreed to become a sponsor'.[115] We could add that it was also at Cairo that in calling for 'all states to boycott all South African goods and to refrain from exporting goods', 'to break off diplomatic,

---

[110] A/RES/2131(XX).
[111] A/C.1/L.364 and Add.1.
[112] A/C.1/SR.1401: 283.
[113] Ibid.
[114] Ibid. See the Cairo Programme for Peace and International Co-Operation, especially its sections on 'Concerted Action for the Liberation of Countries Still Dependent: Elimination of Colonialism, Neo-colonialism, and Imperialism', 'Racial Discrimination and the Policy of Apartheid', and 'Peaceful Co-Existence and the Codification of its Principles by the United Nations', in A/5763: 1–37.
[115] See A/C.1/L.353 and Add.1.

consular, and other relations', and 'to give their support to the special bureau set up by the Organisation of African Unity for the application of sanctions against South Africa', the non-aligned countries also affirmed 'their absolute respect for the right of ethnic or religious minorities to protection in particular against the crimes of genocide'.[116]

As the Liberian delegate put it, to internationally respect the principle of non-intervention was also to internationally protect and promote human rights:

> The most complete manifestation of intervention was colonialism, which was an intrusion into the most vital aspects of the lives of other peoples. He used the word 'peoples' advisedly, because there was a tendency to think of intervention chiefly in terms of interference by one state in the internal affairs of another. Actually it was the impact of intervention on the lives of peoples which made it not only a juridical issue but a political and moral issue of the highest order. *Intervention was thus more than a violation of the rules governing the relations of states; what it amounted to was the domination of one people by another, and it therefore constituted a challenge to the most fundamental principles of human rights.*[117]

The kind of historical interpretation of the 1965 Declaration that should interest us, then, consisted of two basic steps. These two steps had appeared before (at Bandung, at Belgrade, at Havana, and beyond) but it is significant that they now informed arguments of Asian, African, and Latin American states concerning a major UN declaration on the subject.

The first step had to do with the obligations of sovereign states to responsibilities and commitments higher than themselves. It involved a dynamic understanding of domestic jurisdiction and the scope of sovereign privilege. One amendment submitted by Pakistan sought to declare that: 'The principle of non-intervention should not serve as an excuse for the evasion of obligations accepted by states under international agreements or United Nations resolutions.'[118] Pakistan's argument was perhaps a warning for certain academic and political tendencies of recent decades: 'A chaotic position would result if the Assembly were to formulate the principle of non-intervention in a way that would throw into doubt the binding nature of obligations undertaken in international treaties.'[119]

---

[116] A/5763: 12.
[117] A/C.1/SR.1401: 288.
[118] A/C.1/SR.1404: 305. See A/C.1/L.352.
[119] A/C.1/SR.1404: 305. I return to this point in Chapter 6.

Such an interpretation of non-intervention was intended to counter, at this time, Western practices of non-intervention and uses of Article 2 (7) that amounted to an impunity to be enjoyed by colonial powers implicated in mass atrocities: 'There were states which denied their peoples the most fundamental human rights and which, when condemned, hid behind the perversely interpreted principle of non-intervention ... To consolidate their rule and crush the will of the people, they did not hesitate to employ measures amounting to genocide.'[120] A previous twenty-seven-power draft declaration—submitted and sponsored by non-aligned countries—applied clearly the anti-colonial theory when it specified, for instance, that:

> the policies of apartheid and racial discrimination are policies contrary to the principle of non-intervention, due to the fact that these policies not only impair the free will of the people who suffer from these policies, but they moreover deny them their inalienable right to freely choose their own political, economic, social, and cultural systems.[121]

The same draft declared 'the duty of all states not to interfere or hinder the legitimate exercise by any other people, presently under colonial and foreign domination, of their sacred right to self-determination and independence', and in a separate clause that 'use of force to dislocate people and the denial to them of their national identity were direct violations of their inherent rights and were inconsistent with the principle of non-intervention'.[122]

So the notion that non-intervention permits or should ever have permitted a shield for genocidaires or perpetrators of crimes against humanity is flatly rejected in international-societal discourse in the 1960s—precisely against a background of the concept's recent abuse. Continued Pakistan: '[w]hen the world community expressed its concern at such barbarous acts those states [as perpetrators of such acts] pleaded that such matters were essentially within their domestic jurisdiction', and this ought to 'be condemned in clear and unequivocal terms in the proposed declaration'.[123] The point might have been taken ever further: in the 1960s, genocide was a manifestation of intervention as an act, and it was seen here as a supreme denial of the human rights, including the right to self-determination, of an affected people. To deny national identity by the use of mass violence constituted intervention in the domestic affairs of states at its most sinister. Because of

---

[120] Pakistan, in ibid.
[121] See A/C.1/L.353/Rev.4 and Add.1.
[122] Ibid.
[123] A/C.1/SR.1404: 305.

the meaning of intervention at this moment in history, then, it was difficult if not inconceivable to construe intervention as genocide prevention. To prevent genocide, through overcoming colonialism and extreme racism, was precisely to uphold non-intervention. At times such internationalist action was construed as anti-interventionary, but more essentially it was non-interventionary. This was also true of international action to prevent apartheid, soon to be declared a crime against humanity and a violation of the principles of international law and of the UN Charter.[124] Legitimate and legitimized collective action to prevent such atrocities was neither involvement in domestic affairs nor an act of intervention.

The second step, then, was more positive and had to do with a vindication of international anti-colonial action as humanitarian and its legitimacy as mass atrocity prevention. '[I]t would occur to no one', Tunisia was comfortable to argue before the Assembly, 'to accuse of intervention in the domestic affairs of a third country a state which gave active support to the peoples of Southern Rhodesia, the Territories under Portuguese administration, South Africa, Palestine, and all the other countries still under colonial rule which were victims of armed intervention and subject to foreign domination against their will.'[125]

Geneva: 'friendly' intervention

So there might be seen in the first UN Declaration on Non-Intervention, or Resolution 2131 (XX), a kind of refraction of practices, and it was in the mid-1960s that non-intervention in the UN became not only particularly broad in its proscriptions of intervention as an act—more than force and tied to the outcome of self-determined futures—but also, from a Third World reading of institutional change, relatively internationalist and relatively humanitarian.

The extraordinary importance of the Declaration and its solidarist credentials, according to Southern states, should be underlined: after the adoption of Resolution 2131 (XX), the Afghan delegation claimed there had been 'three occasions in the history of the United Nations' which were cause for 'the greatest rejoicing'.[126] First, the United Nations Declaration of Human Rights. Second, the Declaration on the Granting of Independence to Colonial Countries and Peoples. And third, this 'historic moment', the recodification of non-intervention, following from the logic and furthering the aims of the

---

[124] A/RES/3068(XXVIII).
[125] A/C.1/SR.1402: 291.
[126] A/PV.1408: 15.

previous two.[127] Commenting on the draft that would soon be adopted, the Pakistani representative had noted one day earlier with satisfaction 'that the draft unequivocally condemned policies of racial discrimination and included provisions under which Governments practising those inhuman policies would not be able to evade their obligations by claiming the matters in question were domestic affairs', and 'welcomed the reference, in the preamble and in operative paragraph 6, to the "self-determination of peoples"'.[128]

Northern pushback of course came against the most radical readings: most Western states claimed that by virtue of its rejection of subversion the Declaration had also rejected imperialism under the guise of internationalist militarism, so it 'should serve as a warning to those who started so-called wars of liberation; they should take note, in particular, of operative paragraphs 2 and 5 [condemning subversion]'.[129] France observed that 'some representatives had argued that it should be permissible in certain cases to intervene ... on behalf of a given movement or given section of the population', but 'Europeans would remember only too well how the pretext of "assistance to oppressed national minorities" had been used between 1933 and 1940'.[130] Israel described 'certain texts' submitted which 'had left escape clauses that would in fact encourage irredentist movements to serve as a pretext for foreign intervention'.[131] Italy's position exemplified moderation: 'of course no effort should be spared to abolish colonialism and racial segregation as soon as possible ... but no war was lawful, and no one had the right to intervene, in any way, either for or against movements or governments, according to how he judged them'.[132]

It was on account of these concerns that several Western states would come to express doubt about the overall relevance of Resolution 2131 (XX), regretting that parts of the Declaration were 'too vague' and omitted the views of 'experts' in the Sixth Committee, and hence that the resolution was 'merely a statement of political and moral intentions' and 'not a formulation of law; the latter was the task of the Special Committee on Principles of International Law concerning Friendly Relations and Co-operation among States'.[133] '[T]he wisest course would have been to transfer the item for further consideration to the Special Committee', since, for instance, the resolution's use

---

[127] Ibid.
[128] A/C.1/SR.1422: 433.
[129] United States in A/C.1/SR.1423: 436.
[130] A/C.1/SR.1405: 319–320.
[131] A/C.1/SR.1404: 307–308.
[132] A/C.1/SR.1402: 296.
[133] United States, A/C.1/SR.1423: 436; Belgium, ibid.; Israel, ibid.; United States, ibid.

152 Intervention before Interventionism

of the word '"peoples" was imprecise'.[134] In sum, Western votes had been cast in favour, but only 'on the clear understanding' that the resolution was based 'more on concepts of international morality than on a rigorous juridical analysis' and 'should not in any circumstances be invoked as a precedent in the Sixth Committee [Legal Committee] or in the Special Committee [on Friendly Relations]'.[135]

But the Declaration in fact did become the template for future discussions in both the UN's Sixth and Special Committees. And, from a certain Third World view, international morality, politics, and law were linked in all legal orders, and so much to the benefit of the powerful that a project of decolonizing law became less an apology for the weak than a correction of historical politicization.[136] At times the position rested on a controversial argument that the agreements of the UN General Assembly were of considerable legal significance.[137] As a matter of discursive practice, the key point is that the contestation of intervention in the Special Committee largely resembled the encounter underneath Resolution 2131 (XX). To understand the basic reordering of the intervention problem attempted at Bandung, then, is also to understand much of struggle over the meaning of intervention in the Special Committee.

In October and November 1965, during the Sixth Committee's consideration of the final report of the Mexico City meetings of 1964, two key statements were made that should be quoted in full. The first belonged to the Malaysian delegation:

> Disagreement seemed to have centred on the question of how far states were bound not to interfere in the internal affairs of another state and what constituted matters within the domestic jurisdiction of a state. The liberation of non-self-governing territories and the rights of minorities were two main examples that had been put forward as justifiable reasons for intervention.[138]

The second belonged to Mali:

> It should be clearly understood that his delegation considered that practices contrary to the Purposes of the Charter and the provisions of the Universal

---

[134] Canada, A/C.1/SR.1422: 433.
[135] France, ibid.: 432.
[136] See e.g. the comments of Vanderpuye of Ghana on 'the Committee's task ... to transform Western international law into universal international law' and the legal significance of Resolution 2131 (XX) in A/AC.125/SR.72: 12–14. A clear discussion and critique of anti-colonial legalism is contained in Moyn 2021. For a comprehensive analysis, and on decolonization as a 'battle for international law', see Bernstorff and Dann 2019.
[137] See Higgins 1963. For another key discussion from the period see Anand 1962.
[138] A/C.6/SR.878: 223.

Declaration of Human Rights, such as apartheid and genocide, did not come within the domestic jurisdiction of a state. The principle of non-intervention should be invoked only for acts of bad faith. Intervention aimed at restoring human dignity and freeing populations which were still under foreign domination should be considered as an act tending to free humanity from a source of international tensions. Moreover, any subject of discord ceased to be an internal affair when it had international repercussions and came within the purview of the United Nations by virtue of Chapter VII of the Charter.[139]

The Special Committee, submitting its reports to the Sixth Committee for recommendation to the General Assembly, would formally consider non-intervention on three more occasions: New York in 1966, Geneva in 1967, and Geneva again in 1970. In each case the battle was in fact more or less the same: the debate was explicitly about whether the Committee's understanding of non-intervention, as a principle of friendly relations, should adopt or modify the formulation contained in Resolution 2131 (XX).

In New York, a majority considered that formulation an essential instrument for the facilitation of the Committee's work.[140] Southern and socialist draft proposals explicitly reaffirmed that 'by virtue of the number of states which voted in its favour, the scope and profoundness of its contents, and in particular the absence of opposition or reservations reflects a universal legal conviction which already constitutes an authentic and definite principle of international law'.[141] Chile, 'together with all the countries of the Latin American continent', and joined by the countries of Asia and Africa, was 'resolutely and totally in favour of the text of the General Assembly's Declaration as a formulation of non-intervention ... [b]asically, resolution 2131 (XX) was not political but juridical'.[142] Nothing was to be done, according to this group, that would impair its value. What the Committee could do instead is offer 'additional paragraphs for consideration in connection with the text of General Assembly Resolution 2131 (XX)', like the one contained in the revised joint proposal by India, Lebanon, the United Arab Republic, Syria, and Yugoslavia: 'aid and assistance given to peoples under any form of colonial domination does not constitute intervention'.[143]

The voting record on proposals like this one reveals, again, a sharp South–North divide, and anti-colonial politics were at the root of this split.[144]

---

[139] A/C.6/SR.882: 249–250.
[140] A/6230: 152–159.
[141] Ibid.: 153. See e.g. the joint proposal by Chile and the United Arab Republic in A/AC.125/L.17; the draft resolution of Czechoslovakia is in A/AC.125/L.20.
[142] A/AC.125/SR.10: 11.
[143] A/AC.125/L.12.
[144] For the full 1966 report of the Special Committee see A/6230, especially 124–160.

A Western view—that the word of the General Assembly was not 'sacrosanct', that the Special Committee was entitled to 'undertake an examination of the principle of non-intervention on bases quite different from those of resolution 2131 (XX)', that it had been discussed in 'a context quite different', that a 'universal legal conviction could not be brought about by legislation, particularly by legislation adopted by a mere majority'—cast doubt on 'whether the Member States had really reached agreement' just one year earlier.[145] In any total or very deep way, universal agreement had of course not been reached the Declaration's adoption being a story of compromise, not ideal consensus, especially in relation to the positive face of non-intervention. But what matters, from a longer genealogical view, is that the framework of global debate was shifting.

To document this point in the context of the Special Committee, consider the following arguments being made from a loose Northern group: that 'peoples did not necessarily constitute states under international law' and that 'the aspirations of peoples to acquire collectively the capacity to act as states' was a matter 'of self-determination, not of non-intervention'; that paragraphs containing expressions like 'national identity' were hence mistakes; that if phrases concerning 'aid and assistance' to dependent nations were merely a euphemism for 'armed aid and assistance', then they could never be accepted, as they appeared 'to give a state complete freedom to intervene' wherever there was 'foreign domination'; and as long as there 'was no objective procedure under international law for determining what constituted "foreign domination"' the wording of particular paragraphs might appear to offer a 'loop-hole for intervention by armed force or subversive activities.'[146]

The United States had the 'gravest misgivings with regard to paragraph 6 [of the six-power proposal: "[a]id and assistance given to peoples under any form of foreign domination does not constitute intervention"], for its effect would be to give legal sanction to a form of intervention by force.'[147] Then there was the risk of abuse: surely there were 'a number of cases in which sovereign states whose indigenous populations were admittedly fully in charge of their own governments had nevertheless been made the object of the use of force under the pretext of "anti-colonialism".'[148] 'As for paragraph 3 ["the use of force to deprive peoples of their national identity constitutes a violation of

---

[145] Sweden, A/AC.125/SR.11: 14; France, A/AC.125/SR.12: 5; ibid.; United States, A/6230: 159; France, A/AC.125/SR.12: 5.
[146] United States, A/AC.125/SR.13: 8–9; ibid.; Sweden, A/AC.125/SR.12: 10–11; UK, A/AC.125/SR.10: 9; Canada, A/AC.125/SR.13: 8; UK, A/AC.125/SR.10: 9. On international law and the use of force by national liberation movements and on behalf of national liberation movements abroad, see Wilson 1988.
[147] A/AC.125/SR.13: 13. See A/AC.125/L.12.
[148] United States, A/AC.125/SR.13: 13.

their inalienable rights and of the principle of non-intervention"]', argued the United Kingdom, 'the question seemed at first sight to arise whether such a paragraph was not out of place in a text on non-intervention, for it seemed to deal with domestic matters such as human rights and the rights of minorities'.[149]

By 1967 the General Assembly had instructed the Special Committee to consider proposals with the aim of 'widening the area of agreement already expressed in General Assembly resolution 2131 (XX)'—though the parameters of that existing area of agreement were themselves a matter of debate.[150] To 'widen' agreement was not necessarily to widen the scope of the principle, nor even to 'abide by' the Declaration, but to take account of it, and to realize through it a more generally acceptable legal enunciation of non-intervention.

What we need to recognize here is that the first meeting in Geneva reflected again the tensions afflicting New York: between the full text of the Declaration (Resolution 2131 [XX]) and closely related Southern drafts on the one hand, and a set of Western drafts on the other, the purpose of which were to 'seek to identify those elements in resolution 2131 (XX) which were directly relevant to the principle of non-intervention, having in mind that that resolution contained provisions which were not directly relevant to non-intervention as such, but which might be regarded as subsumed in the texts relating to other principles'.[151] The British delegation 'noted a large number of statements, particularly of the African, Asian, and Eastern European delegations and also, to a lesser extent, of certain delegations from Latin America' had been critical of his delegation's proposal and a main complaint was that 'it was designed to "torpedo" resolution 2131 (XX)'.[152] From the view of the Indian delegation, the positions taken by the Western group would 'tear up resolution 2131 (XX)' with a supposed 'view to improving on it', and present a 'diminutive' and 'distorted' understanding of non-intervention: for instance, 'there were no provisions in the United Kingdom proposal corresponding to paragraphs 3 [concerning the use of force to deprive peoples of their national identity as a violation of non-intervention] and 6 [concerning the right of self-determination, absolute respect for human rights, and the contribution of all states to the complete eradication of racial discrimination and colonialism] of the resolution [2131 (XX)]'.[153]

---

[149] A/AC.125/SR.10.
[150] See A/RES/2181(XXI).
[151] A/AC.125/SR.73: 20–21. Compare e.g. A/AC.125/L.54 with A/AC.125/L.13 and A/AC.125/L.44.
[152] Ibid. See A/AC.125/L.44.
[153] India, A/AC.125/SR.72: 10–11.

The Soviet Union made a related argument: to 'torpedo' by way of the British draft would be to ignore the ways in which the international community and its members had managed since the end of the Second World War to transfer 'certain matters to the international plane' and remove them from the 'sphere of purely internal competence'.[154] 'On the basis of freedom and equality', states had come to 'assume certain obligations to take international action, for example under the Convention on the Prevention and Punishment of the Crime of Genocide' or 'the Declaration on the Elimination of All Forms of Racial Discrimination'.[155] '[A] State violating such obligations incurred international responsibility'.[156]

At the same time, there was renewed vigilance among moderates against any reading of solidarist internationalism as a strand of proletarian internationalism. In this context the Tricontinental Conference was explicitly discussed in the Special Committee. Claimed Argentina: 'in open defiance of resolutions 2131(XX) and 2225(XXI), a conference which called itself a Latin American "Solidarity" Conference had recently met in the capital of Cuba and advocated subversion in all its forms on the American continent'.[157] These 'events showed the need to reaffirm the terms of resolution 2131 (XX), which had been adopted at the world level', and lay bare a ploy for 'generalized intervention involving the use of force' at the expense of legitimate independent states.[158] The Mexican representative also condemned the Tricontinental as having floated a subversive interventionism totally incompatible with the principles of the UN Charter, and drew 'attention to the fact that on 11 February 1966 the permanent representative of Mexico to the United Nations had circulated, as an official document, a declaration on an event which the Mexican delegation considered to be the first specific case calling for the application of resolution 2131 (XX): the so-called "Tricontinental Peoples' Solidarity Conference", from which had emanated threats of intervention and seditious propaganda.'[159] Mexico's letter of 11 February 1966 condemned 'the deliberations and decisions of the so-called Tricontinental Solidarity Conference of Peoples' and quoted the speech of Foreign Minister Antonio Carrillo Flores delivered months earlier at the Second Extraordinary Inter-American Conference held at Rio de Janeiro: 'We do indeed recognize that international solidarity has gradually created new institutions which we

---

[154] A/AC.125/SR.71: 10.
[155] Ibid.
[156] Ibid.
[157] A/AC.125/SR.72: 15.
[158] Ibid.: 16.
[159] A/AC.125/SR.72. See S/7142.

have forged into worldwide or regional instruments. We have never doubted, therefore, that the principle of non-intervention is compatible with collective action exceptionally and specifically provided for in treaties.'[160] But only within such parameters: 'What we cannot agree to is that, without the formality of a treaty which is subject to a strict negotiating and control procedure in all our countries, international bodies should arrogate to themselves powers which our peoples have not granted to them.'[161]

What was the institutional upshot to all this competition, and all this contestation? At the last session of the Special Committee, in Geneva in 1970, member states did strike a compromise, notably doing so under various pressures, including due to the progress made in relation to the other six principles of friendly relations. The final formula reflected concessions made by both a Western group that had gathered around the UK proposal of 1967 and a Southern group that insisted on a text resembling Declaration 2131 (XX).

The Friendly Relations Declaration would forbid 'armed intervention and all other forms of interference or attempted threats against the personality of the State or against its political, economic and cultural elements', as well as the use, or encouragement of the use, of 'economic, political or any other type of measures to coerce another State in order to obtain from it the subordination of the exercise of its sovereign rights and to secure from it advantages of any kind'.[162] And while, absolutely, 'no State or group of States has the right to intervene, directly or indirectly, for any reason whatever, in the internal or external affairs of any other State', 'the use of force to deprive peoples of their national identity constitutes a violation of their inalienable rights and of the principle of non-intervention', with the proviso that 'no State shall organize, assist, foment, finance, incite or tolerate subversive, terrorist or armed activities directed towards the violent overthrow of the regime of another State, or interfere in civil strife in another State'.[163] The text of paragraph 6 of Resolution 2131 (XX)—'all states shall contribute to the complete elimination of racial discrimination and colonialism in all its forms and

---

[160] A/AC.125/SR.72.
[161] Ibid. One year earlier the Inter-American Juridical Committee had issued a legal opinion on collective action distinguished from intervention. For a discussion and analysis of that opinion, see Caminos 1998: 204–208. For an argument from a key member of the Inter-American Juridical Committee that intervention and collective action 'are as different as night and day', and for a warning against 'sophistry', see Murdock 1962: 500.
[162] A/RES/2625(XXV).
[163] Ibid. For a fuller discussion of the Friendly Relations Declaration in relation to the idea that a 'third state can treat with liberation movements, assist and even recognize them *without this being considered a premature recognition or constituting an intervention in the domestic affairs of the colonial government*', see Abi-Saab 1962. Emphasis added.

manifestations'—was missing, though reference to the duty to bring a 'speedy end' to colonialism through 'joint and separate action' appeared elsewhere in the Declaration.[164]

Co-living in peace with one another as good neighbours

The Friendly Relations Declaration has been called a 'peculiar document' and a 'patch-and-mend aggregation of bits and pieces of conceptual furniture', rather than a 'crystalline conceptual blueprint'.[165] Yet it is precisely the conflicts and internal tensions that reveal how far states had sought to move away from a UN that projected a morally narrow vision of the 'Alliance of the Victorious Powers' of the Second World War.[166] The Declaration's significance has less to do with universally resolving the intervention question—to the contrary, provisions relating to coercive struggles for national liberation would remain among the most controversial in international law and politics—than with how, from within the history of its writing and against its final wording, we can triangulate changes in globally influential discursive practice.

'The whole question of intervention', observed Liberia in the pivotal UN debates of 1965, amounted to 'confrontation between great and small powers. It was in terms of that division rather than exclusively in terms of ideological divisions that the whole problem should be approached.'[167] The fact of this divide was clearly seized upon by the Soviet Union (if the Special Committee was to succeed, claimed the Soviet delegation, 'an adequate formula must be found which reflected the vital importance of the principle of non-intervention for the peoples of Latin America, Asia, and Africa').[168] But the more important point, from the longer view, is that the 'new' states had arrived as agents in themselves who, through international organizing that spurned Cold War polarizations and the threat of global-institutional fragmentation, broke away from oppressive descriptions of what it is to intervene.

In Chapter 2 we saw that the state-based non-interventionism of the San Francisco Conference looked more like the Rooseveltian vision of the 'Good Neighbor' at Montevideo than the Good Neighbor Policy as further developed, for example, at Buenos Aires, Chapultepec, and Bogotá.

[164] Ibid.
[165] Moyn and Özsu 2020.
[166] Abi-Saab 2020.
[167] A/C.1/SR.1401: 288.
[168] A/AC.119/SR.30: 19–20.

In Chapter 3 we explored the emergence of Afro-Asian and non-aligned emphasis on particular principles of peaceful coexistence. Through the Friendly Relations process, a loose Western coalition had by now abandoned two arguments in the face of ongoing non-Western protest that encompassed an arguably more progressive view both of inter-American good neighbourly relations and of Third World conceptions of peaceful coexistence. The first was that Article 2 (7) could be used to negate international obligations to promote human rights, including self-determination in favour of decolonization, and the international prevention of mass atrocities, including apartheid and genocide. The second was that the boundaries of a duty of interstate non-intervention were simply those of Article 2 (4), which encapsulated a classical theory of intervention as coercive interference. It is not that, through the 1960s, a Western practice—what we have called dictatorial intervention—had been totally substituted by a Southern practice—anticolonial intervention—in some singular, universal way. We have seen how certain elements or iterations of solidarist internationalism remained fiercely resisted by colonial powers of international society. And yet the more general framework in which intervention was debated and understood in the UN had substantially changed; once-hegemonic formulations had made way for interpretations better suited for a new context of international relations and morality in which extreme racism and empire, for instance, were no longer matters of domestic jurisdiction.

I want to finish this chapter by quoting at length a speech made by UK Ambassador to the UN Sir Gladwyn Jebb in 1952, during the UN General Assembly's consideration of the 'race conflict in South Africa resulting from policies of apartheid of the Government of the Union of South Africa'.[169] The purpose of doing so is to illustrate just how far the society of states had moved by 1970.

> I have been asked by the leader of my delegation to explain our general attitude towards the competence of the Assembly to consider the question now before us because I was—in the distant and, shall I say, rather more hopeful days of 1944 and 1945—closely connected with the preparation of the Charter and may therefore be thought perhaps to have some special knowledge of the circumstances surrounding the negotiation and meaning of what is now Article 2, paragraph 7, of the Charter, dealing, as we know, with the question of domestic jurisdiction ...
> *It is quite true that, in our respective organized national societies, we are all, perforce, to some extent at any rate, our brothers' keepers, but in the present state of*

[169] A/PV.381.

international society it is simply not possible for any particular philosophy or morality to be imposed by one group of States on another State or group of States ... With this brief introduction, may I say quite bluntly that my Government entertains no doubt at all that, quite irrespective of the merits ... this particular item on the internal racial policy of the Government of the Union of South Africa is one which the Assembly is not competent to consider and which it ought not to discuss ... For my part, I can think of nothing more clearly and obviously a matter of a country's domestic jurisdiction than the relationship which, as a matter of State, it has rightly or wrongly decided to maintain between persons of varying races living within its own borders ... The General Assembly must be said to intervene in the internal affairs of a Member State when it not only places an item concerning those affairs on the agenda, but also proceeds to consider it and discuss it and, whether by means of a formal draft resolution or otherwise, attempts to indicate to a Member State concerned what policy it ought to pursue. If such an action does not constitute intervention, then it is indeed difficult to know what the term can possibly mean.[170]

Martin Wight, in 1956, came to a similar conclusion in his review of 'the power struggle between the have-nots and the status quo powers' in the UN, which seemed to be shaking the foundations of the organization, and of international society itself:

The limits of Article 2, Paragraph 7, were first explored in the case of South Africa. The question was this: if South Africa infringes human rights, can the General Assembly infringe South African domestic jurisdiction? The Afro-Asians argued that respect for human rights overrides juridical limitations ... Dr Malan [of South Africa] responded by describing the United Nations as 'a cancer eating at the peace and tranquility of the world', the closest thing yet in the history of the United Nations to what Hitler used to say about the League ... The development of the United Nations in these directions is remarkable. *It was not contemplated at San Francisco that the United Nations should be an organization for collective intervention in the domestic affairs of its members.*[171]

Thirteen years later, in the General Assembly's First Committee, the Ecuadorian delegation observed: '[t]here is no doubt that we are going through a period of transition characterized, among other visible phenomena, if not by the collapse of the outmoded concept of absolute state sovereignty, at least by

---

[170] A/PV.381: 60–62.
[171] Wight 1978: 236.

the adaptation of that concept'.[172] Ecuador continued: 'this transitional stage is also marked by the emergence of a basic principle of international authority which has resulted in the struggle against colonialism and its immediate corollary, the birth of new independent states'.[173]

A Bandung meaning of intervention, to be discerned in a context of dynamic domestic jurisdiction and the evolving human rights regime, and as the outcome of pressure against self-determined futures, had decentred older interpretations in the practices of states. It came, to a much greater extent than before, to be inscribed in key documents of the UN—including the First Declaration on Non-Intervention of 1965 and the Friendly Relations Declaration of 1970. And it was bound up in anti-colonial politics and an anti-colonial moment, wherein the superpowers, though experimenting with détente, competed for the support of newly independent states, in a society of states that was increasingly anti-hierarchical. If an older formula approached intervention as a matter of traditional security, a newer global meaning of intervention, from the beginning to the end of the Friendly Relations process, came to take on a broader discretion: the problem of intervention encompassed an alternative theory of international freedom, one that would be frequently applied in cases of extreme foreign and racist domination. In Chapter 5 I will show how intervention in its anti-colonial interpretation took on additional dimensions, a process which became especially apparent over the 1970s, and which might be seen to culminate in the UN's adoption of a Second Declaration on Non-Intervention in 1981.

---

[172] A/PV.1340: 1.
[173] Ibid.

5
Emancipatory intervention and the New International Orders

A panel on covert intervention convened on 25 April 1975 at the American Society of International Law's annual meeting in Washington, DC. Richard Falk was there, Tom Farer was there, Dean Rusk was there, they were citing R. J. Vincent (whose *Nonintervention and International Order* had been published one year before).[1] Panellist David Stern was presenting a review of the state of the concepts of sovereignty and intervention. He had come to a firm conclusion: that in 1975 'neither concept is any longer as monolithic as it once might have been and that the challenge of the entirety of what we so glibly call the Third World has been to break down the neat formalistic compartments that had formerly been erected'.[2] Thirty years earlier, when he had first come into the field, the rules of intervention in international life 'were relatively fixed, reasonably limited in scope, and almost totally cast in the cultural tradition of Western Europe and its culturally related territories'.[3]

No longer so; a Third World protest was being staged, intervention had been cast and recast in the play of multiple discursive practices. Stern was right to observe that 'old standards that we inherited and took for granted are no longer the standards by which we have to operate'.[4] 'I feel that the older concepts of both sovereignty and intervention, originating as they did in the essentially European tradition, have not yet been able to confront and accommodate the overwhelming demands for a system of acceptable standards which will protect the legitimate interests of the emerging nations.'[5]

Because if 'intervention was originally conceived and dealt with in many international agreements as the direct military threat to the territorial integrity of a sovereign member of the international community', then by 1975 it seemed as if it had 'taken on a completely new meaning'.[6] Pronounced

---

[1] American Society of International Law 1975.
[2] Stern, Borosage, and Farer 1975: 200.
[3] Ibid.
[4] Ibid.
[5] Ibid.
[6] Ibid.

Intervention before Interventionism. Patrick Quinton-Brown, Oxford University Press. © Patrick Quinton-Brown (2024).
DOI: 10.1093/oso/9780198886457.003.0006

Stern: 'I would suggest that given the present state of *international economic relations* it is impossible to fix with any precision the meaning of that term.'[7] He could have taken the point further: by 1975 it was the state of international economic relations, yes, but also the state of international-communicative and information-technological relations that played a new role in ordering the intervention concept. And yet these transformations were neglected in the study of International Relations; in 1984, when Hedley Bull edited his major volume on intervention, the focus remained on the Oppenheim-Lawrence notion of 'dictatorial or coercive interference' and contributors like Philip Windsor preoccupied themselves with the Brezhnev and modified Monroe Doctrines, thereby obstructing non-aligned and Third World redescriptions of the intervention problem that aimed precisely to escape such Cold War mentalities.[8]

From the 1970s into the early 1980s the problem of intervention in international society linked up to the declarations of two new international orders: the New International Economic Order (NIEO) and the New World Information and Communication Order (NWICO). In the 1970s and early 1980s, this alternative formulation gained considerable prominence—we see this reflected in a second non-intervention declaration, which expanded on Resolution 2131 (XX).[9] Yet unlike the First Declaration, this second one would not be unanimously adopted in the General Assembly. It drew ire in a more outright way: in 1981 the resolution passed with a vote of 120 to 22, with 6 abstentions.[10] A South–North divide is very much evident here; the records show that all those voting against belonged to a Western group, with only one exception (Venezuela).

Of course the NIEO and NWICO are widely considered to have been failures—failures insofar as they did not achieve their objectives of fundamentally reshaping actual international-economic and -communicative structures, and of redistributing actual economic and communicative fortunes.[11] But I would recall here a maxim of any genealogy and historical analysis in discursive practice: what interests us is not just the success of the

---

[7] Ibid.
[8] Bull 1984c: 1; see Windsor 1984. The revised Monroe Doctrine would soon be known as the Reagan Doctrine.
[9] A/RES/36/103.
[10] See A/36/PV.91: 1630–1631.
[11] For instance, on the Third World's use of international law in a struggle for permanent sovereignty over natural resources, and its eventual subsumption within new regulatory frameworks dealing with foreign investment, see Pahuja 2011: 95–171. Sundhya Pahuja is surely right to say that rather than rehearsing 'yet another version of the argument that the Third World was misguided, unlucky and ultimately not sufficiently unified', the 'episode may be understood heuristically' in the context of broader changes in doctrines and institutions (ibid: 96).

protest, but the record of the confrontation itself, and the normative logics or strategies to be pulled from its battles. Again it is the meanings themselves that seem useful and revelatory. We ought to better see how they came to be bound up in processes of legitimizing political action and how they sought to reorder existing sources of international legitimacy. Through the 1970s and 1980s there was a reconstitution that did not 'win', but which nevertheless seems an important feature of large-scale normative change, and large-scale normative change historically.

To capture its mood and bent, and to differentiate it from the formulations recovered in previous chapters, we might call this a problematization along the lines of an emancipatory intervention. The logic of the emancipatory overlaps of course with the anti-colonial as described in previous chapters—it makes claims to non-intervention as premised on self-determination, and as expressive of a commitment to various forms of autonomy (particularly autonomy as distinct from formal independence), but I want to hold that there are conceivable differences which are also important to understand. A new part of the formula or design had to do with intervention in terms of foreign-imposed underdevelopment, structural economic dependence, and actions taken by transnational corporations.[12] And another newly important part of the answer had to do with foreign-imposed communicative conditions and information flows, including via electronic means and through the distribution of what was being called, even then, 'false' and 'distorted' news.[13] As it is repractised, non-intervention, ordered by a commitment to autonomy that is more than a commitment to formal independence, explicitly forbids some international actions and sanctions others. In this chapter I want to map out and explain some of the most important versions of those actions, which come to inform the content, for instance, of the Second Declaration on Non-Intervention adopted in 1981.

After Friendly Relations

The next UN resolution (but not yet the Second Declaration) on non-intervention was passed in 1976.[14] There was hesitancy towards another appraisal of non-intervention—circulating through UN committee debates

---

[12] On intervention as an economic issue, including in relation to debt traps, tied aid, and the IMF (International Monetary Fund), see Thomas 1985: 122–156. See also e.g. Williams 2013. On the NIEO, see Murphy 2005 and the 2015 special issue of *Humanity* (volume 6, issue 1).

[13] For an introduction to the NWICO and problems of international power as problems of information and communication, see Alleyne 1995. See also Nordenstreng and Schiller 1979.

[14] A/RES/31/91.

Emancipatory intervention and the New International Orders 165

for nearly a decade was the basic argument of the United States, which was repeated almost verbatim in every case: that 'effective measures to strengthen the commitment of the international community to this principle [non-intervention]' would be best achieved by 'universal adherence to the principles and purposes of the United Nations Charter and to the Declaration on the Principles of International Law Concerning Friendly Relations and Cooperation among States'.[15] But while Friendly Relations was a kind of truce, it did not mark a total cessation of hostilities. The 1976 resolution was the first of five similar resolutions pushed by the non-aligned states and adopted in the General Assembly, each titled 'Non-Interference in the Internal Affairs of States', the fifth being followed by the 1981 Declaration.[16]

We know too little about these resolutions, and I want to show that we would be wrong to assume they were mere repetitions of older forms, rather than attempts at taking forward the anti-colonial theory of intervention in new directions. A draft text of the 1976 resolution presented before the First Committee suggests that a set of far more ambitious concerns was on the minds of its non-aligned co-sponsors.[17] Ratne Deshapriya Senanayake, the Sri Lankan delegate and a former Secretary-General of the Afro-Asian Writers' Bureau, explained:

> The erratic meanderings of the international money market in recent years have amply demonstrated the extent to which economic disequilibrium can affect even the most highly developed countries in the world. How much worse could be the impact of economic destabilization on developing countries whose resources are scarce, which depend largely, if not entirely, on commodity exports to earn the money sorely needed for their development, and whose economic survival is already beset with problems over which they have little or no control? *It is against this background that I introduce draft resolution A/C.1/31/L.41* [Non-Interference in the Internal Affairs of States, 1976].[18]

The reference was to the recent 'Nixon Shock', the unilateral decision by the American President to, among other things, suspend the convertibility of the US dollar to gold—effectively bringing an end to the Bretton Woods system of fixed international financial exchange that was established at the end of the Second World War.[19]

---

[15] See e.g. A/33/216: 32.
[16] A/RES/31/91; A/RES/32/153; A/RES/33/74; A/RES/34/101; A/RES/35/159; A/RES/36/103.
[17] See A/C.1/31/PV.55: 18–21.
[18] Ibid.: 21. Emphasis added.
[19] See e.g. Eichengreen 2019: 126–133.

It is not of course that previously analysed beliefs regarding nonintervention and the national liberation struggle were disappearing, but that the liberation thesis was being amended to reach into the international-economic and, soon, the international-communicative and information-technological in ways it had not before.[20] The 1976 resolution—adopted by 106, with 14 abstentions (a Western group)—reasserted that the use of force to deprive peoples of their national identity was a violation of non-intervention, but it also condemned a 'wide range of direct and indirect techniques, including withholding assistance and the threat of withholding assistance, subtle and sophisticated forms of economic coercion, subversion and defamation with a view to destabilization, [that] are being mobilized against governments which seek to free their economies from foreign control and manipulation', especially those seeking 'to exercise permanent sovereignty over their natural resources'.[21]

In the resolution's sixth paragraph we can identify an integral part of the Non-Aligned Movement's campaign strategy that would follow: a request that the Secretary-General invite all member states to express their views on the principle and formally report back to the General Assembly the following year.[22] Paragraph six was the beginning of what became a multiyear project: by successive resolutions, the Secretary-General would invite substantive views on the principle and prepare reports in 1977, 1978, and 1979.[23] In 1980 an ad-hoc working group composed of member states was established for the purpose of writing a new declaration on non-intervention that would complement or supersede the 1965 declaration.[24]

We should note, first, that a Western group of about fifteen states abstained on the 1977, 1978, and 1979 resolutions, and that a Western-dominated group of twenty-five abstained on the 1980 resolution (all other members of the UN voted in favour of all five resolutions).[25] And we should note, second, that states abstaining on these resolutions also, in their comments published in related reports of the Secretary-General for example, warned against further elaboration of the non-intervention concept beyond the formulation contained in the Friendly Relations Declaration, as to do so would 'lead to a certain confusion and cast doubt upon the interpretation and scope of the already-existing prohibitions against interference'.[26] The question, for our

---

[20] On the politics of development and the NIEO project as a meta-narrative at Bandung, see Weber 2016.
[21] A/RES/31/91; see A/31/PV.98: 1478–1479.
[22] A/RES/31/91.
[23] A/32/164; A/32/165; A/34/192.
[24] See A/RES/34/101.
[25] Recorded votes in A/32/PV.106: 1736–1737; A/33/PV.85: 1501–1502; A/34/PV.103: 1897; A/35/PV.94: 1665.
[26] Sweden, A/34/193 and Add.1–2: 12.

purposes, is: which elaborations were casting doubt or leading to a 'certain confusion' upon earlier interpretations and scopes of the concept? Were they simply reassertions the text of Resolution 2131 (XX) or were they breaking new ground?

To reconvene on non-intervention might have been acceptable to the industrialized North if not for the role being played by self-determination, and—this part was not wholly new, but of new significance in the global debate on intervention—non-aligned visions of self-determination with proliferating economic and cultural effects, including in relation to various forms of property. Exemplary was a note, submitted by Panama, which appeared in the second report of the Secretary-General in 1978.[27] Panama claimed that intervention had to be understood on 'the basis of three fundamental pillars of the system established in accordance with the Charter of the UN for the effective exercise of the right to self-determination of peoples', namely:

I. The magna carta of decolonization (Resolution 1514 (XV))
II. The Declaration of Permanent Sovereignty Over Natural Resources (Resolution 1803 (XVII))
III. The Declaration on the Establishment of a New International Economic Order (Resolution 3201 (SVI))[28]

The first pillar has already been addressed (see Chapter 3). To conceive of intervention in terms of the 'magna carta' that was the Declaration on the Granting of Independence to Colonial Countries and Peoples (Resolution 1514 (XV)) was to legitimize certain types of international action against colonialism, for the promotion of human rights, as consistent with non-intervention.[29] It is for this reason that Panama called for special attention and study to be devoted to three documents presented at the 15th summit of the OAU in Khartoum earlier that year: 1) Resolution 37 (of 22 July 1978) on military intervention in Africa and measures to be taken against neocolonialist manoeuvres and intervention in Africa—a condemnation especially of the use of mercenaries as proxies for 'imperialist powers' seeking to 'impede the process of decolonization', 2) Resolution 38, of the same date, on measures to be taken against neocolonialist manoeuvres and foreign military intervention—a call, by now very routine in OAU resolutions, to increase its support and assistance to liberation movements in Southern Africa, including via material assistance dispensed by the OAU's Liberation Committee based in Dar es Salaam, and 3) Resolution 39, also of the same date, on the

---
[27] A/33/216: 10–11.
[28] Ibid.: 11.
[29] Ibid.: 18.

establishment of what had been called, by France and Francophone African states, an 'inter-African military intervention force', but was described more generally in the OAU as an 'inter-African military force' or pan-African 'task force'—adopted with the understanding that such a force could 'be envisaged only within the context of the OAU's objectives and priorities for the elimination of the racist minority regimes of Southern Africa, the total liberation of the continent, and the safeguarding of the independence, sovereignty and territorial integrity of member states'.[30]

The second pillar had to do with how, as it was tied to the self-determination of peoples, the principle of non-intervention also entailed respect for the 'inalienable right of all states freely to dispose of their natural wealth and resources', and a set of related economic rights and duties, including the right of a state 'to nationalization or transfer of ownership to its nationals'.[31] The conclusion of the 1962 Declaration on Permanent Sovereignty Over Natural Resources was that the 'violation of the rights of peoples and nations to sovereignty of their natural wealth and resources is contrary to the spirit and principles of the Charter of the United Nations', and Resolution 32/154, adopted on 19 December 1977, stated that 'any measure or pressure directed against any state while exercising its sovereign right freely to dispose of its natural resources constitutes a flagrant violation of the right of self-determination of peoples and the principle of non-intervention'.[32] Deliberations over the control of the Panama Canal was one example—the Torrijos-Carter Treaties having been signed in September 1977.[33]

And the third pillar referred to the New International Economic Order.[34] In 1974, 70 per cent of the world's population accounted for just 30 per cent of the world's income—the General Assembly had proclaimed a NIEO to 'correct inequalities and redress existing injustices', to 'eliminate the widening gap between the developed and the developing countries', and to 'ensure steadily accelerating economic and social development and peace and justice'.[35] It was to be guaranteed by a set of core understandings and substantive recommendations. Among them were: the elimination of colonialism, apartheid, racial discrimination, and neocolonialism as nothing less than a 'prerequisite for development'; 'restitution and full compensation for the exploitation and depletion of, and damages to, the natural and all other

---

[30] Ibid.: 14. The texts of OAU Resolutions 37 and 39 are contained in Legum 1980: C19, C16. Resolution 39 was a reply to a French-led proposal, supported by Francophone African states, to establish a pan-African defence or military force outside of OAU authority. For a discussion see Powell 2016.
[31] A/33/216: 18.
[32] See A/RES/3171(XXVIII); A/RES/32/154.
[33] On the sovereign right to natural resources and the Panama Canal, see e.g. the 'Latin American Issues' section of the Non-Aligned Movement's Colombo Declaration in A/31/197: 40.
[34] A/33/216: 25–26.
[35] A/RES/S-6/3201.

resources' of nations under colonial or neocolonial rule; a 'just and equitable relationship between the prices of raw materials, primary commodities, manufactured, and semi-manufactured goods' exported and imported by developing states; 'extension of active assistance to developing countries' with no strings attached, as well as international aid 'free of any political or military conditions'; international monetary reform to promote 'an adequate flow of real resources'; and the facilitation of producers' associations in the world economy.[36]

Not explicitly mentioned in the 1974 Declaration, but described four years later by the Non-Aligned Movement as an 'integral part of the struggle for the NIEO', was the need to address imbalanced information and communication flows between North and South.[37] The breaking down of colonial and neocolonial structures in mass media, in the distribution and content of news, and in the control of communication networks was also necessary to ensure economic and social development and peace and justice—'a new international order in the fields of information and mass communication is as vital as a new international economic order'.[38] These objectives came to be associated with the call for a New World Information and Communication Order (NWICO), located then under pillar three of Panama's note.

I will say more about the NWICO later on. But for now, we should note that its origins are usually found in the 1973 Algiers and 1976 Colombo Declarations of the non-aligned countries.[39] Notably it was also at Colombo that the Non-Aligned Movement adopted for the first time a special chapter specifically on non-intervention.[40] In that special chapter we find the following specifications:

> The Non-Aligned commitment to the principle of true independence of states, *as distinct from merely formal sovereignty*, means that the Non-Aligned are opposed to any form of interference in the internal affairs of states ... The Conference expressed alarm at the increasing evidence of the resort to forms of aggression by foreign powers and other political and economic agencies or institutions, *official as well as private, such as transnational corporations*, aimed at preserving and protecting their special interests and dominant influence in order to obstruct and thwart the processes of political, economic, and social transformation. These

---

[36] See the full list in ibid.
[37] 'Belgrade Declaration of the Conference of Non-Aligned Foreign Ministers' in A/33/206: 63.
[38] 'Colombo Political Declaration' in A/31/197: 50.
[39] The Declarations are contained in A/9330 and A/31/197, respectively. 'The Non-Aligned Summit in Algiers of that year [1973] recommended the formation of a Non-Aligned News Agencies Pool as an alternative to the "Big Five" news agencies, and it produced an Action Programme for Economic Cooperation which pointed to a link between colonialism and communication' (Alleyne 1995: 121).
[40] 'Interference in the Internal Affairs of States' in A/31/197: 46–47.

policies of aggression are for the most part being implemented by a wide range of indirect and highly subtle and sophisticated techniques such as *economic aggression, subversion, and defamation of governments* directed at destabilization of states and their institutions.[41]

'Although the process of decolonization had made significant headway', independence 'as distinct from merely formal sovereignty' seemed endangered by 'indirect and highly subtle and sophisticated techniques', including through economic means ('official as well as private') and in informational and communicative dimensions ('defamation of governments').[42] Two years later it was during a meeting of the Foreign Ministers of the Non-Aligned Movement that interference was described not just as 'one of the most serious problems in the world today', but as 'carried out by means of state power and through other national and international political and economic organizations and institutions, of an official or private nature, *especially the transnational corporations and mass media on a global scale*'.[43]

This meeting is suggestive of a trajectory of the intervention debate that seems underappreciated. In light of new problems—including the 'instability of the international monetary situation', fractured faith in a world economy that seemed Northern at its core, and, as I will discuss, the infrastructure and implications of advancements in information and communication technologies—a NIEO and NWICO were to be built into the society of states.[44] But instead of asking 'what were the historical meanings of the NIEO or NWICO?', the next question for our purposes must be: 'what was, in more or less substantive terms, the discursive relationship of the intervention concept to these new international orders?'[45]

Permanent sovereignty over natural resources and the transnational corporations

As for the developed countries, the concept of human solidarity should cause them to feel repugnance at the fact that a group of corporations can with impunity interfere in the most vital workings of the life of a nation, even going so far as to disrupt it completely...

---

[41] Ibid.: 46. Emphasis added. Sri Lanka references the special chapter in its call for a second non-intervention declaration in A/C.1/32/PV.55: 43.
[42] A/31/197: 46.
[43] A/33/206: 17. Emphasis added.
[44] Sri Lanka, A/C.1/31/PV.55: 10.
[45] On the meanings of the NIEO and NWICO, see e.g. Murphy 2005 and Alleyne 1995 respectively. On the Non-Aligned Movement and its role in the creation of these new orders, see Singham and Hune 1986: 25–32.

International action must be directed towards serving the man who enjoys no privileges but who suffers and toils: the miner in Cardiff and the *fellah* in Egypt; the cocoa farmer in Ghana or the Ivory Coast, and the peasant of the plateaux of South America; the fisherman in Java and the coffee farmer in Kenya or Colombia … It is the peoples, all the peoples south of the Río Bravo, that stand up to shout, 'Enough—no more dependence', 'an end to intervention'; to affirm the sovereign right of all developing nations freely to dispose of their natural resources.[46]

Chilean President Salvador Allende was speaking before the General Assembly in December 1972. Non-intervention, from the viewpoint of Chile, of Peru, of Latin America, of the South more generally, had come to serve a distinct international-economic purpose; the G77 declared repeatedly that 'international economic relations should be based on full respect for the principles of equality among states and non-intervention in internal affairs'.[47]

And in the General Assembly, echoing discursive practice at UNCTAD (UN Conference on Trade and Development), the concept was being specified in terms of nationalization, transfer, regulation, and supervision of foreign investment and property, usually in regard to transnational corporations—each of the 1977, 1978, and 1979 Secretary-General reports on non-interference contained references to the transnational corporations and misappropriated natural wealth.[48] In the Programme of Action on the Establishment of a NIEO, 'non-interference' appears explicitly—in its section on 'regulation and control over the activities of transnational corporations'— and in the Charter of Economic Rights and Duties (Article 2, Chapter 2 of that Charter), it is declared that, given the right of every state to full sovereignty over its wealth, natural resources, and economic activities, 'transnational corporations shall not intervene in the internal affairs of a host state'.[49] The international-economic uses of non-intervention were of course not limited to these themes, but it is with them that the concept entered into a practical relationship. They provide one of the clearest illustrations of the use of intervention language in the context of the NIEO.[50]

Allende had anchored his UN speech in an account of what he called a 'historic act of reclamation'—'we have nationalized our basic resources. We have nationalized copper'.[51] 'Our economy could no longer tolerate the state of subordination implied in the 80 percent of its exports in the hands of a small

---

[46] A/PV.2096: 9.
[47] See e.g. 'Manila Declaration and Programme of Action' in UNCTAD 1977: 109–127.
[48] A/32/164; A/32/165; A/33/216; A/34/193; A/35/505. See e.g. Suriname in A/32/164: 9–10.
[49] A/RES/3202(S-VI); A/RES/3281(XXIX).
[50] On intervention as a language to protest, among other things, debt traps and exploitative forms of tied aid, see e.g. Thomas 1985.
[51] A/PV.2096: 2.

group of large, foreign companies', companies that had 'exploited Chile's copper for many years, in the last 42 years alone taking out more than $4,000 million in profits although their initial investment was no more than $30 million'.[52] He gave an extreme contrast: 'in my country there are 700,000 children who will never be able to enjoy life in a normal human way because during the first eight months of life they did not receive the minimum amount of protein'.[53] '[W]e have not confiscated the great foreign copper-mining companies ... however, we have put right a longstanding injustice by deducting from the amount of compensation the profits over 12 per cent per annum which those companies have obtained since 1955', and hence nationalized copper mines 'with scrupulous regard for domestic legislation but also respect for the norms of international law'.[54]

Were norms of non-intervention among them? We should see again that members of international society did not provide a universal reply to this problem, but rather gave multiple and conflicting answers; the fate of foreign investment and the riches as much as the authority of the transnational corporations opened up another front in ongoing contestation.[55] If to the host state the act of nationalization was a reclamation of what was rightfully theirs, then from the perspective of an aggrieved guest or visitor that wrongful act was a matter of private property protection or—less frequently, but crucially still—the well-being, security, even the human rights and property rights of citizens abroad who, went one legal argument at the time, were harmed by alleged expropriations.[56] In this respect, was not the nationalizing of Chile's mining companies akin to a kind of larceny, theft, or robbery in domestic life—under the threat of domestic courts backed by police and military might, and without the payment of 'adequate, prompt, and effective' compensation, did not such a 'confiscation' constitute an interference in affairs for which the United States was primarily responsible?[57]

One prominent reply from the G77 states often went as follows: an act of nationalization by an impoverished state was not an act of intervention, but rather 'an act of development'.[58] At bottom, it was 'an act of reaffirmation of sovereignty' that was an 'unavoidable motive force behind development' as well as the realization of a NIEO.[59] Algerian President Houari Boumédiène in

[52] Ibid.
[53] Ibid.
[54] Ibid.
[55] See e.g. Pahuja 2011: 95–171.
[56] See generally Fleming 1973.
[57] For the US-aligned response, see e.g. comments of John Rehm, Assistant Legal Adviser for the Department of State, in Rehm 1967. See Fleming 1973.
[58] On the right to development, see Whelan 2015.
[59] Cuba, A/PV.2227: 4.

the General Assembly's Sixth Special Session: nationalization was a 'means of liberation' aimed at 'freeing our natural resources from foreign domination', becoming in this way a 'fundamental requisite to economic development'.[60] The argument at times was related to a status of underdevelopment called a function of the structural injustices and dispossessions of formal colonialism.[61] But it was also about the denial of sovereign equality on account of ongoing or more recent arrangements. Nationalization was owed a special status as non-intervention because of contemporary machinations of private companies in host states' domestic affairs at the expense of self-determination: it 'tears down the barrier that a foreign company erects between us, as producers, and our clients and suppliers' and accommodates a 'transition from relations of exploitation to relations of equality'.[62]

There were at this time three prevalent ways of categorizing the transnational corporations in international-societal debate: first, as agents of states—as if the West 'accepted the principle of the right of people to self-determination only when they had succeeded in setting up the institutions and machinery that would perpetuate the system of pillage established in the colonial era'; second, as agents of themselves, as nomadic subjects with some substantial degree of independence—as in, 'Merchants have no country of their own … they have no ties with the soil. All they are interested in is the source of their profits'; and third, as extensions of international-economic structure—as manifestations of an unfettered capitalist system and the 'tragedy of underdevelopment'.[63] The most important point is that by the mid-1970s it was increasingly believed that not only governments but also 'foreign companies and consortia' were independently capable of undertaking intervention, operating at times above or between states, in addition to below or as state proxies.[64] If one part of the argument was about stolen profits and inhibited economic diversification—the so-called corporate hammer to 'the nails of foreign dependency'—then the other was about corporate will to systematically influence or subvert the operation of host states' systems of law, or to sabotage and replace governments that dared to restrict their freedom of action.[65] Allende himself cited documents before the General Assembly revealing 'dark designs' of the International Telephone and Telegraph Corporation, which proved that the corporation itself had 'suggested to the United

---

[60] Algeria, A/PV.2208: 6.
[61] See e.g. the comments of Peru in A/PV.2213: 1–4.
[62] Ibid.: 6.
[63] 'Merchants have no country of their own …'. These were the words of Thomas Jefferson, quoted by Allende in A/PV.2096: 6.
[64] Chile: '[t]here can also be intervention by foreign companies or consortia' (A/33/216: 7).
[65] Cuba, A/PV.2227.

States Government', not the other way around, that the CIA 'should intervene in the political events in Chile' so as to 'overthrow my government within a period of six months'.[66] 'I have in my briefcase the document, dated October 1971, which contains the 18 points of that plan.'[67]

There was knowledge, then, of non-intervention as reining in the transnational corporations, of disciplining and keeping a closer watch on their activities. Left to their own devices, or to the devices of their own governments, the corporations were known to have failed to respect the sanctity of both national responsibilities and international commons—they were liable for vast exploitations of natural resources, yes, but also for having failed to respect the self-determination of peoples. Existing international-economic structures provided tacit incentives for this sort of behaviour, rewarding the transnational corporations when they ought to have penalized them, and contributing to their growth and expansion at the expense of the nations and peoples for whom the foreign corporations were supposed to have played guests, not de facto hosts. And yet to demand a kind of international code of conduct for corporations and their resource extraction was not clearly to withdraw from economic globalization.[68]

There was knowledge, too, of the positive face of this new non-interventionism, of legitimate international actions to be taken to uphold or even enforce shared responsibilities. To illustrate again through the Chilean case: there was to be established a 'permanent machinery for protection and solidarity regarding copper', which, like the Organization of Petroleum Exporting Countries (OPEC), could in ideal circumstances form the 'nucleus of what should be an organization of all third world countries to protect and defend all commodities, mineral, and hydrocarbons as well as agricultural'.[69] To quote Juan Velasco Alvarado of Peru: if 'the buyers' marts set the cold and inhuman machinery of international trade in motion' then the producers' associations sought to break a cycle of foreign control over the economic destinies of the exploited, and to use their common economic pull to serve the broader cause of human rights and development, often as part of a protest against racism and colonialism.[70]

The international action of OPEC was hence described in Third World practice both as 'an example and a source of hope'.[71] '[N]o action could have

---

[66] A/PV.2096: 4.
[67] Ibid.
[68] On the nature of the NIEO as an expression of, not a retreat from, globalization, see Bockman 2015. See also Gilman 2015.
[69] A/PV.2096: 8.
[70] A/PV.2213: 2.
[71] Algeria, A/PV.2208: 4.

fitted more neatly into the logic of the basic concerns of the developing countries than what was undertaken by the oil-exporting countries.'[72] According to this strain of argument, through its price-setting, production targets, and embargoes, OPEC was to its members an 'exercise of their sovereignty', and a 'common front' to 'challenge the omnipotence of the monopolies and the imperialist states' that were 'unscrupulously interfering' in 'the domestic affairs' of underdeveloped states, depriving peoples of their fundamental human rights.[73] Seemingly interventionary action was practised as internationalist, not interventionist; for example it was called by Libyan oil minister 'Izz al-Din al-Mabruk a most legitimate 'collective action' taken on the basis of UN resolutions on the subject of 'the permanent sovereignty of nations over their natural wealth and resources'.[74]

The critique of OPEC-driven international pressure is well known, the debate over the NIEO at large having been marred by the 1973–1974 oil crisis and 1973 Arab–Israeli War.[75] 'The oil weapon' was a bludgeon outlawed if not by the Charter itself then surely by agreements like the Friendly Relations Declaration.[76] In 1979, after the adoption of that year's General Assembly resolution on non-interference, a related resolution on the 'inadmissibility of the policy of hegemonism' was being debated.[77] Yehuda Zvi Blum, the delegate for Israel and Professor of International Law, took the floor. If non-intervention recalled the duty of states to refrain, inter alia, from 'economic coercion', and even from 'all forms of pressure', then the Israeli delegation held that 'Arab oil-exporting countries have been guilty of all such actions, especially since the onset of the energy crisis in 1973, which they deliberately created.'[78] Arab 'petro-hegemonism' was inviting 'global economic chaos'; oil producers were 'using economic coercion in order to control peoples and relations between states'—in short, they had 'frequently interfered through the use of the oil weapon in the internal affairs of sovereign states'.[79]

And we would be remiss if we failed to mention that an argument was also made in favour of legitimate counter-intervention, including in the most extreme forms, to secure essential natural resources. While it remained largely in the realm of the hypothetical, the threat did hang over much of the debate. In one 1975 interview, for example, Henry Kissinger would maintain

---

[72] Ibid.
[73] Cuba, A/PV.2227: 1–2. On OPEC generally, see Garavini 2019.
[74] His 1970 speech to unnamed oil executives is quoted in Dietrich 2015: 73.
[75] See generally Dietrich 2015.
[76] See e.g. Kissinger 1975. See Luttwak 1984.
[77] Eventually adopted as A/RES/34/103.
[78] A/34/PV.103: 1898.
[79] Ibid.

that should the squeeze on oil become extreme—should there be a 'strangulation of the industrialized world'—the coercive interference of the OPEC countries might prompt the use of force in self-defence.[80] Edward Luttwak, writing some years later and partly as a reply to a 1975 study on the subject by the Congressional Research Service of the Library of Congress, would claim that self-described intervention for natural resources might be 'morally and legally justifiable' in the event of 'a political embargo', with the understanding that 'oil is indeed a special case, indeed unique', and that 'no conclusive case can be established which would deny the opportunity for illegal justification' when legal reasoning fails.[81]

Mass media and free flows of information on a global scale

Discursive shifts in relation to the economic occurred simultaneously with shifts in the informational-communicative. The period experienced a technological revolution—the appearance of hundreds of broadcast satellites, for instance, marked the advent of an era of advanced electronic systems that would knit states and peoples closer together, coinciding with the proliferation of colour television and, by the mid-1980s, the home computer. Such technologies generated new degrees of interdependence and complicated claims of domestic jurisdiction. Insofar as satellites were concerned in the 1970s, the problem of their ordering was related to the earlier attempts at managing outer space, particularly space as the 'province of all', to be protected from annexation by sovereign states.[82]

And yet side by side with every innovation arrived practices that were unwilling to let go of national oversight and control, or of self-determination in construing the principle of non-intervention. While outer space might have been imagined as part of the global commons, the use and effects of instruments and devices located in that zone were conceived in terms of action said to penetrate essentially domestic affairs.[83] To be sure, the problem of communicative and informational interventions by electronic means had of course appeared before—consider the controversies over shortwave

---

[80] Kissinger 1975: 172-173. In a December 1974 interview with *Business Week*, Kissinger held that the use of force against oil producers, for the purposes of securing essential natural resources, could not be ruled out 'in the gravest emergency'. Quoted in Dietrich 2017: 293.
[81] Luttwak 1984: 79, 94. See Congressional Research Service of the Library of Congress 1975.
[82] e.g. A/RES/2222(XXI).
[83] Comparisons of the problems of outer space law were being made to those of the law of the sea.

radio, for instance.[84] But they were being elevated to new levels of importance given the rapid technological progress at this moment in history. The problem was of renewed interest to international lawyers, for instance, some of whom were beginning to use the language of 'broadcast interventions' in the affairs of others.[85]

We should use this issue of broadcasting—more specifically of direct satellite broadcasting (DSB)—to give expression to a more general form. It is not that DSB was the only communicative method of concern, but, as with the issue of permanent sovereignty over natural resources and the use of intervention language in the NIEO, it provides an important illustration of the ways in which the idea of intervention was becoming entangled with the accusation of an ongoing 'colonisation of information' that underpinned the NWICO.[86] In particular the relatively simple model of the one-directional broadcast can be used to introduce the period's overarching 'free flow of information' debate.[87]

The puzzle—to quote the language that would appear in the General Assembly's 1982 declaration on the principles of international direct television broadcasting—was about ordering DSB in a 'manner compatible with the sovereign rights of states, including the principle of non-intervention, as well as the right of everyone to seek, receive, and impart information and ideas as enshrined in the relevant UN instruments' including in relation to human rights.[88] In 1972 a Soviet draft resolution on the subject appeared in the General Assembly.[89] A few months later UNESCO (UN Educational, Scientific and Cultural Organization) adopted a Declaration of Guiding Principles on the Use of Satellite Broadcasting for the Free Flow of Information, the Spread of Education and Greater Cultural Exchange.[90]

Among statespeople the following sorts of questions—all too familiar to us in the twenty-first century—were being debated: what were legitimate flows of information? What was the meaning of objectivity in international news? What is the relationship of truth to universal free speech and processes of communication? We might not normally think of diplomats as directly engaged with the question of truth, but interstate arguments along these lines, at times self-described as rooted in philosophical thought, were also claims

---

[84] 'Broadcast satellites open up the possibility of broadcast interventions on television similar to those achieved by shortwave on radio. The potential for abuse, however, is more frightening' (Gold 1971: 77).
[85] Ibid.
[86] See Sauvant 1981; Schiller 1986: 47–76; Stevenson 1988. For a recent take on the NWICO, particularly as a contestation of a liberal vision of the free flow of information, see Cong 2022.
[87] On free versus balanced flows, particularly in the context of DSB, see Dizard 1980.
[88] A/RES/37/92.
[89] A/8771.
[90] The Declaration is contained in A/AC.105/104.

about the meaning of intervention in the context of a NWICO. There were at least two sides to the interpretive contest as it related to DSB as a technological innovation transcending physical borders.

On the one hand was a kind of laissez-faire approach: that true freedom of information, and truth in free information, was freedom of information without international regulation. George H. W. Bush—serving, in 1972, as UN Ambassador—appeared before the General Assembly to invoke John Stuart Mill in *On Liberty*: 'truth has no chance but in proportion as every side of it, every opinion which embodies any fraction of the truth, not only finds advocates, but is so advocated as to be listened to'.[91] The many sides of truth would reveal themselves only through transactions of information without inhibition; to interfere with the 'free market of ideas' would be to interfere with a process producing ever more truthful results. There could hence be 'no adequate basis for drawing up definitive international arrangements to govern satellite community broadcasts, let alone direct broadcasts'.[92] The United States could not accept a proposal that called into question its 'strong 200-year-old belief in the free exchange of information' that served as 'a primary basis for the maintenance of democratic institutions' and for prosperity in global interdependence.[93]

A crude form of the argument was that the more discussion was added, the greater the reflection, the closer to truth and to democracy we would come. A more sophisticated version suggested that at least some minimum unregulated area of thought was a necessary condition for the attainment of truth and greater freedom.[94]

Now, there can be no doubt that the Non-Aligned Movement and Third World project disagreed with an unlimited notion of 'letting be'—of leaving states to broadcast internationally in any way that they wished—but I want to note that on DSB a number of Western and allied states were also deviating from the American line in influential ways.[95] Spanish representative José Luis López-Schümmer praised references to John Stuart Mill, but invited his fellow delegates to consider at least equally the writings of another great European thinker, José Ortega y Gasset, who said: 'Life like freedom,

---

[91] A/C.1/PV.1861: 6.
[92] Ibid.
[93] Ibid.
[94] Mark Alleyne notably argued in 1995 that such a free flow argument can be seen as rooted in liberal-democratic but also liberal trade theory. See Alleyne 1995: 39–65.
[95] Alleyne quotes David Gallick, former Chief of Public Sector Broadcasting Policy in the Canadian Department of Communications, on American dominance in the sphere of DBS: 'It is a strong challenge to Canada's cultural identity and economic development. Perhaps it is not an overstate to suggest it is a threat to Canada's sovereignty as well' (Alleyne 1995: 7, 8). See also, on e.g. South Korea's ambivalent attitude to the NWICO, Kang 1988.

Emancipatory intervention and the New International Orders 179

in the political sense, is what man [sic] lives within the framework of his chosen institutions.'[96] International-political freedom had emerged and ought to emerge, argued López-Schümmer, within a richly institutionalized framework involving both the 'principle of non-interference' and that of 'freedom of information'.[97] '[I]n view of the new reality which the conquest of space denotes, conventional and detailed regulations' around international information and communication were to prevent 'hegemony', to ensure 'small and medium-sized nations or groups of nations or States will be protected'.[98]

From no side was it being argued that freedom of information was to be denied or restricted; rather from every side came an argument about how freedom was to be achieved, and the delineation of the non-intervention principle in relation to that particular freedom (freedom of information). Flows of information were free only when they were just and balanced. To quote Chile at the time: 'Obviously, we agree with such a principle [freedom of information], but the meaning attached to it by free men and peoples is very different from the meaning attached to it by imperialist monopolies.'[99] And to quote El Salvador: 'Information should be free, and in order to guarantee that freedom, which would be jeopardized by excesses and mystifications, it has to be regulated.'[100] To be sure, then, both smaller-power and Great Power conceptions of free flows of information implied information without intervention, but intervention, in non-aligned practice, was not to be conflated with international rules or international responsibility. To uphold shared responsibilities, to draw up and adopt international rules to govern DSB, was not to intervene; often it was precisely the opposite of intervention insofar as those responsibilities and rules protected sovereign equality and the UN-based human rights regime.

By what logic then was 'intervention' to be ascertained in free and global information flows? In a Southern design the most basic organizing principle was consent including the consent of affected states. 'No country could agree to broadcasts by satellite from other States of television programmes into its territory without its control and agreement. Such actions would constitute flagrant intervention in the internal affairs of States.'[101] They were often 'defended on the pretext of the free circulation of information and ideas', but as the history of radio broadcasting had shown—the Vietnamese delegation cited specifically the history of 'Radio Liberty, Radio Free Europe, the Voice

[96] A/C.1/PV.1868: 14.
[97] Ibid.
[98] Ibid.
[99] A/C.1/PV.1867: 12.
[100] A/C.1/PV.1868: 2.
[101] Mongolia, A/SPC/36/SR.19: 4.

of Israel', to which Radio Moscow might have been added—information exchange risked becoming a 'battle for the mind'.[102] The Ministers of Education of the Andean Region—Bolivia, Chile, Colombia, Ecuador, Peru, and Venezuela—met at Bogotá to declare as much. During UN debate the Colombian representative read from their agreements:

> Unilateral management of broadcasts via satellite, whether practised by one State or by non-governmental bodies, might easily lend itself to abuses disturbing the customs, scales of values, and the cultures of the receiving countries, thus entailing intervention in affairs exclusively within the competence of States ... Satellite broadcasting from one State to another, even when carried on by non-governmental bodies, should take place only with the prior and explicit consent of the Governments of the receiving countries.[103]

'Freedom of information is invoked', Chile acknowledged, 'but that freedom is the exclusive right of the transmitter and not the receiver ... The latter's freedom is not taken into account.'[104] This was the Andean position but it was also the non-aligned and Soviet position, its application giving rise to unresolved questions regarding, for instance, the risk of signal spillover from a consenting neighbor into a non-consenting one, in light of technical limitations—now long superseded—related to the cylindrical shape of transmissions.[105]

But perhaps even more interesting to note is that intervention was being constituted here on account of theories having to do with truth and truth-telling. Non-aligned states referred to a right and duty, described as non-interventionist, to combat the dissemination from outside of 'false or distorted news' and for a state to 'fully develop its system of information and mass media as an integral part of its overall national progress and with the aim of realizing its right to inform and be informed in an objective and integrated manner'.[106] To quote El Salvador: 'All countries have a right to ensure that information disseminated in which they are involved be objective, complete, and well-balanced.'[107] Notions of 'objectivity', 'completion', and 'balance' invited complex philosophical questions, of which state delegations were aware, and to which references were made.[108] But what basically

---

[102] Vietnam, A/SPC/36/SR.16: 10; see e.g. Ukraine, A/C.1/PV.1866: 9; Saudi Arabia, A/C.1/PV.1862: 12.
[103] A/PV.2081: 6–7.
[104] A/C.1/PV.1867: 12.
[105] See e.g. El Salvador in A/C.1/PV.1868: 4.
[106] See the non-aligned draft resolution in A/34/827: 10. A/C.1/34/L.56.
[107] El Salvador, A/C.1/PV.1868: 3.
[108] See e.g. ibid.

needs to be understood is that, in non-aligned practice, false information and existing structures of communication were a function, to quote former Jamaican Prime Minister Michael Manley on dependence and destabilization in the Caribbean, of 'the skill with which empire fashions the mind of the governed'.[109]

One tactic then was to explain an international 'lack of objectivity' as linked fundamentally to the maintenance of foreign rule and neocolonialism. The 'survival of the colonial era', wrote Tunisian Minister of Information Mustapha Masmoudi, was 'reflected in the often tendentious interpretation of news concerning the developing countries.'[110] 'Tendentious interpretation' consisted, for example, 'in highlighting events whose significance, in certain cases, is limited or even non-existent' and 'in collecting isolated facts and presenting them as a "whole"'.[111] By 'keeping silent on situations unfavourable to the interests of the countries of origin of these media', coverage of 'world events' and shared international experiences became coverage in favour of the 'interests of certain societies ... distorted by reference to moral, cultural, or political values peculiar to certain states, in defiance of the values or concerns of other nations'.[112] And in sharp contrast to the domestic laws of many industrialized societies, there was no 'right of correction' of false information in international society.[113]

Observed Pakistan in the First Committee: '[f]rom the debate it is clear that misgivings exist not only with regard to freedom of dissemination' (a freedom to be understood primarily in terms of consent of the receiver, to recall the first point I have been making in this section) 'but also with regard to its quality and extent'.[114] Now we can see how 'quality and extent' might have referred to regulation on falsehoods (a second point I am making). But 'quality and extent' might also have referred to values outside of the straightforwardly 'false' or the fake. To add a third key point: what was non-interventionist information was information aimed 'not at increasing tensions among states but at decreasing them; at increasing understanding among peoples', at achieving good neighbourliness and friendly relations.'[115]

Several delegations clarified that freedom of information was not a 'freedom to misinform', but nor did it constitute 'freedom of propaganda for ideas of hostility, violence, racial hatred' or freedom for 'pirate broadcasts whereby

---

[109] Manley's *Jamaica: Struggle in the Periphery*, published in 1982, is quoted in Alleyne 1995: 11.
[110] Masmoudi 1979: 174.
[111] Ibid.
[112] Ibid.
[113] Ibid.: 175.
[114] A/C.1/PV.1868: 16.
[115] Soviet Union, A/C.1/PV.1861: 8.

the stronger mercilessly infringe the economic interests of the less strong'.[116] In discussions of the Secretary-General's third report on non-intervention, Sri Lanka laid out a conception of intervention as defamation, which was not necessarily related to truth: it was 'very significant, because there are ways whereby the reputation, prestige, and standing of leaders in countries are undermined or attacked' so as to 'induce the people of those countries to replace them by others' amenable to foreign interest.[117]

The groundwork had been laid one year earlier at a ministerial conference of the non-aligned countries on the field of information, held in New Delhi from 8 to 13 July 1976. Indian Prime Minister Indira Gandhi delivered the inaugural address: 'in spite of political sovereignty, most of us who have emerged from a colonial or semi-colonial past continue to have a rather unequal cultural and economic relationship with our respective former overlords'.[118] She set the tone for the deliberations, having in mind perhaps, it was observed at the time, Allende's overthrow of 1973 and the military dictatorship of Augusto Pinochet:

> The media of the powerful countries want to depict the governments of their erstwhile colonies as inept and corrupt and their people as yearning for the good old days. This cannot be attributed entirely to the common human failing of nostalgia. To a large extent there is a deliberate purpose. Leaders who uphold their national interests and resist the blandishments of multinational corporations and agencies, are denigrated and their image falsified in every conceivable way.[119]

Unacceptable, then, were transmissions not just propagandistic but also chauvinistic; that sought objectives incompatible with friendly relations, including objectives that imposed themselves on the self-determination of the people. The 'principle of the free flow of information should not authorize technically advanced states to use satellites to disseminate to other states television programmes that might affect their cultural identity'; 'such a practice would be ... an obvious interference in its internal affairs'.[120] When the

---

[116] See Bulgaria, A/C.1/PV.1862: 11; Mongolia, A/C.1/PV.1868: 8; ibid.
[117] A/C.1/32/PV.55: 41.
[118] Quoted in Trần 1976: 44.
[119] Quoted in ibid. Trần Văn Dĩnh, the Temple University Professor of Politics and Communications and former South Vietnamese diplomat who had attended the Bandung Conference, argued in a paper on 'cultural imperialism' and the NWICO that non-aligned countries 'must have had in mind the case of Chile' where 'a combination of economic strangulation and mass communication manipulations' contributed to the success of the CIA-supported *coup d'état*. He quoted the *New York Times* of 5 December 1975: 'the CIA covertly channeled $11.5 million to El Mercurio, the largest paper in Chile, to insure anti-Allende coverage'. See ibid.: 48.
[120] Tunisia, A/SPC/35/SR.18: 13. See also e.g. Indonesia's citing of 'reasonable restraints to safeguard the cultural identity of the peoples of the recipient states' in A/SPC/34/SR.19: 12.

Belgian representative spoke in terms of a 'free flow of information', the argument from Yakov Malik, the Soviet Ambassador to the UN, was in short: whose free flow, in promotion of whose values, and what rights for the receiving state?[121] No one had the right to instil 'polluted' flows of information 'in the minds of other peoples to whom these new "ethical values" are completely alien'.[122] He 'fully agreed with the representative of Brazil who was quite right in saying that freedom of information must also entail respect for the sovereignty of states'.[123]

But, as with the NIEO, there was also a positive face to the intervention concept as it fit into a NWICO. A NWICO meant regulating out interventionist information considered false and unfriendly, but also regulating in solidarist news and information perceived to be both true and emancipatory. Smaller-power designations were turning again to a logic of self-determination, domestic jurisdiction, and human rights such that NWICO commitments were construed by others as infringing upon areas protected by the non-intervention principle. In all this then, non-intervention in the context of a particular interpretation of 'free information' chimed with a particular interpretation of 'free trade' (in fact Argentina was defending a right of states to 'dispose freely of information' in the same breath as a corresponding right of states to 'dispose freely of their natural resources').[124]

As the Indian delegation explained at the Tunis Symposium on the Mass Media in March 1976: if the 'one-sided and loaded flows of information from the industrialized nations to the developing world' had come to be seen, in an 'elitist neocolonial link-up', as 'the very epitome of the flow of information', then 'any interference in this unequal flow comes to be viewed by this section as an interference with its freedom'.[125]

Yet a more positive freedom of information meant 'the right of each nation to inform the world public about its interests, its aspirations, and its social and cultural values', which would imply the elimination of monopolies—state-based and transnational private—on information flows through the international establishment and promotion of a 'plurality of sources and channels of information'.[126] Masmoudi claimed that '80 percent of world

---

[121] A/C.1/PV.1870: 9–10; the Belgian delegate's comments in ibid.: 6–7.
[122] Soviet Union, ibid.: 9.
[123] Ibid. See the comments of the Brazilian delegate in ibid.: 7–8.
[124] A/SPC/33/SR.9: 12.
[125] The records of the Tunis Symposium on the Mass Media, co-organized by Cuba, Mexico, Sri Lanka, Tunisia, and Yugoslavia, are quoted in Schiller 1978: 37–38.
[126] See the MacBride Resolution (Resolution 4/19), named after Irish former Foreign Affairs Minister and Nobel Laureate Seán MacBride, who served as President of the Commission, adopted at the 1980 UNESCO General Conference, reprinted in UNESCO 1980: 68–71. See International Commission for the Study of Communication Problems 1980.

news was emanating from major transnational agencies' based in the industrialized North, and in terms of content, only '20 to 30 percent of news coverage' was devoted to the developing countries, countries which represented over 75 per cent of the world's population.[127] Almost totally captured were the radio frequencies—the developed countries controlled 90 per cent of the entire spectrum.[128] The Declaration of the Ministerial Conference of Non-Aligned Countries on Decolonization of Information, adopted at New Delhi on 13 July 1976, hence affirmed that if the old system of information confined 'what should be known, and how it should be made known, into the hands of the few', and reduced non-aligned countries 'to being passive recipients of information', the new system was to encourage 'constructive and wide-ranging co-operation among themselves for achieving greater collective self-reliance'.[129]

In one such act of international co-operation, Ministers of Information and news agency directors from sixty-two non-aligned states moved to establish the Non-Aligned News Agencies Pool (NANAP) with the understanding that it 'would supplement and expand the existing flow of news' that was Northern-dominated.[130] By 1983, the Pool had grown to more than eighty-three news agencies from Africa, Asia, Latin America, and Eastern Europe.[131] And earlier, in places like Sarajevo in 1977, non-aligned states were founding similar initiatives like the Broadcasting Organizations of the Non-Aligned Countries for the exchange of alternative radio and television programmes.[132] We can see then how 'acts of free information' were much like Boumédiène's 'acts of development', which in upholding the duty to promote human rights and the self-determination of peoples, were anti-colonial in a broad sense that we might call emancipatory. The press pool of the non-aligned states was not just, in a negative formulation, a kind of censorship board. More positively, it was a medium for 'stating positions on critical confrontation issues' perceived as often marginalized by Western-dominated press, and for 'countering tendentious reporting and mass media campaigns'.[133] Here we need to recall that the Mass Media Declaration adopted at the UNESCO Paris Conference—the

---

[127] Masmoudi 1979: 185.
[128] Ibid.
[129] 'Declaration of the Ministerial Conference of Non-Aligned Countries on Decolonization of Information' in Nordenstreng, Manet, and Kleinwächter 1986: 287.
[130] Yugoslavia, A/SPC/33/SR.45: 3. See Non-Aligned News Agencies Pool (Coordinating Committee) 1983.
[131] For an assessment, including of the 'Western counterattack' against the news agency pool of the non-aligned countries and related initiatives, see Nordenstreng and Hannikainen 1984: 3–36.
[132] See e.g. Popović 1977.
[133] Pinch 1987: 169; this 'countering' language comes from the declaration of the 8th non-aligned summit, A/41/697: 130.

outcome of eight years of consultations pushed by non-aligned campaigns, 'a triumph of patient efforts' according to then-Director-General of UNESCO Amadou-Mahtar M'Bow, when the 'probabilities of failure seemed great'—also referred to the contributions by mass media to the 'promotion of human rights and to countering racism, apartheid, and incitement to war', which could not be seen as interventionary against the background of 'international relations in accordance with the new conditions and demands of the contemporary world'.[134] And at the Havana Summit of the Non-Aligned Movement in 1979, the adopted final declaration took note of a number of related recommendations of the Intergovernmental Coordinating Council in the Field of Information of Non-Aligned Countries. It ultimately requested:

> member countries of the Movement to support, through their information media, the liberation movements, particularly those in Southern Africa, with a view to putting an end to the negative and biased information about them, and to support the initiative to organize the year of information about their struggle.[135]

At the Havana Summit, ninety-five non-aligned states also welcomed the creation of a pan-African news agency, one that would contribute to the 'just cause of the African liberation struggle, thus contributing to the establishment of a new international information order'.[136]

Revisiting the UN's Second Declaration on Non-Intervention

It is from the standpoint of the new international orders and a commitment to a more total emancipation that we should approach the UN's Second Declaration on Non-Intervention. We need to see 1981 as the coming together of a series of recommendations reflective of the NIEO and NWICO that extended the anti-colonial theory of intervention as it had to do with support for national liberation, previously discussed in the context of the First Declaration on Non-Intervention of 1965 and the Friendly Relations Declaration of 1970. The decisive diplomatic moves for a second declaration on non-intervention were made during the twentieth anniversary of the Non-Aligned Movement—the point was to institutionalize, in the UN, designs that had figured into newer practices of intervention and non-intervention in the

---

[134] Quoted in UNESCO 1983: 13; see the comments of Yugoslavia in A/SPC/33/SR.45: 2.
[135] A/34/542: 93.
[136] Ibid.: 94.

movement, and to hence institutionalize types of knowledge that, according to non-aligned practitioners, followed from previous agreements and needed more explicit recognition.

'Why we consider a declaration to be necessary in spite of all those that we have is so that the forms of interference and intervention to which we take exception ... may be clearly identified', explained Sri Lanka in the First Committee.[137] 'Also a declaration could contain a specific and clear indication of the measures that states might take and the means they might adopt to prevent any form of interference in the external or internal affairs of other states.' That is, the new declaration could also enumerate positive formulations of non-intervention and internationalist duties to be upheld by states and the international community.[138]

In 1979 a draft declaration, sponsored by Algeria, Botswana, Cuba, Cyprus, Ethiopia, Madagascar, Sri Lanka, and Yugoslavia (subsequently also by Bangladesh and Vietnam), made its rounds through the UN.[139] It held that non-intervention comprehended five parts. One part had to do with all types of interference taken against the 'personality of the state', another part with protecting against subversion, including the recruitment of mercenaries for use against other states.[140] The third, also familiar, concerned the obligation of all states to 'observe, promote, and respect all human rights and fundamental freedoms'.[141] This part stated clearly that: *'[e]fforts by the international community to accord priority to causes and cases, recognized by the General Assembly of the United Nations, of massive and flagrant violations of human rights of peoples and persons shall not be considered as interference in the internal affairs of states*'.[142] The same part specified that 'nothing' in the declaration was to prejudice 'the right of self-determination, freedom, and independence of peoples under colonial or racist regimes' or forms of 'alien' or 'foreign' occupation, as well as 'their right to wage both political and armed struggle' and to 'seek and receive support in accordance with the principles of the Charter'.[143]

Two final parts then focused on concerns of the NIEO and NWICO respectively.[144] The first looked to the economic, holding that 'every state has the sovereign and inalienable right to freely determine its own economic

---

[137] A/C.1/32/PV.55: 42.
[138] Ibid.
[139] Draft in A/34/827: 5–11. A/C.1/34/L.56.
[140] A/34/827: 7, 9.
[141] Ibid.: 10.
[142] Ibid. Emphasis added.
[143] Ibid.
[144] Ibid.: 8, 10.

Emancipatory intervention and the New International Orders 187

system and to develop its international economic relations in accordance with the will of its people'.[145] To that end, the declaration named a number of substantive provisions, a few of which deserve our attention:

- No state should be subjected to action which ... denies to it the right to exercise permanent sovereignty over its natural resources
- The denial of economic assistance or the withholding of economic assistance aimed at influencing the path of economic development chosen by a state, is contrary to the principle of non-interference
- No state or other political or economic agency or institution shall interfere in the sovereign right of states to regulate their foreign economic activity and exercise their authority over foreign investment within their national jurisdiction[146]

If the first of these two parts paraphrased logics common to debates regarding natural resources and the NIEO, then the second applied the same treatment to international information flows and the NWICO. '[E]very state has the right to fully develop its system of information and mass media as an integral part of its overall national progress' in accordance with 'its right to inform and to be informed in an objective and integrated manner'.[147] To this end:

- No state or group of states shall interfere with the right of other states to develop their information system and to combat the monopolizing of information
- States shall respect the right of all states and peoples to be informed in a rapid, objective, and complete manner
- States have the right and duty to combat ... the dissemination of false or distorted news[148]

In light of failures to collectively agree on this ten-power draft, a working group was set up that replaced annual Secretary-General reports on this subject matter with a view of 'finalizing the elaboration of a declaration'.[149] But in fact what we eventually saw in the 1981 Declaration was very much an extension of the ten-power draft.

In the adopted form of the Second Declaration on Non-Intervention, the fuller meaning of the principle of non-intervention was resolved in not five

---

[145] Ibid.: 8.
[146] Ibid.: 8–9.
[147] Ibid.: 10.
[148] Ibid.
[149] See A/RES/35/159.

but three categories: rights of states; duties of states; and matters of both rights and duties.[150] Operative paragraphs under category one stressed the sovereign and inalienable right of a state 'to exercise permanent sovereignty over its natural resources'.[151] The very next paragraph was about:

> the right of states and peoples to have free access to information and to develop fully, without interference, their system of information and mass media and *to use their information media in order to promote their political, social, economic, and cultural interests and aspirations*, based, inter alia, on the relevant articles of the Universal Declaration of Human Rights and the principles of the new international information order.[152]

Under category two was the duty 'of a state to abstain from any defamatory campaign' or other measures which 'constitute interference or intervention in the internal or external affairs of another state', including 'the duty of a state not to use its external economic assistance programme or adopt any multilateral or unilateral economic reprisal or blockade', and to 'prevent the use of transnational and multilateral corporations under its jurisdiction and control as instruments of political pressure or coercion'.[153] Category three specified 'the right and duty of states to combat, within their constitutional prerogatives, the dissemination of false or distorted news', interpreted as 'interference in the internal affairs of other states' and 'harmful to the promotion of peace, cooperation, and friendly relations among states and nations'.[154]

And once again, non-intervention was to serve as a bulwark in an international struggle against colonialism and apartheid, a move cast in the language of universal human rights. 'Nothing' was to prejudice in any manner the right to self-determination of 'peoples under colonial domination, foreign occupation or racist regimes', and 'nothing' was to prejudice the right of those peoples to 'seek and receive' international support for their struggle.[155] All states had a right and duty to 'fully support' these struggles, which were understood in the context of the broader 'right and duty of states to observe, promote, and defend all human rights and fundamental freedoms within their own national territories', and to 'work for the elimination of mass and

---

[150] A/RES/36/103: 78–80.
[151] Ibid.: 79.
[152] Ibid. Emphasis added.
[153] Ibid.: 80.
[154] Ibid.
[155] Ibid.

flagrant violations of the right of nations and peoples … in particular, for the elimination of apartheid and all forms of racism and racial discrimination'.[156]

A Northern, and in this case Western, position on the last of these parts has been discussed in detail in Chapters 3 and 4. On the provisions that were newer, encompassing the NIEO and NWICO, the West was flatly rejectionist.

The delegation of the United States noted in this respect that while there was 'much to commend' in the text, it was 'seriously flawed in many respects', among them the issue that it 'purports to create new rights and duties', which were not 'contained in the UN Charter or in international law'.[157] 'For example, in its paragraph on a new international information order and on the dissemination of information, the text directly contradicts the principles of the Universal Declaration on Human Rights, notably Article 19 of that Declaration, which affirms the right of everyone to receive and impart information across frontiers'.[158] It purported also 'to define new and hitherto unrecognized duties of states with regard to economic assistance and multinational corporations'—neither 'realistically' nor 'equitably'.[159]

In explanations of their negative votes, these states doubted 'the necessity of a new declaration on this subject [to supplement the Declaration of 1965]', noting the draft's 'highly controversial elements'.[160] No doubt the most controversial elements were those amenable to radical anti-colonial readings, in ways that I have discussed in previous chapters. For instance, the Irish delegation announced that it would not 'associate itself with the inclusion of an explicit endorsement of armed struggle' in a UN Declaration.[161] Also opposed was the resolution's call to 'refrain from any measure which would lead to the strengthening of existing military blocs'.[162]

But a vote against the Declaration was also a vote against 'a just and equitable international economic order' and the 'principles of the new international information order'.[163] Greece, for instance, made reference to 'elements to which we cannot subscribe', such as a paragraph limiting the 'right to information'.[164] Finland, abstaining, objected 'specifically to the way in which questions concerning human rights, the dissemination of information,

---

[156] Ibid.
[157] A/C.1/36/PV.51: 56.
[158] Ibid.
[159] Ibid.
[160] Austria, ibid.: 59–60.
[161] Ibid.: 61.
[162] 'I shall confine myself to referring to the absolute opposition of the French delegation to paragraph (ix) of part II of the draft declaration. This provision is aimed at dissuading states from collectively organizing their defense and security.' France, ibid.: 46–47.
[163] A/RES/36/103.
[164] A/C.1/36/PV.51: 57.

and the economic aspects of the principle of non-interference are dealt with.'[165] 'Had those paragraphs been put to separate vote, my delegation would have voted against them.'[166] The Second Declaration on Non-Intervention was adopted on 9 December 1981.[167]

1981: non-intervention beyond the superpower doctrines

What I have not done in this chapter is to assess the material outcomes of the NIEO and NWICO, and I have not tried to account for the origins of these proposals, except in relation to a global debate on intervention. In this new ordering of things, the NIEO and NWICO served as interlocking institutional geometries in a novel articulation of the anti-colonial theory of intervention in international society. And while of course the new international orders did not achieve their aims, it seems wrong to remember them simply as dead ends. They remind us that human rights and self-determination once seemed very hard to disentangle from the idea of what it is to intervene—across an increasing number of social dimensions.

An emancipatory theory of non-intervention, as it pertained to ongoing economic and cultural subordination, was not simply an interdiction, but also a prescription of international protective and humanitarian actions, including developmentalist actions. The way intervention was understood in the international-economic dimension was often similar to the way it was understood in international-information and international-communicative dimensions: a 'right to communicate' seemed comparable to a 'right to develop', rooted in claims about shared humanitarian duties of the international community. Here things like non-aligned producers' associations were constituted much like news agency pools. Located across both visions of international order—visions of the NWICO and NIEO—were the transnational corporations. If transnational corporations—media conglomerates as much as mining companies—were conceived as proxies of interventionist governments or agents in themselves, capable of meddling in domestic affairs, their global regulation and coordination realized the proper import of the non-intervention principle and UN-based human rights regime. To believe as much was to call into question the line often drawn between the public and private spheres.

---

[165] Ibid.: 58.
[166] Ibid.
[167] A/RES/36/103.

Moreover, the defeat of the emancipatory agenda of the intervention concept was not simply a function of persuasion. A significant part of the explanation has to do with political manoeuvres that deviated from a deliberative ideal; often, the rejoinder was withdrawal. We should take note here of the first formal American withdrawal from UNESCO in 1984. (President Reagan wrote in a letter to Congress dated 17 September 1981: 'We recognize the concerns of certain developing countries regarding imbalances in the present international flow of information and ideas. But we believe that the way to resolve these concerns does not lie in silencing voices or restricting access to the means of communication ... We do not feel we can continue to support a UNESCO that turns its back on the high purposes this organization was originally intended to serve.')[168] And we should find evidence of a withdrawal from the NIEO process, too, this time in the form of smokescreens and deferrals (in a Washington meeting on 24 May 1975, Kissinger to President Ford: 'I want to fuzz it up. I don't want to accept a New Economic Order but I don't want to confront [Boumédiène].' Ford's response: 'I see no reason to talk theory when we can in a practical way just screw up the negotiations.')[169]

To be sure, there are other stories to be told of self-determination and intervention in the 1970s and 1980s. One might have to do with international military actions justified, by a minority, as internationalist but condemned by most as severely interventionary, which in some cases delivered humanitarian outcomes of the highest order, and in others did much the opposite.[170] The illegitimacy of the Soviet use of force in Afghanistan from 1979 onwards and its condemnation in the General Assembly, including by a large majority of developing states, should not be obfuscated by Cuba's chairpersonship, at the time, of the Non-Aligned Movement.[171] But nor should it be remembered solely in terms of the Brezhnev Doctrine. In the eyes of many, Soviet abuses of the language of self-determination tarnished the promise of solidarist internationalism in general. Along the same lines, we ought to cite abuses of the idea of 'counter-intervention' and human rights protection adopted

---

[168] Quoted in Nordenstreng and Hannikainen 1984: 62. This was not the only reason, but it was an important reason, behind the US withdrawal. See Roach 1987.

[169] Quoted in Dietrich 2017: 289; see FRUS, 1973–1976: XXXI, Document 292.

[170] A theory of intervention as the denial of self-determination provides the basis of a rereading of, for instance, the 1979 cases of Vietnam in Cambodia and of Tanzania in Uganda. To what extent did such cases involve appeals to solidarist-internationalist, not humanitarian-interventionist, logics? Compare with Wheeler 2000: 78–136.

[171] See e.g. Jackson 1983: 66–69. On 14 January 1980 the General Assembly voted overwhelmingly—104 to 18—to demand that the Soviet Union withdraw its troops from Afghanistan. A/RES/ES-6/2.

in the Reagan era—in relation to Contras in Nicaragua and mujahideen in Afghanistan, for example.[172]

The Reagan-Kirkpatrick doctrine, describing itself as a reply to the Brezhnev Doctrine, is undoubtedly, then, part of the picture of this period, but only insofar as it has to do with a malaise in Third World organizing, a slowdown of smaller-power contestation in the UN, and a logic of exception to the rule of sovereign equality at the heart of non-alignment itself. 'A realistic policy which aims at protecting our own interest and assisting the capacities for self-determination of less developed nations', wrote Jeane Kirkpatrick, future US Ambassador to the UN, in the essay that would shape Reaganite foreign policy, 'will need to face the unpleasant fact that, if victorious, violent insurgency headed by Marxist revolutionaries is unlikely to lead to anything but totalitarian tyranny.'[173] Kirkpatrick and Allan Gerson would claim that 'the Reagan Doctrine rests on the claim that legitimate government depends on the consent of the governed and on its respect for the rights of citizens'; 'it was developed in response to Soviet claims of legitimacy in their imperial venture'; 'it expresses solidarity with the struggle for self-government as against one-party dictatorship', and yet also 'rejects the notion that any government must be respected; that is, it rejects the inviolability of sovereignty.'[174]

If the Reagan years coincided with the political demise of the Third World project, they also coincided with the ebb tide of anti-colonial intervention, both as a matter of peaceful coexistence and as a source of international legitimacy in the United Nations.

What I have been saying instead in this chapter is that, in the decades leading up to the end of the twentieth century, intervention as a global debate was not only about the intensification of Cold War dynamics or the capture by Cold Warriors, especially after détente, of vocabularies like intervention, sovereignty, and human rights.[175] Projects like the Reagan Doctrine, soon condemned by both the UN General Assembly and the International Court of Justice, ought not to draw our attention away from contestations associated with the NIEO and NWICO.[176] A compelling story of the non-aligned

---

[172] See e.g. Scheffer 1991.
[173] Kirkpatrick 1979.
[174] Kirkpatrick and Gerson 1991: 23, 21.
[175] Again to quote Kirkpatrick and Gerson: 'The Brezhnev Doctrine preserves foreign influence. The Reagan Doctrine restores self-government ... The desirable norm in a world of sovereign states in which the principle of *democratic self-determination* is respected' (Kirkpatrick and Gerson 1991: 31). Emphasis added.
[176] See Chesterman 2001: 93–94. In the Nicaragua case of 1986, the International Court of Justice found that the United States violated customary international law by 'training, arming, equipping, financing, and supplying the contra forces'. Yet, as the *New York Times* reported, and 'to the surprise of some lawyers, [the Court] then added that this doctrine does not apply to "the process of decolonization," suggesting that wars of national liberation may be justified in international law'. (Lewis 1986). And notably, on 2

initiative that was the Second Declaration on Non-Intervention of 1981, and of the challenge it posed to existing global order, is linked with a meaning of intervention rooted in self-determination and its denial by means of various forms of foreign pressure, but also with economic and cultural structures and technological change, within a politics of anti-colonialism and anti-racism. An emancipatory conception of intervention concerned itself with new international responsibilities of development in the context of a solidarist internationalism. To uphold these human rights-based and humanitarian responsibilities involved insistence on a range of abstract sovereign privilege subsumed by international laws and rules, but not a surrender of sovereign equality, nor a breach of the non-intervention principle. The meaning of the 1981 Declaration is also the meaning of the Bandung Spirit after formal independence had been won by the formerly colonized: a meaning, as ever, about acting 'not just as an adjunct of the First or Second World, but as a player in world affairs' and a meaning more specifically, by the late 1970s, about 'both economic subordination and cultural suppression—two of the major policies of imperialism'.[177]

November 1983, the General Assembly passed a resolution—adopted by 108 to 9 with 27 abstentions—that '[d]eeply deplore[d]' the US-led intervention of Grenada as a flagrant violation of international law (A/RES/38/7). See Chesterman 2001: 99–102.

[177] Prashad 2007: 45–46. See also Prashad 2012.

6
Liberal intervention and the Responsibilities to Protect

In the mid- to late twentieth century the internationalist responsibility to promote human rights and prevent atrocities—including, as a last resort, coercively, and against the wishes of the affected state—was also understood as an international responsibility not to intervene in the domestic affairs of states, as sovereign equals. By the turn of the century, a liberal interventionism largely overtook such positive connotations of what might have been called a solidarist non-interventionism. In this final chapter I reconsider how and to what extent intervention secured an international legitimacy in the post-Cold War period, and the ways in which the idea of the Responsibility to Protect (RtoP) has been contested by developing states.

The dawn of an era of humanitarian intervention, or what I will call liberal intervention for the sake of clarity, has been traced many times before.[1] At the turn of the millennium, discursive practice is said to have moved from a preoccupation with 'sovereignty as a right' to a convergence upon 'sovereignty as a responsibility'—that is, from an understanding of sovereignty 'with no strings attached', even as a 'licence to kill', to one that implied a duty, shared with the international community, to protect populations from large-scale oppression.[2] This shift in the terms of debate overlapped with another shift from 'humanitarian intervention' to 'RtoP', and marked the emergence, argued many, of a norm on which all agreed.[3] RtoP, wrote Ramesh Thakur in 2013, 'is not, and should not be, a North–South issue'.[4] Thakur conceded that in the late 1990s a debate clearly did emerge 'between the Global North, as represented by NATO, and the Global South, as articulated by the Non-Aligned Movement', but a move from 'humanitarian intervention' to the 'Responsibility to Protect' allegedly 're-established an international consensus on the legitimate ends of the use of military power'.[5]

---

[1] Wheeler 2000; Bellamy and Dunne 2016.
[2] See e.g. Glanville 2014: 158; Evans 2008: 11; ICISS 2001.
[3] See e.g. Weiss 2016; Luck 2010; Thakur and Weiss 2009.
[4] Thakur 2019: 130.
[5] Ibid.: 138.

This chapter turns our attention away from the 'right' to 'responsibility' narrative, and not only because, as I have tried to show in previous chapters, the changing character of sovereignty and domestic jurisdiction has long implied duties, including international duties involving forms of coercion, to protect strangers. I want to suggest instead that while liberal-solidarist accounts of 'sovereignty as responsibility' served significant political purposes in the post-Cold War period, they often proved inaccurate as assessments of actual interstate practice, and to focus on agreement alone would be to overlook a deeper, more primary change in meaning, even to miss the point of this recent stage of the global intervention debate. The anticolonial concept of sovereignty was not a 'sovereignty without responsibility', and no solid or broad consensus in international society was reached on the liberal-interventionist concept of conditional sovereignty.[6] There was of course an important type of coming together in the 2000s, but this coming together conceals a set of interpretive differences that make sense against the discursive practices that I have traced in previous chapters.

In 2005, member states of the UN—191 in all—did strike unanimous agreement on Paragraphs 138 and 139 (concerning the idea of RtoP) of the World Summit Outcome Document.[7] And they did begin, especially from the late 1990s onward, to employ the language of permissible intervention to protect populations from genocide, war crimes, ethnic cleansing, and crimes against humanity. A kind of interventionism in the context of 'sovereignty as responsibility' hence achieved considerable international legitimacy, reflected in a series of institutional developments in the UN. But the fundamental problem remained, as ever, 'what precisely does it mean to intervene?', and more specifically, 'what is the relationship of intervention with sovereign equality?'[8] North–South contestation over a liberal interventionist proposal can be seen to have culminated in the clash of two Responsibilities to Protect.

The basic forms of these two responsibilities—one 'Northern', the other 'Southern', particularly in the sense of articulating traditional values associated with the Non-Aligned Movement—preceded the arrival of the ICISS report in 2001, but they also came clearly into view during ongoing consideration of RtoP in the UN General Assembly.[9] The key discrepancy between them refers to the compatibility of intervention with an essential feature of the classical doctrine of humanitarian intervention: the suspension of

---

[6] Glanville 2011: 247.
[7] A/RES/60/1: 30.
[8] On RtoP as a basis of international hierarchy and control, see Getachew 2019a; Whyte 2017; Orford 2011, 2003. See also e.g. Hehir 2013; Cunliffe 2012; Ayoob 2004.
[9] ICISS 2001.

sovereignty, as distinct from its qualification. Sovereignty, according to a theory of liberal intervention that must be seen to encompass both classical humanitarian intervention and a Northern practice of RtoP, becomes conditional or, more clearly still, defeasible in emergency circumstances.[10] And the mechanism by which this process occurs, under the auspices of RtoP, ought not to be known universally as 'sovereignty as responsibility' but rather something more like 'responsibility as control', which has to do with the transfer from the affected state to foreign guardians and the international community of the RtoP, when states are unable or unwilling to protect. So on opposing views of responsibility as control, we find two practices of intervention, or two conceptions of sovereignty as responsibility. On the Southern view, sovereignty implies, as ever, an RtoP shared by the international community, but responsibility does not imply foreign control: intervention, yes, including coercive intervention under Chapter VII as a last resort, but never intervention that fails to respect the sovereign equality of states, or that casts into doubt the equal right of all to freely determine their own political, economic, and cultural futures. Sovereignty remains the prerequisite for and basis of legitimate intervention as international humanitarian protection. A norm of intervention emerged in the post-Cold War period, but the liberal-interventionist notion of conditional or defeasible sovereignty is contested.

To map out these two discursive practices, and to appreciate what it could possibly mean to intervene, not least coercively, without infringing upon sovereignty, we must first understand how self-determination was decoupled from the constitution of intervention as an act. This is the most important argument made in this chapter and, from the longer historical view, the most important change in the conditions of the concept's meaning in international society. We need to understand how, by the end of the 1990s and especially during UN debates over humanitarian assistance, civilian protection, and human rights promotion, the meaning of 'intervention' was loosened. The essence of intervention as an act no longer had to do with the outcome of foreign pressure against self-determination, with the limits and dynamic scope of domestic jurisdiction, or with the threat or use of force, but rather with a much more general impression of international involvement. This particular reconstitution—of what it is to intervene—seems at least as important, from the long view, as the extraordinary rhetorical achievement that was the concept of the Responsibility to Protect itself.

---

[10] The language of defeasibility—an analogy to property law traditions, referring to a right or interest that can be annulled or forfeited in the event of some specified occurrence—is being recovered from Chesterman 2001: 4.

To sum up, the chapter shows how on opposing historical views of sovereignty's defeasibility, we find two discursive practices of intervention in the UN, or two RtoPs. The historic global uptake of the language of 'sovereignty as a responsibility' and the 'responsibility to protect' cannot be conflated with the global uptake of liberal interventionism, not least because so many in the UN, and to such influential political effect, come to describe intervention as something essentially other than the denial of self-determination, the threat or use of force, or the infringement of sovereignty. On the Southern view, sovereignty is the prerequisite for and basis of all legitimate international protective action in the context of shared responsibility; intervention, yes, and even coercive intervention under Chapter VII, but never intervention that fails to respect the sovereign equality of states. Emergency collective action for the protection of civilians, taken in a timely and decisive manner, yet without interference in local-political or essentially domestic affairs, is also an expression of the international RtoP. Sovereignty no doubt comes with strings attached, with restrictions and shared duties, but intervention, in its more ordinary sense of international involvement, is not a licence to break, for example, foundational international norms and rules. Southern contestation provides a platform against both imperialism and gross violations of human rights.

The New International Humanitarian Order

In 1981, just five days after the adoption of the UN's Second Declaration on Non-Intervention, the General Assembly adopted a related resolution on the promotion of 'a new international humanitarian order'.[11] The proposal had been introduced by Prince el-Hassan bin Talal of Jordan on 28 September.[12] 'In recent years, efforts have been made in the framework of the United Nations system to promote a new international economic order [NIEO]', noted an explanatory memorandum submitted to the Secretary-General.[13] 'Similar endeavours have been undertaken in the field of information [NWICO]. Parallel to these efforts, it is proposed, *as an essential complementary task*, to promote a "new international humanitarian order [NIHO]".'[14]

Two years later, the General Assembly noted the establishment of an Independent Commission on International Humanitarian Issues (ICIHI) tasked

---

[11] A/RES/36/136 was adopted without a vote. See A/36/786.
[12] A/36/PV.15: 294.
[13] A/36/245: 1.
[14] Ibid. Emphasis added.

with further study of the idea.[15] As Kurt Herndl, Assistant Secretary-General for Human Rights, explained in his statement on the NIHO: 'the term "humanitarian" could be used to describe the body of "law of The Hague" and "law of Geneva" created around the turn of the 19th century as an approach to problems that emphasized the protection of individuals as opposed to political considerations'.[16] A NIHO, to quote the Jordanian delegate, should fully recognize the efforts of 'the humanitarian institutions, both governmental and non-governmental', in particular 'the work of the International Committee of the Red Cross, as well as UNHCR, UNICEF, and UNDRO'.[17]

A new international humanitarian order would be established by the end of the century, but it was not Jordan's, and it was not 'humanitarian' as Herndl had described it.[18] A liberal-solidarist era would have more to do with ICISS than with ICIHI, and would in fact directly challenge traditions and values at the heart of the 'law of The Hague' and the 'law of Geneva'—particularly insofar as it involved the 'broad and indiscriminate use' of concepts like 'humanitarian intervention' and 'humanitarian assistance' which, as Jacques Forster, Vice President of the International Committee of the Red Cross, put it, risked erasing 'perceptions of the distinct character of international humanitarian law and humanitarian action'.[19]

Jarat Chopra and Thomas Weiss, in a major 1992 article on codifying humanitarian intervention, observed a certain discursive practice of international humanitarian action in UN debates in 1991 concerning emergency humanitarian assistance in wars.[20] They quoted the delegate of the International Committee of the Red Cross: in 'terms of the existing right to assistance', including in situations of 'internal strife', 'humanitarian assistance cannot be regarded as interference. Far from infringing upon the sovereignty of states, humanitarian assistance in armed conflicts, as provided for by international law, is, rather, an expression of that sovereignty'.[21] While states had 'an obligation to facilitate assistance when the urgency of the needs make assistance necessary', and while 'in situations of armed conflict, it is not possible to consider assistance separately from protection', there 'can be no doubt that relief activities, when conducted in conformity with the rules of international humanitarian law, cannot be termed interference'.[22]

---

[15] A/RES/38/125. See Aga Khan and Talal 1988: 208–220.
[16] A/C.3/40/SR.69: 8.
[17] Ibid.: 9. It would alleviate human suffering in both 'man-made' and 'natural disasters' (A/36/245: 2).
[18] A/C.3/40/SR.69: 8.
[19] International Committee of the Red Cross 2000. See also e.g. Ryniker 2001.
[20] Chopra and Weiss 1992.
[21] Quoted in ibid.: 108.
[22] A/46/PV.42: 61.

During the same session, wrote Chopra and Weiss, 'the Soviet Union noted that reservations about "humanitarian intervention" can be addressed by reformulating the issue as "humanitarian solidarity".'[23] At least as important, we must add, was that India and other developing states had also, during the 1991 debates, taken a position in favour of 'solidarity' rather than 'intervention', and at a greater length: 'an approach being propagated is what has come to be known as "humanitarian intervention"', but while humanitarian crises 'demand innovative solutions', '[i]nnovation at the expense of a nation's sovereignty, or innovation calling for a reluctant abridgement of such sovereignty, must be strictly avoided.'[24] In short, in its discursive context, Resolution 46/182, which emerged out of the 1991 debates, and which called for humanitarian assistance to be provided in accordance with the principles of 'sovereignty, territorial integrity, and national unity' as well as 'humanity, neutrality, and impartiality', accommodated a fading solidarist internationalism.[25]

Resolution 46/182 would be reaffirmed in the Jakarta Declaration of the Non-Aligned Movement of the following year as well as, for instance, the Declaration of the South Summit.[26] Yet when we revisit the records of the 1991 debates, we find that while the United States supported the resolution and looked 'forward to considering and benefiting from the views of the Group of 77', it also asserted the need 'to seize the opportunity' for far-reaching change.[27]

David Chandler and others have shown how 'new humanitarian' NGOs (non-governmental organizations) such as Doctors Without Borders reshaped humanitarian policy agendas at the expense of the traditions of the ICRC, whose neutrality was regarded as complicity.[28] And Jessica Whyte has rightly argued that an emerging 'interventionist humanitarianism' was linked to a call by intellectuals, such as Michel Foucault, to recognize a 'right to intervene' belonging to a 'community of the governed'—individuals as well as non-governmental organizations 'like Amnesty International'—for the purposes of 'confronting governments'.[29] A new humanitarianism might hence have seemed like another step into a world in which, to quote Daniel Patrick

---

[23] Quoted in Chopra and Weiss 1992: 108.
[24] A/46/PV.41: 17–18. See also e.g. Tunisia: '[h]umanitarian assistance, which must be considered an expression of the international community's solidarity', should 'in no case violate the principle of national sovereignty' (ibid.: 28).
[25] A/RES/46/182.
[26] A/47/675: 111; A/55/74: 13.
[27] A/46/PV.41: 53.
[28] See e.g. Chandler 2001; Rieff 2002; Foley 2008.
[29] Whyte 2012: 14. Foucault 1994: 474–475.

Moynihan before the American Society of International Law, 'sovereignty is behind us' and the state was withering away.[30]

In fact, a new practice of human rights confronting governments did not become the fulcrum of the disappearance of the state, but rather the basis of sovereign governments using human rights to confront other governments, as unequals. A liberal interventionism, surfacing in the pages of *Foreign Affairs* concurrently with the records of the General Assembly, asserted not the end of the state but that 'the old idea of sovereign equality' and its 'anti-interventionist regime' had 'fallen out of sync with modern notions of justice'.[31] At the international-societal level, the theory did relate to the advocacy of Bernard Kouchner, serving by the late 1980s as France's Minister of State for Humanitarian Action, and Mario Bettati, the esteemed Professor of International Law, for a right and duty to interfere.[32] It involved a critique, similar to Kouchner's of the Red Cross in Biafra in the 1960s, of the mandate and legal import of the Geneva Conventions as accessories to inaction, even indifference, in the face of genocide.[33] Yet the key point is that a 'new humanitarian order' became entrenched in an American-led 'new world order', one that was understood, certainly among many developing countries, as coercive and hierarchical.[34] Theories of intervention for higher purposes, supplanting earlier understandings of dynamic jurisdiction and international responsibility, had been memorably embraced by key NATO members and their leaders: in French Foreign Minister Roland Dumas' proclamation of what he called the 'right to intervene on humanitarian grounds', in the 'humanitarian war' arguments of the Clinton administration, and the 1999 speech of Tony Blair on 'just wars' for 'values', for example.[35]

How then was liberal intervention being contested, and to what extent was it embraced outside of the NATO group, especially in the early 2000s as the theory developed further? To answer this question, we must first take note of one more discursive pivot, which was subtle and has rarely been

---

[30] See Moynihan's scepticism in American Society of International Law 1991: 2. Compare with Urquhart 1991.
[31] Glennon 1999: 2, 4. See Wheeler 2000; Mayall 1996; Chesterman 2001: 112–162.
[32] See Bettati and Kouchner 1987. On this and related 'norm entrepreneurial' initiatives, including the work of Francis Deng, William Zartman, Roberta Cohen, and others as antecedents of a theory of liberal interventionism, see e.g. Crossley 2016: especially 43–72. See Deng et al. 1996; Cohen and Deng 1998.
[33] See e.g. the discussion contained in Weissman 2010.
[34] See e.g. Damrosch and Scheffer 1991. Whyte argues similarly that to trace the trajectory of the 'right of the governed' to intervene is to see how in the end it became 'a new basis for the legitimacy of state militarism, as well as a new foundation of sovereign power' (Whyte 2012: 31).
[35] Dumas 1991; Roberts 1999; Blair 1999. 'Acts of genocide', claimed Blair in his Chicago speech, 'can never be a purely internal matter' (ibid.). For a discussion, see Freedman 2017. For an illustration of how these developments were being understood in much English-language IR in terms of 'emerging norms of justified intervention', see e.g. Reed and Kaysen 1993.

acknowledged, though it was of tremendous importance and already underway by the late 1990s. We can trace it at work at some of the highest levels of the United Nations.

When Kofi Annan delivered a major speech in 1998 at Ditchley Park in Britain, he acknowledged that the title of his address—'Intervention'—must have surprised some in his audience.[36] 'Or if not, you may think I have come to preach a sermon against intervention. I suppose that would be the traditional line for a citizen of a former British colony to take, in an address before senior diplomats and policy makers of the former imperial Power.'[37] Many would also expect as much from a UN Secretary-General, whatever their country of origin.[38]

But Annan had in mind a very different purpose, speaking as he was amid the crisis in Kosovo. He intended rather, as he would recall in his memoirs, to 'set out the case for humanitarian intervention more broadly by examining its history'.[39] Forty-eight months after the Rwandan genocide, and with 'the determination to never again permit another Bosnia', might not the intervention concept be reclaimed for some brighter purpose?[40]

> In other contexts the word 'intervention' has a more benign meaning. We all applaud the policeman who intervenes to stop a fight, or the teacher who prevents big boys from bullying a smaller one. And medicine uses the word 'intervention' to describe the act of the surgeon, who saves life by 'intervening' to remove malignant growth, or to repair damaged organs. Of course, the most intrusive methods of treatment are not always to be recommended. A wise doctor knows when to let nature take its course. But a doctor who never intervened would have few admirers, and probably even fewer patients. So it is in international affairs.[41]

He went on to describe the purposes, principles, and activities of the UN in terms of this redescribed or reconstituted version of the word—an astonishing shift from decades of knowing the 'maintenance of international peace and security', 'peacekeeping', and 'humanitarian assistance', for example, as matters of legitimate collective action, not intervention.[42]

> Why was the United Nations established, if not to act as a benign policeman or doctor? Our job is to intervene: to prevent conflict where we can, to put a stop to

---

[36] SG/SM/6613: 1.
[37] Ibid.
[38] Ibid.
[39] Annan 2013: 91.
[40] SG/SM/6613: 10.
[41] Ibid.: 2.
[42] Ibid.

it when it has broken out, or—when neither of those things is possible—at least to contain it and prevent it from spreading. That is what the world expects of us, even though—alas—the United Nations by no means always lives up to such expectations. *It is also what the Charter requires of us, particularly in Chapter VI, which deals with the peaceful settlement of disputes, and Chapter VII, which describes the action the United Nations must take when peace comes under threat, or is actually broken.*[43]

'My point', Annan would later recall, 'was that intervention was a cause for everyone, and one not limited by any means to the use of military force.'[44] Very crucially, we should now want to show, this use of the concept was also not limited to infringements of sovereignty.

One year later, the same basic move appeared in the Secretary-General's speech before the UN General Assembly (components of which had been published in an article titled 'Two Concepts of Sovereignty' for *The Economist* four days earlier).[45] What needs to be highlighted here is not only Annan's call to reconcile sovereignty with the need to prevent 'gross and systematic violations of human rights with grave humanitarian consequences', though this was certainly in the foreground, and not only that Annan had been using the phrase that 'sovereignty implies responsibility, not just power'.[46] The other discursive achievement of Annan's speech has to do with its re-evaluation of what it is to intervene. There are two key observations to make.

First: though NATO's role in the Kosovo crisis had 'cast in stark relief what has been called the dilemma of humanitarian intervention', Annan argued that '"intervention" should not be understood as referring only to the use of force' (the legacy of humanitarian intervention in its classical sense and of traditional Western practice).[47] Rather it was 'important to define intervention as broadly as possible, to include actions along a wide continuum from the most pacific to the most coercive'.[48] Outside of the category of what he called 'forcible' or 'armed' intervention were 'less perilous actions of intervention than the one we witnessed recently in Yugoslavia'.[49] The international actions included by Annan in his list of 'less perilous actions of intervention' should be carefully noted: 'the commitment of the international

---

[43] Ibid. Emphasis added.
[44] Annan 2013: 91.
[45] A/54/PV.4; Annan 1999.
[46] A/54/PV.4: 2; SG/SM/6613.
[47] A/54/PV.4: 2.
[48] Ibid.: 3.
[49] Ibid.

community to peacekeeping, to humanitarian assistance, and to rehabilitation and reconstruction'.[50]

What might have appeared to be a reference to earlier UN practices of the various means or dimensions of intervention—away from simply dictatorial force, towards a broader range of effects or actions—was in fact a different sort of practice altogether. From a historical Third World perspective, what Annan had dropped from his definition of intervention was reference to self-determination—a concept which, for decades, had underpinned institutionalized UN practice, but which in 1999 had clearly not escaped his consideration.

'Let me say that the Council's prompt and effective action in authorizing a multinational force for East Timor reflects precisely the unity of purpose that I have called for today.'[51] But if prompt authorization of peacekeeping in East Timor was Annan's model case of stepping in rather than standing by, it was also a case of international coercive action that had been clearly requested by the sovereign government in control of the territory in question, and in relation precisely to the international organizing and conducting of a popular consultation regarding autonomy and processes of attaining formal independence. The key agreements were those between Indonesia and Portugal on the 'Question of East Timor' of 5 May 1999 as well as those of the same date between the UN and the governments of Indonesia and Portugal regarding international security arrangements for a direct ballot of the East Timorese.[52] A few key sentences in Annan's article in *The Economist* did not appear in his UN speech: 'In Kosovo a group of states intervened without seeking authority from the United Nations Security Council. In Timor the Council has now authorized intervention, but only after obtaining an invitation from Indonesia ... Neither of these precedents is satisfactory as a model for the new millennium.'[53]

Recognizing that in both cases, '[a]s in Rwanda five years ago, the international community stands accused of doing too little, too late', Annan was calling for a timely reflection in a particular frame.[54] That frame involved a conception of intervention that was no longer, in essence, an infringement

---

[50] Ibid.
[51] Ibid.: 3.
[52] A/53/951; S/1999/513.
[53] Annan 1999.
[54] Ibid. His call in September 1999 was for states 'to find common ground in upholding the principles of the Charter and in acting in defense of our common humanity' (A/54/PV.4: 3). The following year, in his Millennium report, the call was posed slightly differently: 'if humanitarian intervention is, indeed, an unacceptable assault on sovereignty, how should we respond to a Rwanda, to a Srebrenica, to gross and systematic violation of human rights that offend every precept of our common humanity?' (quoted in ICISS 2001: vii).

of sovereignty or a denial of the right to self-determination said to underpin it. To the contrary, Annan was suggesting that only as a last resort might intervention be taken without the consent of the affected state.[55] Intervention seemed then to refer to international involvement in the upholding of humanitarian responsibilities, and involvement in a loose sense, 'along a wide continuum', with or without sovereign consent, in line or not with sovereign will.[56] If so, then logically non-intervention meant non-involvement in the upholding of humanitarian responsibilities. This was a framework of debate that accepted and promulgated the idea that non-intervention, once at the root of the UN-based human rights regime and the anti-colonial movement, meant something very different from—even the opposite of—its historical Third World practice. Only in a new discursive context could non-intervention imply indifference to atrocities, standing idly by in the face of 'wholesale slaughter', or a refuge of 'states bent on criminal behaviour' who must be taught that 'frontiers are not an absolute defence'.[57]

The second key observation to make in relation to 1999 has to do with what Annan called a new shift in the meaning of sovereignty (especially in light of post-war 'forces of globalization and international cooperation') towards an understanding in which the state was the 'servant of its people, and not vice versa'.[58] We will say less about this second move. Annan's two conceptions of sovereignty—what he called 'state sovereignty' and 'individual sovereignty' (by which he meant the 'human rights and fundamental freedoms of each and every individual, as enshrined in our Charter')—has been much discussed elsewhere.[59] But what should be noted is that Annan can be read here as juxtaposing state values and human values in a way similar to that of a cosmopolitan theory of humanitarian intervention.[60] Annan seemed to accept the idea that the 'human rights of each and every individual, as enshrined in our Charter' stood in tension with respect for state sovereignty, as if there had been practised in historical international society a theory of absolute sovereignty, unqualified by humanitarian responsibility.[61]

Such a sweeping reinterpretation—of non-intervention as non-involvement in shared responsibilities and of sovereignty as yielding to, rather than moving through, human rights in emergency circumstances—overlapped with conceptions of non-intervention and sovereignty that

[55] Annan 1999.
[56] A/54/PV.4: 2.
[57] Ibid.: 4, 3.
[58] Ibid.: 1.
[59] Annan 1999. See e.g. Bellamy 2009b.
[60] See e.g. Tesón 2003.
[61] Annan 1999.

had gained ground elsewhere, above all in Western policy circles.[62] Annan had not advocated humanitarian intervention outright, but succeeded in setting a frame within which much future thinking would proceed. A 'New Interventionism' rejected and replaced a proposal for a NIHO. It also overturned a set of international practices and shared understandings developed by non-aligned states in earlier decades by claiming that: '[s]overeignty has impinged upon international relief efforts since the Treaty of Westphalia in 1648', '[t]he new posture recognises the hollowness of this concept [sovereign equality, more particularly]', and the 'death of the restrictive old rules on peacekeeping and peacemaking—under which most bloody conflicts were simply ignored as "domestic matters"—should not be mourned.'[63] To quote Weiss and Chopra in their 1992 proposal to codify humanitarian intervention in international society: 'Future acceptance of "humanitarian intervention" is linked to conceptual and practical capacity to reconcile its *two conflicting halves*. Running through the United Nations Charter are two contradictions: (i) sovereignty and human rights, and (ii) peace and justice.'[64]

Sovereignty versus human rights, peace versus justice

One foreseeable reply to the above point is that this emerging discourse was not just Western, but also Southern; that a liberal interventionism was also being practised in the OAU, and soon the AU, for instance.[65] But we can show now, particularly given the redescriptions mapped out in the previous section, why that response can only be partly right. There emerged in this period two significant discursive practices of intervention—one Northern and one Southern, in the sense of the values and identities of their practitioners—and while, yes, there were overlaps between them, there were also differences, and it is the differences, given what we think we know already, that provide the most illuminating insights on the changing character of international society. Speaking before the General Assembly on the same day as Annan, on 20 September 1999, was then-President of the Democratic Republic of Algeria, Abdelaziz Bouteflika, who offered a response in his capacity as President of the OAU.[66]

---

[62] See Thakur 2016b.
[63] Weiss and Campbell 1991: 453, 454; Glennon 1999: 2, 4.
[64] Chopra and Weiss 1992: 109. Emphasis added.
[65] Consider in this respect e.g. Williams 2007.
[66] A/54/PV.4: 14.

What he called the perspective of the developing world did 'not deny the right of Northern-hemisphere public opinion to denounce the breaches of human rights where they exist. Nor do we deny that the UN has the right and the duty to help suffering humanity.'[67] But inasmuch as 'the sovereign state remains beyond dispute a place of social contract and the context within which human rights should be organized—political rights, as well as economic and social ones—the international community should favour stability as well as concord and the culture of democracy for our developing countries'.[68] For the South, three questions remained unanswered in an overarching context of positive international action: 'first, where does aid stop and interference begin? Second, where are the lines to be drawn between the humanitarian, the political, and the economic? Third, is interference valid only in weak and weakened states or for all states without distinction?'[69] We 'firmly believe that the countries of the South are capable of overcoming their difficulties, so long as solidarity, loyal assistance, and the concern of the developed countries and international community do not fail them'.[70]

There is no doubt that the language of intervention was gaining significant political traction in the UN. But what we did not see, in General Assembly debates between 1999 and 2000 for instance, was consensus on liberal tensions between sovereignty and human rights or between peace and justice. Politically significant contestation had to do not with a clash between absolute sovereigntists and humanitarian interventionists, or between states in favour of the non-use of force and states in favour of bolder modes of protection, as liberal interventionists have tended to suggest, but more with a divide over the defeasibility of sovereignty, often but not exclusively in relation to force, as distinct from its qualification, across multiple interventionisms. Through the turn of the century and into the RtoP debates, what we see is a Third World that drops the role of non-interventionist, while embracing (as it had before) qualified sovereignty, without dropping a commitment to its non-suspension, even in emergency circumstances. In other words all become interventionists, at least in the very general sense that Annan had in mind—according to a meaning of intervention as international involvement, plausibly coercive, for the protection of human rights. The dilemma was: what place for sovereign equality?

The Northern view has received the most attention. We can locate it in statements, recurring in the UN, like the following: 'the last few years of

[67] Ibid.
[68] Ibid.
[69] Ibid.
[70] Ibid.

this century have disproved the notion that people and human freedoms take second place to state sovereignty'.[71] Sovereignty ought to yield to higher imperatives or responsibilities, and there is a culpability to be associated with sovereigns—both for having failed to protect civilians and for having obstructed international action by using sovereignty as a 'shield'.[72]

> There is one lesson to be learned from these years of turmoil: actions to prevent and repress the most serious violations of human rights may take precedence over respect for national sovereignty. No government can hide behind the shield of its own borders.[73]

The claim rested in 1999, during NATO's aerial campaign against Yugoslavia for example, on an assumption about which problems were located within the domestic and which within the international. 'The Kosovo crisis ... obliges us to ask a sensitive question about the limits to the right of the international community to intervene in the *internal affairs* of a state.'[74] Intervention protects human rights, and especially the right to life, in the internal domain as if it were already and exclusively there. To say so was to adopt earlier strands of thinking about the right or duty to interfere associated with the new humanitarian NGOs, but which were now being put to greater use by governments:

> If there is one lesson for our Organization to learn from the twentieth century, it is that for no state can the massacre of its own people be considered an 'internal affair', under any pretext. This legal formalism would ultimately amount to admitting that, as the head of the UN Interim Administration in Kosovo, Bernard Kouchner has said, it would be 'legitimate, although not elegant, to massacre one's own people.'[75]

This retelling of the twentieth century was, as previous chapters have documented, historically misleading—insofar as 'massacre' and 'genocide' were not, in the practices of states, considered 'internal affairs'.[76] Their categorization as international catastrophes and crimes, horrors that states shared a duty to prevent, was repeatedly recognized, including in the course of writing and adopting both UN declarations on non-intervention.[77] But the

---

[71] Italy, A/54/PV.8: 19.
[72] Ibid.
[73] Ibid.: 21.
[74] Belgium, A/54/PV.14: 17. Emphasis added.
[75] Ibid.
[76] See Chapter 3.
[77] See Chapters 4 and 5.

feat of liberal interventionism was never about accurately recalling the past. Rather, what was important was its uptake in a clash of discursive practices that served to legitimate international action: 'we have come to understand that absolute sovereignty and total non-interference are no longer tenable' (as if they had once been)—'this implies a rethinking of the principles … that have governed the community of nations for over three centuries'; the new international order would abolish the 'sovereign right to ethnic cleansing and genocide'; it was time to declare that 'sovereignty cannot mean impunity for genocide and human rights abuses'.[78]

A Northern understanding of intervention, bearing similarities with classical humanitarian intervention but better known as a liberal-interventionist theory, had then three major points. First, that humanitarian disasters were caused by malevolent or negligent agents in the form of state leaders—'dictators and murderers' who used references to non-intervention in internal affairs and sovereignty as 'a shield'.[79] Second, that affairs previously understood to belong to the international were to be shifted into the domestic or internal—that this was legitimate because it was in the domestic and internal, and behind physical borders, that we could find the problem of humanitarian protection. And hence third, that to effectively uphold responsibility and to prevent large-scale human rights abuses, it was necessary to shelve the sovereignty of certain states at certain times. Other changes discussed in the period—unilateral versus multilateral authority, coalitions of the willing, veto restraints—were of course also important, but the density of agreement on them varied, and all mattered less than the logic not of who intervenes, but of the limits of intervention in relation to sovereignty.[80]

And if this overcoming of sovereign equality was a necessary feature of Northern practice, it was at the heart of the South's rejection of that practice. The primary focus of contestation was not about humanitarian duty (all of course agreed that genocide and other mass atrocities had to be stopped). It was about defining the character of legitimate intervening (as international involvement in the prevention of those atrocities and upholding of that duty). An unacceptable foreign imposition occurred when the objectives and activities of international protectors moved from the domain of the international-humanitarian into that of the internal-political. The line between legitimate and illegitimate intervention, like the historical line between legitimate and illegitimate foreign aid, was crossed when

---

[78] Poland, A/54/PV.17: 5; Italy, A/54/PV.8: 20; Poland, A/54/PV.17: 29; ibid.: 6.
[79] Germany, A/54/PV.8: 11.
[80] Consider e.g. Germany's scepticism of unilateral authorization of humanitarian intervention in ibid. 12.

sovereignty became suspended or adjourned; an unacceptable politicization or abuse occurred when the international action in question effected a denial, even for some higher or sacred purpose, of the sovereign equality and self-determined futures of states and peoples.

In its classical sense, 'humanitarian intervention' was clearly rejected by the members of the Non-Aligned Movement. This much has been widely acknowledged.[81] At the 13th Ministerial Conference in Cartagena, 8–9 April 2000, for instance: 'We reject the so-called "right" of humanitarian intervention, which has no legal basis in the United Nations Charter or in the general principles of international law.'[82] And a few days later, at the South Summit, the G77 plus China readopted this rejection verbatim and requested that the chairpeople of the G77 and Non-Aligned Movement jointly coordinate their consideration of the concept.[83]

But to reject humanitarian intervention was neither to reject the international duty to protect civilians and prevent atrocities nor to reject a coercive internationalism. This much has been much less widely acknowledged. In the late 1990s, from a non-aligned perspective, the international problem of genocide prevention, including through forcible measures under Chapter VII, was largely a problem of political will and enforcement, not about an overcoming of sovereignty. To states like Indonesia, it was too easy to exonerate international actors from their liabilities and misplaced resources in relation to previous disasters:

> to blame this principle [sovereignty] for the inability of the Organization to come to the aid of suffering humanity anywhere is to distort the truth. To extend such assistance is a solemn obligation. Indeed it is imperative. However, there are many reasons why the UN often finds itself ineffective in situations that require it to act swiftly and decisively. These include resource constraints, lack of political will, selectivity, misplaced media attention, and dysfunction in the working of such bodies as the Security Council and in implementing mechanisms. These have nothing to do with the principle of sovereignty.[84]

For all the period's references to the Rwanda case, for instance, quickly forgotten was that Nigeria, on behalf of the NAM, had proposed on 13 April 1994 a draft resolution under Chapter VII that would have empowered UNAMIR

---

[81] See e.g. Wheeler 2006.
[82] A/54/917: 49.
[83] The South Summit called instead for emergency humanitarian assistance guided by the principles 'adopted by the General Assembly in its resolution 46/182' (A/55/74: 13).
[84] Indonesia, A/54/PV.33: 7. See also e.g. India, A/54/PV.27: 20.

(UN Assistance Mission for Rwanda) to enforce 'law and order and the establishment of transitional institutions' while protecting civilians.[85] This draft aimed to 'increase the strength of UNAMIR and to revise its mandate'—precisely what Roméo Dallaire considered necessary to stop the killing.[86] The point here is, as the OAU's International Panel of Eminent Personalities would later conclude, that the decision to deprive UNAMIR of capacities to more robustly keep the peace was a function not of some international-legal or -normative conundrum about sovereign equality, but a failure of political leadership to uphold existing duties.[87]

Kishore Mahbubani, Singaporean Ambassador to the UN, noted that '[i]t is puzzling, perhaps even shocking, that there has been no move to have the OAU report discussed by the Security Council'.[88] This and the Brahimi Panel on UN Peace Operations told 'a sobering story of gross ineptitude, the primacy of narrow national interests among key members of the Security Council over everything else'.[89] What was needed to avert another Rwanda or Srebrenica, as the delegate from Pakistan would put it at the World Summit, was not a Northern doctrine—one that suspended, in a unequal world, the rights and freedoms guaranteed by sovereign equality—but the will to invest in commitments already made.[90]

In 1998, at the Durban Summit, the Non-Aligned Movement defined international humanitarian responsibility in the context of UN-based peacekeeping, emergency humanitarian assistance, and development, with an emphasis on the independence of humanitarian action from political or 'partial' objectives and on coercive measures as a last resort, under Chapter VII, for the maintenance of international peace and security.[91] Such a humanitarianism articulated an internationalist agenda integral to historical solidarist organizing of the South:

> In four and a half decades, the world has changed vastly from the days of the Bandung meeting. Yet the principles laid down by the founders of the NAM remain

---

[85] 'Text of NAM Draft (13 April 1994)' in Dobbs 2014.
[86] Ibid. See Dallaire 2003. A special resolution on the Rwanda crisis, adopted at the 11th Ministerial Meeting of the Non-Aligned Countries on 3 June 1994 (see A/49/287), 'strongly urges the United Nations Security Council' to 'urgently take all necessary measures to put an immediate stop to the carnage in Rwanda'. At the same meeting the principle was declared that peacekeeping be of 'non-intrusive and non-interventionist' nature and show 'full respect for the sovereignty and sovereign equality of all states, their territorial integrity, and non-intervention in their internal affairs' (see Ibid.: 17).
[87] Organisation of African Unity 2000.
[88] A/55/PV.35: 30.
[89] Ibid.
[90] 'In Rwanda, Srebrenica and elsewhere, it was the failure of political will that prevented action, not the absence of an interventionist doctrine.' Pakistan in A/59/PV.86: 5.
[91] See A/53/667: especially 129–131.

valid, and the ideas, goals, and vision articulated then, continue to guide our movement. *As we mark the 50th anniversary of the Universal Declaration of Human Rights, nothing should be used as a convenient mask to hide genocide, gross violations of human rights and crimes against humanity, nor should human rights be used as a political instrument for interference in internal affairs.*[92]

Three overlapping points were coming into view: 1) a refusal of the human rights versus sovereignty dichotomy, 2) a reassertion of duties both to prevent gross violations of human rights and to refrain from intervention, and 3) a recollection that these duties were interlocking and consistent, given the dynamic nature of domestic jurisdiction. Consider also the arguments of Qin Huasun, Chinese Ambassador to the UN, during the 1999 debates:

putting an end to these conflicts and crises and eliminating their root causes is the ardent desire of the peoples of the countries concerned, as well as a legitimate concern of the international community. *However, such arguments as 'humanitarian intervention' and 'human rights over sovereignty' that cropped up recently set up human rights against sovereignty.*[93]

Emphasis on the 'ardent desire of the peoples of the countries concerned' in some ways corresponded to earlier logics of self-determination that informed anti-colonial organizing, but notably the vocabulary of self-determination was no longer appearing, explicitly, with the frequency that it once did.[94] Still a right to sovereignty was located at the root of all other human rights: '[t]he history of China and other developing countries shows that a country's sovereignty is the prerequisite for and the basis of the human rights that the people of that country can enjoy.'[95]

Intervention without infringing sovereignty

In 2000 it was through a General Assembly resolution concerning respect for the Charter to achieve 'international cooperation' in 'solving international problems of humanitarian character' that the South rejected a theory of liberal intervention in the UN (the resolution would be reaffirmed and readopted, with requests for recorded votes, many times over the following

---

[92] Ibid.: 11. Emphasis added.
[93] A/54/PV.27: 12. Emphasis added.
[94] Ibid.
[95] China, A/54/PV.8: 16.

seven years).⁹⁶ This resolution and its readoptions have been overlooked; perhaps because the word 'intervention' does not explicitly appear in its text. To clarify, the language did appear in the resolution's draft form—but was removed at the last minute. I want to suggest now that this removal is a historically significant moment in the post-Cold War contestation of intervention in international society. Not only does it help to illustrate key features of a Southern formulation of qualified but indefeasible sovereignty, it also illustrates the increasingly global reach of a historic loosening in the conditions of intervention's meaning, in the sense that the grip of intervention as an outcome of foreign pressure against self-determined futures gave way to a much more general sense of intervention as international involvement. It was at this moment that collective and internationalist actions that previously did not meet the threshold of 'intervention' were absorbed into a much more ordinary use of the term.

Cuba introduced the draft in the Third Committee with the co-sponsorship of fourteen other non-aligned members.⁹⁷ And like Cuba's 1990 draft resolution on 'Strengthening of United Nations Action in the Human Rights Field Through the Promotion of International Co-operation and the Strict Observance of the Principle of Non-Intervention' (later retitled 'Strengthening of United Nations Action in the Human Rights Field Through the Promotion of International Co-operation and the Importance of Non-Selectivity, Impartiality, and Objectivity'), this latest proposal had been modelled on key paragraphs of the 1965 and 1981 non-intervention declarations, as well as the Friendly Relations Declaration.⁹⁸ Its function was to assert that in 'solving international problems of humanitarian character ... no State or group of States has the right to intervene, for any reason whatever, directly or indirectly': that all forms of 'interference or attempted threats against the personality of the State or against its political economic and cultural elements, are in violation of international law'.⁹⁹

But, as with the fate of the 1990 draft, the word 'non-intervention' would not appear in the resolution's adopted form.¹⁰⁰ It was replaced instead with a reference to 'sovereign equality' and more specifically a provision that 'all states in these activities [activities to "solve international problems of a humanitarian character"] must comply with the principles set forth in Article 2 of the Charter, in particular respecting the sovereign equality of all States

---

⁹⁶ A/C.3/55/L.47; A/C.3/55/L.47/Rev.1; A/RES/55/101. See also A/RES/57/217 of 2002, A/RES/58/188 of 2003, A/RES/59/204 of 2004, A/RES/62/166 of 2007.
⁹⁷ A/C.3/55/L.47.
⁹⁸ A/C.3/45/L.82/Rev.1; see A/RES/45/163.
⁹⁹ A/C.3/55/L.47/Rev.1: 2.
¹⁰⁰ A/C.3/45/L.82/Rev.1.

and refraining from the threat or use of force against the territorial integrity or political independence of any State'.[101] Why? Immediately after Chad and Ethiopia were announced as additional co-sponsors, Cuba explained before the Third Committee: 'The direct reference to non-intervention in the affairs of other States had been removed to take into account the concerns expressed, in particular, by African delegations in the light of recent developments on their continent.'[102]

What were these recent developments in Africa? Why had the non-aligned states come to advocate human rights promotion with respect to 'non-selectivity, impartiality, and objectivity' and for sovereign equality, without reference to the time-tested principle of non-intervention?

In the OAU/AU and subregional organizations like ECOWAS and SADC, African states had renounced a duty of what was being called non-intervention and embraced the right of what was termed intervention. Just a few months earlier, at Lomé, there had been declared a regional right of intervention, which became enshrined in Article 4(h) of the AU Constitutive Act: 'the right of the Union to intervene in a Member state pursuant to a decision of the Assembly in respect of grave circumstances, namely: war crimes, genocide, and crimes against humanity'.[103] We should also note that by 1999 ECOWAS had adopted, among other things, the 10 December Protocol Relating to the Mechanism for Conflict Prevention, Management, and Resolution (the 1999 Protocol), which described the Economic Community of Western African States Monitoring Group (ECOMOG) not just as a multilateral armed force but as an 'intervention force' tasked with, among other things, humanitarian disaster relief, 'observation and monitoring', 'peace-keeping and restoration of peace', and 'preventative deployment'.[104]

No doubt the states of Africa had come together as self-described interventionists and qualified sovereigntists. But if we look at the ways in which the act of intervention was being interpreted, it is far from clear that they became liberal interventionists, let alone classical humanitarian interventionists. In the Constitutive Act we also find the following, for example:

(j) the right of Member States to *request intervention* from the Union in order to restore peace and security;[105]

---

[101] A/RES/55/101.
[102] A/C.3/55/SR.55: 6.
[103] AU Constitutive Act.
[104] ECOWAS Protocol Relating to the Mechanism for Conflict Prevention, Management, and Resolution.
[105] AU Constitutive Act.

It is widely agreed that Article 4(j) provides formal support for what is often called 'intervention by invitation'.[106] The classification of this particular mode of intervention—also known as 'intervention upon request' or 'military assistance upon request'—proceeds from the effect of consent to the foreign use of force.[107] And it forms a branch of international-legal debate that clearly did not begin with the 1980s or 1990s (Hall was reviewing 'intervention by invitation' as early as 1890), but which, though incomprehensible from the view of discursive practices of Cold War international society, had been taken up with zeal in post-Cold War books and articles, including in relation to 'law and force in the New International Order'.[108] To listen to international-legal scholars writing at the time: '[e]xamples of such limited operations would include the use of *peacekeeping forces which do not become involved with internal affairs*'.[109] An example was: 'German help given to the Somalian Government in connection with the hijacked airliner at Mogadishu Airport on 18 October 1977'.[110]

Various African subregional organizations were also institutionalizing arrangements compatible with intervention by request. In the 1996 Botswana Communiqué on the SADC Organ on Politics, Defence and Security, for instance, references to 'military intervention of whatever nature' were suggestive of a reading of military intervention inclusive of traditional peacekeeping operations.[111] The ECOWAS Protocol of 1999, too, allowed for intervention upon request, both as pacific settlement and as a collective security tool.[112] Prior consent—as requests, including ad hoc, not *ex ante*, requests by recognized state governments—would over time, as Erika de Wet has shown, become a normal expectation for interventions undertaken by ECOWAS and the SADC, particularly but not exclusively in the form of 'observation and

---

[106] See e.g. de Wet 2015: 981; Kuwali 2015: 249; the comments of Abdulqawi Ahmed Yusuf in Institute of International Law 2007: 343.
[107] See e.g. Damrosch and Scheffer 1991: chapters 9, 10, 11, and 12 on 'Intervention by Invitation'; Doswald-Beck 1985; Mullerson 1991; Wippman 1996. See also Hafner 2009.
[108] Hall 1890: 290; Damrosch and Scheffer 1991. See de Wet 2020; Nolte 2010; Fox 2015. See too Nguyễn 2019.
[109] Doswald-Beck 1985: 189. Emphasis added.
[110] Ibid.
[111] See A/50/1001, Articles 4.1 and 4.2. The SADC Protocol on Politics, Defence and Security Cooperation in Article 11(4)(a): '[i]n respect of both inter- and intra-state conflicts, the Organ shall seek to obtain the consent of the disputant parties to its peacemaking efforts.' De Wet 2020: 178–179.
[112] Article 27: 'The Mediation and Security Council shall consider several options and decide on the most appropriate course of action to take in terms of intervention.' But the modalities include: 'recourse to the Council of Elders, the dispatch of fact-finding missions, political and mediation missions or intervention by ECOMOG'. ECOWAS Protocol Relating to the Mechanism for Conflict Prevention, Management, and Resolution.

monitoring', 'peacekeeping and restoration of peace', 'preventative deployment', and 'peace-building, disarmament, and demobilisation'.[113]

To be clear, the AU was not technically obliged to wait for the consent of the affected state before undertaking intervention, as had been the case for the OAU's Central Organ of the Mechanism for Conflict Prevention, Management and Resolution of Conflicts.[114] But this is not the only point of interest here. Rather, in part by rhetorical means, an 'intervention by invitation' or 'intervention by request' had become a logical idea in the society of states. What it suggested was that non-intervention, in the loose sense of the word as non-involvement, was not the necessary corollary of sovereign equality. African institutional developments were reflective of a deep and foundational change in meaning at the intergovernmental level according to which intervention implied the upholding of international humanitarian responsibilities.

Of course we must remember that the AU's right of intervention was, first, a right belonging strictly to the Union and, second, a right to be exercised towards its members alone.[115] But what I am saying is that by 2001, and as reflected in African institutional change, a contestation had been mounted against earlier discursive practices in international society such that, out of step with peacekeeping and humanitarian assistance practices associated with the 'law of Geneva' and originally conceived as non-interventionary, protection and humanitarian activities with the consent of the affected state were now being described as 'intervention'. Only by letting go of earlier meanings could states come to know humanitarian relief and assistance, as much as peacekeeping or military aid requested by a sovereign government, as intervention. The shift in African security culture would soon be described as one from 'non-interference' to 'non-indifference' and we did witness the rise of an African interventionist discourse, but the extent to which that discourse entailed a retreat from sovereignty, or an embrace of the human rights-sovereignty dichotomy, seems highly questionable.[116]

Briefly I want to return to Resolution 55/101, which has been almost wholly neglected, and which again can be seen as an attempt by non-aligned states to reject, in the UN General Assembly, liberal interventionism but not interventionism generally, particularly because it marked the abandonment of older

---

[113] Article 22 of ibid. There emerged considerable reluctance within the AU to invoke Article 4(h) in the absence of ad hoc consent or Security Council authorization. See de Wet 2014, 2020: chapter 5.
[114] See generally Kioko 2003.
[115] Ibid.
[116] Williams 2007.

developing world logics of 'non-intervention' in solving international problems of a humanitarian character. In the end, the resolution would be adopted by 78 (a non-aligned group) to 51 (primarily a Western group), with 21 abstentions.[117] Tallies on nearly identical resolutions adopted in 2001, 2002, 2004, and 2007 follow the same trends.[118]

In explaining its vote, the Canadian delegation criticized the text for having 'focused too strongly on national sovereignty without including counterbalancing language on human rights, suggesting that sovereignty was a shield behind which human rights could be violated with impunity'.[119] The American delegation, concurring 'with the statement in the Millennium Report of the Secretary-General that "surely no legal principle—not even sovereignty—can ever shield a crime against humanity"', alleged that 'the resolution tried to build just such a shield'.[120] Similarly, France, on behalf of the EU considered the draft 'was actually concerned with something other than encouraging respect for human rights and fundamental freedoms'.[121] New Zealand, the following year, during the resolution's readoption by the G77 and non-aligned states, added that 'state sovereignty should not be promoted over and above other objectives of the United Nations'.[122] And Australia, in 2004, during another readoption believed the text attached 'primary importance to the protection of sovereignty to the detriment of fostering human rights'.[123]

Yet non-aligned co-sponsors and supporters of Resolution 55/101 were neither unqualified sovereigntists nor anti-humanitarians. Overall what needs to be understood is that if non-aligned states were becoming interventionists for humanitarian purposes, in tandem with their African members, then their new (but not New) interventionism had made a claim about which relationship to sovereign equality. At the 13th Ministerial Conference of the NAM in June 2000 it seemed as if a strategy—never flaunted, but deliberate—had been adopted: if 'the interpretation of the Charter is broadened to make room for humanitarian intervention', then 'the modes of that intervention should also be broadened'.[124] The goal was to ensure that 'any new orientation of humanitarian assistance should be based on unconditional respect for the Charter of the United Nations and international law' and 'must be inspired by the basic criteria of neutrality and impartiality'.[125] Foreign Affairs

---

[117] A/C.3/55/SR.55: 7–8.
[118] A/RES/56/152; A/RES/57/217; A/RES/59/204; A/RES/62/166.
[119] A/C.3/55/SR.55: 6.
[120] Ibid.: 8.
[121] Ibid.: 7.
[122] A/C.3/57/SR.53: 6.
[123] A/C.3/59/SR.49: 7.
[124] See the opening speech by Colombian President Andrés Pastrana in A/54/917: 70.
[125] Ibid.

Minister Nkosazana Dlamini-Zuma of South Africa, which was Chair of the Non-Aligned Movement at the time, put it this way: 'We need to define humanitarian intervention, otherwise others will define it for us.'[126]

Responsibility as control

There were a few themes of interest then—to the South—that must have seemed missing from the report of the International Commission on Intervention and State Sovereignty (ICISS), written and largely completed in 2000 but released three months after the attacks of 11 September 2001 on New York and Washington, DC.[127] Developing states had called for the promotion of principles of neutrality, objectivity, and impartiality in international humanitarian action that could feasibly take the form of coercion, under Chapter VII, as a last resort. Yet ideas such as intervention with consent, and the nature and sources of consent in humanitarian emergencies and civil strife, were designated outside the report's purview: 'the kind of intervention with which we are concerned in this report is action taken against a state or its leaders, without its or their consent, for purposes which are claimed to be humanitarian or protective'.[128]

Sponsored by the Canadian government in September 2000, with a membership intended 'to fairly reflect developed and developing country perspectives', the ICISS sought to 'build a broader understanding of the problem of reconciling intervention for human protection purposes and sovereignty' and 'develop global political consensus'.[129] And it set out to do so, as is commonly known, by 'shifting the terms of the debate' such that its 'proposed change in terminology is also a change in perspective': to move from 'humanitarian intervention' to 'a responsibility to protect' was to move from an understanding of 'sovereignty as control' to one of 'sovereignty as responsibility'.[130] But what should be confessed now is that, in proposing a new conception of the duties implied by any historical right to sovereignty, and particularly duties having to do with humanitarian protection, the report

---

[126] Ibid.: 77.
[127] To be clear, the report was not understood to be addressing the problem of such attacks. 'Our report has aimed at providing precise guidance for states faced with human protection claims in other states; it has not been framed to guide the policy of states when faced with attack on their own nationals, or the nationals of other states residing within their borders' (ICISS 2001: viii). On liberal interventionism after 11 September, including implications on RtoP of the 'war on terror' and late justifications of the war against Iraq in 2003, see Pollentine 2012: 140–166.
[128] ICISS 2001: 8.
[129] Ibid.: 2.
[130] Ibid.: 17. For a full discussion, see Pollentine 2012.

sanctioned something else as well: what might usefully be called 'responsibility as control'. And we should show how, on opposing views on 'responsibility as control', we might identify two Responsibilities to Protect, and in this way expose how early decades of contestation in the twenty-first century in fact resembled, in a fundamental way, the South–North contestation of the final decade of the twentieth.

The central theme of the ICISS report comprehended the following: 'sovereign states have a responsibility to protect their citizens from avoidable catastrophe—from mass murder and rape, from starvation—but that when they are unwilling or unable to do so, that responsibility must be borne by the broader community of states'.[131] Still there was some equivocation as to the nature of what it meant for the international community to bear responsibility: yes, three specific responsibilities were implied by the RtoP (to prevent the crisis, to react to its outbreak, to rebuild afterwards), but if, when a state was unable or unwilling to protect, 'it becomes the responsibility of the international community *to act in its place*', exactly what sort of transfer of authority was involved in a transfer of humanitarian responsibility?[132] While the Commission acknowledged that 'the primary responsibility to protect' rested with the state, might the international community, in fulfilling the residual RtoP in extreme circumstances, take on still more national- or local-political responsibilities?[133]

The substance of the RtoP was described by the Commission as 'the provision of life-supporting protection and assistance to populations at risk'.[134] Its relationship with self-determination, territorial integrity, and choice or replacement of governments was discussed in the report's section on 'right intention'.[135]

> The primary purpose of the intervention must be to halt or avert human suffering. Any use of military force that aims from the outset, for example, for the alteration of borders or the advancement of a particular combatant group's claim to self-determination, cannot be justified. *Overthrow of regimes is not, as such, a legitimate objective, although disabling that regime's capacity to harm its own people may be essential to discharging the mandate of protection*—and what is necessary to achieve that disabling will vary from case to case.[136]

---

[131] Ibid.: viii.
[132] Ibid.: 15. Emphasis added.
[133] Ibid.: xi.
[134] Ibid.: 17.
[135] Ibid.: 35–36.
[136] Ibid.: 35. Emphasis added.

Yet just as the ordinary meaning of guardianship has at least two connotations, so too does this seem true of the international RtoP.[137] Might keeping guard of people, through the 'provision of life-supporting protection', also confer the position or office of becoming more generally responsible for the care of those people?[138] The latter meaning seemed to blur into a logic of trusteeship whereby 'taking responsibility' or fulfilling the residual RtoP granted—for a transitional period—a right to control.[139] So by inheriting an RtoP when a state is unable or unwilling to protect their populations, might international actors also inherit a tacit responsibility whereby the guarded were taken into the more general care of the guardians?[140] To say so would be to suspend competing claims to or sources of supreme authority.

In fact, in the 2001 report, this was explicitly admitted: 'Intervention suspends sovereignty claims to the extent that *good governance*—as well as peace and stability—cannot be promoted or restored unless the intervener has authority over a territory.'[141] The Commission did stress that 'the suspension of the exercise of sovereignty is only *de facto* for the period of the intervention and follow-up, and not *de jure*.'[142] But not only was there a concern here about a logic of the international provision of life-supporting protection blurring into a logic of the international provision of good governance, there were also good reasons to doubt the relevance of this particular distinction between the de facto and de jure. For example, cited by the Commissioners was the case of Yugoslavia: 'Yugoslavia could be said to have temporarily had its sovereignty over Kosovo suspended, though it has not lost it de jure.'[143] This was not clearly true as of 2001, and it became much less probably true after Kosovo's declaration of independence from Serbia in 2008. And surely a very central concern, for the South, was always about intent as distinguished from motive—about whether the intent to control internal affairs, even as a means of effecting a good humanitarian result, was ever legitimate.

This basic process of suspending sovereignty, in the course of transferring RtoP from the state to the international community, is what I mean by responsibility as control. Where international responsibility becomes domestic control, sovereignty has already yielded to humanitarian

---

[137] Guardianship as 'the condition or fact of being a guardian; the office or position of guardian', including as a position of legal tutelage, or as 'keeping guard', as 'protection' (*Oxford English Dictionary*, 2nd edition, 1989).
[138] ICISS 2001: 17.
[139] See generally Bain 2003.
[140] ICISS 2001: xi.
[141] Ibid.: 44. Emphasis added.
[142] Ibid.
[143] Ibid.

protection.[144] The language of defeasibility—expressive of a right that is open to forfeiture or annulment in the fulfilment of some condition—is also useful.[145] While qualified sovereignty refers to any strain of sovereignty as responsibility, only defeasible sovereignty is compatible with responsibility as control—with a process by which sovereignty is disabled or suspended. And it is in light of responsibility as control that we can more thoroughly comprehend and patiently document the rejection, in the South, of the first of two RtoPs; it is basically in reference to responsibility as control that states like Venezuela later alleged that the RtoP language is 'full of traps' concealing 'unmentionable motives'.[146]

Intervention was in all cases to endeavour 'to sustain forms of government compatible with the sovereignty of the state' but, from the view of Northern practice, such an undertaking never represented a hard limit. One subsection of the ICISS report was devoted to trusteeship and international administration (paragraph 5.22: 'useful guidelines for the behaviour of intervening authorities during a military intervention in failed states, and in the followup period, might be found in a constructive adaptation of Chapter XII of the UN Charter'; paragraph 5.24: '[t]here is always likely in the UN to be a generalized resistance to *any resurrection of the "trusteeship" concept*'), and elsewhere it was acknowledged that 'occupation of territory may not be able to be avoided' (as long as there was a commitment to 'returning the territory to its sovereign owner at the conclusion of hostilities or, if that is not possible, administering it on an interim basis under UN auspices').[147] In the penultimate chapter of the report—'Responsibility to Rebuild'—returning the RtoP to the state was described not as returning the obligation to defend civilians from threats to life, but '*returning the society* in question to those who live in it, and who, *in the last instance*, must take responsibility together for *its future destiny*'.[148]

RtoP was no doubt a 'linking concept that bridges the divide between intervention and sovereignty', but the way in which the concepts were being linked suggested the possibility of a mechanism by which sovereignty became defeasible, according to which it might be legitimate in the course of protecting lives—its overarching objective—to overthrow governments and regimes, to

---

[144] On related ideas of conditional sovereignty and the 'responsibilization' of the postcolonial state through RtoP, see Getachew 2019a and Whyte 2017 respectively. On RtoP's appeal to protection as the basis of establishing new authority, and on the discourse of humanitarian intervention as depriving the rescued of a de jure and de facto capacity to act on their own behalf, see generally Orford 2011 and Orford 2003.

[145] Chesterman 2001: 4.

[146] Venezuela, A/59/PV.89: 24.

[147] ICISS 2001: 44, 43, 35.

[148] Ibid.: 45. Emphasis added.

approve of foreign occupation such that it was conceivable to return 'the society in question to those who live in it' at a later date.[149] Hence, from a Southern view, had the perspective of ICISS really strayed from that of an 'International Commission on Humanitarian Intervention' (as it was initially called by its sponsors)?[150] If a logic of trusteeship was a defining feature of classical humanitarian intervention, it seemed latent in Northern RtoP. As William Bain would put it in 2003, such a 'new paternalism' stood 'fundamentally opposed to the demands of human dignity as we have come to understand it in contemporary international society' because it proposed 'to treat an equal unequally.'[151] 'It is in this respect that the idea of trusteeship cannot escape its imperial past, no matter how enlightened or well-intentioned it might be, because it belongs to a mode of conduct that is imperial by its nature.'[152]

Much discussed are certain basic transformations of the meaning of RtoP from the ICISS report of 2001 to the World Summit Outcome Document (WSOD) of 2005: the narrowing of its threshold criteria to four 'mass atrocity crimes', for instance, and its restructuring, proposed in the Secretary-General's 2009 report on the subject, around three pillars.[153] Also transformed in 2005, it is said, was the 'question of authority' insofar as the WSOD did not sanction—as the ICISS report had—intervention by 'coalitions of the willing' when 'the Security Council fails to act'.[154] Yet the question of authority is only in part a question of authorization, of 'who will intervene' or 'who will approve of intervention'.[155] The most important changes rather had to do with whether 'to take international responsibility' meant 'to take control', in the course of keeping guard.

Responsibilities to Protect

In 2005, at the World Summit, all UN member states agreed that states and the international community had a 'responsibility to protect' populations from genocide, war crimes, ethnic cleansing, and crimes against humanity.[156] But if we look closely, this was not a Northern interpretation of intervention at the expense of a Southern one, or vice versa. Nor was it a fusion of

[149] Ibid.: 17.
[150] Bellamy 2009a: 36.
[151] Bain 2003: 173.
[152] Ibid.: 192.
[153] A/63/677. See the discussion in Bellamy 2009a: 66–97.
[154] ICISS 2001: 59, 53.
[155] Compare with 'The Question of Authority' in ICISS 2001: 47–56.
[156] See e.g. Bellamy 2009a: 66–97.

the two viewpoints into one, without their preservation. Despite the unanimous adoption of paragraphs 138 and 139, there coexisted, and coexist today, multiple conceptions of sovereignty as responsibility, two of which seem particularly influential in shaping global order and must be laid bare in the records of the UN General Assembly.

C. S. R. Murthy and Gerrit Kurtz have recently argued that the World Summit's endorsement of RtoP was made much more probable because of a 'discursive shift' whereby a 'normative approach of international solidarity', centred around capacity-building and international assistance short of coercion, 'started to replace bitter debates about the legitimacy of military intervention.'[157] This is surely and profoundly right, though it is important not to lose sight of the extent to which the solidarity approach embraced armed and coercive 'intervention' in the ordinary sense of the word which had by now gained a foothold in discursive practice. Southern practice had and would sanction the collective use of force, through the Security Council, for the purposes of protecting civilians and preventing mass atrocity, in situations of non-state but also state-led violence.[158] What it did not sanction was foreign control of the political, cultural, and economic futures of states and their peoples. The WSOD marked and was marked by the continuation of a clash of two discursive practices of intervention that diverged not on the use of force per se, but on the defeasibility of sovereignty.

Accordingly, it was not that the WSOD signalled an ever-increasing convergence among states on the meaning of RtoP as a singular norm. At the Millennium Summit of 2000, during his unveiling of ICISS, Canadian Foreign Affairs Minister Lloyd Axworthy explained the Commission's objectives in distinctly Northern terms:

> Nothing so threatens the United Nations' very future as this apparent contradiction between principle and power; between people's security and governments' interests; between, in short, humanitarian intervention and state sovereignty.[159]

At the World Summit, the Icelandic delegation argued similarly: while 'sovereign equality' and 'the promise of living in peace as good neighbours' were 'valuable principles', 'Iceland has never looked on the United Nations as a mechanism solely for safeguarding sovereignty.'[160] Up to now 'the key commitments to the peoples enshrined in the UN Charter have not been

---

[157] Murthy and Kurtz 2016: 38.
[158] I return, for example, to initial Southern and non-aligned support for no-fly zones and all necessary measures to protect civilians in Libya in 2011, at the end of this chapter.
[159] Canada, A/55/PV.15: 3.
[160] Iceland, A/60/PV.6: 31.

given their due weight' and the WSOD 'makes significant strides towards redressing the imbalance. In particular, we have established the concept of the responsibility to protect.'[161]

Yet patterns of Southern contestation at the Millennium Summit resembled those of the 1999 debates ('we disagree with the assumption that the principles of sovereignty and humanitarian international law are at variance'; where intervention did occur, '[a]ction must be confined to the saving of lives, not the overthrowing of governments', 'intervention ... must never be used as a guise for unwarranted interference in internal state governance').[162]

And at the World Summit again could be heard the Southern thesis that sovereignty as responsibility did imply a qualified sovereignty, but not defeasible sovereignty; yes, a responsibility to protect, but never responsibility as control. It was on account of a second meaning of sovereignty as responsibility, and the use of the word 'intervention' to refer broadly to international involvement, that it was a consistent argument in context, not some muddle or confusion, to say, as Malaysian Prime Minister Abdullah Ahmad Badawi did before the General Assembly in 2005, that 'any intervention must give due recognition to the Charter principles pertaining to sovereignty, territorial integrity, and non-interference in internal affairs'.[163]

Abdullah was serving at the time as Secretary-General of the Non-Aligned Movement. No doubt, as he noted, there was internationally 'a growing consensus to accept the justifiability of the use of force to protect civilian populations from crimes against humanity, such as genocide and ethnic cleansing'.[164] He might have had in mind developments on the African continent, where a version of the international RtoP had been adopted six months earlier in the AU's Ezulwini Consensus.[165] But even here the interventionism of the AU sat uneasily with liberal-interventionist theory: the Ezulwini Consensus stressed that while '[i]t is important to reiterate the obligation of states to protect their citizens', 'this should not be used as a pretext to undermine the sovereignty, independence, and territorial integrity of states'.[166]

In all cases, according to non-aligned leaders like Abdullah, international protection and the RtoP was to be located within a broader development-led humanitarian programme: 'I should like to say that it is equally a crime against humanity to allow poverty and deprivation to persist in these modern

---

[161] Ibid.: 32.
[162] Iraq, A/55/PV.5: 43; Barbados, A/55/PV.13: 25; ibid.
[163] A/60/PV.4: 40.
[164] Ibid.: 41.
[165] See e.g. Aning and Okyere 2016: 355–358.
[166] African Union 2005.

times. How can we continue to stand by while eight million people around the world die each year because they are too poor to stay alive?'[167]

From one view, then, the NAM strategy had not really changed; quietly the aim was to redefine international humanitarian responsibility in a context in which meaning was not settled, in which Northern activism for RtoP was predominant, but also a context in which the WSOD had multiple interpretations. We should note that, at its 2003 summit in Kuala Lumpur, the NAM reiterated its rejection of humanitarian intervention, 'observed similarities between the new expression "responsibility to protect" and "humanitarian intervention"', and 'requested the Co-ordinating Bureau [of the NAM] to carefully study and consider the expression "the responsibility to protect" and its implications' on the basis of respect for 'territorial integrity and national sovereignty of States'.[168] And at Havana in 2006, the NAM agreed to 'remain seized of the matter' while bearing in mind 'the principles of the UN Charter and international law including respect for the sovereignty and territorial integrity of states, non-interference in their internal affairs, as well as respect for fundamental human rights'.[169]

Likewise, contested meaning was the basis on which the NAM opposed the creation in 2008 of a UN Office on RtoP and UN Special Adviser on RtoP at the Undersecretary-General level. On 7 February 2008, the Cuban delegation in the Fifth Committee protested that: '[i]n a letter dated 20 June 2007, the Chairman of the Coordinating Bureau of the Movement of Non-Aligned Countries had requested the Secretary-General to take into account, in any decision on that very sensitive matter'—the sensitive matter of RtoP— 'the fact that Member States had not completed their deliberations'.[170] If there were to be a Special Adviser, their role would be to 'assist the General Assembly in its consideration of the issue rather than to promote the idea of the RtoP' as if the concept had been adequately or wholly formed.[171]

It was precisely because of what the Secretary-General's office itself had described as the 'manifold concerns regarding the conceptual range and application, and the practical implications' of RtoP that its 'crystallized' and more 'concrete form' was understood as a goal or priority of the UN, not yet a fact in the General Assembly.[172] In meetings between 'senior officials of the Executive Office of the Secretary-General' and several permanent representatives of non-aligned countries, as well as during 'discussions attended by

---

[167] A/60/PV.4: 41.
[168] A/57/759: 10.
[169] A/61/472: 19.
[170] Cuba, A/C.5/62/SR.23: 6.
[171] See e.g. Egypt, A/C.5/62/SR.28: 13.
[172] Chef de Cabinet to the UN Secretary-General, ibid.: 12.

the Chairman of the Coordinating Bureau of the Non-Aligned Movement ... permanent representatives had expressed reticence over the "concept" of the "responsibility to protect", arguing that there was no consensus on the matter.'[173] The Special Adviser's work was to carry out an 'examination of how to further the ideas contained in paragraphs 138 and 139'—the WSOD having stressed the 'need for the General Assembly to continue consideration of the responsibility to protect' while 'bearing in mind the principles of the Charter and international law'.[174]

Again the imperative to 'further the ideas' of RtoP was particularly true of its understanding of sovereign equality. As UN Secretary-General Ban Ki-moon came to put it in his 2009 report on the subject, 'the responsibility to protect is an ally of sovereignty, not an adversary.'[175] Yet principled disagreements emerged as to whether a resurrection of trusteeship could ever be anything but adversarial.[176]

'Neither concerns about sovereignty nor the understanding that sovereignty implies responsibility', noted the Secretary-General's report, 'are confined to one part of the world.'[177] Yet the content of concerns, varying across regions, suggested the existence of unsettled tensions beneath its key paragraphs, in one sense literally—as was the case with the footnotes of paragraph 8, which contained articles authored by then-Special Adviser on RtoP Edward Luck.[178] These are writings in which we find references to: 'the conditions under which rulers surrender the right to govern their people and other nations become free to intervene'; Kofi Annan's view (shared in a speech on 12 October 2005 at the New University of Lisbon) that RtoP, as adopted at the World Summit, had produced 'a new equation, with "human life, human dignity, human rights raised above even the entrenched concept of state sovereignty"'; the arguments of Francis Deng et al. (also reaffirmed in the Secretary-General's report's seventh paragraph) that 'living up to the responsibilities of sovereignty becomes in effect the best guarantee of sovereignty'; and a quotation from Hobbes to the effect that when a sovereign can 'no longer fulfill the function for which he or she was given

---

[173] Ibid.: 11.
[174] Ibid.: 12.
[175] A/63/677: 7.
[176] Compare with the influential argument put forward by Alex Bellamy in 2014: 'the key debates are now about how best to implement RtoP, not about whether to accept the principle', and that accordingly there is 'no longer serious principled disagreement between states on the merits of RtoP itself' or 'its meaning and scope' (Bellamy 2014: 11, 3, 12, 11). See also ibid., 58–74.
[177] A/63/677: 6.
[178] See ibid. In particular: Luck 2008, 2009.

power', that sovereign is 'no longer owed obedience, is no longer indeed a sovereign'.[179]

The emergence of a kind of neo-Hobbesian logic to justify a transferring outward of authority—from domestic subjects towards international subjects—seemed to realize some of the worst fears of the developing countries. And their suspicions mounted further with the report's suggestion that 'Member States may want to consider the principles, rules, and doctrine that should guide the application of coercive force in extreme situations relating to the responsibility to protect. This issue was addressed in the 2001 report of the ICISS and by my predecessor, Kofi Annan, in his 2005 report "In larger freedom".'[180]

The problem for developing states had to do with the reach, not the existence, of the concept's third pillar: 'we must continue to think in a concerted way about the third pillar [the international RtoP inherited when a state manifestly fails to protect]' so as to affirm that 'no juridical norm can legally justify humanitarian intervention by the Security Council under Chapter VII of the Charter.'[181] Coercive intervention was acceptable, but had to be 'fully consistent with the Charter. That means, inter alia, recognizing that a State's responsibility to protect does not qualify State sovereignty'—in the sense that sovereign equality was never to be suspended—but also that sovereignty does 'not exempt the state from its obligation to protect its population. On the contrary, it is from that very attribute that such obligation derives.'[182] RtoP 'must be implemented pursuant to premises that do not undermine the guarantees and sovereignty of states', meaning there were purposive limits to the privileges available to foreign protectors, even in crisis zones: 'the implementation of the responsibility to protect should not contravene ... the principle of non-interference in the internal affairs of states'.[183]

Hence 'it is critical that our discussions not be reduced to the simplistic dichotomy of states on the one side insisting on absolute sovereignty and, on the other side, RtoP proponents demanding that states surrender absolute sovereignty.'[184] Clearly 'we are all united behind our fundamental desire to protect innocent people and to prevent another Rwanda.'[185]

---

[179] Luck 2009: 14; Luck 2008: xxxiv, xxxvii. Luck is quoting or citing: Berkowitz 2008: 18; Kofi Annan's comments in SG/SM/10161; Deng et al. 1996: 15; the writings and analysis of Hobbes contained in MacFarlane and Khong 2006: 39.
[180] A/63/677: 7.
[181] Morocco, A/63/PV.98: 13; Cuba, A/63/PV.99: 22.
[182] Brazil, A/63/PV.97: 13.
[183] Ecuador, A/63/PV.98: 9; China, ibid.: 23.
[184] Singapore, ibid.: 7.
[185] Ibid.

To overlook the contested nature of sovereignty as responsibility would be to endorse its capture by liberal-interventionist theory. The Serbian representative could not restrain himself from quoting Martti Ahtisaari, the former President of Finland and subsequent UN Special Envoy for the Kosovo Status Process, who:

> in an interview with CNN on 10 December 2008, gave his view of the Responsibility to Protect. After acknowledging the fact that the General Assembly had 'accepted the principle of RtoP in 2005', he went on to justify it by saying that *'if a dictatorial leadership in any country behaves the way Milosevic and company did vis-à-vis the Albanians in Kosovo, they lose the right to control them anymore'*. We wonder if such interpretations of the noble concept of the Responsibility to Protect truly lead us away from the supposedly defunct concept of humanitarian intervention.[186]

Liberal hegemony and the struggle for sovereign equality

The argument of this chapter has been that the extent to which intervention gained legitimacy in the post-Cold War society of states must be understood in the context of rival discursive practices. A shared meaning or singular norm of intervention cannot be said to have been achieved insofar as it accommodated the content of one of these practices but not the other. While all agreed on the qualified nature of sovereign rule, in the sense that sovereignty implies a responsibility to protect populations from genocide, war crimes, ethnic cleansing, and crimes against humanity, the transfer of the responsibility to protect from the state to the international community in emergency circumstances was not believed by many, even most, to imply a de facto or de jure suspension of sovereignty. A broad and more ordinary use of the vocabulary of intervention in the UN, by which intervention came to mean international involvement in humanitarian crises abroad, provided a rhetorical and political path by which institutionalization was encouraged and achieved in the early 2000s, but it also masked enduring South–North contestation in relation to a more technical import that such use left behind: having to do with the infringement of sovereignty and self-determined futures of states.

As Jennifer Welsh has argued, the contestation of RtoP can be seen as bound up in processes of normative evolution and in terms of a foundational

---

[186] Serbia, A/63/PV.101: 13.

moral challenge posed to sovereign equality.[187] What sovereign equality has tended to resist is 'a move from a horizontal system of sovereign states that demonstrate mutual respect, to a hierarchical system where conduct is subject to oversight and punishment by an unspecified and unaccountable agent of the "international community", with its own legal personality and purposes'.[188] As she puts it, '[i]t is this possibility, which would potentially enable the strong to impose their conception of justice, that has motivated some of the deepest contestation surrounding RtoP'.[189]

As a matter of international practice, I have tried to suggest, the conditionality inherent in RtoP's understanding of sovereignty is a conditionality of strings attached and restrictions of prerogative, but not a conditionality in the sense of defeasibility, particularly insofar as non-aligned theories of international humanitarian protection can be read as claims to RtoP proper. RtoP is often distinguished from humanitarian intervention.[190] But of course the ICISS was formed in the context of the intervention debates of the 1990s and of a new interventionism said to justify NATO action in places like the former Yugoslavia. And what has linked these plausibly distinct concepts in their practice is a theory of an inverse relationship between sovereignty and human rights. That theory has not remained unchallenged, nor was its contestation settled by subsequent UN-based institutionalization. Hence, while a year like 2011 counted as a high-water mark for liberal interventionism in international society, a clash of Northern and Southern practices shows how it did not mark the eclipse of a global programme of responsible sovereignty per se. Furthermore, the language of RtoP seems embedded in a broader normative and institutionalized structure that makes it unlikely to disappear in the near future.[191]

Writing in the *New York Times* days after the end of NATO's intervention in Libya, David Rieff made a solemn declaration: 'RtoP, RIP'.[192] On one level, the assessment was of course correct. Rieff was surely right to say that if the campaign was 'a textbook case of how the new UN doctrine of the Responsibility to Protect (RtoP) was supposed to work', then it had done 'grave, possibly even irreparable, damage to RtoP's prospects of becoming a global norm'.[193] The Security Council resolutions that authorized

---

[187] Welsh 2013: see especially 391–394.
[188] Ibid.: 394.
[189] Ibid.
[190] See e.g. Evans 2016.
[191] Welsh 2019.
[192] Rieff 2011.
[193] Ibid.

intervention to protect civilians in Benghazi did not, claimed Rieff, authorize air strikes that led directly to the overthrow of Muammar el-Qaddafi; in 2011, 'for all intents and purposes, RtoP was NATO-ized'.[194] On another level, it would be a serious mistake to confuse international humanitarian responsibility, to be upheld by collective and coercive action as a last resort, with a theory of liberal intervention alone. By the end of 2011 there was a relative uptake of a version of RtoP that insisted on absolute respect for sovereign equality and reflected historical values and practices of the Global South. Arguably, for all intents and purposes, RtoP had been non-align-ified. To trace intervention in its contestation is to see how implementations of liberal theory came to trigger a backlash against a logic of 'responsibility as control' in the international responsibility to protect.

That is, after all, how NATO's intervention largely came to be depicted by its critics and how subsequent opposition to intervention, in the UN, came to be justified: NATO had gone 'far beyond the letter and spirit of resolution 1973' by '[a]busing the authorization granted by the Council to advance a political regime-change agenda'.[195]

Much has been said of the ensuing anti-interventionism of the BRICS countries, though anti-interventionism might be more accurately described, as Courtney Fung has put it, as an attempt at 'separating intervention from regime change'.[196] Brazil's concept paper on a 'Responsibility While Protecting', circulated as a document of the General Assembly and Security Council, was not only a critique of foreign-imposed political or local-political futures.[197] It also foregrounded long-standing commitments to non-violent prevention, capacity-building, and accountability in resolution implementation, for example.[198] Still it seems theoretically salient to conceive of a responsibility borne by guardians while protecting, and a more responsible form of protection, as a reassertion of the line between essentially domestic and international affairs, and of the thesis that the duty to prevent gross and systematic violations of human rights need not subvert the duty to respect equal rights and the self-determination of peoples. To specify that the use of force should 'abide by the letter and spirit of the mandate conferred by the Security Council or the General Assembly' seems, in a particular discursive context, like a rejection of sovereignty's suspension in the course

---

[194] Ibid.
[195] South Africa, S/PV.6650: 22.
[196] Fung 2018. See also Ruan 2012; Chen 2016; Foot 2016. See generally Fung 2019.
[197] A/66/551.
[198] See e.g. Spektor 2012; Kenkel 2012; Tourinho, Stuenkel, and Brockmeier 2016.

of protection.[199] A story of two RtoPs reasserts the paternalistic nature of trusteeship in all its forms, and provides a corrective to existing understandings: there was a practice of RtoP belonging to 'non-Western stalwarts of sovereignty' in the post-Cold War period and it did not bar, inherently, the use of force, under Chapter VII, as a last resort.[200]

In fact, according to the Southern view, more was to be done on precisely that level of emergency collective action, though in a different chord: to quote the Indian delegation, 'in this context it is pertinent to mention that we find several member states all too willing to expend considerable resources for regime change in the name of protection of civilians', yet 'unwilling to provide minimal resources, like military helicopters, to the United Nations peacekeeping missions'.[201] Where Northern RtoP permitted a process by which, if a state is unwilling or unable to protect its population, 'they lose the right to control them anymore', Southern RtoP drew from traditions of the Non-Aligned Movement and G77, groups for which sovereignty and self-determination have always been more a prerequisite than an adversary of human rights.[202] The divide, in the discursive practices of states, was not fundamentally about coercive international responsibility. Any depiction of a global intervention debate as one between sovereigntists unwilling to endorse collective force in emergencies, and interventionists whose collective force is anti-sovereigntist as a last resort, is also a liberal-interventionist depiction, one that 'loads the dice in favour of intervention [at the expense of sovereignty] before the argument has even begun, by tending to label and delegitimize dissent as anti-humanitarian'.[203]

The ongoing crisis of liberal theory of intervention is best appreciated in terms of what it replaced and of what has come to be forgotten—including, as this chapter has suggested, the vision of a New International Humanitarian Order and a renewed programme of international and coercive humanitarian action in terms of the 'law of The Hague' and 'law of Geneva', rooted in an overarching commitment to development and non-dependence, and an understanding of the ways in which international hierarchy undermines

---

[199] A/66/551. The preambular section of Resolution 1973 reaffirmed 'a strong commitment to the sovereignty, independence, territorial integrity, and national unity of the Libyan Arab Jamahiriya' (S/RES/1973). For a discussion of regime change and its consistency with Resolution 1973, see e.g. Deeks 2018.

[200] Rotmann, Kurtz, and Brockmeier 2014: 361.

[201] S/PV.6650: 18. For a critical view of 'intervention as stabilization' in Africa, and an admonition against regime stabilization more particularly, see Soares de Oliveira and Verhoeven 2018. Still, as C. S. R. Murthy and Gerrit Kurtz argue, '[t]he Force Intervention Brigade in the Democratic Republic of Congo and the UN assistance mission in Mali demonstrate the potential teeth' and the potential just outcomes 'of a consensual solidarist approach to atrocity prevention'. See Murthy and Kurtz 2016: 53.

[202] Martti Ahtisaari quoted by Serbia in A/63/PV.101: 13.

[203] ICISS 2001: 16.

peace and freedom in their interdependence.[204] The post-Cold War period did witness a new political and moral bid for a sovereignty that was responsible. But this bid was also, and much more controversially, for a sovereignty that was defeasible.[205] And while the latter form of sovereignty was more novel in the history of the global international society that followed the end of the Second World War, its considerable normative reach was not a function of reason and persuasion alone. It must be located in the hegemony of a Global Liberal Order that until just recently hung over us all.

---

[204] Kurt Herndl, Assistant Secretary-General for Human Rights, A/C.3/40/SR.69: 8.
[205] The idea of 'Two Responsibilities to Protect' is more fully developed in Quinton-Brown 2023b.

Epilogue

This book has attempted to sketch out a genealogy of intervention in global international society. In particular it has focused on the attempts of statespeople since 1945 to make sense of what it means to intervene in international relations. And it has been looking at historical meaning particularly in the context of a Southern revolt against Western-dominated order, illustrating moments of the concept's reconstitution in global political order, as part of a story that is bound up with where we are now, and where we might be going.

I have tried to suggest that if we are ever to capture the evolving functions of this shared but contested concept in international society, if we are ever to understand intervention as a genuinely global debate, then we must approach intervention in terms of meanings that have been expressed and seized upon by that society's members. What we need to investigate are the links between established historical orders and influential sets of beliefs concerning more professedly just or better orders, or what I have called discursive practices. Pulled together in a narrative of large-scale social change, these practices articulate what I have been calling the conditions of what it is to intervene; they are made up of self-descriptions of statespeople as practitioners, and they are connected to a struggle to legitimize political action and reorganize the transmission of power that is basic to political authority. It is across the practices, and in their competition and institutional uptake, that we find the more or less perennial problem: how to globally manage involvements in the affairs of others.

And it is in light of the genealogy that we might begin to reassess our turbulent present. For the fall of interventionism should no longer be confused with the fate of internationalism or the promise of sovereign and international humanitarian responsibility. The liberal interventionist moment must instead be understood as entailing an elaborate rhetorical redescription and normative contestation, which supplanted previous understandings and brought about a confusion that was also an ideological feat. In global international society and its study, our comprehension of the intervention problem has suffered from a vast amnesia.

Intervention before Interventionism. Patrick Quinton-Brown, Oxford University Press. © Patrick Quinton-Brown (2024).
DOI: 10.1093/oso/9780198886457.003.0008

From within discursive practices of non-alignment, and what came to be known as the Global South, we can begin to recollect the concept's more complete trajectory and just contributions over the past century. The duty not to intervene was originally a function of Great Power politics after the end of the Second World War, and of attempts to rein in the United Nations organization as drawn up at San Francisco. But this fundamental global principle came to be reclaimed in a process of decolonization that took shape at Bandung, where the newly independent states of Asia and Africa advanced anti-colonialism and anti-racism as founding purposes of an alternative UN-based global order. Reappropriated by those previously excluded from the society of states, the ideas of non-intervention and domestic jurisdiction were integrated into a broader solidarist-internationalist design, one that internationally promoted and protected human rights. To intervene was once not simply to use force for higher and humanitarian purposes. To intervene was rather to offend our common humanity. The contradiction, in a Bandung UN and anti-hierarchical international society beset, but not wholly arrested, by superpower competition, was not between sovereignty and human rights, but between intervention and human rights. A series of international actions to promote human freedom were in fact legitimated on the basis of a total non-interventionism; fundamentally, to intervene meant to deny the primary human right of peoples to self-determination.

Had the reach of self-determination been too far, or the scope of domestic jurisdiction been without limits, such a non-interventionism would of course have shackled internationalism and our global institutions. For anti-colonial theorizing no doubt made 'sovereignty without condition'.[1] But that is not to say it made sovereignty without qualification or without responsibility—a defence of the absolutist conception of sovereignty having never been, in actual discursive context, a valid application of the non-intervention principle. The solidarist internationalism of the South rather served to remind us that where domestic jurisdiction ended, and international jurisdiction began, was always a relative question dependent on the development of international relations and society. Nothing was to be used to conveniently hide genocide, crimes against humanity, and gross abuses of human rights; nor was legitimate solidarist-internationalist action to be instrumentalized as interference in essentially domestic or internal affairs. Formulated as such, the shared duty to promote universal human rights moved through freedom from foreign domination and vassalage.

---

[1] Moyn and Özsu 2020: 29.

During the transition into the twenty-first century, however, something changed. In what came to be known as the 'sovereignty–intervention' debate, international humanitarian protection was turned against equal rights and self-determination.[2] In the beliefs and practices of statespeople, the contradiction between intervention and human rights was skillfully inverted. The non-intervention principle would be depicted as something to be despised by all who sought a world free from the worst abuses of human rights. In such arguments intervention would no longer offend humanity but save it. It would no longer break the rules but uphold a higher moral imperative, even a moral imperative said to underpin international law itself, in a global society that would place greater emphasis upon cosmopolitan concerns for individuals.[3] A new programme of human rights came to justify a theory of international humanitarian protection that, by sanctioning a neo-trusteeship in extreme circumstances, implied a resurrection of unequal sovereignty. Such was the high-water mark of a liberal interventionism that was a matter neither of straightforward global consensus nor of ever-increasing convergence.

In this concluding note, I synthesize the previous chapters in terms of a broad recovery of theories displaced and muddled, which provides the basis of an alternative framing of the global intervention debate. I first retrace the most important transformations of what it has meant to intervene in the shared practices of international society to suggest that neglected, if not effaced, insights of Asian, African, and Latin American statespeople accommodated a concern for both peaceful co-existence and the international promotion and protection of human freedom. Second I suggest that if historically contingent meanings and narratives of intervention play a significant role in processes of legitimating, and de-legitimating, controversial forms of political action and authority, then the stakes of getting the language of intervention right seem extremely high. Whither intervention in an increasingly divided and multipolar world? How might we think of intervention in a way that recognizes diversity as a value, and diverse distributions of agency as a momentous international fact, without abandoning shared and existing international responsibilities? I end, briefly, by reflecting on the genealogy as a repertoire for dilemmas of global ordering and crisis management in the present.

---

[2] ICISS 2001: 16.
[3] See e.g. Tesón 1988; Beitz 1979.

Eras of intervention

In 1991, retiring Secretary-General Javier Pérez de Cuéllar, in his final report on the work of the UN organization, warned against 'novel doctrines' and 'new concepts' of international humanitarian protection debated 'among legal experts and political theoreticians' that were 'not only not required on this issue; but can also upset established understandings'.[4] That this report later came to be depicted as having championed a theory of liberal intervention is an astonishing manoeuvre, not least against the background of the discursive practices charted in this book.[5] As Pérez de Cuéllar put it:

> We need not to impale ourselves on the horns of a dilemma between respect for sovereignty and the protection of human rights. The last thing the United Nations needs is a new ideological controversy. What is involved is *not* the right of intervention but the collective obligation of states to bring relief and redress in human rights emergencies.[6]

Yet a new ideological controversy, one that impaled existing conventions on the horns of a dilemma between sovereignty and human rights, is exactly what followed. 'For us to transcend the dictates of sovereignty', proposed liberal interventionists who were leading us into a post-Cold War era, 'we must articulate an ethical vision and so reshape human relations with authority.'[7] The New Interventionist strategy was at times quite explicit: '[d]rawing upon both the analysis of humanitarian intervention and *re-examination of legal meanings of terms in a political context* provides the means to build bridges and act.'[8] The aim was to 'mollify contradictions between human rights and intervention.'[9]

The story I have told helps us to better understand the extent to which the global intervention debate has remained, and remains for many, under the spell of a perhaps once attractive but now very dangerous teleological view of the UN's role in historical international society. This is a vision in which the organization, divided for over forty years between competing blocs, was unable to act and powerless in its pursuit of justice, having been frozen by Cold War dynamics and an extreme sovereigntism of the newly independent

---

[4] A/46/1: 5.
[5] Chopra and Weiss 1992.
[6] A/46/1: 5. Emphasis added.
[7] Chopra and Weiss 1992: 116.
[8] Ibid. Emphasis added.
[9] Ibid.

states.[10] Only with the end of the bipolar era, the demise of the Third World, and the advent of a more centrally regulated society of states in the 1990s, was the UN at last in a position to promote and protect universal human rights. Only then could it break free from the sovereigntism that had suffocated it and uphold a responsibility to protect civilians under the auspices of a liberal hegemon.

Certainly the preceding chapters suggest that such a UN, and such an international society, did not exist. And its continued use as a legitimating element of a political programme of defeasible sovereignty spells disaster in a context of both shifting power relations and shifting perceptions of the moral, and often too the political, failures of key interventions in the twenty-first century. What I have tried to provide in contrast is a view of decolonial contestation that, without denying the failures and deficiencies of the Global South project, traces the descent and institutionalization of what it has been to intervene in the self-interpretations of states. The true conceit, I have suggested, of our late interventionism was not a kind of vanity or hubris, but its distorted portrayal of alternatively solidarist theories of intervention—theories that steered clear of superpower paradigms and progressively developed over the decades.

In fact it was during and through Cold War decolonization that members of international society overcame a once-hegemonic theory of the non-intervention principle that had been used to weaken the hand of the UN; that had been intended to preserve sovereign licences of colonial and racial exploitation; and that had been established in a moment of Great Power unity that accompanied the end of the Second World War.

To review: at San Francisco, a Latin American-led group sought the inclusion of the promotion of human rights and non-intervention as an explicit duty of states in the UN Charter. If Latin American contestation of the Good Neighbor Policy shifted the meaning of intervention from the Lawrence-Oppenheim thesis of 'dictatorial or coercive interference' towards a more Calvo-esque tradition of intervention as the outcome or effect of foreign pressure, then we can see how an inter-American model of non-intervention had been proposed as a global standard to protect smaller states and their 'personalities'.[11] However the attempt to globally institutionalize, as a duty of states, the theory of intervention as effect—a theory understood to have been adopted in major international agreements at Montevideo, Buenos Aires, the Saavedra Lamas Treaty, and Chapultepec—initially failed. Instead the

---

[10] See Roberts and Kingsbury 1993: 4–5.
[11] Victor Andrés Belaúnde in UNCIO 1945: VI, 66–67.

principle of non-intervention came to be, as an interstate duty reflected in Article 2 (4) of the Charter, much more narrowly construed and, as a duty of the organization towards its members reflected in Article 2 (7), more broadly construed. We therefore showed that the extraordinary and most laudable achievement for humanity that was the creation of the UN occurred within a certain commonality of purposes, true, but also a clash of internationalisms.

In many ways Bandung was a reply to San Francisco, originating in the exclusion of African and Asian countries from meetings that had laid out the framework of post-war order, and the fear of those countries that such exclusion might leave them without a role in the making, and only one in the taking, of the rules and norms of international society.[12] Non-intervention, as contained in the Five Principles of Peaceful Coexistence and Panchsheel Treaty between China and India over Tibet, reflected a conception of intervention not as the threat or use of force, but as the effect of pressure. Yet the Ten Principles of Bandung, in recognizing peace and freedom as interdependent, transformed the theory of intervention as effect. At Bandung a more anti-colonial theory of intervention was an absolute defence of sovereign equality, but also an assertion that abuses of the principle of non-intervention were to 'yield before justice, before liberalism, before common sense'.[13] Such a theory of the concept promised to overturn the assertion, popular in the General Assembly at the time, that colonialism and racism, and large-scale colonial and racial violence, were matters in which the UN and its members could never interfere, even by way of speech, because they were domestic matters belonging essentially to their respective metropoles. Bandung's conception of domestic jurisdiction was dynamic, not static, and emphasized the shared responsibility of states and the international community to uphold obligations having to do with universal human rights and self-determination—and particularly self-determination not just as a principle, but itself as a right, eventually an international-legal right.[14] An Afro-Asian language of intervention was hence used to legitimate international anti-colonial action in relation to racism and the treatment of Indians in South Africa, for instance, as well as broader repudiations of white supremacist international hierarchy and related atrocities and crimes against humanity.

The institutional achievements of the First UN Declaration on Non-Intervention, as well as the UN's Friendly Relations process, were also anti-colonial and humanitarian campaigns mounted by Third World

---

[12] Anghie 2017: 535–536; Tan and Acharya 2008.
[13] Muhammad Fadhel al-Jamali in TMPCAAC 1955: 145–147.
[14] See Rajan 1961; Wilson 1988; Getachew 2019b.

majorities in international settings.[15] As a matter of discursive practice, the story of the 1960s was not one of a jealous nationalism versus a benevolent internationalism, but a conflict or encounter between a dictatorial theory of intervention as coercive interference and an anti-colonial theory of intervention as the outcome of pressure at the expense of self-determined futures. The latter was construed as an internationalism that worked through nationalism, and through the solidarity of nations, rather than at the expense of the state. And it is in terms of this encounter, and the apparent success of the latter theory at the expense of the former, that global meanings of intervention were changing. The anti-colonial theory reduced a range of previously permitted actions directed by large states against smaller ones. But at the same moment that it reformulated the shared duty of states to refrain from intervention, absolutely and in any form, it also embraced and extended the shared duty of states to respect and promote universal human rights. In context, then, the international struggle of the 'Bandung powers' was not one of 'collective intervention' but rather collective or internationalist action to deliver populations from oppression and to uphold the right of those populations to control their own fate and well-being.[16] Developing states did not always agree on the reach of such a positive non-alignment—many of course resisted the interpretations of its substance offered by revolutionist groups, for instance—but no one, then or now, would seriously deny that an international responsibility had been established to prevent certain gross abuses of human rights, through multiple means, including coercion in extreme circumstances. No one would seriously deny the evolution through this period of international human rights law and humanitarian law, for instance, or the uses of the UN-based human rights regime in legitimizing international anti-colonial and anti-racist struggle in the very worst of cases, cases which offended and offend every precept of our common humanity.

Such an agenda of international responsibilities and human rights—a global agenda of human emancipation rooted in freedom from intervention, understood as foreign pressure against self-determined futures—was also one of development, of eradicating extreme economic inequality, and of preventing the silent genocide of mass starvation and disease. The UN's Second Declaration of Non-Intervention, we have shown, sought a greater emancipation by linking the intervention problem explicitly to principles of the New International Economic Order (NIEO) and New World Communication and Information Order (NWICO).[17] Intervention as a matter of

---

[15] A/RES/2131(XX); A/RES/2625(XXV).
[16] Wight 1978: 236.
[17] See especially part 1 of the annex of A/RES/36/103.

neocolonial dependence opened up a new front of global debate without closing previous ones. In relation to the NIEO, non-intervention was a protest against economic coercion, tied aid, debt traps, and structural and exploitative relationships within a world economy.[18] In relation to the NWICO, the principle was used to address the issue of 'false' and 'distorted news' through international electronic means, for example.[19] In both cases it accommodated solidarist-internationalist actions understood in terms of liberation and self-determination: the creation of international producers' associations and news agency pools, for example, nationalization on the basis of permanent sovereignty over natural resources, and UN-based attempts at placing international controls on free but unequal flows of information.

A New International Humanitarian Order (NIHO), first mooted in 1981 and notably the subject of an independent study approved by the General Assembly, was conceived as interlocking with the NIEO and NWICO and 'an essential complementary task' in alleviating 'man-made' and 'natural disasters'.[20] It aimed to deepen international cooperation around the 'law of The Hague' and 'law of Geneva'.[21] And it might be compared to the official position of the International Committee of the Red Cross (in favour of humanitarian assistance and protection but against humanitarian intervention) and contrasted with the position of the 'new humanitarian' NGOs, which undertook assistance in terms of a right or duty to interfere.[22]

Yet while there would emerge a new humanitarian order, it would not be the NIHO of the non-aligned states. As a chapter in a longer genealogical story, liberal interventionism was about reconstitutions in a counterstruggle, even a counter-revolt, against Southern-oriented order.

One such reconstitution involved the claim that sovereignty masked or shielded mass atrocities in international society and therefore that actions to prevent the most serious violations of human rights could take precedence over sovereign equality. We can now be very clear: there of course did emerge glaring historical examples in which flagrant breaches of human rights stirred little if any criticism in the UN—or in Southern forums such as the OAU—and in which developing-world perpetrators sought impunity through references to non-intervention and domestic jurisdiction.[23] But it

---

[18] Thomas 1985: 122–155.
[19] Alleyne 1995.
[20] Explanatory memo presented by Jordan to the General Assembly, A/36/245: 1–2. See Aga Khan and Talal 1988.
[21] Kurt Herndl in A/C.3/40/SR.69: 8.
[22] Chandler 2001; Rieff 2002; Foley 2008. See also Whyte 2012.
[23] Oji Umozurike, writing in 1979, gave the example of the OAU's muted response to atrocities committed by Idi Amin in Uganda as compared with the OAU's correct treatment of, and coercive resistance against, apartheid and colonialism, despite South African claims of domestic jurisdiction. OAU as much as

does not follow that an absolutist conception of sovereignty was an expression of solidarist internationalism or a historical feature of the non-aligned vision of anti-hierarchical global order. It rather follows that charter provisions, including OAU Charter provisions, regarding non-intervention were being shamefully misconstrued; from the solidarist-internationalist view, the principle of non-intervention can never be used to violate with impunity the norms and rules of international society.[24]

To invoke non-intervention to shield the commission of mass atrocities would, in short, be just as empty a moral gesture and just as much an abuse as the 'little veto' of Article 2 (7) invoked by major Western powers through the 1950s and 1960s to suppress the UN-based anti-colonial and anti-racist movement.[25] It would contradict an established set of beliefs, promoted by non-aligned states themselves during the adoption of the UN's First Declaration on Non-Intervention, for example, and directly in reference to genocide and crimes against humanity, that non-intervention could never serve as an excuse to evade obligations accepted by states under international law and treaties.[26] In the end it would undermine the true anti-colonial theory of non-intervention by providing its critics with a pretense of ignorance.

A second reconstitutive move encompassed the liberal-interventionist appeal to define intervention as broadly as possible, even so broadly as to sanction the idea, previously inconceivable in the technical meanings of states, of 'intervention by consent' or 'intervention by invitation'.[27] Insofar as intervention might come to mean international involvement, and hence insofar as non-intervention might come to mean non-involvement, the tension between human rights and intervention could be quietly undone. As a rhetorical move, the implications for political and moral debate would be far-reaching: a whole range of internationalist activities in the era of formal decolonization—not least international peacekeeping, an invention remembered by many in terms of the anti-colonialism and non-interventionism of the Suez Crisis—would be recategorized as 'intervention' in UN debate. If we accept that even mediation missions and peacekeeping with sovereign consent eventually did become, in a discourse of states, interventionary action, then we can begin to understand how Southern practice abandoned the language of non-intervention in debates around the international promotion of

---

UN Charter provisions regarding domestic jurisdiction, he suggested, were being 'quoted out of context.' See Umozurike 1979: 207, 197–209.

[24] Ibid.
[25] Chile's rebuke of an anti-internationalist reading of Article 2 (7), quoted in Rajan 1961: 235.
[26] See Chapter 4, especially the last two sections.
[27] See e.g. Damrosch and Scheffer 1991. See generally de Wet 2020.

human rights: for non-intervention had become conflated with indifference to existing international obligations.[28]

Such a new characterization of intervention and sovereignty as potentially allied concepts was at the heart of the proposed Responsibility to Protect (RtoP).[29] But here too we have provided a corrective to the orthodox narrative. While a more ordinary language of intervention in the UN no doubt helped to facilitate the inclusion of RtoP in paragraphs 138 and 139 of the World Summit Outcome Document of 2005, it would be wrong to treat the adoption of those paragraphs as a universal, albeit fleeting, endorsement of liberal interventionism.[30] The RtoP concept was originally intended to reconcile opposing views on humanitarian intervention in a debate 'between the Global North, as represented by NATO, and the Global South, as articulated by the Non-Aligned Movement', its co-authors being of the view that '[t]he proposed change in terminology is also a change in perspective, reversing the perceptions inherent in the traditional language, and adding some additional ones.'[31] Still it is too easy to say that it 're-established an international consensus on the legitimate ends of the use of military power' or that disagreements on the 'meaning and scope' of sovereignty as a responsibility came to fade away.[32] The institutional uptake of RtoP was a historic political agreement on the shared duty of states to protect populations from mass atrocities, but it papered over recurring interpretive disagreements on the suspension of sovereignty. Non-aligned contestations of RtoP, we have seen, sounded much like long-standing arguments against humanitarian intervention, on account of their unyielding defence of sovereign equality while protecting.[33] Taking responsibility could never, from this view, mean taking domestic or local-political control, in the form of a sacred trust or otherwise. The line between Northern and Southern conceptions of sovereignty as responsibility, of ongoing Northern and Southern practices of the Responsibility to Protect, is also a solidarist-internationalist line: of sovereignty with strings attached, but without condition.

From a more global and critical perspective, then, what seems so striking about the past thirty years is not so much the taking on of solidarist concerns having to do with the implementation of existing international and

---

[28] A/RES/55/101. See the section, 'Intervention without infringing sovereignty' in Chapter 6.
[29] ICISS 2001.
[30] Paragraph 139 notably referred to 'collective action', not intervention. See A/RES/60/1.
[31] Thakur 2019: 138; ICISS 2001: 17. It seems hard to imagine a clearer expression of, to quote Srinivasan, the 'paradiastolic gesture' at the heart of worldmaking through modification of our representational practices. Srinivasan 2019: 148. See Skinner 2002: 175–187.
[32] Thakur 2019: 138; Bellamy 2014: 12.
[33] See also Welsh 2013.

humanitarian responsibilities, including by collective action and the use of force as a last resort; it is rather the disappearance of self-determination and domestic jurisdiction as constitutive formula of the intervention concept, such that it became possible to conceive of an age of interventionists, even if not plainly an age of sovereignty's suspension. The history of our present crisis is that of liberal interventionism, but also that of what liberal interventionism replaced.

Intervention after interventionism

Today international society suffers glaringly from a strain and disunity that might seem to render, at first blush, the post-Cold War world a moment of inimitable consensus. But the choices are not as stark as they have recently been presented and, from a properly Southern or solidarist-internationalist perspective, the debate has said too little—not too much—about the international struggle for human freedom in its totality. In contrast to those who see intervention either as a benevolent guardianship or a crusading imperialist ideology, we could continue to develop a picture of the progressive evolution of global order that is inclusive of multiple conceptions of intervention and multiple paths to solidarity.

A genealogy of intervention in the practices of non-aligned statespeople and the norms and rules of international society suggests that, by its nature as a political concept, new rounds of its contestation and reconstitution are to be expected, and ought to be expected, in light of new international dilemmas. One such dilemma hanging over the book is of course the palpable risk of, and the moral and political imperative to resist, sliding into a New Cold War. Other and surely related dilemmas—the recurrence in and through cyberspace of intrusive forms of data and information in domestic life and elections, for instance—appear at a time when problems of cooperation and responsibility in global commons, climate-related above all, have become impossible to neglect. Languages of intervention, sovereignty, human rights, and responsibility relate to each of these domains; debates around environmental degradation and climate change are also debates about domestic jurisdiction and sovereign and shared duties, and the principle of non-intervention is widely, even increasingly, cited in international attempts at governing cyberspace and state-based cyber operations.[34]

---

[34] See e.g. Conca 2015; Huang and Mačák 2017; Mueller 2020.

Yet while in some ways the character of these challenges seems genuinely new, and while the political contexts and players are of course not the same, there must be a sense in which basic logics of intervention are returning to international society, rather than surfacing there for the first time. For while intervention is often treated as a particular type of international event, something that happens through means other than speculation or belief, what we have shown instead is that, at a deeper and more fundamental level, intervention is a socially-meaningful description and evaluation, one that has been tied up not just with the question of force, but that of freedom.[35] Its institutionalization and function is therefore always a matter of the management of inequalities of power and the legitimation, or delegitimation, of political activity, including new and future attempts at the foreign domination of others.

As an illustration, and without offering anything more than an illustration, we might cite the Ukraine Crisis, unfolding at the moment of writing this concluding note—in August 2023. The conflict in Ukraine has clearly shocked the conscience of humanity. Simultaneously the crisis is one in which the self-determined future of a sovereign equal has been jeopardized: in which an international defence against a brutal aggression is a sovereigntist defence rather than a humanitarian intervention, and the appropriate path to freedom and peace is through internationally sustaining, not subduing, sovereignty. Of course divergent conceptions of legitimate statehood and of protection from imperialism and neo-empire have been deployed by all sides. But it is precisely the clash and contestation of such controversial deployments of intervention languages that demand our attention. In this respect the much-publicized speech of Martin Kimani, delivered at an emergency Security Council session, exemplifies a nuanced interpretation of self-determination in a world in which abuses of that concept are again being made.[36] Kimani, Kenya's Ambassador to the UN, should be quoted at length:

> Today, the threat or use of force against the territorial integrity and political independence of Ukraine has been effected. Kenya is gravely concerned by the announcement made by the Russian Federation to recognize the Donetsk and Luhansk regions of Ukraine as independent States … This situation echoes our own history. Kenya and almost every African country were birthed by the ending of empire. Our borders were not of our own drawing. They were drawn in the distant colonial metropoles of London, Paris and Lisbon with no regard for the ancient

---

[35] Compare with Vincent 1974: 1.
[36] S/PV.8970. I thank Nilufer Oral for drawing my attention to this speech when it went viral on social media in late February 2022.

244 Intervention before Interventionism

> nations that they cleaved apart. Today across the border of every single African country live our countrymen with whom we share deep historical, cultural and linguistic bonds. At independence, had we chosen to pursue States on the basis of ethnic, racial or religious homogeneity, we would still be waging bloody wars these many decades later. Instead, we agreed that we would settle for the borders that we inherited, but we would still pursue continental, political, economic and legal integration ... We must complete our recovery from the embers of dead empires in a way that does not plunge us back into new forms of domination and oppression.[37]

Hence has something been unwisely lost since the liberal-interventionist turn, which as I have suggested was really a turn away from alternative practices of thinking about what it means to intervene, that this genealogy has tried to contextualise and explain? Was something swept away that should have stayed?

To be clear: the overall argument of this book has been on the order less of a vindication of what might be called the 'Bandung theory' or anti-colonial theory as a faultless solution to past or present problems than a timely problematization of the ways in which its historical contestation has been hidden from view. Still, what I would propose is that genealogical analysis might serve at least as a repertoire for retheorizing the intervention concept, with the proviso that an apparent global restoration of non-interventionist and sovereigntist discourse is far from stable and demands extreme caution, particularly if it is to avoid degenerating into a crude power politics or bloc mentality. What I hope to have defended, therefore, is a type of a sensibility in approaching the intervention debate now. As the preceding chapters suggest, this sensibility is a pluralist one that, in thinking about the future of global order and justice, is clearly not a retreat to the anti-universalist sovereigntism and shallow morality against which post-Cold War liberalism has been juxtaposed. An alternatively pluralist approach to intervention, in a hyper-connected, twenty-first-century context that necessitates, for both moral and political reasons, a certain solidarism distinct from its contemporary liberal or neo-liberal form, is rather about confronting deep-seated ethnocentricities and building claims for justice out of the discursive practices of global international society. By way of conclusion, there are at least two ideas, drawn from the genealogy, that would seem to have much to contribute to current intervention debates and suit a broadly attractive vision of enduring global governance.

---
[37] Ibid.: 8–9.

First there is a need to appreciate, again and urgently, the difference between intervention and legitimate solidarity, and between intervention and collective action. These distinctions were once widely recognized against the backdrop of an increasingly fragmented and polarized world. Crucial to the historical idea that legitimate international action to prevent crimes against humanity is not an act of intervention, but rather an act of solidarity, is an understanding of the dynamic nature of domestic jurisdiction in international law and society. Intervention—precisely a breach of shared responsibilities: the shared responsibility of states not to intervene in the domestic affairs of others and the shared responsibility of states to respect the self-determination of peoples—must no longer be confused with legitimate implementations of existing international obligations. Accordingly, the reaffirmation of non-intervention and sovereign equality as fundamental principles of international relations is always compatible with collective legal action. The duty not to intervene in the internal affairs of state has not, and cannot, provide a blank cheque to those who within their own borders would seek to violate with impunity the obligations they have undertaken in their agreements with others. Equally there is no necessary tension, and there ought no longer to be cultivated a tension, between the vocabulary of sovereignty and that of universal human rights. Intervention, in short, is a word that should be carefully used in the context in which it has been developed in global international society.

Second and relatedly, there is a need to leave behind at last, in the study of International Relations, the classical definition of intervention as dictatorial or coercive interference. For all its desire to decolonize and to globalize, and for all its critical awareness of the nature of social practice and norms, the discipline retains, we can now clearly see, a definition of one of its most significant and core concepts that is either an anachronism or a tarnishing legacy of turn-of-the-century humanitarian intervention debates. The definition of intervention as a discrete and authority-oriented act of coercive interference, typically understood to refer to the use or threat of force, is not just *originally* a Great Power definition, it is *substantively* one as well. A more historically global definition of intervention would refer to the outcome of foreign pressure in relation to the essentially domestic affairs of states. It would encompass economic pressure, debt traps and severely tied aid, propaganda and electoral interferences, as well as subversion and incitement. And a more radically anti-colonial definition of intervention would refer to foreign pressure at the expense of self-determination. Differentiating intervention from the use or threat of force, and differentiating coercive interventionism from coercive internationalism, seems productive theoretically for the additional reason that global collective security action for the prevention of mass atrocities is consistent with a vision of an anti-hierarchical society of sovereign equals.

Statespeople speak in languages that serve many sides, whose common words contain conflicting meanings, and do not stay the same. But if we are no longer cognizant of the struggles waged over the terms of global-diplomatic discourse, and the historical contexts and conditions of their institutionalization, there is a dangerous risk of distortion both in our analysis and in our understandings of each other. Clearly there are many ways of doing or interpreting intervention, depending on where we stand and when. But I have tried to suggest that the process by which we come to appreciate how we stand, and how we have stood, is not always so clear. In fact, finding ourselves, marking out the normative boundaries of the diplomatic community, and charting the conflicts involved in the historical use and implementation of our concepts requires unlearning much of what we thought to be true.

It is an irony that, for the sake of common interest and shared responsibility, we need to better locate and contextualize our differences. But, particularly now, there is something more worth recovering from the dialogical grist of international society than agreement alone. In an increasingly post-Western world, the preservation of common rules and institutions is also their transformation as part of a longer process of the globalization and decolonization of a single society of states. Ultimately the viability of global order and the pursuit of global justice cannot be secured except by redefining, once again, what it means to intervene.

Bibliography

UN documents

Verbatim records of meetings

A/31/PV.98. Verbatim Records of the UN General Assembly, Thirty-first Session, 98th Plenary Meeting. 14 December 1976.
A/32/PV.106. Verbatim Records of the UN General Assembly, Thirty-second Session, 106th Plenary Meeting. 19 December 1977.
A/33/PV.85. Verbatim Records of the UN General Assembly, Thirty-third Session, 85th Plenary Meeting. 15 December 1978.
A/34/PV.103. Verbatim Records of the UN General Assembly, Thirty-fourth Session, 103rd Plenary Meeting. 14 December 1979.
A/35/PV.94. Verbatim Records of the UN General Assembly, Thirty-fifth Session, 94th Plenary Meeting. 12 December 1980.
A/36/PV.15. Verbatim Records of the UN General Assembly, Thirty-sixth Session, 15th Plenary Meeting. 28 September 1981.
A/36/PV.91. Verbatim Records of the UN General Assembly, Thirty-sixth Session, 91st Plenary Meeting. 9 December 1981.
A/46/PV.41. Verbatim Records of the UN General Assembly, Forty-sixth Session, 41st Plenary Meeting. 11 November 1991.
A/46/PV.42. Verbatim Records of the UN General Assembly, Forty-sixth Session, 42nd Plenary Meeting. 12 November 1991.
A/54/PV.14. Verbatim Records of the UN General Assembly, Fifty-fourth Session, 14th Plenary Meeting. 25 September 1999.
A/54/PV.17. Verbatim Records of the UN General Assembly, Fifty-fourth Session, 17th Plenary Meeting. 29 September 1999.
A/54/PV.27. Verbatim Records of the UN General Assembly, Fifty-fourth Session, 27th Plenary Meeting. 6 October 1999.
A/54/PV.33. Verbatim Records of the UN General Assembly, Fifty-fourth Session, 33rd Plenary Meeting. 11 October 1999.
A/54/PV.4. Verbatim Records of the UN General Assembly, Fifty-fourth Session, 4th Plenary Meeting. 20 September 1999.
A/54/PV.8. Verbatim Records of the UN General Assembly, Fifty-fourth Session, 8th Plenary Meeting. 22 September 1999.
A/55/PV.5. Verbatim Records of the UN General Assembly, Fifty-fifth Session, 5th Plenary Meeting. 7 September 2000.
A/55/PV.13. Verbatim Records of the UN General Assembly, Fifty-fifth Session, 13th Plenary Meeting. 13 September 2000.
A/55/PV.15. Verbatim Records of the UN General Assembly, Fifty-fifth Session, 15th Plenary Meeting. 14 September 2000.
A/55/PV.35. Verbatim Records of the UN General Assembly, Fifty-fifth Session, 35th Plenary Meeting. 27 October 2000.
A/59/PV.86. Verbatim Records of the UN General Assembly, Fifty-ninth Session, 86th Plenary Meeting. 6 April 2005.
A/59/PV.89. Verbatim Records of the UN General Assembly, Fifty-ninth Session, 89th Plenary Meeting. 8 April 2005.

248 Bibliography

A/60/PV.4. Verbatim Records of the UN General Assembly, Sixtieth Session, 4th Plenary Meeting. 14 September 2005.
A/60/PV.6. Verbatim Records of the UN General Assembly, Sixtieth Session, 6th Plenary Meeting. 15 September 2005.
A/63/PV.97. Verbatim Records of the UN General Assembly, Sixty-third Session, 97th Plenary Meeting. 23 July 2009.
A/63/PV.98. Verbatim Records of the UN General Assembly, Sixty-third Session, 98th Plenary Meeting. 24 July 2009.
A/63/PV.99. Verbatim Records of the UN General Assembly, Sixty-third Session, 99th Plenary Meeting. 24 July 2009.
A/63/PV.101. Verbatim Records of the UN General Assembly, Sixty-third Session, 101st Plenary Meeting. 28 July 2009.
A/75/PV.3. Verbatim Records of the UN General Assembly, Seventy-fifth Session, 3rd Plenary Meeting. 21 September 2020.
A/C.1/PV.1861. Verbatim Records of the UN General Assembly, First Committee, 1861st Meeting. 12 October 1972.
A/C.1/PV.1862. Verbatim Records of the UN General Assembly, First Committee, 1862nd Meeting. 13 October 1972.
A/C.1/PV.1866. Verbatim Records of the UN General Assembly, First Committee, 1866th Meeting. 18 October 1972.
A/C.1/PV.1867. Verbatim Records of the UN General Assembly, First Committee, 1867th Meeting. 18 October 1972.
A/C.1/PV.1868. Verbatim Records of the UN General Assembly, First Committee, 1868th Meeting. 19 October 1972.
A/C.1/PV.1870. Verbatim Records of the UN General Assembly, First Committee, 1870th Meeting. 20 October 1972.
A/C.1/31/PV.55. Verbatim Records of the UN General Assembly, Thirty-first Session, First Committee, 55th Meeting. 8 December 1976.
A/C.1/32/PV.55. Verbatim Records of the UN General Assembly, First Committee, Thirty-second Session, 55th Meeting. 7 December 1977.
A/C.1/36/PV.51. Verbatim Records of the UN General Assembly, First Committee, Thirty-sixth Session, 51st Meeting. 3 December 1981.
A/PV.381. Verbatim Records of the UN General Assembly, Seventh Session, 381st Plenary Meeting. 17 October 1952.
A/PV.1340. Verbatim Records of the UN General Assembly, Twentieth Session, 1340th Plenary Meeting. 28 September 1965.
A/PV.1408. Verbatim Records of the UN General Assembly, Twentieth Session, 1408th Plenary Meeting. 21 December 1965.
A/PV.2081. Verbatim Records of the UN General Assembly, Twenty-seventh Session, 2081st Plenary Meeting. 9 November 1972.
A/PV.2096. Verbatim Records of the UN General Assembly, Twenty-seventh Session, 2096th Plenary Meeting. 4 December 1972.
A/PV.2208. Verbatim Records of the UN General Assembly, Sixth Special Session, 2208th Plenary Meeting. 10 April 1974.
A/PV.2213. Verbatim Records of the UN General Assembly, Sixth Special Session, 2213th Plenary Meeting. 12 April 1974.
A/PV.2227. Verbatim Records of the UN General Assembly, Sixth Special Session, 2227th Plenary Meeting. 24 April 1974.
S/PV.6650. Verbatim Records of the UN Security Council, Sixty-sixth Year, 6650th Meeting. 9 November 2011.
S/PV.8970. Verbatim Records of the UN Security Council, Seventy-seventh Year, 8970th Meeting. 21 February 2022.

Summary records of meetings

A/AC.119/SR.3. Summary Records of the UN General Assembly, Special Committee on Principles of International Law Concerning Friendly Relations and Co-operation among States, 3rd Meeting. 16 October 1964.

A/AC.119/SR.8. Summary Records of the UN General Assembly, Special Committee on Principles of International Law Concerning Friendly Relations and Co-operation among States, 8th Meeting. 16 October 1964.

A/AC.119/SR.10. Summary Records of the UN General Assembly, Special Committee on Principles of International Law Concerning Friendly Relations and Co-operation among States, 10th Meeting. 16 October 1964.

A/AC.119/SR.17. Summary Records of the UN General Assembly, Special Committee on Principles of International Law Concerning Friendly Relations and Co-operation among States, 17th Meeting. 21 October 1964.

A/AC.119/SR.25. Summary Records of the UN General Assembly, Special Committee on Principles of International Law Concerning Friendly Relations and Co-operation among States, 25th Meeting. 23 October 1964.

A/AC.119/SR.28. Summary Records of the UN General Assembly, Special Committee on Principles of International Law Concerning Friendly Relations and Co-operation among States, 28th Meeting. 21 December 1964.

A/AC.119/SR.29. Summary Records of the UN General Assembly, Special Committee on Principles of International Law Concerning Friendly Relations and Co-operation among States, 29th Meeting. 23 October 1964.

A/AC.119/SR.30. Summary Records of the UN General Assembly, Special Committee on Principles of International Law Concerning Friendly Relations and Co-operation among States, 30th Meeting. 26 October 1964.

A/AC.119/SR.31. Summary Records of the UN General Assembly, Special Committee on Principles of International Law Concerning Friendly Relations and Co-operation among States, 31st Meeting. 26 October 1964.

A/AC.119/SR.32. Summary Records of the UN General Assembly, Special Committee on Principles of International Law Concerning Friendly Relations and Co-operation among States, 32nd Meeting. 26 October 1964.

A/AC.125/SR.10. Summary Records of the UN General Assembly, Special Committee on Principles of International Law Concerning Friendly Relations and Co-operation among States, 10th Meeting. 25 July 1966.

A/AC.125/SR.11. Summary Records of the UN General Assembly, Special Committee on Principles of International Law Concerning Friendly Relations and Co-operation among States, 11th Meeting. 25 July 1966.

A/AC.125/SR.12. Summary Records of the UN General Assembly, Special Committee on Principles of International Law Concerning Friendly Relations and Co-operation among States, 12th Meeting. 25 July 1966.

A/AC.125/SR.13. Summary Records of the UN General Assembly, Special Committee on Principles of International Law Concerning Friendly Relations and Co-operation among States, 13th Meeting. 25 July 1966.

A/AC.125/SR.71. Summary Records of the UN General Assembly, Special Committee on Principles of International Law Concerning Friendly Relations and Co-operation among States, 71st Meeting. 4 December 1967.

A/AC.125/SR.72. Summary Records of the UN General Assembly, Special Committee on Principles of International Law Concerning Friendly Relations and Co-operation among States, 72nd Meeting. 4 December 1967.

A/AC.125/SR.73. Summary Records of the UN General Assembly, Special Committee on Principles of International Law Concerning Friendly Relations and Co-operation among States, 73rd Meeting. 4 December 1967.

Bibliography

A/BUR/SR.103. Summary Records of the UN General Assembly, General Committee, 103rd Meeting. 22 September 1955.

A/C.1/SR.538. Summary Records of the UN General Assembly, First Committee, 538th Meeting. 6 December 1952.

A/C.1/SR.830. Summary Records of the UN General Assembly, First Committee, 830th Meeting. 4 February 1957.

A/C.1/SR.834. Summary Records of the UN General Assembly, First Committee, 834th Meeting. 6 February 1957.

A/C.1/SR.839. Summary Records of the UN General Assembly, First Committee, 839th Meeting. 8 February 1957.

A/C.1/SR.936. Summary Records of the UN General Assembly, First Committee, 936th Meeting. 13 December 1957.

A/C.1/SR.937. Summary Records of the UN General Assembly, First Committee, 937th Meeting. 13 December 1957.

A/C.1/SR.1396. Summary Records of the UN General Assembly, First Committee, 1396th Meeting. 3 December 1965.

A/C.1/SR.1397. Summary Records of the UN General Assembly, First Committee, 1397th Meeting. 6 December 1965.

A/C.1/SR.1398. Summary Records of the UN General Assembly, First Committee, 1398th Meeting. 6 December 1965.

A/C.1/SR.1401. Summary Records of the UN General Assembly, First Committee, 1401st Meeting. 8 December 1965.

A/C.1/SR.1402. Summary Records of the UN General Assembly, First Committee, 1402nd Meeting. 8 December 1965.

A/C.1/SR.1404. Summary Records of the UN General Assembly, First Committee, 1404th Meeting. 9 December 1965.

A/C.1/SR.1405. Summary Records of the UN General Assembly, First Committee, 1405th Meeting. 9 December 1965.

A/C.1/SR.1422. Summary Records of the UN General Assembly, First Committee, 1422nd Meeting. 20 December 1965.

A/C.1/SR.1423. Summary Records of the UN General Assembly, First Committee, 1423rd Meeting. 20 December 1965.

A/C.3/40/SR.69. Summary Records of the UN General Assembly, Third Committee, Fortieth Session, 69th Meeting. 6 December 1985.

A/C.3/55/SR.55. Summary Records of the UN General Assembly, Third Committee, Fifty-fifth Session, Third Committee, 55th Meeting. 29 November 2000.

A/C.3/57/SR.53. Summary Records of the UN General Assembly, Third Committee, Fifty-seventh Session, 53rd Meeting. 16 December 2002.

A/C.3/59/SR.49. Summary Records of the UN General Assembly, Fifty-ninth Session, Third Committee, 49th Meeting. 31 January 2005.

A/C.5/62/SR.23. Summary Records of the UN General Assembly, Fifth Committee, Sixty-second Session, 23rd Meeting. 7 February 2008.

A/C.5/62/SR.28. Summary Records of the UN General Assembly, Fifth Committee, Sixty-second Session, 28th Meeting. 17 April 2009.

A/C.6/SR.878. Summary Records of the UN General Assembly, Sixth Committee, 878th Meeting. 18 November 1965.

A/C.6/SR.882. Summary Records of the UN General Assembly, Sixth Committee, 882nd Meeting. 24 November 1965.

A/SPC/33/SR.9. Summary Records of the UN General Assembly, Special Political Committee, Thirty-third Session, 9th Meeting. 18 October 1978.

A/SPC/33/SR.45. Summary Records of the UN General Assembly, Special Political Committee, Thirty-third Session, 45th Meeting. 4 December 1978.

A/SPC/34/SR.19. Summary Records of the UN General Assembly, Special Political Committee, Thirty-fourth Session, 19th Meeting. 1 November 1979.
A/SPC/35/SR.18. Summary Records of the UN General Assembly, Special Political Committee, Thirty-fifth Session, 18th Meeting. 29 October 1980.
A/SPC/36/SR.16. Summary Records of the UN General Assembly, Special Political Committee, Thirty-sixth Session, 16th Meeting. 28 October 1981.
A/SPC/36/SR.19. Summary Records of the UN General Assembly, Special Political Committee, Thirty-sixth Session, 19th Meeting. 3 October 1981.

Letters, reports, draft resolutions, and draft amendments

A/31/197. Letter Dated 1 September 1976 from the Permanent Representative of Sri Lanka to the United Nations Addressed to the Secretary-General. Documents of the Fifth Conference of Heads of State or Government of Non-Aligned Countries, Held at Colombo, Sri Lanka, from 16 to 19 August 1976. 8 September 1976.
A/32/164. Non-interference in Internal Affairs of States. Report of the Secretary-General. 2 September 1977.
A/32/165. Implementation of the Declaration on the Strengthening of International Security. Report of the Secretary-General. 2 September 1977.
A/33/206. Letter Dated 6 September 1978 from the Chargé d'Affaires Ad Interim of the Permanent Mission of Yugoslavia to the United Nations Addressed to the Secretary-General. Documents of the Conference of Ministers for Foreign Affairs of Non-Aligned Countries, Held at Belgrade, Yugoslavia, from 25 to 30 July 1978. 6 September 1978.
A/33/216. Non-interference in Internal Affairs of States. Report of the Secretary-General. 21 September 1978.
A/34/192. Non-interference in Internal Affairs of States. Report of the Secretary-General. 4 October 1979.
A/34/193. Implementation of the Declaration on the Strengthening of International Security. Report of the Secretary-General. 4 October 1979.
A/34/542. Letter Dated 1 October 1979 from the Permanent Representative of Cuba to the United Nations Addressed to the Secretary-General. Documents of the Sixth Conference of Heads of State or Government of Non-Aligned Countries, Held in Havana, Cuba, from 3 to 9 September 1979. 11 October 1979.
A/34/827. Implementation of the Declaration on the Strengthening of International Security. Report of the First Committee. 13 December 1979.
A/35/505. Review of the Implementation of the Declaration on the Strengthening of International Security. Report of the Secretary-General. 15 October 1980.
A/36/245. Letter Dated 28 October 1981 from the Permanent Representative of Jordan to the United Nations Addressed to the Secretary-General. Explanatory Memorandum: New International Humanitarian Order. 30 October 1981.
A/36/786. New International Humanitarian Order. Report of the Third Committee. 8 December 1981.
A/41/697. Letter Dated 30 September 1986 from the Permanent Representative of Zimbabwe to the United Nations Addressed to the Secretary-General. Documents of the Eighth Conference of Heads of State or Government of Non-Aligned Countries, Held at Harare, Zimbabwe, from 1 to 6 September 1986. 14 October 1986.
A/46/1. Report of the Secretary-General on the Work of the Organization. 13 September 1991.
A/47/675. Letter Dated 11 November 1992 from the Permanent Representative of Indonesia to the United Nations Addressed to the Secretary-General. Documents of the Tenth Conference of Heads of State or Government of Non-Aligned Countries, Held at Jakarta, Indonesia, from 1 to 6 September 1992. 18 November 1992.

Bibliography

A/49/287. Letter Dated 25 June 1994 from the Minister for Foreign Affairs of Egypt Addressed to the Secretary-General. Documents of the Eleventh Ministerial Conference of the Countries of the Non-Aligned Movement, Held at Cairo, Egypt, from 31 May to 3 June 1994. 29 July 1994.

A/50/1001. Letter Dated 8 July 1996 from the Permanent Representative of Botswana to the United Nations Addressed to the Secretary-General. Communiqué issued by the Summit of Heads of State or Government of the Southern African Development Community at Gaborone, Botswana, on 28 June 1996. 19 July 1996.

A/53/667. Letter Dated 7 October 1998 from the Permanent Representative of South Africa to the United Nations Addressed to the Secretary-General. Documents of the Twelfth Conference of Heads of State or Government of Non-Aligned Countries, Held at Durban, South Africa, from 29 August to 3 September 1998. 13 November 1998.

A/53/951. Question of East Timor. Report of the Secretary-General. 5 May 1999.

A/54/917. Letter Dated 6 June 2000 from the Permanent Representative of South Africa to the United Nations Addressed to the Secretary-General. Final Document of the Thirteenth Ministerial Conference of the Movement of Non-Aligned Countries, held at Cartagena, Colombia, on 8 and 9 April 2000. 16 June 2000.

A/55/74. Letter Dated 5 May 2000 from the Permanent Representative of Nigeria to the United Nations Addressed to the President of the General Assembly. Documents of the Group of 77 South Summit, held in Havana, Cuba, from 10 to 14 April 2000. 12 May 2000.

A/57/759. Letter Dated 4 March 2003 from the Chargé d'Affaires Ad Interim of the Permanent Mission of Malaysia to the United Nations Addressed to the Secretary-General. Documents of the Thirteenth Conference of Heads of State or Government of the Non-Aligned Countries, held in Kuala Lumpur, Malaysia, from 20 to 25 February 2003. 18 March 2003.

A/61/472. Letter dated 19 September 2006 from the Permanent Representative of Cuba to the United Nations addressed to the Secretary-General. Documents of the Fourteenth Conference of Heads of State or Government of the Non-Aligned Countries, held in Havana, Cuba, from 11 to 16 September 2006. 29 September 2006.

A/63/677. Implementing the Responsibility to Protect. Report of the Secretary-General. 12 January 2009.

A/66/551. Letter dated 9 November 2011 from the Permanent Representative of Brazil to the United Nations addressed to the Secretary-General. Responsibility While Protecting: Elements for the Development and Promotion of a Concept. 11 November 2011.

A/3673. Letter Dated 20 September 1957 from the Chairman of the Delegation of the Union of Soviet Socialist Republics, Addressed to the President of the General Assembly. Explanatory Memorandum: Declaration on the Principles of Peaceful Co-existence between States. 20 September 1957.

A/5356. Consideration of Principles of International Law Concerning Friendly Relations and Cooperation among States in Accordance with the Charter of the United Nations. Report of the Sixth Committee. 14 December 1962.

A/5746. Consideration of Principles of International Law Concerning Friendly Relations and Cooperation among States in Accordance with the Charter of the United Nations. Report of the Special Committee on Principles of International Law Concerning Friendly Relations and Cooperation among States. 16 November 1964.

A/5763. Letter Dated 28 October 1964 from the Permanent Representative of the United Arab Republic to the United Nations Addressed to the Secretary-General. Programme for Peace and International Co-operation Adopted by the Second Conference of Heads of State or Government of the Non-Aligned Countries, Held at Cairo, United Arab Republic, from 5 to 10 October 1964. 29 October 1964.

A/6230. Consideration of Principles of International Law Concerning Friendly Relations and Cooperation among States in Accordance with the Charter of the United Nations. Report of the 1966 Special Committee on Principles of International Law Concerning Friendly Relations and Co-operation among States. 27 June 1966.

A/6700 (Part II). Report of the Special Committee on the Situation with Regard to the Implementation of the Declaration on the Granting of Independence to Colonial Countries and Peoples. 2 October 1967.

A/8771. Letter Dated 8 August 1972 from the Minister for Foreign Affairs of the Union of Soviet Socialist Republics Addressed to the Secretary-General. Draft: Convention on Principles Governing the Use by States of Artificial Earth Satellites for Direct Television Broadcasting. 9 August 1972.

A/9330. Letter Dated 22 November 1973 from the Permanent Representative of Algeria to the United Nations Addressed to the Secretary-General. Documents of the Fourth Conference of Heads of State or Government of the Non-Aligned Countries, Held at Algiers, Algeria, from 5 to 9 September 1973. 22 November 1973.

A/AC.105/104. Draft Declaration of Guiding Principles on the Use of Satellite Broadcasting for the Free Flow of Information, the Spread of Education and Greater Cultural Exchange, Transmitted by the Director-General of UNESCO to the Secretary-General. 15 November 1972.

A/AC.119/L.6. Special Committee on Principles of International Law Concerning Friendly Relations and Co-operation among States. Czechoslovakia: Proposal. 29 August 1964.

A/AC.119/L.7. Special Committee on Principles of International Law Concerning Friendly Relations and Co-operation among States. Yugoslavia: Proposal. 31 August 1964.

A/AC.119/L.8. Special Committee on Principles of International Law Concerning Friendly Relations and Co-operation among States. United Kingdom: Proposal. 31 August 1964.

A/AC.119/L.24. Special Committee on Principles of International Law Concerning Friendly Relations and Co-operation among States. Mexico: Proposal. 21 September 1964.

A/AC.119/L.26. Special Committee on Principles of International Law Concerning Friendly Relations and Co-operation among States. United States: Amendment to United Kingdom Proposal. 21 September 1964.

A/AC.119/L.27. Special Committee on Principles of International Law Concerning Friendly Relations and Co-operation among States. Ghana, India, and Yugoslavia: Proposal. 21 September 1964.

A/AC.125/L.12. Special Committee on Principles of International Law Concerning Friendly Relations and Co-operation among States. Joint Proposal by India, Lebanon, the United Arab Republic, Syria, and Yugoslavia. 25 July 1996.

A/AC.125/L.13. Special Committee on Principles of International Law Concerning Friendly Relations and Co-operation among States. Joint Proposal by Australia, Canada, France, Italy, the United Kingdom of Great Britain and Northern Ireland, and the United States of America. 16 March 1966.

A/AC.125/L.17. Special Committee on Principles of International Law Concerning Friendly Relations and Co-operation among States. Joint Draft Resolution by Chile and the United Arab Republic. 27 June 1966.

A/AC.125/L.20. Special Committee on Principles of International Law Concerning Friendly Relations and Co-operation among States. Draft Resolution by Czechoslovakia. 27 June 1966.

A/AC.125/L.44. Special Committee on Principles of International Law Concerning Friendly Relations and Co-operation among States. Draft Declaration Submitted to the Special Committee by the United Kingdom. 19 July 1967.

A/AC.125/L.54. Special Committee on Principles of International Law Concerning Friendly Relations and Co-operation among States. Joint Draft Resolution by Argentina, Cameroon, Chile, Czechoslovakia, Ghana, Guatemala, India, Kenya, Mexico, Nigeria, Poland, the Union of Soviet Socialist Republics, and Venezuela. 19 August 1967.

A/C.1/L.343/Rev.1. Union of Soviet Socialist Republics: Draft Declaration on the Inadmissibility of Intervention in the Domestic Affairs of States and the Protection of their Independence and Sovereignty. 3 December 1965.

A/C.1/L.350. United States of America: Amendments to Document A/C.1/L.343/Rev.1. 3 December 1965.

254   Bibliography

A/C.1/L.351. United Kingdom of Great Britain and Northern Ireland: Amendments to Document A/C.1/L.343/Rev.1. 6 December 1965.

A/C.1/L.352. Pakistan: Amendments to Document A/C.1/L.343/Rev.1. 6 December 1965.

A/C.1/L.353 and Add.1. United Arab Republic and United Republic of Tanzania: Draft Resolution on the Inadmissibility of Intervention in the Domestic Affairs of States and the Protection of their Independence and Sovereignty. 8 December 1965.

A/C.1/L.353/Rev.4 and Add.1. Algeria, Burma, Burundi, Cameroon, Cyprus, India, Iraq, Jordan, Kenya, Kuwait, Lebanon, Libya, Malawi, Mali, Mauritania, Nigeria, Rwanda, Saudi Arabia, Sudan, Syria, Togo, Uganda, United Arab Republic, United Republic of Tanzania, Yemen, Yugoslavia, and Zambia: Revised Draft Declaration on the Inadmissibility of Intervention in the Domestic Affairs of States and the Protection of their Independence and Sovereignty. 11 December 1965.

A/C.1/L.364 and Add.1. Afghanistan, Algeria, Argentina, Bolivia, Brazil, Burma, Burundi, Cameroon, Chile, Colombia, Congo (Brazzaville), Congo (Democratic Republic of), Costa Rica, Cyprus, Dahomey, Ecuador, El Salvador, Ethiopia, Gabon, Guinea, Guatemala, Haiti, Honduras, India, Iran, Iraq, Ivory Coast, Jordan, Kenya, Kuwait, Lebanon, Libya, Malawi, Mali, Mauritania, Mexico, Nicaragua, Niger, Nigeria, Panama, Paraguay, Peru, Rwanda, Saudi Arabia, Sierra Leone, Syria, Trinidad and Tobago, Togo, Tunisia, United Arab Republic, Uganda, United Republic of Tanzania, Uruguay, Venezuela, Yemen, Yugoslavia, and Zambia: Draft Declaration on the Inadmissibility of Intervention in the Domestic Affairs of States and the Protection of their Independence and Sovereignty. 20 December 1965.

A/C.1/34/L.56. Algeria, Botswana, Cuba, Cyprus, Ethiopia, Guyana, Madagascar, Sri Lanka, and Yugoslavia: Draft Declaration on the Inadmissibility of Intervention and Interference in Interference in the Internal Affairs of States. 3 December 1979.

A/C.3/45/L.82. Report of the Economic and Social Council. Cuba: Draft Resolution. Strengthening of United Nations Action in the Human Rights Field through the Promotion of International Co-operation and the Strict Observance of the Principle of Non-intervention. 26 November 1990.

A/C.3/45/L.82/Rev.1. Report of the Economic and Social Council. Cuba: Revised Draft Resolution. Strengthening of United Nations Action in the Human Rights Field through the Promotion of International Co-operation and the Strict Observance of the Principle of Non-intervention. 3 December 1990.

A/C.3/55/L.47. Belarus, Burundi, China, Cuba, Democratic People's Republic of Korea, Democratic Republic of the Congo, Iran (Islamic Republic of), Iraq, Lao People's Democratic Republic, Libyan Arab Jamahiriya, Myanmar, Nigeria, Russian Federation, Sudan, and the United Republic of Tanzania: Draft Resolution. Respect for the Purposes and Principles Contained in the Charter of the United Nations to Achieve International Cooperation in Promoting and Encouraging Respect for Human Rights and for Fundamental Freedoms and in Solving International Problems of Humanitarian Character. 2 November 2000.

A/C.3/55/L.47/Rev.1. Belarus, Burundi, China, Cuba, Democratic People's Republic of Korea, Democratic Republic of the Congo, Iran (Islamic Republic of), Iraq, Lao People's Democratic Republic, Libyan Arab Jamahiriya, Myanmar, Nigeria, Russian Federation, Sudan, and the United Republic of Tanzania: Revised Draft Resolution. Respect for the Purposes and Principles Contained in the Charter of the United Nations to Achieve International Cooperation in Promoting and Encouraging Respect for Human Rights and for Fundamental Freedoms and in Solving International Problems of Humanitarian Character. 8 November 2000.

A/C.6/L.492. Afghanistan, Cambodia, Ceylon, Czechoslovakia, Dahomey, Ghana, Indonesia, Iraq, Libya, Romania, United Arab Republic, and Yugoslavia: Draft Resolution. Future Work in the Field of the Codification and Progressive Development of International Law. 2 December 1961.

A/C.6/L.505. Czechoslovakia: Draft Resolution. Consideration of Principles of International Law concerning Friendly Relations and Co-operation among States in Accordance with the Charter of the United Nations. 26 October 1962.

S/7123. Letter Dated 7 February 1966 Addressed to the President of the Security Council from the Representatives of Argentina, Bolivia, Brazil, Chile, Colombia, Costa Rica, Dominican Republic,

Ecuador, El Salvador, Guatemala, Haiti, Honduras, Nicaragua, Panama, Paraguay, Peru, Uruguay, and Venezuela. 8 February 1966.
S/7134. Letter Dated 10 February 1966 from the Chargé d'Affaires Ad Interim of Cuba Addressed to the Secretary-General. 11 February 1966.
S/7142. Letter Dated 11 February 1966 from the Permanent Representative of Mexico Addressed to the Secretary-General. 15 February 1966.
S/1999/513. Question of East Timor. Report of the Secretary-General. 5 May 1999.
SG/SM/6613. Secretary-General Reflects on 'Intervention' in Thirty-fifth Annual Ditchley Foundation Lecture. 26 June 1998.
SG/SM/10161. World Summit Achieved Concrete, Significant Gains in Human Rights, Rule of Law, Secretary-General Says in Address to Universidade Nova de Lisboa. 12 October 2005.

Resolutions

A/RES/1236(XII). Peaceful and Neighbourly Relations Among States. 14 December 1957.
A/RES/1514(XV). Declaration on the Granting of Independence to Colonial Countries and Peoples. 14 December 1960.
A/RES/1815(XVII). Consideration of Principles of International Law Concerning Friendly Relations and Co-operation Among States in Accordance with the Charter of the United Nations. 18 December 1962.
A/RES/2131(XX). Declaration on the Inadmissibility of Intervention in the Domestic Affairs of States and the Protection of Their Independence and Sovereignty. 21 December 1965.
A/RES/2151(XXI). Question of Southern Rhodesia. 17 November 1966.
A/RES/2181(XXI). Consideration of Principles of International law Concerning Friendly Relations and Co-operation Among States in Accordance with the Charter of the United Nations. 12 December 1966.
A/RES/2222(XXI). Treaty on Principles Governing the Activities of States in the Exploration and Use of Outer Space, including the Moon and Other Celestial Bodies. 19 December 1966.
A/RES/2225(XXI). Status of the Implementation of the Declaration on the Inadmissibility of Intervention in the Domestic Affairs of States and the Protection of Their Independence and Sovereignty. 19 December 1966.
A/RES/2625(XXV). Declaration on Principles of International Law Concerning Friendly Relations and Co-operation Among States in Accordance with the Charter of the United Nations. 24 October 1970.
A/RES/3068(XXVIII). International Convention on the Suppression and Punishment of the Crime of Apartheid. 30 November 1973.
A/RES/3171(XXVIII). Permanent Sovereignty over Natural Resources. 17 December 1973.
A/RES/3201(S-VI). Declaration on the Establishment of a New International Economic Order. 1 May 1974.
A/RES/3202(S-VI). Programme of Action on the Establishment of a New International Economic Order. 1 May 1974.
A/RES/3281(XXIX). Charter of Economic Rights and Duties of States. 12 December 1974.
A/RES/31/91. Non-interference in the Internal Affairs of States. 14 December 1976.
A/RES/32/153. Non-interference in the Internal Affairs of States. 19 December 1977.
A/RES/32/154. Implementation of the Declaration on the Strengthening of International Security. 19 December 1977.
A/RES/33/74. Non-interference in the Internal Affairs of States. 15 December 1978.
A/RES/34/101. Non-interference in the Internal Affairs of States. 14 December 1979.
A/RES/34/103. Inadmissibility of the Policy of Hegemonism in International Relations. 14 December 1979.
A/RES/35/159. Non-interference in the Internal Affairs of States. 12 December 1980.

A/RES/36/103. Declaration on the Inadmissibility of Intervention and Interference in the Internal Affairs of States. 9 December 1981.
A/RES/36/136. New International Humanitarian Order. 14 December 1981.
A/RES/37/92. Principles Governing the Use by States of Artificial Earth Satellites for International Direct Television Broadcasting. 10 December 1982.
A/RES/38/7. The Situation in Grenada. 2 November 1983.
A/RES/38/125. New International Humanitarian Order. 16 December 1983.
A/RES/45/163. Strengthening of United Nations Action in the Human Rights Field Through the Promotion of International Co-operation and the Importance of Non-selectivity, Impartiality and Objectivity. 18 December 1990.
A/RES/46/182. Strengthening of the Coordination of Humanitarian Emergency Assistance of the United Nations. 19 December 1991.
A/RES/55/101. Respect for the Purposes and Principles Contained in the Charter of the United Nations to Achieve International Cooperation in Promoting and Encouraging Respect for Human Rights and for Fundamental Freedoms and in Solving International Problems of a Humanitarian Character. 2 March 2001.
A/RES/56/152. Respect for the Purposes and Principles Contained in the Charter of the United Nations to Achieve International Cooperation in Promoting and Encouraging Respect for Human Rights and for Fundamental Freedoms and in Solving International Problems of a Humanitarian Character. 13 February 2002.
A/RES/57/217. Respect for the Purposes and Principles Contained in the Charter of the United Nations to Achieve International Cooperation in Promoting and Encouraging Respect for Human Rights and for Fundamental Freedoms and in Solving International Problems of a Humanitarian Character. 27 February 2003.
A/RES/58/188. Respect for the Purposes and Principles Contained in the Charter of the United Nations to Achieve International Cooperation in Promoting and Encouraging Respect for Human Rights and for Fundamental Freedoms and in Solving International Problems of a Humanitarian Character. 22 December 2003.
A/RES/59/204. Respect for the Purposes and Principles Contained in the Charter of the United Nations to Achieve International Cooperation in Promoting and Encouraging Respect for Human Rights and for Fundamental Freedoms and in Solving International Problems of a Humanitarian Character. 20 December 2004.
A/RES/60/1. 2005 World Summit Outcome. 16 September 2005.
A/RES/62/166. Respect for the Purposes and Principles Contained in the Charter of the United Nations to Achieve International Cooperation in Promoting and Encouraging Respect for Human Rights and for Fundamental Freedoms and in Solving International Problems of a Humanitarian Character. 18 December 2007.
A/RES/ES-6/2. The Situation in Afghanistan and its Implications for International Peace and Security. 14 January 1980.
A/RES/S-6/3201. Declaration on the Establishment of a New International Economic Order. 1 May 1974.
S/RES/1973. United Nations Security Council Resolution 1973 (On the Situation in the Libyan Arab Jamahiriya). 17 March 2011.

Additional documentary sources

John F. Kennedy Presidential Library and Museum, Boston, MA. Lincoln Gordon Personal Papers.
St Antony's College Library, Oxford. Transcripts of the Meetings of the Political Committee of the Asian-African Conference Held at Bandung, 20 April 1955 (originals). Cited as TMPCAAC.

Published sources

Abi-Saab, Georges M. 'The System of the Friendly Relations Declaration'. In *The UN Friendly Relations Declaration at 50: An Assessment of the Fundamental Principles of International Law*, edited by Jorge E. Viñuales, 12–22. Cambridge: Cambridge University Press, 2020.
Abi-Saab, Georges M. 'War of National Liberation and the Laws of War'. *Annals of International Studies* 3 (1972): 93–117.
Abi-Saab, Georges M. 'The Newly Independent States and the Rules of International Law: An Outline'. *Howard Law Review* 8 (1962): 93–117.
Abi-Saab, Georges M. 'The Newly Independent States and the Scope of Domestic Jurisdiction'. *Proceedings of the American Society of International Law (1921–1969)* 54 (1960): 84–90.
Accioly, Hildebrando. *Manual de Direito Internacional Público*. 8th edn. São Paulo: Saraiva, 1968.
Acharya, Amitav. *Constructing Global Order: Agency and Change in World Politics*. Cambridge: Cambridge University Press, 2018.
Acharya, Amitav. 'Who Are the Norm Makers? The Asian-African Conference in Bandung and the Evolution of Norms'. *Global Governance* 20 (2014): 405–417.
Acharya, Amitav. 'The R2P and Norm Diffusion: Toward a Framework of Norm Circulation'. *Journal of the Responsibility to Protect* 5, no. 1 (2013): 466–479.
Acharya, Amitav, and Barry Buzan. *The Making of Global International Relations: Origins and Evolution of IR at its Centenary*. Cambridge: Cambridge University Press, 2020.
Adebajo, Adekeye. 'The Revolt Against the West: Intervention and Sovereignty'. *Third World Quarterly* 37, no. 7 (2016): 1187–1202.
Adelman, Jeremy and Gyan Prakash, eds. *Inventing the Third World: In Search of Freedom for the Postwar Global South*. London: Bloomsbury, 2023.
Adler, Emanuel, and Vincent Pouliot. *International Practices*. Cambridge: Cambridge University Press, 2011.
African Union. *The Common African Position on the Proposed Reform of the United Nations: The Ezulwini Consensus*. Addis Ababa: African Union, 2005.
Aga Khan, Sadruddin, and Hassan bin Talal. *Winning the Human Race?: The Report of the Independent Commission on International Humanitarian Issues*. London: Zed Books, 1988.
Alden, Chris, Sally Morphet, and Marco Antonio Vieira. *The South in World Politics*. London: Palgrave Macmillan, 2010.
Alleyne, Mark D. *International Power and International Communication*. London: Palgrave Macmillan, 1995.
Allison, Roy. *Russia, the West, and Military Intervention*. Oxford: Oxford University Press, 2013.
Allison, Roy. *The Soviet Union and the Strategy of Non-Alignment in the Third World*. Cambridge: Cambridge University Press, 1988.
American Society of International Law. *Proceedings of the American Society of International Law at its Eighty-Fifth Annual Meeting*. Washington, DC: American Society of International Law, 1991.
American Society of International Law. *Proceedings of the American Society of International Law at its Sixty-Ninth Annual Meeting*. Washington, DC: American Society of International Law, 1975.
Anand, R. P. *New States and International Law*. Delhi: Vikas, 1972.
Anand, R. P. 'Role of the "New" Asian-African States in the Present International Legal Order'. *American Journal of International Law* 56, no. 2 (1962): 383–406.
Anderson, Carol. *Eyes off the Prize: The United Nations and the African American Struggle for Human Rights, 1944–1955*. Cambridge: Cambridge University Press, 2003.
Anghie, Antony. 'Bandung and the Origins of Third World Sovereignty'. In *Bandung, Global History, and International Law*, edited by Luis Eslava, Michael Fakhri, and Vasuki Nesiah, 535–551. Cambridge: Cambridge University Press, 2017.
Anghie, Antony. 'Whose Utopia? Human Rights, Development, and the Third World'. *Qui Parle: Critical Humanities and Social Sciences* 22, no. 1 (Fall/Winter 2013): 63–80.
Anghie, Antony. *Imperialism, Sovereignty and the Making of International Law*. Cambridge: Cambridge University Press, 2005.

Aning, Kwesi, and Frank Okyere. 'The African Union'. In *The Oxford Handbook on the Responsibility to Protect*, edited by Alex Bellamy and Tim Dunne, 355-372. Oxford: Oxford University Press, 2016.

Annan, Kofi. *Interventions: A Life in War and Peace*. London: Penguin Books, 2013.

Annan, Kofi. 'Two Concepts of Sovereignty'. *The Economist* 352, no. 8137 (1999): 49-50.

Ansprenger, Franz. *The Dissolution of the Colonial Empires*. London: Routledge, 1989.

Aptheker, Herbert, ed. *The Correspondence of W. E. B. Du Bois*. Vol. III, *Selections 1944-1963*. Amherst, MA: University of Massachusetts Press, 1978.

Arrighi, Giovanni. *Adam Smith in Beijing: Lineages of the 21st Century*. London: Verso, 2007.

Ayoob, Mohammed. 'Third World Perspectives on Humanitarian Intervention and International Administration'. *Global Governance* 10, no. 1 (2004): 99-118.

Bain, William. 'Pluralism and Solidarism'. In *International Society: The English School*, edited by Cornelia Navari, 95-108. London: Palgrave, 2021.

Bain, William. *Between Anarchy and Society: Trusteeship and the Obligations of Power*. Oxford: Oxford University Press, 2003.

Baldwin, David. 'The Concept of Security'. *Review of International Studies* 23, no. 1 (1997): 5-26.

Baldwin, David. 'Foreign Aid, Intervention, and Influence'. *World Politics* 21, no. 3 (1969): 425-447.

Barkawi, Tarak. 'Decolonising War'. *European Journal of International Security* 1, no.2 (2016): 199-214.

Barraclough, Geoffrey. *An Introduction to Contemporary History*. Harmondsworth: Penguin, 1967.

Bartelson, Jens. *A Genealogy of Sovereignty*. Cambridge: Cambridge University Press, 1995.

Bass, Gary. *Freedom's Battle: The Origins of Humanitarian Intervention*. New York: Knopf, 2008.

Beitz, Charles R. 'Nonintervention and Communal Integrity'. *Philosophy and Public Affairs* 9, no. 4 (1980): 385-391.

Beitz, Charles R. 'Bounded Morality: Justice and the State in World Politics'. *International Organization* 33, no. 3 (1979): 405-424.

Bellamy, Alex J. *The Responsibility to Protect: A Defence*. Oxford: Oxford University Press, 2014.

Bellamy, Alex J. *The Responsibility to Protect: The Global Effort to End Mass Atrocities*. Cambridge: Polity Press, 2009a.

Bellamy, Alex J. 'Kosovo and the Advent of Sovereignty as Responsibility'. *Journal of Intervention and Statebuilding* 3, no. 2 (2009b): 163-184.

Bellamy, Alex J. 'Humanitarian Intervention and the Three Traditions'. *Global Society* 17, no. 1 (2003): 3-20.

Bellamy, Alex J., and Tim Dunne, eds. *The Oxford Handbook on the Responsibility to Protect*. Oxford: Oxford University Press, 2016.

Beloff, Max. 'Reflections on Intervention'. *Journal of International Affairs* 22, no. 2 (1968): 198-207.

Berkowitz, Peter. 'Leviathan Then and Now'. *Policy Review* 151 (October/November 2008): 3-20.

Bernstorff, Jochen von, and Philipp Dann, eds. *The Battle for International Law: South-North Perspectives on the Decolonization Era*. Oxford: Oxford University Press, 2019.

Bettati, Mario, and Bernard Kouchner, eds. *Le devoir d'ingérence*. Paris: Denoël, 1987.

Bevir, Mark. 'Contextualism: From Modernist Method to Post-analytic Historicism'. *Journal of the Philosophy of History* 3, no. 3 (2009): 211-224.

Bevir, Mark. 'What is Genealogy?' *Journal of the Philosophy of History* 2, no. 3 (2008): 263-275.

Bevir, Mark. *The Logic of the History of Ideas*. Cambridge: Cambridge University Press, 1999.

Bevir, Mark, and Jason Blakely. *Interpretive Social Science: An Anti-Naturalist Approach*. Oxford: Oxford University Press, 2018.

Bevir, Mark, and Ian Hall. 'The English School and the Classical Approach: Between Modernism and Interpretivism'. *Journal of International Political Theory* 16, no. 2 (2020): 153-170.

Bevir, Mark, and Asaf Kedar. 'An Anti-Naturalist Critique of Qualitative Methodology'. *Perspectives on Politics* 6, no. 3 (2008): 503-517.

Bilgin, Pinar. 'Thinking Past "Western" IR?' *Third World Quarterly* 29, no. 1 (2008): 5-23.

Blair, Tony. 'The Doctrine of International Community'. Speech to the Economic Club, Chicago, 22 April 1999, https://web.archive.org/web/20170301204740/www.pbs.org/newshour/bb/international-jan-june99-blair_doctrine4-23/ (accessed 10 November 2023).

Bockman, Johanna. 'Socialist Globalization against Capitalist Neocolonialism: The Economic Ideas behind the NIEO'. *Humanity: An International Journal of Human Rights, Humanitarianism, and Development* 6, no. 1 (2015): 109–128.

Booth, Ken. 'Human Wrongs in International Relations'. *International Affairs* 71, no. 1 (1995): 103–126.

Bossuyt, Marc. 'Human Rights and Non-intervention in Domestic Matters'. *Review of the International Commission of Jurists* 35 (1985): 45–52.

Boutros-Ghali, Boutros. 'The Five Principles'. *Chinese Journal of International Law* 3, no. 2 (2004): 373–378.

BRICS. 'BRICS Joint Statement on Strengthening and Reforming the Multilateral System.' 1 June 2021, https://web.archive.org/web/20230402031810/https://www.mea.gov.in/bilateral-documents.htm?dtl/33888/BRICS_Joint_Statement_on_Strengthening_and_Reforming_the_Multilateral_System (accessed 29 November 2023).

Brownlie, Ian. 'Humanitarian Intervention'. In *Law and Civil War in the Modern World*, edited by John N. Moore, 217–251. Baltimore, MD: Johns Hopkins University Press, 1974.

Brownlie, Ian. 'Thoughts on Kind-Hearted Gunmen'. In *Humanitarian Intervention and the United Nations*, edited by Richard B. Lillich, 138–148. Charlottesville, VA: University Press of Virginia, 1973.

Brownlie, Ian. *International Law and the Use of Force by States*. Oxford: Oxford University Press, 1963.

Bull, Hedley. *Justice in International Relations*. Waterloo, ON: University of Waterloo, 1984a.

Bull, Hedley. 'The Revolt Against the West'. In *The Expansion of International Society*, edited by Hedley Bull and Adam Watson, 217–228. Oxford: Oxford University Press, 1984b.

Bull, Hedley. 'Introduction'. In *Intervention in World Politics*, edited by Hedley Bull, 1–6. Oxford: Clarendon Press, 1984c.

Bull, Hedley, ed. *Intervention in World Politics*. Oxford: Clarendon Press, 1984d.

Bull, Hedley. 'Intervention in the Third World'. *The Non-Aligned World* 1, no. 3 (1983): 307–323.

Bull, Hedley, and Adam Watson, eds. *The Expansion of International Society*. Oxford: Oxford University Press, 1984.

Burke, Roland. *Decolonization and the Evolution of Human Rights*. Philadelphia, PA: University of Pennsylvania Press, 2010.

Buzan, Barry, and Lene Hansen. *The Evolution of International Security Studies*. Cambridge: Cambridge University Press, 2009.

Byrne, Jeffrey James. 'The Romance of Revolutionary Transatlanticism. Cuban–Algerian Relations and the Diverging Trends within Third World Internationalism'. In *The Tricontinental Revolution: Third World Radicalism and the Cold War*, edited by R. Joseph Parrott and Mark Atwood, 163–190. Cambridge: Cambridge University Press, 2022.

Cabral, Amilcar. 'The Weapon of Theory: Address to the First Tricontinental Conference'. In *Selected Texts by Amilcar Cabral: Revolution in Guinea*, translated and edited by Richard Handyside, 90–112. New York: Monthly Review Press, 1970.

Calvo, Carlos. *Le droit international théorique et pratique*, Vol. I. 5th edn. Paris: Arthur Rousseau, 1896.

Caminos, Hugo. 'The Role of the Organization of American States in the Promotion and Protection of Democratic Governance'. *Académie du Droit International, Recueil de Cours* 273 (1998): 103–238.

Canadian Department of External Affairs. *Report on the United Nations Conference on International Organisation held at San Francisco, 25 April–26 June 1945*. Ottawa: King's Printer, 1945.

Caney, Simon. *Justice Beyond Borders: A Global Political Theory*. Oxford: Oxford University Press, 2005.

Cardoso, Fernando Henrique, and Enzo Faletto. *Dependency and Development in Latin America*, translated by Marjory Mattingly Urquidi. Berkeley, CA: University of California Press, 1979.

Cardozo, Michael. 'Intervention: Benefaction as Justification'. In *Essays on Intervention*, edited by Roland J. Stranger, 63–85. Columbus, OH: Ohio State University Press, 1964.

Carnegie Endowment for International Peace. *The International Law of the Future: Postulates, Principles, and Proposals*. Washington, DC: Carnegie Endowment for International Peace, 1944.

Carnegie Endowment for International Peace. *International Conferences of American States: Supplement 1933–1940*. Washington, DC: Carnegie Endowment for International Peace, 1940.

Cassese, Antonio. *Self-determination of Peoples: A Legal Reappraisal*. Cambridge: Cambridge University Press, 1995.

Čavoški, Jovan. *Non-Aligned Movement Summits: A History*. London: Bloomsbury, 2022.

Ceadel, Martin. 'Enforced Pacific Settlement or Guaranteed Mutual Defence? British and US Approaches to Collective Security in the Eclectic Covenant of the League of Nations'. *International History Review* 35, no. 5 (2013): 993–1008.

Chandler, David. 'The Road to Military Humanitarianism: How the Human Rights NGOs Shaped a New Humanitarian Agenda'. *Human Rights Quarterly* 23, no. 3 (2001): 678–700.

Chen, Yifeng. 'Bandung, China, and the Making of World Order in East Asia'. In *Bandung, Global History, and International Law*, edited by Luis Eslava, Michael Fakhri, and Vasuki Nesiah, 177–195. Cambridge: Cambridge University Press, 2017.

Chen, Zheng. 'China Debates the Non-Interference Principle'. *Chinese Journal of International Politics* 9, no. 3 (2016): 349–374.

Chesterman, Simon. *Just War or Just Peace?: Humanitarian Intervention and International Law*. Oxford: Oxford University Press, 2001.

Chopra, Jarat, and Thomas G. Weiss. 'Sovereignty is No Longer Sacrosanct: Codifying Humanitarian Intervention'. *Ethics and International Affairs* 6, no. 1 (1992): 95–117.

Claude, Inis. 'Collective Legitimation as a Political Function of the United Nations'. *International Organization* 20, no. 3 (1966): 367–379.

Cohen, Roberta, and Francis M. Deng. *Masses in Flight: The Global Crisis of Internal Displacement*. Washington, DC: Brookings Institution, 1998.

Conca, Ken. *An Unfinished Foundation: The United Nations and Global Environmental Governance*. Oxford: Oxford University Press, 2015.

Cong, Wanshu. 'Contesting Freedom of Information: Capitalism, Development, and the Third World'. *Asian Journal of International Law* 13, no. 1 (2022): 46–75.

Congressional Research Service of the Library of Congress. *Oil Fields as Military Objectives: A Feasibility Study*. Washington, DC: U.S. Government Printing Office, 1975.

Connell-Smith, Gordon. *The Inter-American System*. Oxford: Oxford University Press, 1966.

Connolly, William E. *The Terms of Political Discourse*. Oxford: Blackwell Publishers, 1993.

Cooley, Alexander, and Daniel Nexon. *Exit from Hegemony: The Unraveling of the American Global Order*. Oxford: Oxford University Press, 2020.

Cot, Jean-Pierre. 'History of the United Nations Charter'. In *Max Planck Encyclopedia of Public International Law* (online edition), edited by Rüdiger Wolfrum. Oxford: Oxford University Press, 2011.

Crawford, Neta. *Argument and Change in World Politics: Ethics, Decolonization, and Humanitarian Intervention*. Cambridge: Cambridge University Press, 2002.

Crossley, Noële. *Evaluating the Responsibility to Protect: Mass Atrocity Prevention as a Consolidating Norm in International Society*. London: Routledge, 2016.

Cunliffe, Philip. *Critical Perspectives on the Responsibility to Protect: Interrogating Theory and Practice*. New York: Routledge, 2012.

Cutler, Lloyd. 'The Right to Intervene'. *Foreign Affairs* 64, no. 1 (1985): 96–112.

Dallaire, Roméo. *Shake Hands with the Devil: The Failure of Humanity in Rwanda*. Toronto: Vintage, 2003.

Damrosch, Lori Fisler, and David J. Scheffer, eds. *Law and Force in the New International Order*. Boulder, CO: Westview Press, 1991.

Davies, D. J. Llewelyn. 'Domestic Jurisdiction: A Limitation on International Law'. *Transactions of the Grotius Society* 32 (1946): 60–67.
Deeks, Ashley. 'The NATO Intervention in Libya—2011'. In *The Use of Force in International Law: A Case-Based Approach*, edited by Tom Ruys and Olivier Corten, 749–759. Oxford: Oxford University Press, 2018.
Deng, Francis, Sadikiel Kimaro, Terrence Lyons, Donald Rothchild, and I. William Zartman. *Sovereignty as Responsibility: Conflict Management in Africa*. Washington, DC: Brookings Institution Press, 1996.
De Wet, Erika. *Military Assistance on Request and the Use of Force*. Oxford: Oxford University Press, 2020.
De Wet, Erika. 'The Modern Practice of Intervention by Invitation in Africa and Its Implications for the Prohibition of the Use of Force'. *European Journal of International Law* 26, no. 4 (2015): 979–998.
De Wet, Erika. 'The Evolving Role of ECOWAS and the SADC in Peace Operations: A Challenge to the Primacy of the United Nations Security Council in Matters of Peace and Security?' *Leiden Journal of International Law* 27, no. 2 (2014): 353–369.
Dietrich, Christopher. *Oil Revolution: Anticolonial Elites, Sovereign Rights, and the Economic Culture of Decolonization*. Cambridge: Cambridge University Press, 2017.
Dietrich, Christopher. 'Mossadegh Madness: Oil and Sovereignty in the Anticolonial Community'. *Humanity: An International Journal of Human Rights, Humanitarianism, and Development* 6, no. 1 (2015): 63–78.
Dinkel, Jürgen. *The Non-Aligned Movement: Genesis, Organization, and Politics*. Leiden: Brill, 2019.
Dizard, Wilson P. 'The US Position: DBS and Free Flow'. *Journal of Communication* 30, no. 2 (1980): 157–168.
Dobbs, Michael, ed. *National Security Archive Electronic Briefing Book No. 472*. Washington, DC: National Security Archive, 2014.
Dörr, Oliver, and Albrecht Randelzhofer. 'Article 2 (4)'. In *The Charter of the United Nations: A Commentary*, edited by Simma Bruno, Daniel-Erasmus Khan, Georg Nolte, and Andreas Paulus, 200–234. Oxford: Oxford University Press, 2012.
Doswald-Beck, Louise. 'The Legal Validity of Military Intervention by Invitation of the Government'. *British Yearbook of International Law* 56, no. 189 (1985): 189–252.
Doyle, Michael W. *The Question of Intervention: John Stuart Mill and the Responsibility to Protect*. New Haven, CT: Yale University Press, 2015.
Dozer, Donald Marquand, ed. *The Monroe Doctrine: Its Modern Significance*. Tempe, AZ: Center for Latin American Studies, Arizona State University, 1976.
Du Bois, W. E. B. 'To the Nations of the World'. In *W. E. B. Du Bois: A Reader*, edited by David Levering Lewis, 639–641. New York: Henry Holt, 1995.
Dugard, C. J. R. 'The Organisation of African Unity and Colonialism: An Inquiry into the Plea of Self-Defence as a Justification for the Use of Force in the Eradication of Colonialism'. *International and Comparative Law Quarterly* 16, no. 1 (1967): 157–190.
Dulles, John Foster. 'Conceptions and Misconceptions Regarding Intervention'. *Annals of the American Academy of Political and Social Science* 144, no. 1 (1929): 102–104.
Dumas, Roland. 'La France et le droit d'ingérence humanitaire'. *Relations internationales et stratégiques* 1, no. 3 (1991): 55–66.
Dunne, Tim, and Christian Reus-Smit. *The Globalization of International Society*. Oxford: Oxford University Press, 2017.
Edward, George. *The Cuban Intervention in Angola, 1965–1991: From Che Guevara to Cuito Cuanavale*. London: Frank Cass, 2005.
Eichengreen, Barry. *Globalising Capital: A History of the International Monetary System*. Princeton, NJ: Princeton University Press, 2019.
Elias, Taslim Olawale. 'The Era of Protectorates, Colonies, and Capitulations'. In *The International Court of Justice and Some Contemporary Problems: Essays in International Law*, 300–316. The Hague: Martinus Nijhoff, 1983.

Ellis, Ellen. 'Intervention as a Sanction of International Law'. *Proceedings of the American Society of International Law* 27 (1933): 78–88.
Eslava, Luis, Michael Fakhri, and Vasuki Nesiah, eds. *Bandung, Global History and International Law: Critical Pasts and Pending Futures*. Cambridge: Cambridge University Press, 2017.
Evans, Gareth. 'Responsibility to Protect: The Next Ten Years'. In *The Oxford Handbook on the Responsibility to Protect*, edited by Tim Dunne and Alex J. Bellamy, 913–931. Oxford: Oxford University Press, 2016.
Evans, Gareth. *The Responsibility to Protect: Ending Mass Atrocity Crimes Once and for All*. Washington, DC: Brookings Institution Press, 2008.
Ewing, Cindy. 'The Colombo Powers: Crafting Diplomacy in the Third World and Launching Afro-Asia at Bandung'. *Cold War History* 19, no. 1 (2019): 1–19.
Falk, Richard. 'Intervention and National Liberation'. In *Intervention in World Politics*, edited by Hedley Bull, 119–134. Oxford: Clarendon Press, 1984.
Falk, Richard, ed. *The Vietnam War and International Law*, Vol. 1. Princeton, NJ: Princeton University Press, 1968.
Falk, Richard. 'The New States and International Legal Order'. *Académie du Droit International, Recueil de Cours* 118 (1966): 1–102.
Falk, Richard. 'Historical Tendencies, Modernizing and Revolutionary Nations and the International Legal Order'. *Howard Law Journal* 8, no. 2 (1962): 128–151.
Fanon, Frantz. *The Wretched of the Earth*, translated by Constance Farrington. New York: Grove Press, 1963.
Fenwick, Charles G. 'Intervention: Individual and Collective'. *American Journal of International Law* 39, no. 4 (1945): 645–663.
Fenwick, Charles G. 'Intervention by Way of Propaganda'. *American Journal of International Law* 35, no. 4 (1941): 626–631.
Fidler, David P., Sung Won Kim, and Sumit Ganguly. 'Eastphalia Rising? Asian Influence and the Fate of Human Security'. *World Policy Journal* 26, no. 2 (2009): 53–64.
Finnemore, Martha. *The Purpose of Intervention: Changing Beliefs about the Use of Force*. Ithaca, NY: Cornell University Press, 2003.
Fisher, Roger. 'Intervention: Three Problems of Policy and Law'. In *Essays on Intervention*, edited by Roland Stranger, 464–471. Columbus, OH: Ohio State University Press, 1964.
Fleming, John. 'The Nationalisation of Chile's Large Copper Companies in Contemporary Interstate Relations'. *Villanova Law Review* 18, no. 4 (1973): 593–647.
Foley, Conor. *The Thin Blue Line*. London: Verso, 2008.
Foot, Rosemary. 'The State, Development, and Humanitarianism: China's Shaping of the Trajectory of R2P'. In *The Oxford Handbook on the Responsibility to Protect*, edited by Tim Dunne and Alex Bellamy, 932–947. Oxford: Oxford University Press, 2016.
Foot, Rosemary, John Lewis Gaddis, and Andrew Hurrell, eds. *Order and Justice in International Relations*. Oxford: Oxford University Press, 2003.
Forbes, Ian, and Mark Hoffman. 'Introduction: Intervention and Sovereignty in the International System'. In *Political Theory, International Relations, and the Ethics of Intervention*, edited by Ian Forbes and Mark Hoffman, 1–12. London: Macmillan, 1993.
Fortin, Carlos, Jorge Heine, and Carlos Ominami. *Latin American Foreign Policies in the New World Order: The Active Non-Alignment Option*. London: Anthem Press, 2023.
Foucault, Michel. *Society Must be Defended: Lectures at the Collège de France, 1975–76*, translated by David Macey. New York: Picador, 2003.
Foucault, Michel. 'Confronting Governments: Human Rights'. In *Essential Works of Foucault 1954–1984*. Vol 3, *Power*, edited by James D. Faubion and translated by Robert Hurley, 474–475. London: Penguin, 1994.
Fox, Gregory. 'Intervention by Invitation'. In *Oxford Handbook of the Use of Force in International Law*, edited by Marc Weller, 816–840. Oxford: Oxford University Press, 2015.
Frank, André Gunder. *Capitalism and Underdevelopment in Latin America*. New York: Monthly Review Press, 1967.

Franck, Thomas M. *The Power of Legitimacy among Nations*. Oxford: Oxford University Press, 1990.
Freeden, Michael. *Ideologies and Political Theory: A Conceptual Approach*. Oxford: Oxford University Press, 1996.
Freedman, Lawrence. 'Blair's Chicago Speech and the Criteria for Intervention'. *International Relations* 31, no. 2 (2017): 107–124.
Friedman, Jeremy. *Shadow Cold War: The Sino-Soviet Competition for the Third World*. Chapel Hill, NC: University of North Carolina Press, 2015.
Friedmann, Wolfang. 'Intervention and the Developing Countries'. *Virginia Journal of International Law* 10, no. 2 (1969): 205–222.
Fung, Courtney J. *China and Intervention at the UN Security Council: Reconciling Status*. Oxford: Oxford University Press, 2019.
Fung, Courtney J. 'Separating Intervention from Regime Change: China's Diplomatic Innovations at the UN Security Council Regarding the Syria Crisis'. *China Quarterly* 235 (2018): 693–712.
Gadamer, Hans-Georg. *Truth and Method*, 2nd revised edn, translated by Joel Weinsheimer and Donald Marshall. New York: Continuum, 2004.
Gallie, W. B. 'Essentially Contested Concepts'. *Proceedings of the Aristotelian Society* 56 (1955–56): 167–198.
Garavini, Giuliano. *The Rise and Fall of OPEC in the Twentieth Century*. Oxford: Oxford University Press, 2019.
Gellman, Irwin F. *Good Neighbour Diplomacy: United States Policies in Latin America, 1933–1945*. Baltimore, MD: Johns Hopkins University Press, 1979.
Getachew, Adom. 'The Limits of Sovereignty as Responsibility'. *Constellations* 29, no. 2 (2019a): 225–240.
Getachew, Adom. *Worldmaking after Empire: The Rise and Fall of Self-Determination*. Princeton, NJ: Princeton University Press, 2019b.
Gilman, Nils. 'The New International Economic Order: A Reintroduction'. *Humanity: An International Journal of Human Rights, Humanitarianism, and Development* 6, no. 1 (2015): 1–16.
Gilmour, D. R. 'The Meaning of "Intervene" within Article 2 (7) of the United Nations Charter: An Historical Perspective'. *International and Comparative Law Quarterly* 16, no. 2 (1967): 330–351.
Glanville, Luke. *Sovereignty and the Responsibility to Protect: A New History*. Chicago, IL: Chicago University Press, 2014.
Glanville, Luke. 'The Antecedents of "Sovereignty as Responsibility"'. *European Journal of International Relations* 17, no. 2 (2011): 233–255.
Gleijeses, Piero. *Visions of Freedom: Havana, Washington, Pretoria and the Struggle for Southern Africa 1976–1991*. Chapel Hill, NC: University of North Carolina Press, 2016.
Gleijeses, Piero. *Conflicting Missions: Havana, Washington, and Africa, 1959–1976*. Chapel Hill, NC: University of North Carolina Press, 2003.
Gleijeses, Piero. *The Dominican Crisis: The 1965 Constitutionalist Revolt and American Intervention*. Baltimore, MD: Johns Hopkins University Press, 1978.
Glendon, Mary Ann. 'The Forgotten Crucible: The Latin American Influence on the Universal Human Rights Idea'. *Harvard Human Rights Journal* 16 (2003): 27–39.
Glennon, Michael. 'The New Interventionism: The Search for a Just International Law'. *Foreign Affairs* 78, no. 3 (1999): 2–7.
Gold, Martin. 'Direct Broadcast Satellites: Implications for Less-Developed Countries and for World Order'. *Virginia Journal of International Law* 12, no. 1 (1971): 66–91.
Goodrich, Leland M., and Edward Hambro. *Charter of the United Nations: Commentary and Documents*. Boston, MA: World Peace Foundation, 1949.
Goodwin, Geoffrey. 'An International Morality?' In *The Morality of Politics*, edited by Bhikhu Parekh and R.N. Berki, 99–113. London: Allen and Unwin, 1972.
Gowan, Peter. 'US: UN'. *New Left Review* 24 (November–December 2003), https://newleftreview.org/issues/II24/articles/peter-gowan-us-un/ (accessed 31 October 2023).

Grandin, Greg. *Empire's Workshop: Latin America, the United States, and the Rise of the New Imperialism*. New York: Henry Holt and Company, 2006.
Grovogui, Siba N'Zatioula. 'This State of Independence Shall Be: Africa, the West, and the Responsibility to Protect'. *Relaciones Internacionales* 26 (2014): 13–31.
Grovogui, Siba N'Zatioula. 'A Revolution Nonetheless: The Global South in International Relations'. *Global South* 5, no. 1 (2011): 175–190.
Grovogui, Siba N'Zatioula. *Sovereigns, Quasi Sovereigns, and Africans: Race and Self-Determination in International Law*. Minneapolis, MN: University of Minnesota Press, 1996.
Haass, Richard. *Intervention: The Use of American Military Force in the Post-Cold War World*. Washington, DC: Brookings Institution, 1999.
Hafner, Gerhard. 'Present Problems of the Use of Force in International Law: Intervention by Invitation'. *Yearbook of the Institute of International Law* 73 (2009): 227–267.
Hall, Ian. 'The "Revolt Against the West" Revisited'. In *The Globalization of International Society*, edited by Tim Dunne and Christian Reus-Smit, 345–361. Oxford: Oxford University Press, 2017.
Hall, William Edward. *A Treatise on International Law*. Oxford: Clarendon Press, 1890.
Halpern, Manfred. 'The Morality and Politics of Intervention'. In *International Aspects of Civil Strife*, edited by James Rosenau, 249–288. Princeton, NJ: Princeton University Press, 1964.
Hehir, Aidan. *Humanitarian Intervention: An Introduction*. London: Red Globe Press, 2013.
Heinze, Eric. *Waging Humanitarian War: The Ethics, Law, and Politics of Humanitarian Intervention*. New York: State University of New York Press, 2009.
Henkin, Louis. 'Force, Intervention, and Neutrality in Contemporary International Law'. *Proceedings of the American Society of International Law* 57 (1963): 147–173.
Heraclides, Alexis, and Ada Dialla. *Humanitarian Intervention in the Long Nineteenth Century: Setting the Precedent*. Manchester: Manchester University Press, 2015.
Hershey, Amos Shartle. *The Essentials of International Public Law and Organization*. New York: Macmillan, 1927.
Hershey, Amos Shartle. 'The Calvo and Drago Doctrines'. *American Journal of International Law* 1, no. 1 (1907): 26–45.
Higgins, Rosalyn. 'Intervention and International Law'. In *Intervention in World Politics*, edited by Hedley Bull, 29–44. Oxford: Oxford University Press, 1984.
Higgins, Rosalyn. *The Development of International Law Through the Political Organs of the UN*. Oxford: Oxford University Press, 1963.
Hilderbrand, Robert C. *Dumbarton Oaks: The Origins of the United Nations and the Search for Postwar Security*. London: University of North Carolina Press, 1990.
Hobbes, Thomas. *Leviathan*, edited by J. C. A. Gaskin. Oxford: Oxford University Press, 1996.
Hoffmann, Stanley. 'The Problem of Intervention'. In *Intervention in World Politics*, edited by Hedley Bull, 7–28. Oxford: Oxford University Press, 1984.
Holzgrefe, J. L., and Robert Keohane, eds. *Humanitarian Intervention: Ethical, Legal, and Political Dilemmas*. Cambridge: Cambridge University Press, 2003.
Huang, Zhixiong, and Kubo Mačák. 'Towards the International Rule of Law in Cyberspace: Contrasting Chinese and Western Approaches'. *Chinese Journal of International Law* 16, no. 2 (2017): 271–310.
Hurrell, Andrew. 'Beyond the BRICS: Power, Pluralism, and the Future of Global Order'. *Ethics and International Affairs* 32, no. 1 (2018): 89–101.
Hurrell, Andrew. 'Towards the Global Study of International Relations'. *Revista Brasileira de Política Internacional* 59, no. 2 (2016): 1–18.
Hurrell, Andrew. *On Global Order: Power, Values and the Constitution of International Society*. Oxford: Oxford University Press, 2007.
ICISS (International Commission on Intervention and State Sovereignty). *The Responsibility to Protect*. Ottawa: International Development Research Centre, 2001.
Ignatieff, Michael. 'The Responsibility to Protect in a Changing World Order: Twenty Years since its Inception'. *Ethics and International Affairs* 35, no. 2 (2021): 177–180.

Ikenberry, John G. *A World Safe for Democracy: Liberal Internationalism and the Crises of Global Order*. New Haven, CT: Yale University Press, 2020.

Imobighe, T. A. 'An African High Command: The Search for a Feasible Strategy of Continental Defence'. *African Affairs* 79, no. 315 (1980): 241–254.

Indonesia. *Asia-Africa Speaks from Bandung*. Jakarta: Indonesian Ministry of Foreign Affairs, 1955.

Institute of International Law. *Sub-group on Intervention by Invitation, 10th Commission, Present Problems of the Use of Force in International Law, Session de Santiago*. Paris: Pedone, 2007.

International Commission for the Study of Communication Problems. *Many Voices, One World: Towards a New, More Just, and More Efficient World Information and Communication Order*. London: Kogan Page, 1980.

International Committee of the Red Cross. '"Humanitarian Intervention" and International Humanitarian Law'. Keynote address by Jacques Forster, Vice President of the International Committee of the Red Cross, presented at the Ninth Annual Seminar on International Humanitarian Law for Diplomats accredited to the United Nations, Geneva, 8–9 March 2000, 12 September 2000, https://www.icrc.org/en/doc/resources/documents/statement/57jqjk.htm (accessed 10 November 2023).

Jackson, Richard L. *The Non-Aligned, the UN, and the Superpowers*. New York: Praeger, 1983.

Jackson, Robert H. *Quasi States: Sovereignty, International Relations and the Third World*. Cambridge: Cambridge University Press, 1990.

Jahn, Beate. 'Humanitarian Intervention: Justifying War for a New International Order'. In *The Justification of War and International Order: From Past to Present*, edited by Lothar Brock and Hendrik Simon, 355–378. Oxford: Oxford University Press, 2021.

Jansen, Godfrey. *Afro-Asia and Nonalignment*. London: Faber, 1966.

Jensen, Steven L. B. *The Making of International Human Rights: The 1960s, Decolonization, and the Reconstruction of Global Values*. Cambridge: Cambridge University Press, 2016.

Kang, Joon-Mann. 'The New World Information Order: The South Korean Case'. *Journal of Contemporary Asia* 18, no. 1 (1988): 77–88.

Keene, Edward. 'International Hierarchy and the Origins of the Modern Practice of Intervention'. *Review of International Studies* 39, no. 5 (2013): 1077–1090.

Keene, Edward. 'The Development of the Concept of International Society: An Essay on Political Argument in International Relations Theory'. In *Confronting the Political in International Relations*, edited by Michi Ebata and Beverly Neufeld, 17–41. London: Macmillan, 2000.

Kenkel, Kai Michael. 'Brazil and R2P: Does Taking Responsibility Mean Using Force?' *Global Responsibility to Protect* 4, no. 1 (2012): 5–32.

Khan, Daniel-Erasmus. 'Drafting History'. In *The Charter of the United Nations: A Commentary*, edited by Simma Bruno, Daniel-Erasmus Khan, Georg Nolte, and Andreas Paulus, 1–24. Oxford: Oxford University Press, 2012.

Kim, Sung Won. 'Eastphalia Revisited: The Potential Contribution of Eastphalia to Post-Westphalian Possibilities'. *Pacific Focus* 33, no. 3 (2018): 434–545.

Kim, Sung Won, David Fidler, and Sumit Ganguly. 'Eastphalia Rising? Asian Influence and the Fate of Human Security'. *World Policy Journal* 26, no. 2 (2009): 53–64.

Kioko, Ben. 'The Right of Intervention under the African Union's Constitutive Act: From Non-interference to Non-intervention'. *International Review of the Red Cross* 85, no. 852 (2003): 807–824.

Kirkpatrick, Jeane. 'Dictatorships and Double Standards'. *Commentary* 68, no. 5 (1979): 34–45.

Kirkpatrick, Jeane, and Allan Gerson. 'The Reagan Doctrine, Human Rights, and International Law'. In *Right V. Might: International Law and the Use of Force*, edited by Louis Henkin, Stanley Hoffmann, Jeane Kirkpatrick, Allan Gerson, William Rogers, and David Scheffer, 19–36. New York: Council on Foreign Relations Press, 1991.

Kissinger, Henry. 'Interview for Bill Moyers' Journal. January 15, 1975'. *Department of State Bulletin* 72, no. 1859 (1975): 165–181.

Klose, Fabian. *The Emergence of Humanitarian Intervention: Ideas and Practice from the Nineteenth Century to the Present*. Cambridge: Cambridge University Press, 2016.

Kuwali, Dan. 'From Stopping to Preventing Atrocities: Actualisation of Article 4(h)'. *African Security Review* 24, no. 3 (2015): 248–269.
Lamb, Robert. 'Recent Developments in the Thought of Quentin Skinner and the Ambitions of Contextualism'. *Journal of the Philosophy of History* 3, no. 3 (2009): 246–265.
Lane, Melissa. 'Doing Our Own Thinking for Ourselves: On Quentin Skinner's Genealogical Turn'. *Journal of the History of Ideas* 73, no. 1 (2012): 71–82.
Lasser, William. *Benjamin V. Cohen: Architect of the New Deal*. New Haven, CT: Yale University Press, 2002.
Lauren, Paul Gordon. *The Evolution of International Human Rights: Visions Seen*. Philadelphia, PA: University of Pennsylvania Press, 2011.
Lawrence, Thomas J. *Principles of International Law*. 7th edn, revised by Percy Winfield. Boston, MA: D. C. Heath, 1920.
Lawrence, Thomas J. *Principles of International Law*. 5th edn. Boston, MA: D. C. Heath, 1913.
Lawson, George, and Luca Tardelli. 'The Past, Present, and Future of Intervention'. *Review of International Studies* 39, no. 5 (2013): 1233–1253.
League of Nations. 'Resolutions adopted by the Assembly during its Seventeenth Ordinary Session (21st September to 10th October 1936)'. *League of Nations Official Journal*, Special Supplement no. 153 (1936): 1–43.
Lee, Christopher J., ed. *Making a World after Empire: The Bandung Moment and its Political Afterlives*. Athens, OH: Ohio University Press, 2010.
Legum, Colin, ed. *Africa Contemporary Record 1978–1979*. New York: Africana, 1980.
Lewis, Paul. 'World Court Supports Nicaragua After US Rejected Judges' Role'. New York Times, 28 June 1986, https://www.nytimes.com/1986/06/28/world/world-court-supports-nicaragua-after-us-rejected-judges-role.html/ (accessed 10 November 2023).
Lillich, Richard, ed. *Humanitarian Intervention and the United Nations*. Charlottesville, VA: University of Virginia Press, 1973.
Lillich, Richard. 'Intervention to Protect Human Rights'. *McGill Law Journal* 15, no. 2 (1969): 205–219.
Lillich, Richard. 'Forcible Self-Help by States to Protect Human Rights'. *Iowa Law Review* 53 (1967): 325–351.
Linklater, Andrew. *The Transformation of Political Community: Ethical Foundations of the Post-Westphalian Era*. Columbia, SC: University of South Carolina Press, 1998.
Linklater, Andrew, and Hidemi Suganami. *The English School of International Relations: A Contemporary Reassessment*. Cambridge: Cambridge University Press, 2006.
Little, Richard. 'Revisiting Intervention: A Survey of Recent Developments'. *Review of International Studies* 13, no. 1 (1987): 49–60.
Little, Richard. *Intervention: External Involvement in Civil Wars*. London: Rowman & Littlefield, 1975.
Lorca, Arnulf Becker. *Mestizo International Law: A Global Intellectual History, 1842–1933*. Cambridge: Cambridge University Press, 2015.
Louis, William Roger. 'The Suez Crisis and the British Dilemma at the United Nations'. In *The United Nations Security Council and War: The Evolution of Thought and Practice since 1945*, edited by Vaughan Lowe, Adam Roberts, Jennifer Welsh, and Dominik Zaum, 280–297. Oxford: Oxford University Press, 2008.
Lowe, Vaughan. *International Law*. Oxford: Oxford University Press, 2007.
Luck, Edward. 'Building a Norm: The Responsibility to Protect Experience'. In *Mass Atrocity Crimes: Preventing Future Outrages*, edited by Robert Rotberg, 108–127. Washington, DC: Brookings Institution Press, 2010.
Luck, Edward. 'Sovereignty, Choice, and the Responsibility to Protect'. *Global Responsibility to Protect* 1, no. 1 (2009): 10–21.
Luck, Edward. 'The Responsible Sovereign and the Responsibility to Protect'. In *Annual Review of United Nations Affairs*, edited by Joachim Müller and Karl Sauvant, xxxiii–xliv. Oxford: Oxford University Press, 2008.

Lüthi, Lorenz M. 'Non-Alignment, 1946–1965: Its Establishment and Struggle against Afro-Asianism'. *Humanity: An International Journal of Human Rights, Humanitarianism, and Development* 7, no. 2 (2016): 201–223.

Luttwak, Edward N. 'Intervention and Access to Natural Resources'. In *Intervention in World Politics*, edited by Hedley Bull, 79–94. Oxford: Clarendon Press, 1984.

MacFarlane, Neil S. *Intervention in Contemporary World Politics*. Adelphi Paper 350. London: International Institute for Strategic Studies, 2002.

MacFarlane, Neil S. *Superpower Rivalry and Third World Radicalism: The Idea of National Liberation*. London: Croom Helm, 1985a.

MacFarlane, Neil S. *Intervention and Regional Security*. Adelphi Paper 196. London: International Institute for Strategic Studies, 1985b.

MacFarlane, Neil S., and Yuen Foong Khong. *Human Security and the UN: A Critical History*. Bloomington, IN: Indiana University Press, 2006.

Mackie, Jamie. *Bandung 1955: Non-Alignment and Afro-Asian Solidarity*. Singapore: Didier Millet, 2005.

Macmillan, John. 'Intervention and the Ordering of the Modern World'. *Review of International Studies* 39, no. 5 (2013): 1039–1056.

Macron, Emmanuel. 'A New Initiative for Europe', Speech at Sorbonne University, 26 September 2017, https://web.archive.org/web/20230705092256/https://www.elysee.fr/en/emmanuel-macron/2017/09/26/president-macron-gives-speech-on-new-initiative-for-europe (accessed 29 November 2023).

Mahler, Anne Garland. *From the Tricontinental to the Global South: Race, Radicalism, and Transnational Solidarity*. Durham, NC: Duke University Press, 2018.

Malik, Charles. *The Problem of Coexistence*. Evanston, IL: Northwestern University, 1955.

Mallavarapu, Siddharth. 'Colonialism and the Responsibility to Protect'. In *Theorising the Responsibility to Protect*, edited by Ramesh Thakur and William Maley, 305–322. Cambridge: Cambridge University Press, 2015.

Malmvig, Helle. *State Sovereignty and Intervention: A Discourse Analysis of Interventionary and Non-Interventionary Practices in Kosovo and Algeria*. London: Routledge, 2006.

Mani, V. S. *Basic Principles of Modern International Law: A Study of the United Nations Debates on the Principles of International Law Concerning Friendly Relations and Cooperation Among States*. New Delhi: Lancer Books, 1993.

Mantena, Karuna. *Alibis of Empire: Henry Maine and the Ends of Liberal Imperialism*. Princeton, NJ: Princeton University Press, 2010.

Masmoudi, Mustapha. 'The New World Information Order'. *Journal of Communication* 29, no. 2 (1979): 172–185.

Mayall, James. *The New Interventionism, 1991–1994*. Cambridge: Cambridge University Press, 1996.

Mayall, James. *Nationalism and International Society*. Cambridge: Cambridge University Press, 1990.

Mazower, Mark. *Governing the World: The History of an Idea*. New York: Penguin, 2012.

Mazower, Mark. *No Enchanted Palace: The End of Empire and the Ideological Origins of the United Nations*. Princeton, NJ: Princeton University Press, 2009.

Mazrui, Ali. 'The United Nations and Some African Political Attitudes'. *International Organization* 18, no. 3 (1964): 499–520.

Mazrui, Ali. 'Consent, Colonialism and Sovereignty'. *Political Studies* 11, no. 1 (1963): 36–55.

Mazzini, Giuseppe. 'Non-Intervention'. In *Life and Writings of Giuseppe Mazzini*, Vol. VI, 300–308. London: Smith, Elder, & Co., 1870.

McDougal, Myres S., and Harold D. Lasswell. 'The Identification and Appraisal of Diverse Systems of Public Order'. *American Journal of International Law* 53, no. 1 (1959): 1–29.

McDougal, Myres D., and W. Michael Reisman. 'Rhodesia and the United Nations: The Lawfulness of International Concern'. *American Journal of International Law* 62 (1968): 1–19.

McNemar, Donald. 'Intervention and the Developing States—Regional Meeting'. *American Journal of International Law* 63, no. 2 (1969): 306–311.

McPherson, Alan. *A Short History of US Interventions in Latin America and the Caribbean*. Chichester, West Sussex: Wiley-Blackwell, 2016.

McPherson, Alan. *The Invaded: How Latin Americans and their Allies Fought and Ended US Occupations*. New York: Oxford University Press, 2014.

McPherson, Alan. *Yankee No!: Anti-Americanism in US–Latin American Relations*. Cambridge, MA: Harvard University Press, 2004.

McWhinney, Edward. 'The "New" Countries and the "New" International Law: The United Nations' Special Conference on Friendly Relations and Co-operation among States'. *American Journal of International Law* 60, no.1 (1966): 1–33.

Menon, Rajan. *The Conceit of Humanitarian Intervention*. Oxford: Oxford University Press, 2016.

Minter, William, and Elizabeth Schmidt. 'When Sanctions Worked: The Case of Rhodesia Re-examined'. *African Affairs* 87, no. 347 (1988): 207–237.

Mišković, Nataša, Harald Fischer-Tiné, and Nada Boškovska, eds, *The Non-Aligned Movement and the Cold War: Delhi, Bandung, Belgrade*. New York: Routledge, 2014.

Mononi, Asuka-Ngongo. 'The OAU Liberation Committee: The Rhetoric of African Liberation'. Doctoral Dissertation. Department of Political Science, Indiana University, 1975.

Moore, John Norton, ed. *Law and Civil War in the Modern World*. Baltimore, MD: Johns Hopkins University Press, 1974.

Moore, John Norton. 'Intervention: A Monochromatic Term for a Polychromatic Reality'. In *Law and the Indo-China War*, 119–150. Princeton, NJ: Princeton University Press, 1972.

Moore, John Norton. 'The Control of Foreign Intervention in Internal Conflict'. *Virginia Journal of International Law* 9, no. 2 (1969): 205–264.

Morgenthau, Hans. 'To Intervene or Not to Intervene'. *Foreign Affairs* 45, no. 3 (1967): 426–436.

Moyn, Samuel. 'The High Tide of Anticolonial Legalism'. *Journal of the History of International Law* 23, no. 1 (2021): 5–31.

Moyn, Samuel. 'Review of Luke Glanville, Sovereignty and the Responsibility to Protect: A New History'. *Law and History Review* 33, no. 1 (2015): 269–271.

Moyn, Samuel. *The Last Utopia: Human Rights in History*. Cambridge, MA: Harvard University Press, 2010.

Moyn, Samuel, and Umut Özsu. 'The Historical Origins and Setting of the Friendly Relations Declaration'. In *The UN Friendly Relations Declaration at 50: An Assessment of the Fundamental Principles of International Law*, edited by Jorge E. Viñuales, 23–48. Cambridge: Cambridge University Press, 2020.

Mueller, Milton. 'Against Sovereignty in Cyberspace'. *International Studies Review* 22, no. 4 (2020): 779–801.

Mullerson, Rein. 'Intervention by Invitation'. In *Law and Force in the New International Order*, edited by Lori Fisler Damrosch and David J. Scheffer, 127–134. Boulder, CO: Westview Press, 1991.

Murdock, James Oliver. 'Collective Security Distinguished from Intervention'. *American Journal of International Law* 56, no. 2 (1962): 500–503.

Murphy, Craig N. 'What the Third World Wanted: The Meaning of the NIEO'. In *Global Institutions, Marginalization and Development*, edited by Craig N. Murphy, 103–117. London: Routledge, 2005.

Murphy, Sean D. *Humanitarian Intervention: The United Nations in Evolving World Order*. Philadelphia, PA: University of Pennsylvania Press, 1996.

Murthy, C. S. R., and Gerrit Kurtz. 'International Responsibility as Solidarity: The Impact of the World Summit Negotiations on the R2P Trajectory'. *Global Society* 30, no. 1 (2016): 38–53.

Mussolini, Benito. *Scritti e Discorsi di Benito Mussolini*. Vol. X, *Scritti e Discorsi dell'Impero*. Milan: Hoepli, 1936.

Nabulsi, Karma. *Traditions of War: Occupation, Resistance and the Law*. Oxford: Oxford University Press, 1999.

Nguyễn, Quốc Tấn Trung. 'Rethinking the Legality of Intervention by Invitation: Toward Neutrality'. *Journal of Conflict and Security Law* 24, no. 2 (2019): 201–238.
Nietzsche, Friedrich. *On the Genealogy of Morals and Ecce Homo*, translated by Walter Kaufmann. New York: Random House, 1989.
Nolte, Georg. 'Intervention by Invitation'. In *Max Planck Encyclopedia of International Law*. Oxford: Oxford University Press, 2010.
Non-Aligned News Agencies Pool (Coordinating Committee). *News Agencies Pool of Non-Aligned Countries: A Perspective*. New Delhi: Indian Institute of Mass Communication for Coordinating Committee, 1983.
Nordenstreng, Kaarle, and Lauri Hannikainen. *The Mass Media Declaration of Unesco*. Norwood, NJ: Ablex Publishing Corporation, 1984.
Nordenstreng, Kaarle, Enrique González Manet, and Wolfgang Kleinwächter, eds. *New International Information Order Sourcebook*. Prague: International Organization of Journalists, 1986.
Nordenstreng, Kaarle, and H. I. Schiller, eds. *National Sovereignty and International Communication*. Norwood, NJ: Ablex, 1979.
Oberdorfer, Don. 'Noninterventionism, 1967 Style'. *New York Times*, 17 September 1967, https://www.nytimes.com/1967/09/17/archives/noninterventionism-1967-style-noninterventionism-cont.html/ (accessed 10 November 2023).
Obregón, Liliana. 'Between Civilisation and Barbarism: Creole Interventions in International Law'. *Third World Quarterly* 27, no. 5 (2006): 815–832.
Oppenheim, Lassa. *International Law: A Treatise*. 7th edn, edited by Hersch Lauterpacht. 1905/06. London: Longmans, 1948.
Oppenheim, Lassa. *International Law: A Treatise*. 5th edn, edited by Hersch Lauterpacht. London: Longmans, 1937.
Oppenheim, Lassa. *International Law: A Treatise*. 2nd edn. London: Longmans, Green and Co., 1912.
Orford, Anne. *International Authority and the Responsibility to Protect*. Cambridge: Cambridge University Press, 2011.
Orford, Anne. *Reading Humanitarian Intervention: Human Rights and the Use of Force in International Law*. Cambridge: Cambridge University Press, 2003.
Organisation of African Unity. *Rwanda, The Preventable Genocide: The Report of the International Panel of Eminent Personalities to Investigate the 1994 Genocide in Rwanda and the Surrounding Events*. Addis Ababa: Organisation of African Unity, 2000.
Organisation of African Unity. *Proceedings of the Summit Conference of Independent African States*, Vol. I, Sect. I. Addis Ababa: Organisation of African Unity, 1963a.
Organisation of African Unity. *Proceedings of the Summit Conference of Independent African States*, Vol. I, Sect. II. Addis Ababa: Organisation of African Unity, 1963b.
Organization of American States. *Report on the First Afro-Asian-Latin American Peoples' Solidarity Conference and Its Projections ('Tricontinental Conference of Havana'): New Instrument of Communist Intervention and Aggression*, Vol. II. Washington, DC: Pan American Union, 1966.
OSPAAAL (Organization of Solidarity with the Peoples of Asia, Africa, and Latin America). *The First Solidarity Conference of the Peoples of Africa, Asia, and Latin America: Proceedings*. Havana: Executive Secretariat of the OSPAAAL, 1966.
Pahuja, Sundhya. *Decolonising International Law: Development, Economic Growth, and the Politics of Universality*. Cambridge: Cambridge University Press, 2011.
Pan-American Union. *Inter-American Juridical Yearbook, 1948*. Washington, DC: Pan American Union, 1949.
Pan-American Union. *Inter-American Conference on Problems of War and Peace: Handbook for the Use of Delegates*. Washington, DC: Pan American Union, 1945.
Parrott, Joseph R., and Mark Atwood Lawrence, eds. *The Tricontinental Revolution: Third World Radicalism and the Cold War*. Cambridge: Cambridge University Press, 2022.
Pasha, Mustapha Kamal, ed. *Globalization, Difference, and Human Security*. London: Routledge, 2016.

Peak, Thomas. *Westphalia from Below: Humanitarian Intervention and the Myth of 1648*. London: Hurst, 2021.
Phạm, Quỳnh N., and Robbie Shilliam, eds. *Meanings of Bandung: Postcolonial Orders and Decolonial Visions*. London: Rowman & Littlefield, 2016.
Phillips, Andrew, and Chris Reus-Smit, eds. *Culture and Order in World Politics*. Cambridge: Cambridge University Press, 2020.
Pinch, Edward T. 'The Flow of News: An Assessment of the Non-Aligned News Agencies Pool'. *Journal of Communication* 28, no. 4 (1987): 163–171.
Pollentine, Marc. 'Constructing the Responsibility to Protect'. Doctoral Dissertation. School of European Languages, Translations, and Politics, Cardiff University, 2012.
Popović, Mirko. 'Cooperation Among Non-Aligned Countries in Radio Broadcasting'. *Review of International Affairs* 28, no. 663 (1977): 1–3.
Powell, Nathaniel. 'Saving Mobutu: Zaire, the West, and the Inter-African Force, 1978–1979'. In *Conflict, Politics, and Human Rights in Africa*. Working Paper No. 3, 1–42. Boston, MA: African Studies Center, Boston University, 2016.
Prashad, Vijay. *The Darker Nations: A People's History of the Third World*. New York: New Press, 2007.
Prashad, Vijay. *The Poorer Nations: A Possible History of the Global South*. London: Verso, 2012.
Quinton-Brown, Patrick. 'Interventionist or Internationalist? Coercion, Self-determination, and Humanitarianism in Third World Practice'. *International Relations* 37, no. 2 (2023a): 251–273.
Quinton-Brown, Patrick. 'Two Responsibilities to Protect'. *Millennium: Journal of International Studies* 51, no. 2 (2023b): 405–430.
Quitter, John H. A. 'Editor's Foreword. Intervention and World Politics'. *Journal of International Affairs* 22, no. 2 (1968): ix–x.
Rajan, M. S. *Nonalignment and Nonaligned Movement: Retrospect and Prospect*. New Delhi: Vikas, 1990.
Rajan, M. S. *United Nations and Domestic Jurisdiction*. London: Asia Publishing House, 1961.
Rajan, M. S. 'The Question of Defining "Domestic Jurisdiction"'. *International Studies* 1, no. 3 (1959): 248–279.
Ramgotra, Manjeet K. 'Postcolonial Republicanism and the Revival of a Paradigm'. *Good Society* 26, no. 1 (2017): 34–54.
Recchia, Stefano, and Jennifer M. Welsh, eds. *Just and Unjust Military Interventions: European Thinkers from Vitoria to Mill*. Cambridge: Cambridge University Press, 2013.
Reed, Laura, and Carl Kaysen, eds. *Emerging Norms of Justified Intervention*. Cambridge, MA: American Academy of Arts and Social Sciences, 1993.
Rehm, John B. 'Expropriation of American Investments Abroad'. In *Digest of International Law*, Vol. VIII, edited by Marjorie Whiteman, 1143–1163. Washington, DC: US Government Printing Office, 1967.
Reus-Smit, Chris. *On Cultural Diversity*. Cambridge: Cambridge University Press, 2018.
Reus-Smit, Chris. 'The Concept of Intervention'. *Review of International Studies* 39, no. 5 (2013a): 1057–1076.
Reus-Smit, Chris. *Individual Rights and the Making of the International System*. Cambridge: Cambridge University Press, 2013b.
Rieff, David. 'R2P, R.I.P.'. New York Times, 7 November 2011, http://www.nytimes.com/2011/11/08/opinion/r2p-rip.html/ (accessed 10 November 2023).
Rieff, David. *A Bed for the Night: Humanitarianism in Crisis*. London: Vintage, 2002.
Roach, Colleen. 'The US Position on the New World Information and Communication Order'. *Journal of Communication* 37, no. 4 (1987): 36–51.
Roberts, Adam. 'The So-Called Right of Humanitarian Intervention'. *Yearbook of International Humanitarian Law* 3 (2002): 3–51.
Roberts, Adam. 'NATO's "Humanitarian War" Over Kosovo'. *Survival* 41, no. 3 (1999): 102–123.
Roberts, Adam. 'Humanitarian War: Military Intervention and Human Rights'. *International Affairs* 69, no. 3 (1993): 429–449.

Roberts, Adam and Benedict Kingsbury, eds. *United Nations, Divided World: The UN's Roles in International Relations*. Oxford: Oxford University Press, 1993.

Rodogno, Davide. *Against Massacre: Humanitarian Interventions in the Ottoman Empire, 1815–1914*. Princeton, NJ: Princeton University Press, 2012.

Romulo, Carlos P. *Forty Years: Third World Soldier at the UN*. New York: Greenwood Press, 1986.

Romulo, Carlos P. *I Walked with Heroes*. New York: Holt, Rinehart and Winston, 1961.

Romulo, Carlos P. *The Meaning of Bandung*. Chapel Hill, NC: The University of North Carolina Press, 1956.

Rosenau, James N. 'Intervention as a Scientific Concept'. *Journal of Conflict Resolution* 13, no. 2 (1969): 149–171.

Rosenau, James N. 'The Concept of Intervention'. *Journal of International Affairs* 22, no. 2 (1968): 165–176.

Roth, Brad. *Governmental Illegitimacy in International Law*. Oxford: Oxford University Press, 2000.

Rotmann, Philipp, Gerrit Kurtz, and Sarah Brockmeier. 'Major Powers and the Contested Evolution of a Responsibility to Protect'. *Conflict, Security and Development* 14, no. 4 (2014): 355–377.

Ruan, Zongze. 'Responsible Protection: Building a Safer World'. *China International Studies* 34 (2012): 19–41.

Russell, Ruth B. *A History of the United Nations Charter*. Washington, DC: Brookings Institute, 1958.

Ryniker, Anne. 'The ICRC's Position on "Humanitarian Intervention"'. *International Review of the Red Cross* 83, no. 842 (2001): 527–532.

Sabaratnam, Meera. *Decolonising Intervention: International Statebuilding in Mozambique*. London: Rowman & Littlefield, 2017.

Šahović, Milan. *Principles of International Law Concerning Friendly Relations and Cooperation*. Belgrade: Institute of International Politics and Economics, 1972.

Sauvant, Karl P. 'From Economic to Socio-Cultural Emancipation: The Historical Context of the New International Economic Order and the New International Socio-Cultural Order'. *Third World Quarterly* 3, no. 1 (1981): 48–61.

Sauvy, Alfred. 'Trois mondes, une planète'. *Vingtième Siècle. Revue d'historie*, no. 118 (1989): 81–83.

Scarfi, Juan Pablo. *The Hidden History of International Law in the Americas: Empire and Legal Networks*. Oxford: Oxford University Press, 2017.

Scheffer, David. 'The Great Debate of the 1980s'. In *Right v. Might: International Law and the Use of Force*, edited by Louis Henkin, Stanley Hoffmann, Jeane Kirkpatrick, Allan Gerson, William Rogers, and David Scheffer, 1–18. New York: Council on Foreign Relations Press, 1991.

Schiller, Herbert. *Information and the Crisis Economy*. Oxford: Oxford University Press, 1986.

Schiller, Herbert. 'Decolonization of Information: Efforts toward a New International Order'. *Latin American Perspectives* 5, no. 1 (1978): 35–48.

Schlesinger, Stephen C. *Act of Creation: The Founding of the United Nations*. Cambridge, MA: Westview Press, 2003.

Scott, Andrew. 'Nonintervention and Conditional Intervention'. *Journal of International Affairs* 22, no. 2 (1968): 208–216.

Searle, John R. *The Construction of Social Reality*. London: Penguin, 1995.

Senaratne, Kalana. 'Internal Self-Determination in International Law: A Critical Third-World Perspective'. *Asian Journal of International Law* 3, no. 2 (2013): 305–339.

Seybolt, Taylor B. *Humanitarian Military Intervention: The Conditions for Success and Failure*. Oxford: Oxford University Press, 2007.

Sherwood, Marika. 'There is No New Deal for the Blackman in San Francisco: African Attempts to Influence the Founding Conference of the United Nations'. *International Journal of African Studies* 29, no. 1 (1996): 71–94.

Shilliam, Robbie. 'Intervention and Colonial-modernity: Decolonising the Italy/Ethiopia Conflict through Psalms 68:31'. *Review of International Studies* 39, no. 5 (2013): 1131–1147.

Shilliam, Robbie, ed. *International Relations and Non-Western Thought: Imperialism, Colonialism and Investigations of Global Modernity*. New York: Routledge, 2011.

Shimazu, Naoko. 'Diplomacy as Theatre: Staging the Bandung Conference of 1955'. *Modern Asian Studies* 48, no. 1 (2014): 225–252.

Shimazu, Naoko. *Japan, Race, and Equality: The Racial Equality Proposal of 1919*. London: Routledge, 2009.

Shirer, William L. *The Rise and Fall of the Third Reich: A History of Nazi Germany*. New York: Simon & Schuster, 1960.

Shue, Henry. 'Limiting Sovereignty'. In *Humanitarian Intervention and International Relations*, edited by Jennifer Welsh, 11–29. Oxford: Oxford University Press, 2004.

Sikkink, Kathryn. 'Latin America's Protagonist Role in Human Rights'. *Sur International Journal on Human Rights* 12, no. 22 (2015): 207–219.

Simms, Brendan, and D. J. B. Trim, eds. *Humanitarian Intervention: A History*. Cambridge: Cambridge University Press, 2011.

Singham, Archibald W., and Shirley Hune. *Non-Alignment in an Age of Alignments*. Harare: College Press, 1986.

Singham, Archibald W. and Trần Văn Dĩnh, eds. *From Bandung to Colombo*. New York: Third Press Review, 1976.

Skinner, Quentin. *Visions of Politics*. Vol. I, *Regarding Method*. Cambridge: Cambridge University Press, 2002.

Skinner, Quentin. 'Some Problems in the Analysis of Political Thought and Action'. In *Meaning and Context: Quentin Skinner and his Critics*, edited by James Tully, 97–118. Princeton, NJ: Princeton University Press, 1988.

Smith, Gaddis. *The Last Years of the Monroe Doctrine, 1945–1993*. New York: Hill & Wang, 1994.

Soares de Oliveira, Ricardo, and Harry Verhoeven. 'Taming Intervention: Sovereignty, Statehood and Political Order in Africa'. *Survival* 60, no. 2 (2018): 7–32.

Socher, Johannes. 'Lenin, (Just) Wars of National Liberation, and the Soviet Doctrine on the Use of Force'. *Journal of the History of International Law* 19, no. 2 (2017): 219–245.

Spektor, Matias. 'Humanitarian Interventionism Brazilian Style?' *America Quarterly* 6, no. 3 (2012): 54–59.

Srinivasan, Amia. 'Genealogy, Epistemology and Worldmaking'. *Proceedings the Aristotelian Society* 119, no. 2 (2019): 127–156.

Stern, David S., Robert Borosage, and Tom Farer. 'Covert Intervention and Third World Ideas'. *Proceedings of the Annual Meeting of the American Society of International Law* 69 (April 1975): 200–216.

Stevenson, Robert. *Communication, Development, and the Third World: The Global Politics of Information*. New York: Longman, 1988.

Swatek-Evenstein, Mark. *A History of Humanitarian Intervention*. Cambridge: Cambridge University Press, 2020.

Tan, Kok-Chor. 'Enforcing Cosmopolitan Justice: The Problem of Intervention'. In *Cosmopolitanism in Context: Perspectives from International Law and Political Theory*, edited by Rolad Pierik and Wouter Werner, 155–178. Cambridge: Cambridge University Press, 2016.

Tan, See Seng, and Amitav Acharya, eds. *Bandung Revisited: The Legacy of the 1955 Asian-African Conference for International Order*. Singapore: National University of Singapore Press, 2008.

Taylor, Charles. 'Comparison, History, Truth'. In *Philosophical Arguments*, 148–151. Cambridge, MA: Harvard University Press, 1995.

Taylor, Charles. 'Self-Interpreting Animals'. In *Human Agency and Language*, 45–76. Cambridge: Cambridge University Press, 1985.

Tesón, Fernando R. 'The Liberal Case for Humanitarian Intervention'. In *Humanitarian Intervention: Ethical, Legal, and Political Dilemmas*, edited by J. L. Holzgrefe and Robert O. Keohane, 93–129. Cambridge: Cambridge University Press, 2003.

Tesón, Fernando R. *Humanitarian Intervention: An Inquiry Into Law and Morality*. Dobbs Ferry, NY: Transnational Publishers, 1988.

Thakur, Ramesh. *Reviewing the Responsibility to Protect: Origins, Implementation, and Controversies*. London: Routledge, 2019.
Thakur, Ramesh. 'Atrocity Crimes'. In *Why Govern: Rethinking Demand and Progress in Global Governance*, edited by Amitav Acharya, 138-156. Cambridge: Cambridge University Press, 2016a.
Thakur, Ramesh. 'Rwanda, Kosovo, and the International Commission on Intervention and State Sovereignty'. In *The Oxford Handbook on the Responsibility to Protect*, edited by Alex Bellamy and Tim Dunne, 94-113. Oxford: Oxford University Press, 2016b.
Thakur, Ramesh, and William Maley, eds. *Theorising the Responsibility to Protect*. Cambridge: Cambridge University Press, 2015.
Thomas, Ann van Wynen, and A. J. Thomas Jr. *Non-Intervention: The Law and its Import in the Americas*. Dallas, TX: Southern Methodist University Press, 1956.
Thomas, Caroline. *New States, Sovereignty and Intervention*. Aldershot: Gower, 1985.
Tickner, Arlene B. and Ole Wæver. *International Relations Scholars Around the World*. London: Routledge, 2009.
Tourinho, Marcos, Oliver Stuenkel, and Sarah Brockmeier. 'Responsibility While Protecting: Reforming RtoP Implementation'. *Global Society* 30, no. 1 (2016): 134-150.
Trần Văn Dĩnh. 'Nonalignment and Cultural Imperialism'. *Black Scholar* 8, no. 3 (1976): 39-49.
Tully, James. 'The Pen is a Mighty Sword: Quentin Skinner's Analysis of Politics'. *British Journal of Political Science* 13, no. 4 (1983): 489-509.
Umozurike, U. Oji. 'The Domestic Jurisdiction Clause in the OAU Charter'. *African Affairs* 78, no. 113 (1979): 197-209.
UNCIO (United Nations Conference on International Organization). *Documents of the United Nations Conference on International Organization*, Vols I-XXI. New York and London: United Nations Information Organizations, 1945.
UNCTAD (United Nations Conference on Trade and Development). *Proceedings of the United Nations Conference on Trade and Development, Fourth Session*, Vol. I. New York: UNCTAD, 1977.
UNESCO (United Nations Educational, Scientific and Cultural Organization). *Historical Background of the Mass Media Declaration (New Communication Order 9)*. Paris: UNESCO, 1983.
UNESCO (United Nations Educational, Scientific and Cultural Organization). *Records of the General Conference, 21st Session, Belgrade, 23 September to 28 October 1980*, Vol. I. Paris: UNESCO, 1980.
United Nations Department of Public Information. *Yearbook of the United Nations*, Vol. XIX. New York: UN Department of Public Information, 1965.
United Nations Department of Public Information. *Yearbook of the United Nations*, Vol. IV. New York: UN Department of Public Information, 1950.
United States Department of State. *The Tricontinental Conference: A Staff Study*. Washington, DC: Government Printing Office, 1966.
United States Department of State. *Charter of the Organization of American States, 9th International Conference of American States at Bogota, Columbia, 30 March-2 May 1948, Report of Delegation of the US*. Washington, DC: Government Printing Office, 1948.
United States Department of State. *Charter of the United Nations: Report to President on the Results on the San Francisco Conference, by the Chairman of the US Delegation, the Secretary of State, 26 June 1945*. Washington, DC: Government Printing Office, 1945.
United States Department of State. *Report of the Delegation of the United States of America to the Inter-American Conference for the Maintenance of Peace, Buenos Aires, Argentina, December 1-23, 1936*. Washington, DC: Government Printing Office, 1937.
United States Department of State. *Report of the Delegates of the United States of America to the Seventh International Conference of American States, Montevideo, Uruguay, 3-26 December 1933*. Washington, DC: Government Printing Office, 1934.
United States Department of State. *Papers Relating to the Foreign Relations of the United States [FRUS], 1904-1976*. Washington, DC: Government Printing Office, 1904-1976.
Urquhart, Brian. *Ralph Bunche: An American Life*. New York: W. W. Norton, 1998.

Urquhart, Brian. 'Sovereignty vs. Suffering'. New York Times, 17 April 1991, https://www.nytimes.com/1991/04/17/opinion/sovereignty-vs-suffering.html (accessed 10 November 2023).

Vincent, R. J. *Human Rights and International Relations*. Cambridge: Cambridge University Press, 1986.

Vincent, R. J. *Nonintervention and International Order*. Princeton, NJ: Princeton University Press, 1974.

Vincent, R. J., and Peter Wilson. 'Beyond Non-intervention'. In *Political Theory, International Relations, and the Ethics of Intervention*, edited by Ian Forbes and Mark Hoffman, 122–132. London: Macmillan, 1993.

Viñuales, Jorge E., ed. *The UN Friendly Relations Declaration at 50: An Assessment of the Fundamental Principles of International Law*. Cambridge: Cambridge University Press, 2020.

Vitalis, Robert. 'The Midnight Ride of Kwame Nkrumah and Other Fables of Bandung'. *Humanity: An International Journal of Human Rights, Humanitarianism, and Development* 4, no. 2 (2013): 261–288.

Von Bernstorff, Jochen. 'The Battle for Wars of National Liberation'. In *The Battle for International Law: South–North Perspectives on the Decolonization Era*, 52–70. Oxford: Oxford University Press, 2019.

Walzer, Michael. *Just and Unjust Wars: A Moral Argument with Historical Illustrations*. Philadelphia, PA: Basic Books, 1977.

Wang, Jeffrey, trans. 'Record of the Second Meeting between Premier Zhou and Prime Minister U Nu', 29 June 1954. PRC FMA 203-00007-03, 46–57. Wilson Center Digital Archive, 2014, https://digitalarchive.wilsoncenter.org/document/record-second-meeting-between-premier-zhou-and-prime-minister-u-nu (accessed 10 November 2023).

Weber, Cynthia. *Simulating Sovereignty: Intervention, the State, and Symbolic Exchange*. Cambridge: Cambridge University Press, 1995.

Weber, Heloise. 'The Political Significance of Bandung for Development: Challenges, Contradictions, and Struggles for Justice'. In *Meanings of Bandung*, edited by Quỳnh N. Phạm and Robbie Shilliam, 153–164. London: Rowman & Littlefield, 2016.

Weber, Heloise, and Poppy Winanti. 'The Bandung Spirit and Solidarist Internationalism'. *Australian Journal of International Affairs* 70, no. 4 (2016): 391–406.

Weiss, Thomas G. 'The Turbulent 1990s: R2P Precedents and Prospects'. In *The Oxford Handbook on the Responsibility to Protect*, edited by Alex Bellamy and Tim Dunne, 56–73. Oxford: Oxford University Press, 2016.

Weiss, Thomas G. *Humanitarian Intervention: Ideas in Action*. Cambridge: Polity Press, 2007.

Weiss, Thomas G., and Kurt M. Campbell. 'Military Humanitarianism'. *Survival* 33, no. 5 (1991): 451–464.

Weissman, Fabrice. '"Not in Our Name": Why Doctors Without Borders Does Not Support the "Responsibility to Protect"'. *Criminal Justice Ethics* 29, no. 2 (2010): 194–207.

Welsh, Jennifer. 'Norm Robustness and the Responsibility to Protect'. *Journal of Global Security Studies* 4, no. 1 (2019): 53–72.

Welsh, Jennifer. 'Norm Contestation and the Responsibility to Protect'. *Global Responsibility to Protect* 5, no. 4 (2013): 365–396.

Welsh, Jennifer. 'A Normative Case for Pluralism: Reassessing Vincent's Views on Humanitarian Intervention'. *International Affairs* 87, no. 5 (2011): 1193–1204.

Welsh, Jennifer, ed. *Humanitarian Intervention and International Relations*. Oxford: Oxford University Press, 2004.

Westad, Odd Arne. *The Global Cold War: Third World Interventions and the Making of Our Times*. Cambridge: Cambridge University Press, 2005.

Wheeler, Nicholas. 'The Humanitarian Responsibilities of Sovereignty: Explaining the Development of a New Norm of Military Intervention for Humanitarian Purposes in International Society'. In *Humanitarian Intervention and International Relations*, edited by Jennifer Welsh, 29–52. Oxford: Oxford University Press, 2006.

Wheeler, Nicholas. *Saving Strangers: Humanitarian Intervention in International Society.* Oxford: Oxford University Press, 2000.

Wheeler, Nicholas. 'Pluralist or Solidarist Conceptions of International Society: Bull and Vincent on Humanitarian Intervention'. *Millennium: Journal of International Studies* 21, no. 3 (1992): 463–487.

Whelan, Daniel J. '"Under the Aegis of Man": The Right to Development and the Origins of the New International Economic Order'. *Humanity: An International Journal of Human Rights, Humanitarianism, and Development* 6, no. 1 (2015): 93–108.

Whyte, Jessica S. 'Always on Top?: The Responsibility to Protect and the Persistence of Colonialism'. In *The Postcolonial World*, edited by Jyotsna G. Singh and David D. Kim, 308–324. London: Routledge, 2017.

Whyte, Jessica S. 'Human Rights: Confronting Governments? Michel Foucault and the Right to Intervene'. In *New Critical Legal Thinking: Law and the Political*, edited by Matthew Stone, Illan Rua Wall, and Costas Douzinas, 11–31. London: Routledge, 2012.

Wight, Martin. *Power Politics*, edited by Hedley Bull and Carsten Holbraad. Leicester: Leicester University Press, 1978.

Wight, Martin. 'Power Struggle Within the United Nations'. *Proceedings of the Institute of World Affairs* 32 (1957): 247–259.

Willetts, Peter. *The Non-Aligned Movement: The Origins of a Third World Alliance.* London: Frances Pinter, 1978.

Williams, David. 'Development, Intervention, and International Order'. *Review of International Studies* 39, no. 5 (2013): 1213–1231.

Williams, John. *Ethics, Diversity, and World Politics: Saving Pluralism From Itself?* Oxford: Oxford University Press, 2015.

Williams, Paul D. 'From Non-Intervention to Non-Indifference: The Origins and Development of the African Union's Security Culture'. *African Affairs* 106, no. 423 (2007): 253–279.

Wilson, Heather. *International Law and the Use of Force by National Liberation Movements.* New York: Oxford University Press, 1988.

Windsor, Philip. 'Superpower Intervention'. In *Intervention in World Politics*, edited by Hedley Bull, 45–66. Oxford: Oxford University Press, 1984.

Winfield, Percy. 'History of Intervention in International Law'. *British Yearbook of International Law* 3 (1922): 130–149.

Wippman, David. 'Military Intervention, Regional Organizations and Host State Consent'. *Duke Journal of Comparative & International Law* 7, no. 1 (1996): 209–240.

Wood, Bryce. *The Making of the Good Neighbour Policy.* New York: Columbia University Press, 1961.

Wriggins, Howard. 'Political Outcomes of Foreign Assistance: Influence, Involvement, or Intervention?' *Journal of International Affairs* 22, no. 2 (1968): 217–230.

Wright, Quincy. 'The Goa Incident'. *American Journal of International Law* 56, no. 3 (1962): 617–632.

Wright, Quincy. *The Role of International Law in the Elimination of War.* Manchester: Manchester University Press, 1961.

Wright, Quincy. 'Subversive Intervention'. *American Journal of International Law* 54, no. 3 (1960): 521–535.

Wright, Quincy. 'Is Discussion Intervention?' *American Journal of International Law* 50, no. 1 (1956): 102–110.

Yugoslavia. *The Conference of Heads of States or Government of Non-Aligned Countries, Belgrade, September 1–6, 1961.* Belgrade: Belgrade Publishing House, 1961.

Index

For the benefit of digital users, indexed terms that span two pages (e.g., 52–53) may, on occasion, appear on only one of those pages.

Abboud, Ibrahim 105
Abi-Saab, Georges 8–9
Azm, Khalid al- 100–101
absolute non-interventionism 8–10, 124
absolute sovereignty 8–10, 160–161, 204, 207–208, 226
Accioly, Hildebrando 42–43
Acharya, Amitav 91
Active Non-Alignment 4
Additional Protocol Relative to Non-Intervention (Buenos Aires Protocol of 1936) 68, 70–71, 95–96
Adebajo, Adekeye 123–124
Aden Adde (Aden Abdullah Osman) 105–106
Afghanistan 1–2, 20–21, 191–192
    Soviet invasion of 20–21, 191–192
Africa 86–87, 98, 109–110, 117–118, 167–168, 213
    Central 21–22, 139–140
    Northern 21–22, 96
    Southern 10–11, 108–109, 121–122, 167–168, 184–185
African Union (AU) 22, 205, 213, 215, 223
    Constitutive Act 213–214
Afro-Asia 7–8, 15, 18, 91, 92–93, 95–96, 104–105, 113
    'collective intervention' led by 29–30, 160, 237–238
    the intervention concept and its interpretation in *see* Bandung, theory of intervention; anti-colonial intervention
Afro-Asian Peoples' Solidarity Movement 18–19, 111
Afro-Asian Writers' Bureau 165
agency
    contingent 13
    globalization of political 7–8, 143–144, 234
    situated 12–13
    redistributed 6, 46–47
aggression 57–58, 64–65, 73–74, 113, 114–115, 169

colonialism as permanent 113–115
contested meaning and codification of 27, 37–38, 73–74, 90–91, 169
Ahtisaari, Martti 227
aid, foreign or international 30, 54–55, 73–74, 98, 100–101, 106–107, 135, 164, 168–169, 171, 206, 210, 215, 238–239, 245–246
    anti-colonial 153
    difference between intervention and legitimate 153, 206, 210, 215
    emergency 136
    military 73–74, 117–118, 154, 215
    tied or conditional 30, 54–55, 164, 168–169, 171, 238–239, 245–246
Albania 127–128
Algeria 96–101, 107, 127–128, 186
Allende, Salvador 171–174, 182
American Mercury 85
American Society of International Law 42, 199–200
analytic meaning 32, 37–38, 48–51 *see also* naturalism
Anghie, Antony 89–90
Angola 108–109, 116, 121–122
Annan, Kofi 22, 201, 202–206, 225–226
anti-colonial intervention 85 *see also* Bandung, theory of intervention; solidarist internationalism
    attempts at institionalizing in the UN a theory of 123, 162
    vs dictatorial intervention in the UN 123, 162
    as distinguished from effective intervention 89
    in relation to emancipatory intervention 164
    moderate and radical strains of 102–109
    relative uptake in historical international society 158–161

anti-colonial redescription of
    intervention 10–11, 18, 86–87,
    237–238
anti-colonialism 89–90, 103–104, 118–119,
    144–145, 154–155, 192–193, 240–241
anti-interventionism 229–230 *see also*
    non-interventionism
anti-naturalism 26, 50–51
anti-racism 27–28, 89–90, 103–104, 118–119,
    192–193, 233
anti-solidarism 15, 142
apartheid 87–88, 107–108, 147–150, 152,
    158–159, 188–189
Arab League 143
Argentina 156–157, 183
Argentine Pact (Treaty of Non-Aggression and
    Conciliation) 72 *see* Saavedra Lamas
    Treaty
armed force 54–57, 65–66, 68–69, 77–78, 134,
    143–145 *see also* force
    threat or use of 60, 65–66, 78, 112
Arrighi, Giovanni 7–8
Asia 2–3, 7–8, 11–12, 86, 111, 113, 117–118,
    122
Asian-African Conference *see* Bandung,
    Conference
assistance, international
    economic 136, 186–187, 189
    humanitarian *see* humanitarian assistance
    military 103–104, 112, 154
    to peoples under colonial domination 103,
        147–148, 151, 153–155
    technical 30, 61–62
atrocities 115, 124–125, 149–150, 194,
    203–204, 208–209, 237
    colonial 87–88, 121–122
    mass 10–12, 149, 150, 221, 222, 240, 241,
        245–246
Australia 76, 79, 80, 99–100, 216
authority
    as distinguished from authorization of
        intervention 218–221
    ethical visions, practices, and the re-shaping
        of 13, 235 *see also* worldmaking
    intervention as directed at changing the
        structure of 35–37, 40
    global organization and re-organization
        of 6, 232, 234
    power and 6, 232, 234
Axworthy, Lloyd 222

Badawi, Abdullah Ahmad 223–224
Bain, William 220–221

balance of power 4–5, 111–112
Baldwin, David 30, 33
Bandung 2, 15, 123–128, 136, 137–138, 143,
    152, 192–193, 233, 237–238, 244
    Conference (Asian-African Conference of
        1955) 89–96, 136, 137–138, 143, 152,
        233, 237
    Political Committee 90, 92, 93, 95–96, 98,
        100–101
    powers 8–9, 127–128, 237–238
    Principles as progressively developing the
        Panchsheel (Five Principles of Peaceful
        Coexistence) 89
    Principles (Ten Principles of
        Bandung) 88–89, 93–95, 104, 237
    Spirit 18, 85, 93–94, 120, 192–193
    theory of intervention 85, 244 *see also*
        anti-colonial intervention; solidarist
        internationalism
    UN 87–88, 121, 233
Bangladesh 186
Ban Ki-moon 225
Barraclough, Geoffrey 7–8
Beavogui, Louis Lansana 105–108
Belaúnde, Viktor Andrés 74
Belgrade 18–19, 86, 104–105, 116, 118–119,
    136, 137–138, 143
    Conference (First Conference of Heads of
        State or Government of Non-Aligned
        Countries, 1961) 104–109
    Declaration 106–107
beliefs 2–3, 5–6, 34–35, 45–47, 49–50, 52, 232,
    234
Beloff, Max 29–30
Bettati, Mario 200
Biafra, the International Committee of the Red
    Cross in 200
Big Three 56–15
Black, Cyril 27, 40–41
Blair, Tony 200
bloc politics 22–23, 104
Blum, Yehuda Zvi 175
Bogotá 68–69, 95–96, 132, 134, 143, 158–159,
    179–180
    Charter (Charter of the Organization of
        American States, 1948) 68–69, 95–96,
        132, 134, 143, 158–159
Bogra, Mohammad Ali 93
Bolívar, Simon 120
Bolivia 73–74, 99–100, 179–180
Bosnia and Herzegovina 201

Botswana 186, 214–215
  Communiqué on the SADC Organ on Politics, Defence and Security 214–215
Boumédiène, Houari 172–173, 184–185, 191
Bouteflika, Abdelaziz 205
Bowman, Isaiah 75
Brahimi Panel 210
Brazil 1–2, 58, 60–61, 71, 77, 182–183, 229–230
Brecher, Michael 36
Brexit 1–2
Brezhnev Doctrine 162–163, 191–192
BRICS (Brazil, Russia, India, China, and South Africa) 1–2, 229–230
Brijuni Islands 104
Brzeziński, Zbigniew 27–28
Buenos Aires 17, 68–71, 75, 82–83, 95–96, 143, 158–159, 236–237
  Conference (Inter-American Conference for the Maintenance of Peace, 1936) 17, 68–69, 75, 143, 158–159, 236–237
  Protocol of 1936 *see* Additional Protocol Relative to Non-Intervention
Bull, Hedley 4, 42–43, 162–163
Burke, Roland 94
Burma (Myanmar) 89, 92, 133
Bush, George H. W. 178
Byrne, Jeffrey 111

Cabral, Amílcar 112
Cadogan, Alexander 59–60
Cairo (Second Conference of Heads of State or Government of Non-Aligned Countries, 1964) 143, 147–148
Calvo, Carlos 17, 42–43, 55, 65–66, 91, 95–96, 134, 136
  Doctrine 42–43, 65–68
  theory of intervention (as effect or outcome of foreign pressure) 70, 87, 95–96, 236–237 *see also* effective intervention
Canada 72–73, 133, 216–218
capacity-building 222, 229–230
capitalism 5–6, 30–31, 173–174
Cardozo, Michael 30
Carrillo Floes, Antonio 156–157
Cartagena (13th Ministerial Conference of the Movement of Non-Aligned Countries, 2000) 209
Cassin, René 98–99
Castro, Fidel 116–120
Ceylon 89, 97 *see also* Sri Lanka
Chad 212–213

Chandler, David 199–200
Chapter VII (of the UN Charter) 78–80, 195–197, 209–210, 226, 229–230
Chapultepec 17, 63, 64–65, 69, 70, 74, 75, 82–83, 95–96, 143, 158–159, 236–237
  Act of 63, 74, 82–83, 236–237
  Conference (Inter-American Conference on Problems of War and Peace, 1945) 64–65, 69, 70, 75, 95–96, 143, 158–159
  effective intervention and 63
Chiang Kai-shek 56–57
Chile 58, 99–100, 153, 171–174, 179–180
China 1–2, 56–58, 89, 90, 92, 209, 211
Chopra, Jarat 198–199, 204–205
Churchill, Winston 56–57
civilizing mission 53, 66–67
civil war 27, 40
civil strife 92, 146, 157–158, 217
civilians 206–207, 209, 220, 228–230, 235–236
  protection of *see* protection of civilians
Clark Memorandum 66–67
coercion 14–15, 29–30, 39, 55–56, 121, 131–132, 188, 195 *see also* force; armed force
  armed 28–29, 39
  economic 166, 175, 238–239
  intervention defined as an act of
  international 28–29, 39 *see also* dictatorial intervention; Oppenheim-Lawrence theory
  physical 125, 141, 146
coercive interference 14–16, 40, 41–43, 236–238, 245–246 *see also* dictatorial intervention; Oppenheim-Lawrence theory
coercive internationalism 22, 115, 121–122, 209, 245–246 *see also* internationalists and interventionists distinguished
coercive intervention 48, 50–51, 195–197, 226 *see also* coercive interference
coexistence 15, 90, 108
  peaceful *see* peaceful coexistence
Cohen, Benjamin 59–60
Cold War 1–2, 8, 16, 18, 20–22, 51, 104, 116–117, 143–145, 162–163, 192–193
  global 103–104, 144–145
  New 2, 242
collective action 8–11, 54–55, 87–88, 103, 122, 142, 156–157, 197, 201, 241–242, 245
  distinguished from intervention 122, 149–150, 156–157, 201, 245
  emergency 197, 230

legitimate 122, 142, 149–150, 162
collective security 63–65, 214–215, 245–246 *see also* self-defence, collective
   regional 64–65
Colombia 58, 170, 179–180
Colombo 89, 95, 121–122, 169
   Conference of 1954 89, 95
   Conference of 1976 (Fifth Conference of Heads of State or Government of Non-Aligned Countries) 121–122, 169
colonialism 26, 94–95, 101–102, 107, 108, 113, 146–148, 157–158 *see also* empire; imperialism
   as an atrocity and/or violation of fundamental human rights 87–88, 95, 121–122, 167–168 *see* Declaration on the Granting of Independence to Colonial Countries and Peoples
   classical academic understanding of intervention and its complicities with 26, 32–43, 51, 245–246
   contested meanings and manifestations of 98–102, 106, 120, 148, 181, 183, 220–221, 234
   dictatorial intervention and its complicities with 51, 87–88, 127–128, 134–136
   effective intervention and its complicities with 87–88, 96–97, 127–128, 134–137
   in the fields of information and mass communication 166, 169, 176, 181, 183
   ideological origins of the UN and 83
   in the international economic order 166, 168–170
   liberal intervention as a resurrection of 15, 219–221
   as 'permanent aggression' 113–115
   the Responsibility to Protect and 219–221
   shared duty of all states to contribute to the complete elimination of 10–11, 87–88, 106, 144–146, 157–158, 168–169, 188–189
colonial oppression 10–11, 120, 140, 142, 147
colonial powers 85–86, 96–97, 103–104, 106–107, 118–119, 149, 158–159
colonial rule 19–20, 85–88, 107–108, 119, 150
colonized peoples 89–90, 96, 103, 112
colour line, global 10, 85
Committee of Five 76–77, 79–80, 127
common interest 2, 89, 246
commons, international 22–23, 174, 176–177, 242
communism 27–28, 113–114

companies 171–174, *see also* corporations
   mining 172, 190
conditional sovereignty 3, 6–7, 195–196 *see also* defeasible sovereignty
conflict 14–15, 43–44, 81–82, 104, 158, 201, 243, 246
   armed 198
   normative 19–20, 237–238, 246
   prevention of 213, 215
Congo (Brazzaville) 109–110
Connally, Tom 79, 81
Connell-Smith, Gordon 68
consensus 20, 38–39, 82, 142, 147–148, 195, 206, 224–225, 234
   Ezulwini 223
   international 194, 241
consent 16, 22, 30, 179–181, 214, 215, 217
   and aid or assistance 30, 136
   of the governed 192
   international communications and 179–181
   intervention with *see also* intervention by invitation
   intervention without 203–204, 217
   legal significance of 30
contestation 4, 6–7, 20–21, 24, 132–133, 206, 227–229, 242
   of global order 12, 110–111, 128–129, 143–144
   normative 15–16, 104–105, 232
   as reconstitution 24, 26, 46–47, 52, 242
   in relation to processes of legitimating political action 45–47
contested concepts 32, 37–38, 232
contextualism 44–45
control
   donor 30–31
   foreign 166, 174, 195–196, 222
   responsibility as 195–196, 217, 228–229
   sovereignty as 217–218
cooperation 92, 135, 164–165, 188, 242
   international 136, 184–185, 212
Coordinating Bureau of the Non-Aligned Movement 224–225
Córdova, Roberto 69–70
corporations 170, 173–174
   transnational *see* transnational corporations
cosmopolitanism 3, 6, 15, 20, 25–26, 47–48, 234 *see also* liberal solidarism
Cot, Jean-Pierre 76

crimes 8, 10–11, 114, 147–150, 221–224, 237, 240
  against humanity 10–11, 87–88, 139, 149–150, 195, 210, 213, 221–223, 237, 240
  war 195, 213, 221–222, 227
Cuba 28–29, 65, 68, 99–100, 104–105, 116, 118, 121–122, 212–213, 224
communitarianism 15
cyberspace 242
Cyprus 186
Czechoslovakia 53, 126, 129, 133

Dadzie, Kenneth 140
Dallaire, Roméo 209–210
Declaration of Guiding Principles on the Use of Satellite Broadcasting for the Free Flow of Information, the Spread of Education and Greater Cultural Exchange 177
Declaration of Lima 63
Declaration of the Heads of State or Government of Non-Aligned Countries *see* Belgrade, Declaration
Declaration of the Ministerial Conference of Non-Aligned Countries on Decolonization of Information 183–184
Declaration of the Rights and Duties of Nations 73
Declaration of the South Summit (2000) 199
Declaration on Fundamental Principles concerning the Contribution of Mass Media to Strengthening Peace and International Understanding, to the Promotion of Human Rights and to Countering Racialism, Apartheid and Incitement to War (UNESCO Mass Media Declaration) 184–185
Declaration on Permanent Sovereignty Over Natural Resources 167–168
Declaration on the Elimination of All Forms of Racial Discrimination 156
Declaration on the Establishment of a New International Economic Order 167
Declaration on the Granting of Independence to Colonial Countries and Peoples 9–10, 106–108, 110, 150–151, 167–168
Declaration on the Principles of International Law Concerning Friendly Relations and Cooperation among States *see* Friendly Relations Declaration

Declaration on the Problem of Subversion 145–146
decolonization 6–7, 10, 27, 40, 43, 83–84, 138–139, 167–168, 170, 183–184
  of the concept of intervention 5–6, 37–38, 245–246
  and formal empire 27, 170
  of global order 6–7, 10
  of information 183–184
  of international law 138–139, 152
  of the Responsibility to Protect 228–231
  in and through the UN 83, 138–139
defamation 20–21, 166, 169–170, 181–182
defeasible sovereignty 6–7, 195–196, 206, 219–220, 222, 223, 236 *see also* conditional sovereignty
democracy 37–38, 78, 114, 178, 206
  and anti-colonialism 98–99, 119
  contested meaning of 37–38
  and freedom of information 178–179
Deng, Francis 225–226
dependence 4–5, 16, 30–31, 55–56, 93–94, 108–109, 180–181
dependency theory 30–31, 173–174
developing states/countries/world 10–12, 33, 168–169, 183–184, 191–192, 199, 206, 226 *see also* Global South; Third World
development (economic) 20–21, 78, 123–124, 136, 137–139, 168–169, 172–173, 212–213
de Wet, Erika 214–215
dictatorial interference 20, 24, 43, 77, 130, 143 *see also* coercive interference; dictatorial intervention; Oppenheim-Lawrence theory
dictatorial intervention 17, 19, 49, 72–73, 86–87, 98, 121–122, 125–126, 128, 129–131, 142, 158–159
  abandonment during the Friendly Relations process 129–136
  vs anti-colonial intervention in the UN 123, 162
  and Article 2 (4) of the UN Charter 61–62, 74, 75, 90–91, 130
  Bandung's rejection of 89
  complicities with colonialism 51, 87–88, 127–128, 134–136
  vs effective intervention in the founding of the UN 53
  and the double ordering of intervention in the UN Charter 75
  Latin American-led revolt against 70
diplomatic community 5–6, 14–15, 107, 246

direct satellite broadcasting *see* DSB
disarmament 104, 108, 214–215
discourse 4–5, 14, 37–39, 49, 50–52, 244, 246 *see also* discursive practice; representational practice
 global-political 14, 38–39
discursive practice 15–16, 46–47, 54, 56, 194–196, 232, 233 *see also* representational practice
Ditchley Park 201
diversity 13, 37, 46–47, 52, 234, 246 *see also* pluralism
Dlamini-Zuma, Nkosazana 216–217
dollar diplomacy 30–31
domestic affairs 64–65, 82–83, 87–88, 97, 98–101, 149–150, 245–246 *see also* domestic jurisdiction; internal affairs
domestic jurisdiction 8–9, 79–81, 87–88, 96–97, 121, 132, 139, 158–160, 233 *see also* domestic affairs; internal affairs
 anti-colonial intervention as resting on a dynamic theory of 121, 128, 138–140
 and the criterion of international law 61, 78, 80–81, 138–140
 dynamic nature of 8–9, 80–81, 87–88, 98, 110, 113, 121, 138, 139–140, 211, 245
 liberal intervention and suspensions of 22, 196–197
 static *vs* dynamic theory of 97, 207–208, 237
Dominican Republic 28–29, 65–68, 118
donor control 30–31
Dorticós Torrado, Osvaldo 116
DSB (direct satellite broadcasting) 177–179
Du Bois, W. E. B. 85–86
Dulles, John Foster 62–63, 80–81
Dumas, Roland 200
Dumbarton Oaks (Conference, 1944) 56–64, 75, 76 *see also* United Nations, Charter
 Joint Formulation Group 59
 Proposals 57, 71, 78, 80–81
Durban (12th Conference of Heads of State or Government of Non-Aligned Countries, 1998) 210

East Timor 203
ECOMOG (Economic Community of Western African States Monitoring Group) 213
economic assistance 136, 186–187, 189 *see also* aid, foreign or international; assistance, international
economic coercion 166, 175, 238–239 *see also* coercion
Economic Community of Western African States *see* ECOWAS
 Monitoring Group *see* ECOMOG
economic sanctions 29, 54–55 *see also* economic coercion
ECOSOC *see* United Nations, Economic and Social Council
ECOWAS (Economic Community of Western African States) 213–215
Ecuador 70–71, 160–161, 179–180
Eden, Anthony 97
effective intervention 54, 69–70, 77, 87, 90–91, 97–99, 133, 136–137 *see also* Calvo, Carlos, theory of intervention
 and Article 2 (7) of the UN Charter 78–80
 vs dictatorial intervention in the evolution of the Good Neighbor Policy 65–70
 vs dictatorial intervention in the founding of the UN 53
 distinguished from anti-colonial intervention 89
 and the double ordering of intervention in the UN Charter 75
 and the Panchsheel (Five Principles of Peaceful Coexistence) 90–91
Egypt 94–95, 103–104, 170
elections 70, 72–73, 242
Ellis, Ellen 42
El Salvador 179–181
emancipatory intervention 162
 as extending and overlapping with the anti-colonial theory of intervention 164
 influence on the Second UN Declaration on Non-Intervention 185
 political defeat of the agenda of 190–69
 positive face of 174, 183, 190
 relationship with the NIEO and NWICO 168–170
emergency humanitarian assistance 198, 210
empire 15, 85, 86, 102, 103–104, 111, 127–128, 158–159 *see also* colonialism; imperialism
 white-supremacist 101–102, 120–122
enforcement 11–12, 20, 48, 78, 79–80, 88–89, 115–116, 121–122, 209
English School (of International Relations Theory) 5–6, 16, 40–41, 43, 47–48, 50–51
equality 27, 62–63, 98–99, 115, 156, 171, 172–173
 sovereign *see* sovereign equality
Ethiopia 53, 186, 212–213

ethnic cleansing 195, 207–208, 221–223, 227
ethnic conflict 92–93
Evatt, Herbert 79–82
Ezulwini Consensus 223

Fairmont Hotel 56, 76 *see also* Committee of Five
Faisal bin Abdulaziz Al Saud 82
fake/false news 20–21, 180–181, 187, 188, 238–239
Falk, Richard 40–41, 162
Farer, Tom 162
Finland 189–190, 227
Finnemore, Martha 47
First UN Declaration on Non-Intervention (1965) 19–20, 142, 148, 161, 163, 166, 185–186, 240
Five Principles of Peaceful Coexistence *see* Panchsheel
force *see also* armed force
Ford, Gerald 191
Forster, Jacques 198
Foreign Affairs 200
foreign aid *see* aid, foreign or international; *see also* assistance, international
foreign pressure 19–20, 29–30, 33, 55–56, 79–81, 91, 101, 245–246
  intervention as the effect or outcome of 63 *see also* effective intervention; Carlos, Calvo, theory of intervention
Foucault, Michel 199–200
France 56, 76, 89–90, 96, 97–99, 119
freedom 20, 83, 93–95, 109–110, 120, 178–179, 181–182
  human 93–94, 206–207, 233, 234, 242
  of information 178–183
  as interdependent with peace 93–96, 114, 121–122, 230–231, 237
  intervention fundamentally as a problem of 20, 243
free flows of information, global 176
free information 178, 183, 184–185
free trade 183
'friendly' intervention 123
  as a conception of intervention as a problem of freedom to determine one's own future, rather than of freedom from physical violence 20, 161
  as an era of global debate and institutionalization characterized by the displacement of the dictatorial theory of intervention 125–126, 158–159
  as a formulation of the intervention concept expressed in the Friendly Relations Declaration 150, 157–158
friendly relations 19–20, 123–128, 151–153, 164 *see also* Friendly Relations Declaration; Special Committee on Friendly Relations
Friendly Relations Declaration 19, 123, 125–126, 128–129, 157–158, 161, 164–167 *see also* Special Committee on Friendly Relations
Fulbright, J. William 27–28
Fung, Courtney 229–230

G77 (Group of 77) 2, 8, 20–21, 171, 172–173, 199, 209, 216
Gandhi, Indira 182
genealogy 3–4, 12–13, 38–39, 45–47, 51, 232, 244
  as a corrective to naturalist accounts 17, 38–39, 50
  critical 12–13, 38–39, 45–46
  definition of 12–13
  discursive practices and 47
  processes of legitimating political action and 13, 15–16, 234
  as a repertoire 244
  techniques of conceptual change and 13, 45–47
  worldmaking and 12–13
General Assembly (UN) 19–20, 78, 79–80, 143–145, 153–154, 159–161, 177, 224–225
Geneva 123–124, 128–129, 150, 153, 155, 157
  Agreements/Accords on Vietnam (1954) 89–90, 114
  Conventions 200
  law of 197–198, 215, 230–231, 239
  Special Committee on Friendly Relations, 1967 and 1970 discussions at 150
genocide 147–150, 156, 207–209, 221–223
  Convention on the Prevention and Punishment of the Crime of 156
  prevention 149–150, 209
  Rwandan 201
Germany 53, 104
  Nazi 104
Gerson, Allan 192
Ghana 129, 133, 134–135, 140, 170
Gildersleeve, Virginia 75, 77
global governance 2, 52, 244

global international society 43–44, 63–64, 230–232, 244–245 *see also* international society
globalization 6–8, 45–46, 83, 116–117, 140, 143–144, 174, 204
  of international society 7–8, 45–46
  non-intervention as consistent with 140, 174
  of political agency 7–8, 143–144
Global Liberal Order 230–231
Global North 88–89, 194, 241
global order 2–6, 49–50, 70, 242, 244, 246 *see also* international order
Global Sixties 27–28
global society 17, 234
  of individuals 234
  of states 17 *see* global international society
Global South 8, 10–12, 86, 88–89, 98–99, 120–122 *see also* Third World
Good Neighbor Policy 67, 69–70, 73, 77, 82–83, 158–159, 236–237
good neighbourliness 20–21, 63–64, 66–67, 93, 126–127, 158, 181
Great Powers 31, 56, 58–59, 78, 81–83, 233, 236
  and the meaning of intervention 39
Greece 99–100, 144–145, 189–190
Grenada 192–193
Gromyko, Andrei 59–60, 79–80, 82
Group of 77 *see* G77
Guinea 105–108

Hackworth, Green 75, 77
Hague, law of the 197–198, 230–231, 239
Haile Selassie 105–106, 108–109
Haiti 28–29, 67–68, 99–100
Hallstein Doctrine 131–132
Hall, William Edward 214
Halpern, Manfred 27
Hartley, Robert 75
Havana 111–112, 116, 117, 148, 184–185, 224
  Conference (Fourteenth Conference of Heads of State or Government of Non-Aligned Countries, 2006) 224
  Solidarity Conference of the Peoples of Africa, Asia, and Latin America (1966) *see* Tricontinental
  Summit (Sixth Conference of Heads of State or Government of Non-Aligned Countries, 1979) 184–185
hegemony 4, 26–27, 48, 178–179, 230–231
  exit from 4
hegemonism 175

Henkin, Louis 42
Herndl, Kurt 197–198
hierarchy, international 4, 10, 14–15, 32, 86, 89–90, 227–228, 230–231, 237
  contestation of 4, 10, 83, 89–90, 227–228, 237
  racial 10, 83, 102
  white-supremacist 237
Hitler, Adolf 53, 160
Hobbes, Thomas 225–226
Hoffmann, Stanley 32
host states 171–174
Hull, Cordell 58, 61–62, 66–68, 76
humanitarian assistance 196, 198–199, 201, 202–203, 216–217, 239
  emergency 198, 210
humanitarian intervention 43–44, 47–48, 194, 199, 202–205, 216–217, 241 *see also* liberal intervention; liberal solidarism
  classical theory of 21–22, 195–196, 208, 213, 220–221
  distinguished from RtoP 194, 228
  inherent in Northern RtoP 195–196, 220–221, 228
humanitarian interventionism 3–4, 59–60, 110 *see also* liberal interventionism
humanitarianism 15, 83–84, 210
  interventionist 199–200
  non-interventionist and internationalist 88–89, 194
humanitarian NGOs, new 199–200, 207, 239
humanitarian responsibility and/or duty, international 9–12, 73, 86–88, 99–100, 107, 139, 144–145, 190, 203–204, 210, 218, 232, 233, 237–238, 241–242
humanitarian solidarity 199
'humanitarian war' 47–48, 200
humanity 59, 152, 199, 206, 209, 233, 236–238, 243
human rights 20–22, 94–95, 98–101, 189–190, 204–205, 216, 233–235
  abuses 9–11, 91, 147, 207–208
  Interventional Covenants on 94, 105–106
  and self-determination 18, 92–93, 102, 190
  self-determination as the primary human right or 'essence' of all 94, 107, 233
  vs sovereignty 8, 205, 228, 233, 235, 245
  through sovereignty and sovereignty through 55, 100–101, 204–205, 233, 245
  UN-based regime 179, 190, 203–204, 237–238

human rights (*Continued*)
  universal 83–86, 88–89, 91, 94, 233, 235–238
  Universal Declaration of 105–106, 150–152, 187–188, 210
human values 10–11, 124, 204
Hurrell, Andrew 7–8

Iceland 99–100, 222–223
ICIHI (Independent Commission on International Humanitarian Issues) 197–198
ICISS (International Commission on Intervention and State Sovereignty) 198, 217–218, 220–222, 226, 228
  report 195–196, 218, 220–221
ICRC (International Committee of the Red Cross) 197–200, 239
identity 87–88, 154
  cultural 182–183
  non-intervention as the non-use of force to deprive national 146, 149, 155, 157–158
  Global South or Third World as an 86, 92
ideology 2–3, 10, 12–13, 22–23, 116–117, 120, 232, 235, 242
  Cold War 10, 116–117, 143–144
  and the 'correct' use of normative terms 45
  genealogy as a critique of 13
impartiality 199, 212, 213, 216–217
imperialism 5–6, 100–101, 111–112, 114, 116–117, 192–193, 197 *see also* colonialism; empire
impunity 149, 170, 207–208, 216, 239–240, 245
independence 55–56, 64–65, 73, 106–110, 119, 167–168
  formal 164, 192–193, 203
  political 57, 62–65, 74, 76, 87–88, 129, 130
Independent Commission on International Humanitarian Issues *see* ICIHI
India 85, 89, 90, 92, 98–100, 133–135, 139, 155, 183, 230
Indonesia 89, 95–96, 203, 209
inequality 4, 51, 81–82, 243
information 169, 177–185, 187–190 *see also* NWICO
  decolonization of 183–184
  dissemination 180–183, 187, 188–190
  false 180–181
  flows 164, 179–180, 183–184, 187
  free 178, 183, 184–185

  freedom of 178–183
institutionalization 13, 17, 49–50, 85, 88–89, 123–124, 243, 246
interdependence 2, 70–71, 94–95, 114, 176, 178, 230–231
interference *see* intervention
Intergovernmental Coordinating Council in the Field of Information of Non-Aligned Countries 184–185
internal affairs 72–73, 90–92, 152, 164–165, 171, 186, 207–208 *see also* domestic affairs; domestic jurisdiction
  and external affairs belonging to the state 42–43, 64–66, 68, 73, 143, 146, 157–158, 188 *see also* domestic affairs; domestic jurisdiction
International Commission on Intervention and State Sovereignty *see* ICISS
International Committee of the Red Cross *see* ICRC
international community 186, 194, 195–196, 206, 207, 218, 219–220, 227–228
International Court of Justice 69, 75, 192–193
international humanitarian action and/or protection 21–22, 195–196, 217, 228, 234, 235
  as distinguished from intervention 21–22, 198
international involvement 22, 136–137, 196–197, 203–204, 206, 208–209, 211–212, 223
internationalism 10–12, 22–23, 88–89, 110, 111, 236–238
  coercive 22, 115, 121–122, 209, 245–246
  proletarian 10, 111–112, 156–157
  solidarist 18, 118–119, 121–122, 191–193, 233, 238–240
internationalists and interventionists distinguished 96, 117, 245
international law 42, 61, 78, 128, 129–130, 137–140, 154, 199–200
  definition of intervention in 42
international legitimacy 6–7, 47–48, 163–164, 192, 194–195
international norms 26, 197
international order 4, 39, 40–41, 53, 64–65, 87–88, 162, 190 *see also* global order; international society
international organizations 53–54, 56–57, 62–64, 70–71, 113
International Relations (IR), academic discipline 6–7, 11–12, 33–34, 37–39, 41–42, 44–45, 162–163, 245–246

international society 6–8, 12–14, 41–42, 45–50, 158–160, 204–205 *see also* global order; international order
  genealogy, discursive practices, and 4–5, 12, 43, 51
  global 43–44, 63–64, 230–232, 244–245
  globalization of 7–8, 45–46
  large-scale change in 2–3, 10–11, 38–39, 46–47, 232
  post-Western 10, 22–23, 122, 246
interpretivism 12, 45, 50–51
intervention *see also* non-intervention
  academic definitions of 24
  analytic meaning of *see* analytic meaning
  classical definition of 39, 51, 245–246
  as a contested concept 32
  as an evaluation of action 14, 26, 243
  as an event 13–15, 28, 39, 44–45, 52
  as a normative-political concept practiced and repracticed in international discourse 33–34, 50–52
  anti-colonial theory of *see* anti-colonial intervention
  Bandung theory of *see* Bandung, theory of intervention
  definition in international law 42
  as the denial of or pressure at the expense of self-determination 20, 88–89, 102–103, 113–114, 118–119, 197, 203–204, 237–238, 245–246
  dictatorial theory of *see* dictatorial intervention
  direct and indirect 29, 69, 72–73
  effective theory of *see* effective intervention
  emancipatory theory of *see* emancipatory intervention
  and the 'friendly' era of global debate *see* 'friendly' intervention
  humanitarian *see* humanitarian intervention
  by invitation 22, 214–215, 240–241
  liberal *see* liberal intervention
  ordinary meaning of *see* international involvement
  subversive 29, 156–157
interventionism *see also* non-interventionism
  as distinguished from internationalism 96, 117, 245
  liberal *see* liberal intervention; liberal interventionism
  post-Cold War arrival of 1, 194, 232
Iran 72–73
Iraq 98–100
Ireland 189

Israel 103–104, 151, 175, 179–180
Italy 53, 151

Jakarta Declaration (of the Tenth Conference of Heads of State or Government of Non-Aligned Countries, 1992) 199
Jamali, Muhammad Fadhel al- 98
Japan 53, 79, 85–86
Jebb, Gladwyn 159
Johnson, Lyndon B. 27–28
Journal of International Affairs 4–5, 48–49
Jordan 197–198
jurisdiction 59, 79, 98–99, 124–125, 188
  domestic *see* domestic jurisdiction
  international 11–12, 80, 233
justice 2, 6, 43–44, 46–47, 59, 98–99, 138–140, 168–169, 204–211, 235–237, 244, 246
  vs order 43–44
just war 28–29, 40, 114, 200

Kenya 170, 243
Khan, Daniel-Erasmus 76
Khrushchev, Nikita 141
Kimani, Martin 243
Kirkpatrick, Jeane 192
Kissinger, Henry 175–176, 191
Kosovo 3, 201, 202–203, 207, 219, 227
Kotelawala, John 101
Kouchner, Bernard 200, 207
Kuala Lumpur (Thirteenth Conference of Heads of State or Government of Non-Aligned Countries, 2003) 224
Kurtz, Gerrit 222

Laos 143–144
Latin America 70, 75, 86–87, 111, 117–118, 120, 121–122
Lauterpacht, Hersch 131, 134
law
  of Geneva 197–198, 215, 230–231, 239
  of the Hague 197–198, 230–231, 239
  international *see* international law
Lawrence, T. J. 17, 55–56, 82–83, 134
League of Nations 53, 57, 58–59, 61, 73–74, 80–81
  Covenant 53, 57, 58–59, 61, 72–74, 78, 80–81, 132
Lebanon 107–108, 153
legitimacy 6–7, 12, 41–45, 227
  constraining role of 44–45
  legitimation processes and political language 45–47

legitimacy (*Continued*)
  normative contestation and shifts in
    international 6–7, 10–11, 194
  power and 44–45
Leninism 30–31, 114
liberal hegemony 227, 235–236
liberal intervention 194 *see also* humanitarian
    intervention; liberal solidarism
  defeasible sovereignty and 6–7, 195–196,
    219–220
  the disappearance of self-determination
    and 197, 241–242
  compared to humanitarian
    intervention 195–196
  human rights *vs* sovereignty dichotomy
    and 204–205, 211, 222, 235
  compared to Northern RtoP 195–196,
    220–221, 228
  as a resurrection of trusteeship or
    colonialism 15, 219–221
  suspension of sovereign equality and 200,
    204–205, 219–220, 222–223, 227–228
  treatment of the concept of domestic affairs
    and the nature of domestic
    jurisdiction 204–208
liberal interventionism 12, 15, 194, 197, 205,
    207–208, 239, 241–242 *see also* New
    Interventionism
  conceit of 15, 207–208, 235–236
  as a revolt against solidarist
    internationalism 11–12, 194, 230–231
  as a skillful inversion of the contradiction
    between intervention and human
    rights 204–205, 235
liberal solidarism 8, 47, 48, 51
Liberation Committee (OAU) 110–111,
    167–168
Liberia 78, 148, 158
Libya 1–2, 228–229
Linklater, Andrew 48
Little, Richard 30, 41–42
'little veto' 96–97, 127–128, 240 *see also*
    non-intervention, as a shield
Lomé (Thirty-sixth Ordinary Session of the
    Assembly of Heads of State and
    Government of the OAU, 2000) 213
López-Schümmer, José Luis 178–179
Luck, Edward 225–226
Luttwak, Edward 175–176

Mabruk, 'Izz al-Din al- 174–175
McNamara, Robert 27
McWhinney, Edward 137

Madagascar 138, 186
Mahbubani, Kishore 210
Malaysia 152
Mali 152
Malik, Charles 93–94
Malik, Yakov 182–183
Manley, Michael 180–181
Mao Zedong 28–29
Marshall Plan 36–37
Marxism 30–31, 192
Masmoudi, Mustapha 181, 183–184
mass atrocities 10–12, 149, 150, 221, 222, 240,
    241, 245–246
mass media 169–170, 180–181, 183, 184–185,
    187–188
  and global free flows of information 176
Mass Media Declaration 184–185
Mazrui, Ali 113
M'Bow, Amadou-Mahtar 184–185
Menon, Krishna 98–99, 113
Mexico 58, 69–73, 134, 140, 156–157
Mexico City (First Session of the Special
    Committee on Friendly Relations,
    1964) 129
military aid 117–118, 215 *see also* aid, foreign
    or international; assistance,
    international
military force 4–5, 29, 30, 42–43, 202, 218 *see
    also* force; armed force
Mill, John Stuart 178–179
*Millennium: Journal of International
    Studies* 47–48
Millennium Summit (UN Millennium
    Summit, 2000) 222–223
minorities 53, 92–93, 191–192
  rights 152, 154–155
Mishra, Brajesh 134, 136
Mohieddin, Khaled 115
Molotov, Vyacheslav 85
Monod, Philippe 131–133
Monroe Doctrine 65–66, 111–114, 162–163
  for Africa 109–110
  Roosevelt Corollary 28–29, 65–66
Monrovia group 110–111
Montevideo (Seventh International
    Conference of American States,
    1933) 17, 65, 66–68, 70, 75, 95–96, 143
  Convention on the Rights and Duties of
    States 67, 70–71, 127
morality 44–46, 122, 141, 147–148, 151–152,
    158–159
'moral violence of nations' 102
Morgenthau, Hans 30

Morocco 96–97
Moscow Declaration on General Security 62–63
Moynihan, Daniel Patrick 199–200
multipolarity 22–23, 52, 234
mutual security 65, 89 *see also* collective security
Murthy, C. S. R. 222
Mussolini, Benito 53

NAM *see* Non-Aligned Movement
NANAP *see* Non-Aligned News Agencies Pool
Nasser, Gamal Abdel 96, 103–104, 107–108
national identity 10–11, 87–88, 113–114, 146, 149–150, 154–155, 157–158
non-intervention as the non-use of force to deprive 146, 149, 155, 157–158
nationalism 1–2, 10, 237–238
Nationality Decrees in Tunis and Morocco case 138–140 *see also* domestic jurisdiction, dynamic nature of
nationalization 20–21, 168, 171–173, 238–239
as an 'act of development' 172–173, 184–185
national liberation 10–11, 19–20, 94–95, 110, 112, 143–146, 154
national liberation movements 18–19, 103, 118–119, 127–128, 145–146
NATO (North Atlantic Treaty Organization) 47–48, 194, 200–203, 207, 228–229, 241
naturalism 14–15, 26, 35, 38–39, 41–42, 49, 50–51
natural resources 166–168, 170, 171–176
Nazi Germany 104
Nehru, Jawaharlal 83, 90–93, 95, 101, 104, 107–108
neo-colonialism 8, 116–118, 168–169, 181 *see also* colonialism
neo-trusteeship 234 *see also* trusteeship
neutralism 89, 104
neutrality 4, 104, 199–200, 216–217
as distinguished from non-alignment 104–105, 108
New Delhi (Ministerial Conference of the Non-Aligned Countries on Decolonization of Information, 1976) 182–184
New International Economic Order *see* NIEO
New International Humanitarian Order *see* NIHO
New International Information Order *see* NWICO

New Interventionism 26–27, 204–205, 228 *see also* liberal intervention; liberal interventionism; liberal solidarism
news agency pools 20–21, 190, 238–239
New World Information and Communication Order *see* NWICO
New World Order 8, 89–90, 200 *see also* Global Liberal Order
New York 123–124, 128–129, 142, 153–157
adoption of the First UN Declaration on Non-Intervention (1965) in 142
meetings of the Special Committee on Friendly Relations (1966) in 153–157
New York Times 27–28, 228–229
New Zealand 216
NGOs, new humanitarian 199–200, 207, 239
Nicaragua 28–29, 67–68, 191–192
Nicaragua v. United States case 131, 191–192
NIEO (New International Economic Order) 20–21, 163, 167–171, 197, 238–239
Nietzsche, Friedrich 45
Nigeria 209–210
NIHO (New International Humanitarian Order) 197, 230–231, 239
Nixon Shock 165
Nkrumah, Kwame 104–105, 108, 109–111
non-aggression 72, 90–91
non-aligned countries/states 106–107, 147–148, 183–185, 215–217, 224–225, 239
Non-Aligned Movement (NAM) 2, 169–170, 209–210, 216–217, 223, 224–225
Non-Aligned News Agencies Pool (NANAP) 184–185
non-alignment 88, 103–105, 124–125, 137–138, 192, 233
Active 4
anti-colonialism as the basis of 89, 103–104, 116–117
meanings of 103–105, 108, 137–138, 192
distinguished from neutrality 104–105, 108
positive 237–238
as a rival to the politics of an evolving Afro-Asianism 104–105, 111
non-interference *see* non-intervention
non-intervention *see also* intervention
academic definitions of 24
categorical 7–10, 19–20
as a contested concept 32
as a continuation of the UN-based human rights regime 8–9, 85, 150–151, 179, 190, 203–204, 244

non-intervention see also intervention (*Continued*)
  corollary of sovereignty 8–10, 138, 215
  declarations on *see* First UN Declaration; Second UN Declaration
  denial or withholding of economic assistance aimed at influencing path of economic development chosen by a state as contrary to 186–187
  double ordering in the UN Charter of 75
  as a duty of states to combat fake/false news and 176, 187
  as a duty of states to contribute to the elimination of colonialism and extreme racism 85, 146
  as good neighbourliness 1, 66–70, 90, 93, 126, 158
  within the NIEO and NWICO *see* emancipatory intervention
  as non-interference in civil strife 146, 150
  as non-involvement *see* intervention, ordinary meaning of; liberal interventionism
  as the non-use of force *see* dictatorial intervention
  as the non-use of foreign pressure *see* effective intervention
  normative foundation of non-alignment and the Global South 2, 70–71, 91, 105–106, 113–114, 117, 150–151, 195–197, 210
  pressure directed against a state while exercising its sovereign right to its natural wealth and resources as a violation of 162, 168
  principle 2, 8–9, 30, 39, 57, 58–59, 69, 77, 87–88, 98, 117–118, 137, 179, 183, 190, 234, 242
  as a problem of freedom to determine one's own future, rather than of freedom from physical violence *see* 'friendly' intervention
  racial discrimination and apartheid as contrary to the principle of 138–140, 152, 188–189
  as respect for or the non-use of pressure at the expense of self-determination 10
  see also anti-colonial intervention; Bandung, theory of intervention; solidarist internationalism
  as a return to old-style power politics and sovereigntism 2, 244
  as a shield 8, 121, 149–150, 206–208, 240
  see also 'little veto'
  the use of force to deprive national identity as a violation of 146, 149, 155, 157–158
non-interventionism *see also* interventionism
  absolute 8–10, 124
  return in international society of 1–2, 6–7, 242
  solidarist 194
non-use of force 3, 120–121, 127–128, 136–137, 206 *see also* force
normative contestation 15–16, 104–105, 232 *see also* contestation
norms 4–10, 51–53, 171–172 *see also* discourse; discursive practice
  global 35–36, 228–229
  shared 2–3, 11–12, 38–39
  singular international 21–22, 26
Northern RtoP 220–221, 230
Norton Moore, John 31–32
Notter, Harley 62–63
NWICO (New World Information and Communication Order) 163–164, 169, 170, 183, 185–187, 190, 238–239
Nyerere, Julius 110

OAS (Organization of American States) 68, 95–96, 117–118, 120, 133–135, 143
  Charter 134–135
OAU (Organisation of African Unity) 22, 109–111, 139, 143, 147–148, 167–168, 205, 215
  Casablanca and Monrovia Groups 110–111
  Charter 109–110, 239–240
  Declaration on the Problem of Subversion 145–146
  Frontline States (ad-hoc committee) 110
  International Panel of Eminent Personalities 209–210
  Liberation Committee 110–111, 167–168
Oberdorfer, Don 27–28
oil-exporting countries 174–175
OPEC (Organization of Petroleum Exporting Countries) 174–176
Oppenheim, Lassa 17, 55–56, 67–68, 82–83, 134
Oppenheim-Lawrence theory (of intervention as coercive or dictatorial interference) 42–43, 70, 91, 95–96, 162–163, 236–237 *see also* coercive interference; dictatorial intervention
order 4, 6–8, 17, 43–44, 51, 75, 82–83, 115–116

global *see* global order
international *see* international order
vs justice 43–44
Organisation of African Unity *see* OAU
Organization of American States *see* OAS
Organization of Petroleum Exporting Countries *see* OPEC
Ortega y Gasset, José 178–179
OSPAAAL (Organization of Solidarity with the Peoples of Asia, Africa and Latin America) 111

Pakistan 89, 94–95, 148, 149–150, 181, 210
Palestine 19–20, 100–101, 150
Pan-Americanism 64
Panama 65, 73, 120, 167–169
  Canal 168
Panchsheel (Five Principles of Peaceful Coexistence) 18, 90–95, 126
  to Ten Bandung Principles 89
  Treaty (1954 Agreement on Trade and Intercourse between the Tibet Region of China and India) 92, 237
Paris 243
  Peace Conference 85–86
Pasvolsky, Leo 76–77
peace 79–80, 93–95, 104–105, 114–115, 137–138, 168–169, 204–211
  as interdependent with freedom 93–95, 114, 230–231, 243
peacebuilding 22
peaceful coexistence 27–29, 104, 105–106, 114–115, 126, 127–128, 158–159
  Bandung and the concept of 90, 93–96
  Five Principles of 90, 95, 237
  Friendly Relations process and 127–128
  non-alignment and 104–106
  Tricontinental Conference and 114–115
peacekeeping 201–205, 213, 214–215, 240–241
  UN-based 22, 210
Pérez de Cuéllar, Javier 235
Permanent Court of International Justice 138–140
permanent sovereignty over natural resources 170
personality, state 17, 55–56, 63, 64–65, 70, 74, 87–88, 95–96, 134
  moral 63, 74
Peru 58, 63, 74, 171, 174, 179–180
Phạm, Quỳnh 89–90
Philippines 73–74, 81, 85–86
Phillips, William 67

physical violence 125, 141, 146 *see also* coercion; force
Pinochet, Augusto 182
Platt Amendment 65
pluralism 13–14, 22–23, 39, 43–44, 48, 244 *see also* diversity
  vs solidarism debate 13–14, 43–44, 48
police action 28–29, 75
populist nationalism 1–2
Portugal 203
Portuguese colonies 19–20, 116, 121–122, 150
post-Cold War period 8, 194, 195–196, 227, 229–231, 242
  early 21–22, 25–26, 51
post-Western world 6–7, 52, 246
power 2, 4, 12–15, 31, 32, 44–47, 111–112, 160, 232–233, 236, 243–244
  authority and 6, 232, 234
  balance of 4–5, 111–112
  inequality 31–32, 243
  institution-making and 13
  legitimation of 13–15, 44–47, 232, 243
  operation through practices 12–13
  politics 2, 244
  redistribution of 2–4, 7–8, 46–47, 236
practice
  discursive 15–16, 46–47, 54, 56, 194–196, 232, 233
  institutionalized 8–9, 13, 124–125
  representational 12–13, 45–47
Prashad, Vijay 104
Prebisch-Singer hypothesis 36–37
pressure 55–56, 90–91, 95–96, 118–121, 130–131, 133–134, 137
  intervention as the effect or outcome of foreign 102–103, 133, 145, 161, 237–238 *see* Carlos, Calvo, theory of intervention; effective intervention
Princeton Conference on Intervention and the Developing States (1967) 16–17, 24
producers' associations 20–21, 168–169, 174, 190, 238–239
proletarian internationalism 10, 111–112, 156–157
  as distinguished from solidarist internationalism 10, 111–112, 156–157
propaganda 20–21, 29–30, 55–56, 73–74, 95–96, 101, 127–128, 181–182 *see also* fake/false news
protection of civilians 196–197, 209, 223

Protocol Relating to Non-Intervention of Buenos Aires (1936) *see* Additional Protocol Relative to Non-Intervention
Protocol Relating to the Mechanism for Conflict Prevention, Management, and Resolution (ECOWAS, 1999) 213
proxy actors 55–56, 167–168, 173–174, 190

Qaddafi, Muammar 228–229
Qin Huasun 211
qualified sovereignty 206, 219–220, 223

race 4–5, 86, 111, 144–145, 159
racial discrimination 95, 107, 108, 121, 146, 149, 150–151, 155–158
  duty of all states to contribute to the complete elimination of 10–11, 87–88, 106, 144–146, 157–158, 168–169, 188–189
racism 15, 101, 115–117, 122, 174, 188–189, 237
  extreme 8–9, 18, 19–20, 83–84, 87–88, 137–138, 147, 149–150
Rajan, M. S. 4–5
Ratsimbazafy, Henri Jux 138–139
Reagan, Ronald 191–192
Reagan(-Kirkpatrick) Doctrine 20–21, 192–193
Recchia, Stefano 48
reconstitution 8, 12, 126, 133, 163–164, 239–240
  contestation as 24, 26, 46–47, 52, 242
  in terms of discursive practices and their partial international institutionalization 126
  as distinguished from regulation 54
  intervention as the thing to be reordered 43
  revolt as 46–47
redescription 45–48, 50–51, 64, 102–103, 205
  anti-colonial 10–11, 18, 86–87
  evaluative 12
  revolt and 45–46
  rhetorical 22–23, 45, 46–47, 232
  Third World 162–163
Reedy, El-Sayed Abdel Raouf el- 137–138
regime change 36–37, 100–101, 229–231
  Southern RtoP and the separation of intervention from 229–230
relativism 15
representational practice 12–13, 45–47 *see also* discursive practice

Resolution 1514 (XV) *see* Declaration on the Granting of Independence to Colonial Countries and Peoples
Resolution 2131 (XX) *see* First UN Declaration on Non-Intervention
Responsibility to Protect *see* RtoP
Responsibility While Protecting 229–230
Review of International Studies 14–15, 48–49
'revolt against the West' 4, 7–8, 11–12
revolution 27, 89, 141, 144–146
revolutionary solidarity 120
rhetorical redescription 22–23, 45, 46–47, 232, 241 *see also* genealogy, techniques of conceptual change and; worldmaking, modification of practices and
Rhodesia (Zimbabwe) 19–20, 110, 115–116, 121–122, 150
Rieff, David 228–229
Rio de Janeiro
  adoption of the Treaty of Non-Aggression and Conciliation (1933) at 72
  Second Extraordinary Inter-American Conference (1965) 156–157
  Third Meeting of Ministers of Foreign Affairs of the American Republics (1942) 73
Roberts, Adam 47–48
Romulo, Carlos P. 81–82, 101
Roosevelt, Franklin D. 58–59, 66–68, 127
Roosevelt, Theodore 58–59, 65–68
  Corollary 28–29, 65–66, 75
Rosenau, James 16–17, 24–26, 32, 33–38, 40, 41–42, 50–51
RtoP (Responsibility to Protect) 22, 47–48, 194
  death of 3–4
  going beyond 3
  international 197, 219, 223, 226
  Northern 220–221, 230
  regime change and 218, 229–230
  residual 218–219
  responsibility as control 195–196, 217, 228–229
  self-determination and 218, 220–221, 234
  Special Adviser on 224–225
  Southern 230
  sovereignty as responsibility 3, 194–197, 217–218
Rusk, Dean 162
Russia 1–2, 243 *see also* Soviet Union
Rwanda 3, 203–204, 209–210, 226
  genocide in 201

Saavedra Lamas Treaty (Treaty of Non-Aggression and Conciliation) 72–74, 236–237
SADC (Southern African Development Community) 213–215
Salam, Saeb 107–108
sanctions 85–86, 108–109, 147–148, 164, 221–222, 240–241
  diplomatic 108–109
  economic 29, 54–55
  mandatory 115–116
  UN-based 121–122
San Francisco (Conference on International Organization) 17, 54, 56–57, 62–63, 68–69, 72–74, 85, 123–124
Saudi Arabia 82
Schwebel, Stephen 131, 134–136
Scott, Andrew 30
Seaton, Earle Edward 147–148
Second UN Declaration on Non-Intervention (1981) 20–21, 161, 164, 192–193, 197, 238–239
security 59–61, 137–139, 210, 213–215
  collective 63–64, 214–215
  contested meaning of 37–38
  mutual 65, 89
  national 27–28, 71
  regional collective 64–65
Security Council 58–60, 78, 115–118, 209, 210, 229–230
self-defence 53, 175–176
  collective 65, 113–114 *see also* collective security; mutual security
  individual 113–114
self-determination 10–12, 20–22, 94–95, 100–104, 113–114, 140–141, 167
  contested logic of 123, 162
  external and internal approaches to 101
  and human rights 18, 92–93, 102, 190
  intervention as the denial of or pressure at the expense of 20, 88–89, 102–103, 113–114, 118–119, 197, 203–204, 237–238, 245–246
  liberal intervention and the disappearance of 197, 241–242
  of peoples 94, 137–138, 141, 150–151, 168, 174, 184–185, 229–230
  as the primary human right or 'essence' of all human rights 94, 107, 233
  as a principle 114, 137–138
  from principle to right 237
  as a right 10–12, 94–99, 118–121, 149–150

self-determined futures 19, 21–22, 87–88, 101, 103–104, 208–209, 211–212, 237–239
Senanayake, Ratne Deshapriya 165
Serbia 219, 227
Shilliam, Robbie 5–6, 89–90
Sinclair, Ian 130
Singer, Hans 30–31, 36–37
Skinner, Quentin 44–46
Smith, Ian 115–116
Smuts, Jan 83
socialism 10, 86, 111
solidarism 43–44, 47, 48, 51, 244
  liberal 8, 47, 48, 51
  vs pluralism debate 13–14, 43–44, 48
solidarist internationalism 18, 118–119, 121–122, 191–193, 233, 238–240 *see also* anti-colonial intervention; Bandung, theory of intervention
solidarity 107, 115, 117–122, 242, 245
South Africa 18–20, 99–100, 108–109, 115, 121–122, 147–148, 159–160
Southern African Development Community *see* SADC
Southern RtoP 230
sovereign equality 1–2, 20, 62–63, 195–196, 208–210, 212–213, 227–228 *see also* sovereignty
sovereign privilege 21–22, 98–99, 118–119, 148
  abstract 11–12, 95–96, 121, 192–193
sovereigntism 2, 15, 235–236, 244
sovereigntists 124–125, 142, 206, 213, 230
  absolute/unqualified 206, 216–217
  qualified 213
sovereignty 7–9, 195–197, 203–205, 219–223, 225–227, 229–231 *see also* sovereign equality
  absolute 8–10, 160–161, 204, 207–208, 226, 233, 239–240
  conditional 3, 6–7, 195–196
  as control 217–218
  defeasible 6–7, 195–196, 206, 219–220, 222, 223, 236
  external and internal 101
  formal 169–170
  vs human rights 8, 205, 228, 233, 235, 245
  through human rights and human rights through 55, 100–101, 204–205, 233, 245
  'intervention' without infringing 211
  as the keystone of interstate relations 138
  legitimate 98–101, 120

sovereignty (*Continued*)
  non-intervention as a corollary of 8–10, 138, 215
  permanent 166–168, 170, 174–175, 177, 186–188
  'as a place of social contract' 206
  'popular' 98–99, 120
  qualified 206, 219–220, 223
  relationship with obligation and the development of international law 138–139
  as responsibility 3, 194–197, 217–218
  as a right 194
  as a shield 206–208, 216, 239–240
  state *vs* individual 204
  as supreme authority 219
  suspension of 11–12, 219–220, 229–230, 241–242
  and territorial integrity 74, 167–168, 224
  without condition 233
Soviet Union 17, 19–21, 56–57, 79–80, 101, 141, 143–145, 158 *see also* Russia
Special Adviser on RtoP 224–225
Special Committee on Friendly Relations 19, 72, 110, 123
Spingarn, Arthur 85
Srebrenica 210
Sri Lanka 165, 181–182, 186
Srinivasan, Amia 12–13, 45–46
Stassen, Harold 75, 77
state sovereignty *see* sovereignty
statespeople 11–17, 33–35, 41–42
Stern, David 162–163
Stettinius, Edward 56, 76, 81–82
subversion 29, 95–96, 101, 120, 127–128, 145–146, 154, 166
subversive intervention 29, 145
subversive interventionism 156–157
Sudan 105
Suez Canal 28–29, 103–104, 240–241
Suganami, Hidemi 48
Sukarno 102–105
superpower doctrines, non-intervention beyond 190
superpowers 29, 40, 89–90, 101, 103–104, 161
  competition/conflict/rivalry 2–3, 8, 233
  proxy conflict 27
Syria 153

Tanzania 147–148
Talal, El-Hassan bin 197
technical assistance 30, 61–62

Ten Principles (Bandung Principles) 88, 93–95, 104, 237
Thailand 98–99, 143–144
Thakur, Ramesh 194
The Economist 202–203
Third World 18–19, 86, 87–88, 104–105, 116–117, 162, 192 *see also* Global South
  as an identity 18, 92
Third World Quarterly 123–124
Thomas, Caroline 4–5
Tibet 90, 92–93, 237
Timor-Leste 203
Tito (Josip Broz) 104–105, 108–109
Torrijos-Carter Treaties 168
trade 31, 36–37, 69–70, 92, 171, 174, 183
transnational corporations 20–21, 164, 169–170, 190
  and mass media 170
  and misappropriated natural wealth 171
  and permanent state sovereignty over natural resources 170
Treaty of Non-Aggression and Conciliation 72
  see also Saavedra Lamas Treaty
Tricontinental (Solidarity Conference of the Peoples of Africa, Asia, and Latin America, 1966) 18–20, 88, 113–119, 156–157
Trump, Donald 1–2
trusteeship 11–12, 219, 220–221, 225, 229–230
  see also colonialism; empire; imperialism
  liberal intervention as a resurrection of 15, 219–221
Trusteeship Council (UN) 85–86
Tunis and Morocco Nationality Decree case 138–140; *see also* domestic jurisdiction, dynamic nature of
Tunisia 19–20, 97, 150, 181
Tunis Symposium on the Mass Media 183

Uganda 110
Ukraine 1–2, 243
Umozurike, Oji 109–110, 240–241
UNAMIR (United Nations Assistance Mission for Rwanda) 209–210
UN-based human rights regime 179, 190, 203–204, 237–238
UN-based peacekeeping 22, 210
UNCTAD (UN Conference on Trade and Development) 171
UNESCO (UN Educational, Scientific and Cultural Organization) 177, 184–185, 191

United Arab Republic 115, 137–138, 147–148, 153
United Kingdom 17, 56–58, 89, 97, 154–155, 157, 201
United Nations 53, 81–82, 98–100, 134–135, 137–138, 160, 201
  Assistance Mission for Rwanda *see* UNAMIR
  Charter 17, 93–94, 97, 106–107, 126, 133–135, 137–138, 204–205 *see also* Dumbarton Oaks
    Chapter VI 201
    Chapter VII 78–80, 195–197, 209–210, 226, 229–230
    Chapter VIII 61, 78
    dictatorial *vs* effective intervention in the writing of 53
    double ordering of intervention in Articles 2 (4) and 2 (7) 75
    perfection as visualized by the small states 81
  Disaster Relief Coordinator (UNDRO) 197–198
  Economic and Social Council (ECOSOC) 78–79, 82–83
  First Declaration on Non-Intervention (1965) 19–20, 142, 148, 161, 163, 166, 185–186, 240
  Friendly Relations Declaration (1970) 19, 123, 125–126, 128–129, 157–158, 161, 164–167
  General Assembly *see* General Assembly
  High Commissioner for Refugees (UNHCR) 197–198
  International Children's Fund (UNICEF) 197–198
  Second Declaration on Non-Intervention (1981) 20–21, 161, 164, 192–193, 197, 238–239
  Security Council 58–60, 78, 115–118, 209, 210, 229–230
  Trusteeship Council 85–86
United Nations Conference on International Organization *see* San Francisco
United States 27–28, 56–57, 67–70, 77, 81, 85, 117–118, 130–131, 134–135, 140, 143–144, 162
Universal Declaration of Human Rights 105–106, 150–152, 187–188, 210
universal human rights 83–86, 88–89, 91, 94, 233, 235–238
Uruguay 58, 72–73, 78

U Nu 92
U Thant 118

values 44–47, 136–137, 179–183, 198, 200
  cultural 74, 183–184
  human 10–11, 124, 204
  reconstitution of 45–46
  state *vs* human 204
Vandenberg, Senator 81
Vanderpuye, William Waldo Kofi 139–140
Vargas, Getúlio 64
Velasco Alvarado, Juan 174
Venezuela 58, 65–66, 72–73, 163, 179–180, 219–220
veto 60, 76, 78, 81–82, 96–97, 208
  Article 2 (7) as a 'little veto' 96–97, 127–128, 240
Vietnam 19–20, 27–28, 40, 89, 114, 117, 143–145, 186
Vilfan, Joža 140
Vincent, R. J. 4–5, 14–16, 39–44, 48–49, 162
violence 7–8, 29, 96, 112–113, 181–182
  colonial 96, 237
  racial 237
  physical 20, 83, 127

Walzer, Michael 40
Wan Waithayakon 98–99
war
  civil 27, 40
  'humanitarian' 47–48, 200
  internal 39, 41
  just 28–29, 40, 114, 200
  laws of 113
  between peoples 106–107
  wars of national liberation 19–20, 110, 113, 143–144
war crimes 195, 213, 221–222, 227
Weiss, Thomas 198–199
Welles, Sumner 68
Welsh, Jennifer 48, 227–228
Western-centrism 6, 13–14
Westphalia 3, 91, 204–205
  Treaty of 204–205
  Westphalian and post-Westphalian politics 3, 91
Wheeler, Nicholas 4–5, 14–16, 42–45, 47–48
Whyte, Jessica 199–200
Wight, Martin 160
Wilson, Woodrow 58–59
Windsor, Philip 162–163
Wood, Bryce 69
World Bank 27

world economy 4–5, 168–170, 238–239
worldmaking 10, 12–13
    modification of practices and 241 *see also* genealogy, techniques of conceptual change and; rhetorical redescription
world order *see* global order; global international society
World Summit (UN World Summit) 210, 221–223, 225–226
World Summit Outcome Document *see* WSOD
Wright, Quincy 29, 140

WSOD (World Summit Outcome Document) 195, 221, 222–225, 241

Xi Jinping 1–2

Yalta 56–57, 60, 104
Youlou, Fulbert 109–110
Yugoslavia 104–105, 129, 133–135, 140, 153, 219

Zhou Enlai 90, 92, 93, 95
Zimbabwe 115–116

The manufacturer's authorised representative in the EU for product
safety is Oxford University Press España S.A. of El Parque Empresarial
San Fernando de Henares, Avenida de Castilla, 2 - 28830 Madrid
(www.oup.es/en or product.safety@oup.com). OUP España S.A. also acts
as importer into Spain of products made by the manufacturer.
Printed and bound by CPI Group (UK) Ltd, Croydon, CR0 4YY

14/04/2025
01844749-0001